The Iroquois Eagle Dance

Laurence M. Hauptman, Series Editor

PLATE 1

Dew Eagle dances on the deer.

(Watercolor by Ernest Smith, Seneca artist of Tonawanda.)

THE IROQUOIS EAGLE DANCE
An Offshoot of the Calumet Dance

WILLIAM N. FENTON
with
**AN ANALYSIS OF
THE IROQUOIS EAGLE DANCE AND SONGS**
by Gertrude Prokosch Kurath

SYRACUSE UNIVERSITY PRESS

Syracuse University Press Edition 1991
91 92 93 94 95 96 97 98 99   6 5 4 3 2 1

This book is published from an edition originally published as *Bulletin* 156 of the Bureau of American Ethnology, the Smithsonian Institution in 1953.

This book is published with the assistance of a grant from the John Ben Snow Foundation.

William N. Fenton is Distinguished Professor Emeritus of Anthropology at the State University of New York at Albany. He is the author of *The False Faces of the Iroquois, The Role Call of the Iroquois Chiefs,* and editor of *Parker on the Iroquois.*

Gertrude Prokosch Kurath was a student of Martha Graham and a pioneer of Dance Ethnology in America. She is a musicologist and lives in Ann Arbor, Michigan.

The paper used in this publication meets the minimum requirements of American National Standard for Information Sciences—Permanence of Paper for Printed Library Materials, ANSI Z39.48-1984. ∞™

Library of Congress Cataloging-in-Publication Data

Fenton, William Nelson, 1908–
    The Iroquois Eagle dance : an offshoot of the Calumet dance /
William N. Fenton. — Syracuse University Press ed.
        p.   cm. — (The Iroquois and their neighbors)
    Reprint. Originally published : Washington, D.C. : Smithsonian
Institution, Bureau of American Ethnology, 1953.
    Includes bibliographical references and index.
    ISBN 0-8156-2533-2 (alk. paper)
    1. Eagle dance.   2. Iroquois Indians—Dances.   3. Iroquois
Indians—Rites and ceremonies.   I.Title.   II. Series.
E99.I7F454   1991
394'.3—dc20   91-4257
                                                                     CIP

Manufactured in the United States of America

CONTENTS

ILLUSTRATIONS

PLATES

(All plates, except frontispiece, following page 222)

1. (Frontispiece.) Dew Eagle dances on the deer. (Watercolor by Ernest Smith, Seneca artist of Tonawanda.)
2. The household of Resting-sky. *Back row:* Resting-sky and Voice-above. *Center:* It-dips-water; and (*front*) her grandson.
3. Sherman Redeye, Snipe Clan, Coldspring Seneca informant.
4. Clara Redeye, Voice-above, Hawk Clan, interpreter, at Coldspring.
5. It-dips-water, Hawk Clan matron, wife of Resting-sky, Coldspring Seneca.
6. Eagle Dance in 1942 for Big-canoe and He-carries-an-ax. *1,* Wood-eater puts tobacco in the fire. *2,* On the last song the dancers lay down the feather fans.
7. Eagle Dance in 1942. *1,* The second round of speeches for Dew Eagle. *2,* The dancers crouch and sway with the song.
8. Eagle Dance in 1942. *1,* Passing the pig head and crying like crows. *2,* Members carry home pails of corn soup.
9. Wood-eater, Bear Clan, Seneca ritualist at Coldspring.
10. Corn-husker, Hawk Clan, Seneca of Coldspring, and his two pet hawks.
11. Twenty-canoes, Bear Clan, and Stick-lodged-in-a-crotch, Deer Clan, guardians of Handsome Lake's message, as delegates from Coldspring to Tonawanda Longhouse.
12. Snorer, Hawk Clan, Seneca of Coldspring.
13. Hemlocks-lying-down, Turtle Clan, conductor and singer of Seneca ceremonies at Coldspring.
14. Earth-hiller, matron of the Wolf Clan, Coldspring.
15. Helper, Sachem chief of the Bear Clan, Tonawanda Seneca.
16. *1,* He-strikes-the-rushes, Snipe Clan, Seneca ritualist, with gourd rattle of the Medicine Company, in the costume of the Federal Period. *2,* Chief Joseph Logan, Onondaga, and Simeon Gibson, Six Nations Reserve, Canada.
17. Djidǫ'gwas, a Seneca of the Wolf Clan, at Coldspring.
18. Yankee Spring, a Seneca of the Beaver Clan, at Tonawanda.
19. Sarah Snow, Seneca of the Bear Clan, Coldspring's clairvoyant and herbalist.
20. Eagle Society Bundles. *1,* Fans and gourd rattles from the bundle of Hemlocks-lying-down. *2,* An old set of fans in New York State Museum.
21. Striped emblem pole of Eagle Society, displayed for a meeting of the Society. (Courtesy New York State Museum.)

*For contents of supplement, see pp. 225-227.

22. Five-feathered fans from Cattaraugus Seneca. (Milwaukee Public Museum photograph.)
23. Water drum and horn rattle, by Clarence White of Coldspring, laid out for Eagle Dance singers.
24. Horn rattles: *Left*, two by Hemlocks-lying-down; *right*, by Corn-husker.
25. Corn-husker's wife leaches white corn for soup.
26. Hulled white corn after three washings.
27. The Seneca Eagle Dance. (Oil painting by Ernest Smith, Seneca artist of Tonawanda.)
28. Cherokee Eagle Dance movements by Will West Long: Approach, holding the fan, and crouch.

FIGURES

INTRODUCTION TO THE 1991 EDITION

THE END OF THE CENTURY

Some fifty-seven years after my first field work among the people of Coldspring Longhouse on the Allegany Reservation of the Seneca Nation of Indians, I revisited Salamanca, New York, a small city of nearly seven thousand population, which occupies lands leased from the Seneca Nation. The great ''Oxbow'' of the Allegheny River flows north out of Pennsylvania, its northern extremity passes through Salamanca, and then it reaches west and south to Sun Fish, Red House, Gahaiine (''Witch's walk'') to Coldspring, and on south to Cornplanter and Kinzua, returning to Pennsylvania. The great terminal moraines of the last ice age still confine the river to its ancient course, mark the outlines of the Indian reservation, and encompass the Allegany State Park; but otherwise man has altered geography with railroads, the Kinzua Dam and reservoir, and a superhighway.

My concerns in revisiting Salamanca were personal. I was interested to learn how the new leases would affect the community. Members of my immediate family rest in Wildwood Cemetery on Indian land now subject to Indian lease. My late wife of fifty years, whom I met when living among the Senecas, had roots in the white community. Our friends were in both camps.

I would see whomever I could find during a brief visit. Indeed, ''Bee Bee'' Ground knew I had recorded the genealogy of her grandparents, Chauncey and Bertha Warrior. I had made copies of it for her, and we spent a rainy morning reviewing it with her husband, Will Ground, from Tonawanda and recalling former times. Traditional roles of ethnologist and informant were reversed. They asked the questions, and I related what the old people told me and recalled events that I experienced during the 1930s. We talked of Tonawanda field days, of Husk Face performances at Coldspring, of museum collections, their care and interpretation. I autographed my book on the False Faces for them, but the Eagle Dance never entered our conversation. At the end of our session, Bee Bee presented me with an eagle feather on a loop of spun bison hair, which hangs above me as I write. She died within a year.

It rained cats and dogs that Monday. Duwayne Leslie Bowen greeted me at the Seneca Iroquois National Museum. I had known his father, Wesley, and the son is one of the gifted Iroquois writers, whose work I had reviewed. Duwayne is an original in the best tradition of Seneca storytellers. His tales of supernatural incidents during his lifetime recall the mists and hills of the Allegheny Oxbow. The Senecas have produced painters like Ernest Smith of Tonawanda and a host of others; and now the new voices supply the want of folklore that was fading a generation ago. Duwayne remarked to me: "You know, I guess, that you are legendary."

George Heron, a former president of the Seneca Nation, had overseen the building of two residential communities—Jimersontown and Steamburg—with compensation received for cultural damages following the Kinzua Dam condemnation of Coldspring and a third of the reservation. A fluent Seneca speaker, George has continued to assist linguists and has taught language classes for young people. I have known him since the 1940s when he played baseball with the "John boys" on one of the great Seneca teams. Later, he and I had served on a committee to explore the feasibility of "Iroquoia," a Seneca Williamsburg, that proved impracticable; but out of it emerged the Seneca Iroquois National Museum. He comes in afternoons to guide visitors through the museum.

George related the sad news that the family of Herb Dowdy, one of the truly great Seneca singers, had that day held his Tenth Day feast, that Herb had died suddenly of a massive coronary attack while resting after working in his garden. Young Herb Dowdy had been an Eagle dancer, he of course knew the songs, and I had planned to ask him how the Eagle Society fared. George also volunteered that the Green Corn ceremony was in progress, that Herb, also known as "Gobit," had been one of the surviving speakers. He concluded, "Next time, come stay with me. I too am alone."

I drove to Steamburg in a monsoon rain. The longhouse was quiet. The heavy rain had quenched the smoke of cooking. No one was in sight, and I found old friends away. None of the ambience of remembered days at Coldspring Longhouse remained. Salamanca and the Allegany Reservation were about to emerge into something new. I wondered whether the ceremonies of the medicine societies such as the Eagle Dance would survive. The dark cloud that hung over Salamanca real estate titles for a generation since the Great Depression, when I first went there, is about to clear. With the lease question settled in favor of the Senecas, individual householders and small shopkeepers will suffer hardships at first; but the real estate boom in nearby Ellicottville, engendered by the winter sports industry, will soon spill over into Salamanca, which is about to be discovered by visitors from Toronto, Buffalo, Cleveland, and Pittsburgh. By their standards, Salamanca real estate will offer bargains.

This not irrelevant note on the contemporary Indian-white community stands in sharp contrast to conditions described in the previous introduction. I had married field observations of two performances of the Eagle Dance, a curing society, to a problem posed in Edward Sapir's seminar at Yale on the "Impact of Culture on Personality." Out of it grew a dissertation. In the course of the investigation, I realized that history operated at several levels. There were individuals whose life histories mirrored participation in culture; the community had a history of its own; the ceremony described varied locally; and the ceremony had evolved relatively recently among the tribes of the Iroquois Confederacy out of a widespread war and peace ritual known as the Calumet Dance. In linking the present to the past I developed an approach that I termed "upstreaming," a term I borrowed from Sir Flinders Petrie of Egyptian prehistory fame, in which I worked steadily backward from my own observations to the historical sources. This approach contributed to the now burgeoning field of ethnohistory. My contribution to that discipline has found support and criticism (see Michael K. Foster, ed., *Extending the Rafters: Interdisciplinary Approaches to Iroquois Studies* [Albany: State University of New York Press, 1984]; and Daniel Richter in *Ethnohistory* 32, no. 4: [1985]363–369).

A recent statement of the genealogy and history of Iroquois studies appears in *The False Faces of the Iroquois* (Norman: University of Oklahoma Press, 1987, pp. 86 ff.). Many of the same people contributed to the two studies, and other Iroquoianists have written on ceremonialism. The previous introduction outlines the problem; it tells just how I worked; and the former picture of life at Coldspring presents a marked contrast to the opening statement of this essay.

New readers may welcome guidance on where to begin. I am an empiricist. As such, I present my observations first before making a general statement. Some readers may wish to begin with "the Eagle Dance as a cultural phenomenon" (p. 75 ff.) and then go back and peruse the accounts of various celebrations. They should also look at the sketches of participating personalities (p. 38 ff.). It is such individuals in a society who affect the performance of set forms; it is their innovations that lead to culture change and determine local diversity.

I usually shun rereading old writing. The present book represents some of my earliest attempts to turn what I saw and heard into prose. Writing is never easy. Thoreau constantly reminds me that every sentence has a long probation. In rereading the book, I was struck by some awkward constructions and other passages that I could not improve on today. The main thing was to put it all down. Field notes of interviews from persons who spoke reservation English and for whom Seneca was their first language resist transformation into standard English. Seneca word order frequently puts the subject after the verb for emphasis after incorporating the root in the verb itself. "Fifty muskrats shot my father," Corn-husker's boast that he spoke English, speaks to this problem. Many concepts are simply untranslatable.

Writing from historical sources presents similar problems. One reads them for light on the topics that interest him. It is tempting to cite what, in the words of Cadwallader Colden, appears "in the Words of the

Registers.'' One gets caught up in the style of the eighteenth-century writers, analysis of what they say destroys the flavor of the message, and it is tempting to quote them verbatim. One loses sight of the problem, and the reader loses his way. History is a dialogue between the scholar and his sources, which he must examine critically. The anthropologist faced with the historian's task becomes an ethnohistorian. He brings to the dialogue concepts of another discipline and the perspective of his own ethnographic field work among the living.

When I entered anthropology, it was customary for ethnologists to map the distribution of culture traits isolated in field work and discovered in the historical literature. Culture areas were then delineated and historical drift inferred. The concepts of age and area were under attack from the functionalists who regarded such history as bogus and concentrated on the interaction of cultural activities and institutions at a given point of time. Radcliffe-Brown and Malinowski were the principal critics of the American historical school. Under the guidance of Clark Wissler and Leslie Spier, I set out to combine the two approaches by seeking the roots of a cultural activity, which I had observed and recorded in a living, functioning society, through both a distributional approach and direct history. In this way, I demonstrated that the Eagle Dance was derived from the Calumet Dance, a widespread phenomena in the seventeenth century; that it originated probably in the Pawnee Hako ceremony; and that it reached the Iroquois in the late seventeenth and early eighteenth centuries only to be transformed into a medicine or curing society in the nineteenth century. The ritual pattern that I had established from all the Iroquois variants afforded clues for identifying related activities among neighboring peoples and for interpreting documentary records of performances.

Gertrude Kurath, a dancer, musicologist, and pioneer in the ethnographic dance, undertook to transcribe the recordings I had made of the Eagle Dance songs. In the course of her field work on Iroquois dance forms, she transformed her previous knowledge of choreographic notation to diagraming Iroquois dance performances. She added to my observations her own observation and analysis of two Eagle Dance celebrations at Six Nations Reserve in Canada. She mapped the ritual movements within the space of the longhouse and illustrated the posture of the dancers with stick figures. The analysis of the music is unique. But not stopping here, she mapped the distribution of similar dance forms throughout the continent. Her analysis of the music and the dance forms taken together with an independent study of historical data confirmed the conclusions that I had reached. The musical and choreographic analyses were carried further than in any previous similar work on American Indians (*United States Quarterly Book Review* 10, no. 2 [June 1954]: 205–206).

The work has generated interest beyond the field of Iroquois studies. Students of the Cherokee in the Southeast, notably Ray Fogelson, have followed its leads; and Plains ethnologists, notably Robert Hall and the late James Howard of Oklahoma, have furthered the connection between the Calumet and the Great Pipe ceremony on the northern plains.

I am confident that somewhere in Iroquoia the Eagle Dance is being performed. Perhaps the reprinting of this monograph will assist native Iroquois in communities where the ceremony has lapsed. Taken together with published recordings, in which they have always manifested intense interest, they now have a how-to book based on what we saw and what the old people told us.

WILLIAM N. FENTON

Slingerlands, New York
September 1990

The Iroquois Eagle Dance

THE IROQUOIS EAGLE DANCE
AN OFFSHOOT OF THE CALUMET DANCE

By WILLIAM N. FENTON

INTRODUCTION

The present monograph stems from a dissertation which was originally presented to the faculty of the Graduate School of Yale University in candidacy for the degree of doctor of philosophy, 1937. The dissertation incorporated ethnographic materials which were gathered during field work in western New York between 1933 and 1936, and these were marshaled in a way to show the bearing of the problem of individual variation in behavior on ethnology. My interest in this problem has continued during 12 years of field investigations among the Iroquois and other tribes while a member of the staff of the Bureau of American Ethnology. For one reason or another the monograph has remained unpublished, and the present draft represents a third rewriting. New material has accumulated, historical perspective has deepened and widened, and methods of handling historical problems call for a different presentation. Experience has indicated that it is best to look at historical sources from the viewpoint of the field and to test early descriptions of Indian behavior against a knowledge of how Indians behave as persons. When I at first proceeded from ethnology to the earlier historical sources and tried to reconcile the two types of data across the chasm of several centuries by reading history chronologically up to the present, I met with small success. It works better to begin with the present and work steadily backward. For this application of the archeologists' method of "direct historic approach" I have borrowed the term "upstreaming," from the classical archeologists.

Ethnology frequently demands historical investigation at different levels. Starting with individual informants, more general levels are the community, the tribe, neighboring tribes, and the area. The theme of this investigation is that the diversity of individual expression in cultural situations reflects the personal history of the individual within the culture of his group. In the Eagle Dance individuals participate differently in a ceremony which is part of their common cultural heri-

1

tage. Much of the individual differences in behavior consists in performing well roles that are shared by several members of the group and delivering certain utterances which are known to several erudite members of the group. Iroquois ceremonies differ locally in detail, and individual ritual custodians cherish local and tribal variants and modify them slightly even after prolonged residence in another community. But everywhere in Iroquoia the Eagle Dance ritual has one underlying ceremonial pattern which sets limits to the expression of individual personality, and this ritual pattern which orders the program of other Iroquois medicine society rites has developed in the long course of Iroquois history. It regiments all of their ceremonies. The Iroquois Eagle Dance, moreover, and its ritual paraphernalia bear a striking resemblance to the Eagle Dance of the Shawnee and the Cherokee, and all of these variants in the Appalachian Highlands derive from the dance in honor of the Calumet which Marquette first encountered among the Illinois at a time when the Iroquois lacked it. The Calumet Dance spread from the Pawnee east, south, and west, and north following 1680, and in an attenuated form it seems to have reached the Iroquois about 1750. Such a cultural phenomenon as the Eagle Dance and its relation to the Calumet Dance, and the spread of the latter, cannot be explained satisfactorily by only using the functional method which studies the interaction of various elements and institutions of culture at a given point of time, for the explanation of individual and of group behavior often lies in history.

Such anthropological theory as I possess I owe to the faculty in anthropology at the Yale Graduate School who contributed to my professional training some years ago. Prof. Edward Sapir and Dr. Clark Wissler, who will not read this bulletin, taught me linguistics, ethnohistory, and a respect for Indians as persons. Dr. Leslie Spier coached my dissertation, and from him I learned how to be a professional ethnographer. Prof. Cornelius Osgood introduced me to the literature on the Americas, and Prof. George Peter Murdock taught me how to test field work in the library. Material culture came alive in the hands of Te Rangi Hiroa (Sir Peter Buck). The students of my age group are now professionals—teachers, museum administrators, and researchers—mostly outside of the Americanist tradition in which we were reared. Anthropology has grown immensely since June of 1933 when Professor Sapir and Dr. Mark May sent me out to the Iroquois from the Institute of Human Relations and subsequently earmarked funds for my research. I should have failed completely were it not for the friendly advice of Dr. Frank G. Speck, who, although I was not enrolled as his student at the University of Pennsylvania, suggested a method of outlining the Seneca ceremonies at Coldspring Longhouse which gave unity to all my later work (Fenton, 1936 b). For my dissertation, he contributed notes on the Cherokee and Cayuga Eagle Dances and read the manuscript. Speck later became a member of the Eagle Society at Coldspring, an honor which I cannot claim, and his Seneca friends performed the rite for him last on January 20, 1950, in an effort to revive him "on the brink of the grave" (Speck, 1950; and The Seneca of Coldspring Longhouse, 1950, pp. 60–61).

From my colleagues in Eastern Woodland studies, Prof. Carl and Dr. Erminie Voegelin of Indiana University, I have received notes on the Өawikila Eagle Dance of the Shawnee. Martha Champion Randle spent a week with us at Tonawanda in 1936, recording Bob Shanks' Eagle songs, which are now transcribed happily by Gertrude P. Kurath of Ann Arbor, Mich., author of the analysis of the dance and songs which supplements my study. Beginning in 1941 recording equipment was made available to me by the Library of Congress, and the Eagle Dance recorded by Chief Joseph Logan of Six Nations Reserve was included in the first album of Iroquois music (Fenton, 1942, pp. 29–30). For a good deal of historical and distributional data I am indebted to Prof. Regina Flannery Herzfeld, of Catholic University of America, and the late Prof. John M. Cooper.

Ethnology among the Iroquois has a long genealogy, which I have recounted several times (Fenton, 1940, pp. 160–164; 1949, pp. 233–234; 1951 a). Lewis H. Morgan, America's great ethnologist, preceded me a century ago at Tonawanda, and I once had access to his journals and field notes at the Rush Rhees Library of the University of Rochester. F. W. Waugh was one of the people for whom Sapir made field work possible at Grand River during the second decade of the century. Waugh's Iroquois Field Notes, in manuscript, was lent to me some years ago by the National Museum of Canada through Dr. Diamond Jenness. The originals are in Ottawa, but a duplicate set of Waugh's folklore collection is now at the American Philosophical Society Library. The Waugh papers contain several references to the Eagle Dance.

Subsequently, Dr. Alexander A. Goldenweiser sent me his Iroquois notebooks, which contain some pointed notes on the Eagle Dance. To Dr. Arthur C. Parker, emeritus director of the Rochester Museum of Arts and Sciences, I am indebted for contributions from his early Newtown Seneca field notes and excerpts from the manuscripts of Laura Wright, and for his kindness in reading a preliminary draft of this monograph.

I once used the reference libraries of Buffalo, incurring debts of gratitude to many persons. I worked mainly at the Buffalo Historical Society where I remember the kindness of Robert W. Bingham to a student, and the help of Miss Alice Pickup, librarian.

Ernest Smith is one of a band of Seneca draftsmen at Tonawanda, and my friend Roy M. Mason, N. A., gave him criticism in painting when Smith set out to illustrate my ethnology. To the New York State Museum and other such institutions I have given credit where due for photographs and permissions to publish. In first preparing this manuscript great credit is due to Olive Ortwine Fenton, who tried to teach me to write coherently and who became my wife.

It is the custom in ethnology to call the bearers of the oral tradition "informants." At Coldspring, Jonas and Josephine Snow were my hosts one summer, as were Sherman and Clara Redeye the next winter and summer. I learned as I ate and lived in the community. Some informants worked for wages by the hour; on principle, I paid them when we worked regularly according to local wage standards. These were my friends at Coldspring, as are those of them who survive to-day (1951): Levi Snow, Charles and Sadie Butler, William, Hattie, and LeRoy Cooper, Chief John Jacobs, Jonas Crouse, Wesley White, Albert Jones, John Jimmerson, Chief Hiram Watt, Chauncey Johnny John, Howard Jimmerson, Henry Redeye, Myron and Lucy Turkey, Chauncey and Geneva Warrior, and others who listened to and patiently answered my questions during two summers at Coldspring. James Crow, Jake Jack, and Jesse Cornplanter, whose ethnological interest dates from childhood memory of his father Edward Cornplanter working with Prof. Frederick Starr, Arthur C. Parker, and M. R. Harrington, introduced me to Seneca customs at Newtown Longhouse, Cattaraugus Reservation.

I cannot mention all of the 600 persons at Tonawanda who made 2½ years among them a unique experience, but Chief Barber Black, Chief Edward Black, Chief Lyman Johnson, Chief Solon Skye, and Chief Henan Scrogg made a policy of seeing that I got things straight; and besides, I tutored under Elijah David, Simeon Skye, Jesse Cornplanter, and Robert Shanks; Cephas Hill and his mother, Jennie Jones, made me always welcome; and Rev. Peter W. Doctor enjoyed going back to his pagan upbringing to enrich my knowledge.

Onondaga information comes principally from Chief David Thomas, his wife, their son, and his friend Floyd Henhawk. I did not witness the Eagle Dance at Newtown or at Onondaga, N. Y. In Canada, the late Simeon Gibson was my interpreter (Fenton, 1944), and Chief Joseph Logan of Onondaga Longhouse recorded for me. Chief Alexander General and Howard Skye of the Cayuga Nation have proved invaluable sources.

In quoting informants and in citing information about them, the text employs English translations of Indian personal names that they hold as members of particular clans and by which they are called on ceremonial occasions. Many of these people who were my friends have already "gone the long trail"; those who are left deserve my wholehearted loyalty. Let those who read this monograph accept it with a clear mind, for it is written without malice aforethought in the spirit of speeches made at Eagle Dance meetings.

THE PROBLEM

Field workers in North America have all experienced the dilemma of the ethnographer trying to resolve data which were obtained from informants who agree only on the patterned aspects of their culture, such as the presence of clans, the function of moieties, and the broad outlines of a calendric series of ceremonies. However, the appreciation that individual variations within the culture pattern or from a supposed norm are legitimate cultural data, which Radin championed in ethnology (Radin, 1920, 1926, 1927, 1933), and which Sapir stimulated in culture-personality psychology (Mandelbaum, 1949), has grown apace with the interest of the role of the individual in the culture of his society (Linton, 1936, 1947; Hallowell, 1946; Fenton,1948; Wallace, A. F. C., 1952). The ethnographic material on the Eagle Dance which follows shows the extent to which individual participation affects cultural situations and what aspects of such behavior can be accounted for with the ordinary techniques of ethnology. The methods and techniques of projective tests were developed after this study was made and were not then available. It is interesting, however, to compare my impressions of Iroquois personality (Fenton, 1948), written under the stimulation of reading Hallowell (1946), with the findings of Wallace (1952), who confirmed my predictions for the Tuscarora.

During the summer of 1933, I conducted my first field work among the Seneca Nation, spending the whole season at Coldspring on the Allegany Indian Reservation, which stretches 40 miles along the Allegheny River in southwestern New York. I went to Allegany Reservation because two previous generations of my family have been acquainted with Seneca families resident there. My father had once taken me to a Green Corn Dance at Coldspring Longhouse, and we had visited among the families of "pagans" in the neighborhood. Corn-husker had made masks for my father and had assisted in assembling an ethnological collection, which was later divided between the United States National Museum and the Museum of the American Indian, Heye Foundation. So Corn-husker took me to board with his family, and I slept out in an umbrella tent which had been lent to me by Scudder Mekeel, who had preceded me at the Institute. Living in the dooryard of a Seneca family had distinct advantages. My host knew about the old culture and he was interested in my welfare. From the vantage point of Corn-husker's dooryard, I observed and noted the goings and comings of his family, their relatives, and friends. In turn we visited other houses to attend meetings of a singing society, to widen my circle of acquaintance, and to get specific information.

I stayed with Corn-husker from June until after the Green Corn Festival in September. As the single White stranger in the community, a member of a race whom the Seneca had come to suspect if not dislike (Sullivan and Brodhead had come against the Seneca in 1779; the Whites had cheated the Indians of their lands at Buffalo Creek in 1838; Yankee farmers lived all around them; and in the city of Salamanca on leased land were merchants and lawyers, railroad workers, and middle-class folks, some friendly and some unfriendly), naturally my ethnological activities were watched and discussed by the Indian individuals and families, who reacted according to their own interests and prejudices, their sentiment for the Longhouse Religion of Handsome Lake, or their belief as Christians that I was giving lip service to the "pagan societies." They grouped me with Corn-husker's family— "that White man who sleeps in a tent at Corn-husker's"—and gradually they regarded me as a person. The ethnologist presented a single personality; to him the community presented many personalities.

Life at Coldspring is a going concern and the longhouse settlement has a culture of its own. Albeit this culture is not the integrated culture of an aboriginal Seneca community, nevertheless faith in the revelation of the Seneca Prophet, Handsome Lake, unites a small autonomous group of families and gives them a sense of belonging to something which is ancient and respectable; and they cherish the last vestiges of that culture, which their somewhat isolated life on the reservation has engendered. I write this knowing that of three railroads crossing the reservation, the Erie has given employment to the men of Coldspring for several generations. The "regular" gang and the "extra" gang comprise two distinct classes of workmen in the community. Work in the woods has given way to construction work, principally on New York State highways, of which two main roads junction at Coldspring. Randolph, Salamanca, and Bradford have supplanted nearby Quaker Bridge, Steamburg, and Red House as shopping centers. And children are transported to State-supported schools. But despite these identifications with rural New York, from their babyhood children are taught Seneca, "the real language" (ǫgw'e' ǫweka·'),[1] which is spoken in Coldspring, and later they learn English (gányǫ· ka·'), the language of the White man, his schools, and his work-a-day world. (Conditions have changed rapidly since my first visit in 1933; it was the period of the depression, there was no work off the reservation, and many old people who spoke little English were yet alive. Change has

---

[1] See phonetic note, p. 12.

accelerated during a Second World War. Now many of the children are not learning Seneca.) Women still pick huckleberries along the tracks and carry them home in splint baskets of their own manufacture. On summer evenings, mutual aid societies meet to compose and rehearse dance songs, there are impromptu social dances, and the members hoe each other's gardens, cut wood, and help the women (Fenton, 1936 a). Men still play lacrosse in summer, although baseball is a keen rival, and snow-snake remains the distinctive Indian winter sport. Nearly everyone attends the stated festivals at the longhouse.

Coldspring used to be noted for its well-kept Indian gardens, although in my time there, both good and poor gardens were common. Corn-husker had a well-kept garden of potatoes, cabbage, corn, pole beans, squash, and pumpkins. At various times the whole family worked in the garden and older women still assumed much of the traditional burden of cultivation. Rude plank and clapboard houses were the rule and well-tended lawns were not exceptional. At Cornhusker's the accessories of the old garden and kitchen culture—corn mortar, dumbbell pestle, washing basket, pack basket, hand baskets—lay where they were left about the dooryard or stood behind the house. There was the inevitable drawshave horse or *schnitzelbank* and a bent white hickory timber for making a lacrosse stick.

Inside the house at night, the kerosene lamp would illumine a mud turtle rattle, a bag of horn rattles, a lacrosse stick hanging on the wall next to a shotgun, and baseball gloves. Indians especially like photographs—individual portraits, group pictures of athletic teams, members of the family as show Indians in costume with some troupe, and a few pictures of movie stars. There is always a calendar advertising Dr. Somebody's patent medicine which gives the phases of the moon and is consequently useful for computing the dates of festivals. An alarm clock stands on the shelf. Overhead, above the stove, snowsnakes, green hickory canes, a bow, and ash darts for the hoop-and-javelin game, extend across drying racks which are improvised by suspending two poles parallel on wire from the ceiling. Gourd and pumpkin rattles fitted with wooden handles hang high on the wall near a bundle of brown paper or floursacking from which protrude two sticks or tufts of feathers, indicating that some member of the Medicine Company lives here.

When members of the family are taken sick, they try various herbal medicines suggested by the elders. If they dream, they consult a clairvoyant, who may suggest joining one of the medicine societies. If they recover, they feel thankful and "put up their societies" and give feasts for the tutelaries of the societies, lest the sickness revert to them or their children.

A Seneca is born into one of eight clans which are divided into two phratries or moieties. At death, the four clans of the other moiety conduct the wake and funeral, supervise the last journey to the longhouse, and bury their "cousin." Such services are reciprocal. Although the Seneca bear patrilineal English family names, they practice double descent, since membership in a clan implies the right to use one of a series of personal names belonging to that clan; it assigns the person automatically to a moiety or side, and he is an enrolled member of the tribe and entitled to receive a Government annuity—all by descent in the female line. Deeds to improvements on the reservation may pass from father to sons, but most personal property is disposed of by the clan at the Ten Days' Feast. And the title to the reservation, which they hold in severalty, ultimately rests in the women.

Such information came to me by observation, in answer to direct questions, as anecdote accompanying genealogies, in conversations at all manner of gatherings and ceremonials, at meals, and while walking on the road. Thus I endeavored to learn rapidly the social and ceremonial affiliation of everyone in the community.

Apart from individual variations in behavior which arise at psychological levels beyond the reach of the ethnologist, I noted first among the Seneca diversity of individual expression which struck me as being the product of the peculiar participation of these individuals in the culture of the group. Men know some things because of personal history. In the first summer, I was continually impressed that individuals differed on the most elementary cultural data: names for baskets, the order for listing clans, and knowledge of the types of masks (Fenton, 1937, p. 216). Members of the same household had separate and often divergent stories for the beginning of a medicine society, and they gave varying accounts of participation in the ceremonies. Men whom I had observed in positions of authority, as ritual conductors of longhouse celebrations or private rites of a society, might know all of the songs and the procedure, but they proved quite ignorant concerning the origin and history of the ceremonies. As time went on, the housemother where I boarded voluntarily commented on possible informants. She had entertained the medicine societies in her home, and although she seldom attended public ceremonies at the longhouse, she knew: "Hemlocks-lying-down is a good singer, and he knows all about medicines; Snorer is the best speaker, he knows the origin legends, and you will have to pay him; Woodeater is proud, he speaks little English, and he may not tell you; I guess my man Corn-husker does not know what his father knew; and old Stick-lodged-in-a-crotch is always asleep and they say he never hears what the speaker says."

I began to realize that within the framework of a simple community of 72 households and 326 persons, individuals participate differently in affairs which are their common social heritage. Also my approach to principal persons carried the feeling-tone of my adopted household.

My first effort was to establish the pattern which underlies the rituals, for many of them presented superficial similarities and seemed to follow a common program (Fenton, 1936 b). The Eagle Dance was among the first medicine society rites which I was privileged to witness that first summer when my enthusiasm for recording all I saw and noting the clan membership of every participant had not been dampened by the criticism of learned informants who soon told me that much of what I noted was really irrelevant to the ritual. My spurious accuracy contrasted with a review of the meeting by Hemlocks-lying-down, who had conducted the ceremony; he corrected my notes and gave me an account of the ceremony which revealed an abstract pattern for the ritual which he knew from many meetings. Later, as better informants and interpreters were secured and I commenced to control the outline of the ritual, I decided that what individuals had to say in these meetings might constitute a body of interesting data.

Sapir's lectures on the "Impact of Culture on Personality," during the next academic year at Yale, stimulated me to pursue data on personality expression in ritual. I was back in Coldspring for the Seneca New Year (January 18 to February 2, 1934). With the ritual pattern firmly in mind, I set about recording the expressions of individual personalities which came to me in the form of life-history data, direct testimony, gossip about others; I noted what individuals took part in the ceremonies and what roles were assigned to them; and I paid particular heed to derogatory speeches which have a formalized place in the Eagle Dance and in the War Dance, which are two of the medicine society meetings. It is in these speeches that one finds individuals reacting to the behavior of others within the formal outline of a ceremony. Within the larger framework of Iroquois ceremonialism the culture has provided this opportunity for individuals to drain off aggression. The speeches made on these occasions reflect personality conflicts, prejudices, humor, and bitterness, and all those varied emanations, such as song, gesture, and etiquette, which result from individual participation in the culture of the group, and are, in short, an individual's own peculiar culture or his personality.

Individuals who participated in the meetings of Eagle Society which I have attended at Coldspring and at Tonawanda have their own personal histories, which are distinct from the history of the Eagle Society. Although their behavior patterns conform mainly to the lines of least resistance within the well-worn grooves of the ritual, nevertheless one individual may tower above his fellows for sheer quality in performing routine tasks, another may feel uncomfortable in the presence of a third, and because of some past incident he may not speak at all, and a fourth person may absent himself entirely. A fifth person may enjoy the situation immensely and rise to joke with his fellow members of Eagle Society who are his neighbors.

There were some five men and a woman whose presence or absence affected the form and content of two Eagle Society meetings at Coldspring. Their case histories seem relevant to this discussion. The cases are pertinent to the first two meetings. The first meeting emphasizes the ritual and is followed by an anniversary celebration of Resting-sky's cure by the Eagle Society. The latter meeting illustrates how the varied personalities participated in the situation, and possibly their behavior, individually as well as together, was the result of historical processes. The notes from this meeting also illustrate how ritual, or progressively abbreviated set forms of behavior, is influenced by variation in individual behavior.

Perhap's like Radin's good investigators (Radin, 1933, p. ix), I am hardly aware of the precise manner in which I gathered the data on the Eagle Dance as a cultural phenomenon. In the season of 1934 and in the 2½ years that followed in the Indian Service, I employed the Coldspring observations as a lever to pry from many informants in several Iroquois communities all I could get on the Eagle Society. That the ethnologist finds out what he already knows is a maxim which all later field work has confirmed. While at Tonawanda I came to use Seneca in daily conversations, and a good deal of the material was noted in phonetic script, especially the prayers which I took in text. But most of the accounts came in "Reservation English" from bilingual informants who shift back and forth between Iroquois and English. I offer their original remarks unaltered except by changes in grammar to render them intelligible to readers.

The approach to ethnographic problems is inevitably that of the ethnologist. I have conscientiously endeavored to present culture from the viewpoint of the Iroquois, keeping my own discussion apart from the data. Ethnography is not a chronological record of researches such as the ethnologist writes in a journal, but is rather a synthesis of material centered on a problem which the ethnologist discovers in the literature and carries to the field, or which, as in the present case, the data themselves suggest. The task of ethnology is the description of a given culture.

Field work progresses from the specific to the general. The observations of specific ceremonies and accounts of the ritual from separate localities and the cases of participating personalities precede the most general chapter which orients the Eagle Society in Iroquois culture. When traditional history is exhausted, documentary history and comparative ethnography give depth and breadth.

A word first about the Tonawanda, Onondaga, and Grand River variants of the Eagle Dance: A ceremonial friendship existed at Tonawanda between Helper, a chief of the Bear Clan, and his younger neighbor, He-is-coming, of the Snipe clan in the other moiety. They chose to renew this friendship in February 1935, shortly after my arrival at Tonawanda. After the meeting, I wrote up my observations, noting obvious differences from the Coldspring version. I consulted the principals and obtained as full accounts as they would give of the doings. Again, certain personalities, whom I came to know well and saw frequently for 2 years, largely determined the content of that meeting. He-strikes-the-rushes, who was reared at Newtown on Cattaraugus Reservation and later lived at Coldspring on Allegany Reservation, had come back to live with his wife at Tonawanda whence his mother had gone to Cattaraugus. Custom has adhered to him as he has adjusted to three localized ceremonial systems. Tonawanda people quite misunderstood him at this meeting when, in the Newtown pattern, he exercised the privileged joking relationship with his father's clansman. The latter misconstrued his meaning because, like everyone else at Tonawanda, he did not know of such a pattern or that it is sometimes employed in the Eagle Dance.

Watching and participating at later meetings of the Society at Tonawanda, Allegany, and Six Nations have served to check first impressions. Too long residence in the field, however, unavoidably brings a certain loss of freshness; it encourages abstraction, and invites the Indian's philosophy of procrastination. Frequent, repeated visits over a span of years yield a series of observations, contributing to mature conclusions.

Because Tonawanda people feel that their local version of the Eagle Dance is correct in those features which stand at variance with the Coldspring Seneca version, the Newtown Seneca version, and the versions current among the Canadian Iroquois, local diversity merits separate treatment. My own data and those of Mrs. Kurath on the Onondaga ceremony on Grand River precede the description of the Cayuga rite, which follows Speck (1949, pp. 111–113).

In placing the Eagle Dance in its ethnographic and historical perspective, two problems arise: first, the abundant historical literature on the Iroquois, so full on other matters, contains so few references to anything resembling the Eagle Dance that the age of its appearance among the Iroquois is uncertain; and second, where was its source?

The Eagle Dance, in all its variants among the related Iroquois,

of traits which, when analyzed and plotted, have separate
s among neighboring peoples. I am not here concerned
distributions. But the patterning of these traits among
ois most closely resembles the Calumet Dance which Mar-
rst encountered among tribes living in the Mississippi Valley
between the Great Lakes and the St. Francis River in Arkansas;
it bears analogies to the Pawnee Hako and its later variants on the
Northern Plains. The Iroquois of the seventeenth century are said
to have disrespected the calumet, by which the French writers meant
the reed and fan. Features of the ancient rite are perpetuated in
the modern Iroquois Eagle Dance, so we may expect that some form
of the widely distributed Calumet Dance diffused to the Iroquois
toward the middle of the eighteenth century either from the Upper
Great Lakes, from the Southeast, at the height of the Cherokee wars,
or directly from the Pawnee, who perpetuated its most elaborate
form.

After the above was written the music and dance were transcribed
by Gertrude Prokosch Kurath. It is interesting to see the analysis
of the dance and the songs bear out the original findings of ethnohistory. Taking the lead from my dissertation, Mrs. Kurath
pursued her study independently and has reached similar conclusions
about the relationship of the Iroquois Eagle Dance to the Pawnee
Hako, the diffusion of the Calumet Dance, and its survival in recent
times. The method of science which submits a problem to independent researchers for testing with separate data and different
methods in this case brings corroboration of the original finding.

PHONETIC NOTE

The orthography employed in this paper is the same as that used
in previous publications (Fenton, 1936 b, 1941 a). It reduces Seneca
transcription to a minimum of characters required by the economy
of the language. The vowels *a* (of English *father*), *ä* (of English
hand) *ε* (of English *met*), *e* (of French *été*), *i* (of French *fini*), and *o*
(of English *mote*) may later be reduced to four: *a*, *e*, *i*, and *o*. They
occur frequently in diphthongs and less frequently triphthongs. Na-
salization is denoted by a hook beneath the vowel. A raised comma
indicates the glottal stop. The character *š* is "*c*" (of English *shoe*);
ž varies between "*dz*" and "*dj*" (of English *adz* and *judge*) depending
on the speaker; *s* and *t* are ordinarily somewhat aspirated; heavily
aspirated *s* and *t* are followed by *h* (e. g., *sh* and *th*), *h* everywhere
indicates aspiration; and *T* indicates a terminal whispered *t* which
is articulated after a terminal glottal stop in a few words.

THE SENECA EAGLE DANCE AT COLDS ALLEGHENY RIVER

A SUMMER MEETING, WITH EMPHASIS ON THE

Hemlocks-lying-down came up the road past Corn-hus dusk, carrying a leatheroid bag. It contained his dru ⊥⊥⊥ horn rattle, and his Eagle Society bundle. He informed me that he was the conductor and singer and so, therefore, he was inviting me to attend an Eagle Dance over at Esther Fatty's across the road.

We sat talking under a maple tree in front of the house until his grandson, who was to be one of the dancers, came along carrying a tin pail. The latter was limping. He said that he heard a screech owl in a pine tree toward the longhouse and that he had turned his ankle. Hemlocks-lying-down remarked that hearing a screech owl is bad luck. Then we picked ourselves up and wandered over cross-lots to Esther Fatty's house. We entered through the south door, going past the kitchen stove where she was cooking soup in a wash boiler.

Francis Bowen (Hawk), Esther Fatty's son, and Corn-husker's second son (Bear), from our house, were in the adjoining room, where the ceremonies were to be held. Two-arrows-flying (Hawk), her grandson, and Sam Fatty (Snipe), 80, her father, came down off the hill from across the Erie tracks. Sam was carrying a lantern.

Presently the room filled with the invited guests, members of the Eagle Society, and they took their places on the chairs and benches which had been placed about the room in readiness. Hemlocks-lying-down, the conductor, seated them according to the accompanying diagram (fig. 1).

Participation in the meeting *	Moiety	Membership
1. Francis Bowen (ska'iyǫwi·yo·'), *recipient of the ceremony*	I	X
2. Esther Fatty, Hawk Clan, *matron and hostess to her son*	I	(?)
3. Hemlocks-lying-down, Turtle Clan, *messenger, conductor, and first singer*	II	X
4. Two-arrows-flying, Hawk Clan, *dancer*	I	X
5. Hemlocks-lying-down's grandson, Beaver Clan, *dancer*	II	X
6. Corn-husker, Hawk Clan, *whooper*	I	X
7. Amos Red Eye, Heron Clan, *presentation speaker*	I	X
8. Wood-eater, Bear Clan, *speaker and priest, and presentation speaker*	II	X
9. Sam Fatty, Snipe Clan, *gift custodian*	I	X
10. William Cooper, Snipe Clan, *second singer*	I	X
11. Stick-lodged-in-a-crotch, Deer Clan	I	X
12. Corn-husker's second son, Bear Clan, *standing*	II	X
13. Wife and baby of dancer 5, Hawk Clan	I	(?)
14. Recipient's young son, Turtle Clan, *reading paper*	II	(?)
15. Son of second singer 10, Bear Clan, *reading paper*	I	(?)
16. W. N. F.		
17. Child asleep on floor.		

*X=member; (?)=status unknown.

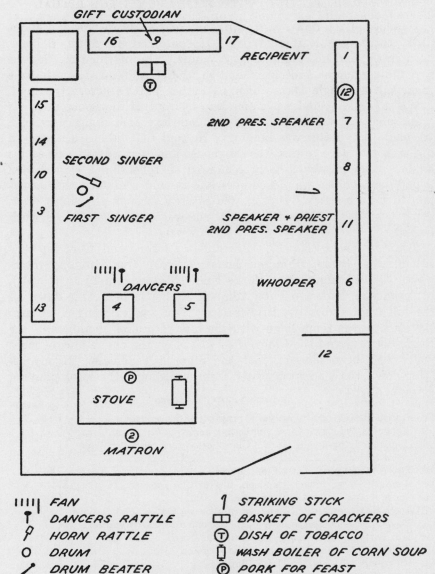

FIGURE 1.—Floor plan of Eagle Dance for Francis Bowen.

Several interesting facts bearing upon the problem of moiety alinement emerge from an analysis of the seating plan. The messenger,
conductor, first singer, speaker, and priest are of the opposite moiety

from the recipient or beneficiary of the ceremony. The dancers, singers, and presentation speakers represent each moiety. Moiety alinement for the whooper and the gift custodian seems unimportant. There is no spatial separation according to moieties in the sense that one moiety sits opposite its "cousins." We note, however, a convenient arrangement of dancers and singers, in general opposite the speakers, with the gift custodian opposite the dancers. The matron or cook is the close relative of the recipient for whom she sponsors the ritual, arranging all details with the conductor in the opposite moiety, who in this instance acted also as first singer and supplied the ritual equipment. The attendants and functionaries are largely composed of the close relatives of the recipient, and all who have any active part are members.

PRELIMINARY

Esther Fatty handed a large market basket full of soda crackers to her son, Francis Bowen, who set it on the floor in the northeast corner.

The two dancers were outside dressing.

The conductor, Hemlocks-lying-down, took from his bag the water drum, with the beater pinned through the selvage of the skin head, together with a black horn rattle, and, removing the beater from the drum, laid it to the right of the drum which he inverted on the floor. He placed the rattle at the left of the drum with the handle toward the second singer.

Hemlocks-lying-down, again as conductor, enlisted the services of several men for specific offices, going about whispering to each one separately. He asked Snorer (Hawk) to be whooper; Amos Red Eye (Heron) to present the fan and rattle to the dancer of his moiety; Wood-eater (Bear) to give the address of thanksgiving to the Great Spirit, to incant the tobacco-throwing prayer, and to present the fan and rattle to the dancer of his moiety; and, finally, Sam Fatty (Snipe) to take charge of distributing gifts—crackers—to the dancers following the speeches.

THANKSGIVING TO ALL THE SPIRIT-FORCES

Wood-eater delivered the Thanksgiving to the Spirit-forces, returning thanks especially for the tobacco.

TOBACCO PRAYER TO THE DEW EAGLE

Going to the kitchen, accompanied by the conductor carrying the tobacco in a saucer, Wood-eater held the wands and rattles and punctuated his prayer by committing pinches of tobacco to the flames (p. 145).

When the tobacco prayer was ended, the conductor set the balance of the tobacco on the floor and presently a member filled his pipe and passed the dish to another. All the members who wish may smoke the Indian tobacco. The conductor puts the balance in his pouch or shares it with the priest.

Now the feather wands were brought in from the kitchen with the tiny gourd rattles appended to the handles. Hemlocks-lying-down, the conductor, handed one to Wood-eater (Bear) and the other one to Amos Red Eye (Heron), for the other moiety.

THE RITUAL

(1) *Whoop and Song I.*[2] (Here begins the Eagle Dance proper.)— Corn-husker whooped and all echoed weakly. Hemlocks-lying-down (now as head singer) struck the drum twice and commenced the first song; William Cooper joined the antiphony using the horn rattle. The dancers are seated in their chairs at this dance side by side, instead of facing.

Toward the end of the song, Wood-eater took the striking stick and struck the floor, stopping the singing. He spoke and presented the fan and rattle to Hemlocks-lying-down's grandson (Beaver), the dancer of his moiety. The dancer, who remained seated in receiving it, disengaged the rattle from the fan handle, holding it in his right hand and taking the fan in his left. The members reply "It is well" (nyoh), and the drummer strikes the drum once whenever the Creator or Dew Eagle is mentioned, or they are requested to be of one mind with their host.

(2) *Whoop and Song II.*—Amos Red Eye performed the same function for the other moiety, giving the wand and rattle to Two-arrows-flying (Hawk), who in turn took the wand in his left hand and the rattle in his right.

(3) *Whoop and Song III.*—Sam Fatty (Snipe) reached for the stick,[3] struck the floor vehemently, and, standing, addressed the host and members, taking charge of the crackers.

Second round.—The next three speeches repeat the order of the first three speeches. They are delivered by the same men.

(4) *Whoop and Song IV.*—The dance begins here. Immediately the dancers commence swaying from side to side in their chairs, fluttering the calumet fans which they hold extended horizontally in their left hands, and beating time with their rattles. During the second part of the song, they crouch on the floor advancing and turning from side to side in imitation of birds. Halfway in the song they bend over, imitating birds scratching in the gravel and eating. Finally the head

---

[2] "At Newtown," according to He-strikes-the-rushes, "a presentation address is made by the conductor, giving the drum and rattles to the singers so they can sing. Two slow songs follow and the wands are presented. Frequently the first two songs are sung over by the priest as he finishes burning tobacco." Wood-eater sometimes does this at Allegany.

[3] The conductor is also acting as head singer, so there is no one left to hand the stick to the members. They have to pass it to each other, snaking it across the floor.

is down below one knee. Then they retreat jumping, tu
to either side, and they end with three short beats of
return to their chairs.

Eagle dancing is a tremendous muscular strain, and
required agility the role usually devolves upon younger men and boj
Among the Seneca there are still old men who are remembered for
having been agile dancers. John Armstrong is crippled with rheuma-
tism, but even the younger children know he was once a gifted dancer.

The dancers and singers are expected to continue until someone
strikes the signal pole, or floor; then they sit and all whoop softly.

The second round of speeches is addressed to the host.

Wood-eater struck the floor and spoke a second time. He distributed crackers which, according to Hemlocks-lying-down, was the
first time. He made the mistake of commencing the distribution in
the clockwise direction, but Hemlocks-lying-down corrected him.

Food distribution commences at the second round of speeches, then
the dance starts. Presents must be given to the dancers.

(5) *Whoop and Song V.*—The songs are composed by burden syllables, according to Hemlocks-lying-down, and they have no meaning.

Amos Red Eye (Heron) hit the floor and spoke.

This second round of speeches is really the first of the speeches
addressed to the host, hoping he will have good luck, etc.

(6) *Whoop and Song VI.*—Sam Fatty grabbed the stick and beat
the floor. Silence followed; and he stood to speak, as each of the
others had. Taking the basket by the handle he presented five
crackers each to the first and second singers, eight to each of the
dancers, and five each to the rest of the active members. The singers and dancers were provided with boxes, as they would get most
of them. The others put them in their pockets or on the bench
behind them. This being done, the ceremony was resumed.

(7) *Whoop and Song VII.*—Stick-lodged-in-a-crotch (Deer), being
nearly asleep, if not entirely, did not reach for the striking stick
quite quickly enough; and a dancer (whether or not it was because
he was nearest to him, or because he was of the opposite moiety, I
am not sure) commenced jumping toward him, only stopping and
retreating when the old man struck the floor. Everyone laughed.
The dancers are supposed to continue until the signal is given to
stop, and therefore theoretically, the speaker must anticipate the
end of the song. "He is supposed to strike before the whoop, or
cry, or at the end of the song." However, Stick-lodged-in-a-crotch
was sleepy. He distributed crackers.

This is the first speech by an active member who was not an official.

(8) *Whoop and Song VIII.*—Wood-eater (Bear), struck the floor,
spoke and distributed crackers. This was his third speech.

(9) *Whoop and Song IX.*—Corn-husker (Hawk), the whooper, struck the floor and spoke. He spoke only once. Most of the others spoke at least twice. He said afterward that he was sleepy, having worked hard all day.

The crackers were well-nigh distributed.

(10) *Whoop and Song X.*—Amos Red Eye (Heron) also spoke for the third time. It is noteworthy that the original three speakers are continuing in order, but that the whooper has inserted his speech between them, and a member has previously spoken between their second and third group of speeches. It amounts to there being but one member present who has not fulfilled an official role, namely, Stick-lodged-in-a-crotch, who is partly asleep. Further, the second singer, William Cooper, did not speak; speaking is not required of singers.[4]

(11) *Whoop and Song XI.*—Sam Fatty (Snipe), keeper of the crackers, making his third speech, distributed the last of the crackers from the basket. By this time the portions had diminished.

Here Hemlocks-lying-down arose and, as conductor, announced that there would be two more songs before the dancers "laid down their fans and rattles" and departed. The headman makes this announcement when the gifts are nearly distributed; then any additional speakers must provide their own presents. Otherwise, they sing the last song which always precedes laying down the feather fans.

(12) *Whoop and Song XII.*—Stick-lodged-in-a-crotch (Deer), struck the floor, spoke and donated to the dancers the last of the crackers which had been given to him.

(13) *Whoop and Song XIII.*—Wood-eater (Bear) beat the floor, spoke, made fun of Stick-lodged-in-a-crotch for having been asleep, and then presented his crackers to Stick-lodged-in-a-crotch, who had given all of his to the dancers.

(14) *Whoop and Song XIV.*—Following the dance, the birds laid down their ritual implements parallel on the floor, each placing the wand with its handle pointing toward his left hand with the fan feathers to the left, and the rattle handle pointing toward his right hand. They departed to dress. The conductor picked up the fans, suspended the rattles from the fan handles by loops attached to the rattle handles, and took the equipment into the kitchen where he rolled it into a bundle in a newspaper wrapper.

Wood-eater, the preacher or speaker, returned thanks to those who had participated and asked the Spirit-forces to guide them and protect them from accident while returning home. This ended the ritual.

[4] According to He-strikes-the-rushes, "when the messenger notifies the members, he assigns duties. He says to one, 'you shall go and strike the stick and speak,' meaning he shall merely speak; or at second thought, 'you shall be the one who shouts'; or 'you shall be singer.' The singers are not supposed to make speeches; singing is enough." (See invitation texts, p. 136.)

An interim followed while the conductor and the hostess were arranging the feast.

Francis Bowen, recipient of the ritual, spoke long and emotionally, almost repentantly, about the trouble he had been having with his neighbors.

During the winter his children had stoned the neighbors' children while returning from school. Later, two of these children died of measles. The parents consulted an old clairvoyant, who said that Francis had bewitched the children. Meanwhile he had been having trouble with his wife, and he beat her several times. She left him. Soon all her clansmen gathered forces with the irate neighbors and beat Francis until he was nearly dead.

Soon after I arrived in the settlement, I was warned to avoid his place at night because he was carrying a gun and shooting at all prowlers. We heard shots on several occasions. Finally, one night in July, the neighbors were drunk, and we were awakened again by shots and the old Seneca war cry. There was swearing and the noise of gravel disturbed by running feet going east along the road toward the neighbors, but there were no casualties.

This time Esther Fatty consulted the clairvoyant. "Francis was having trouble with his head." He could not sleep. Hemlocks-lying-down conducted several rituals at her request. They met one morning at dawn and sang (gano'iowi'') for him, because his mind was distraught with worry. Again, one evening Hemlocks-lying-down conducted the Bear Society dance for him. This present Eagle Dance was the third attempt to find a cure for his troubled mind.

Toward the close of Francis' remarks Sam Fatty (Snipe), his mother's father; Wood-eater (Bear) (opposite moiety), priest and preacher of the Handsome Lake Revelation; Stick-lodged-in-a-crotch (Deer); and Amos Red Eye (Heron) (of the same moiety as Francis) successively walked over to him, grasped his hand and talked to him, giving advice and telling him to mend his ways, to take care of his family, and try to make up with his neighbors, to stay sober, and be of good mind, etc. In this manner they pledged their friendship. Their behavior was not patterned by membership in either moiety, but their role was rather that of old men and chiefs who traditionally act as counselors and peacemakers between the younger people.

The power of Eagle Society ritual to cement social bonds of friendship is by no means small. It is, however, noteworthy that certain men present—Francis' clansman and neighbor Corn-husker (Hawk), the whooper; William Cooper (Snipe), the second singer; and the headman, Hemlocks-lying-down (Turtle), either through dislike or diffidence did not pledge their friendship. However, all except Hemlocks-lying-down, who was acting as conductor and head singer, and the second singer and the dancers spoke during the meeting.[5]

THE FEAST

Meanwhile, Esther Fatty (Hawk), hostess, and the conductor had arranged the feast. A side of baked pork was brought in a pan and fed first to the dancers, who cried like a couple of crows, as one after the other they picked over it and tore off the best cuts. Hemlocks-lying-down passed it, going counterclockwise, to the members and finally to the dancers again, because they clamored for more. They were fed.

The host, Francis Bowen, helped the conductor carry a wash boiler of corn soup, which they set in the middle of the room. At a signal from the conductor, "Come now set down the pails," everyone present slid a pail across the floor toward the soup.

The recipient of the ritual, Francis Bowen, stirred the soup with a maple paddle and dished several ladlefuls into the conductor's pail.

Then the conductor filled each of the pails in turn, proceeding in a methodical counterclockwise direction, a ladleful to a pail until the soup was gone. Two pails were filled for the house. Each member rescued his pail and departed, taking along the few crackers which he still had. The dancers, by this time, however, had most of them.

Discussion.—We have purposely noted the clan membership and moiety alinement of those who attended. We find the principal ritual functionaries in the opposite moiety from the recipient and his mother, the sponsor. Informants specify that this must be. We have already noted absence of any spatial separation of the moieties. Although speakers joke with one another and offer gifts to the dancers and other speakers by way of recompense for the evil things they have said about them, in but one case (between Wood-eater and Stick-lodged-in-a-crotch) did ridicule cross moiety lines; Hemlocks-lying-down and other Coldspring informants claim this was accidental. Hemlocks-lying-down remembers speeches in ridicule of the other clan at Cattaraugus, but he has never observed the practice at Coldspring. Then, it would seem, the personalities involved are more important than membership in a particular clan. Wood-eater ridiculed Stick-lodged-in-a-crotch, not because he was a Deer, but because he went to sleep.

It is perhaps unfair to lay bare the therapeutic powers of a Seneca medicine society in the light of modern medical knowledge. Nevertheless, when I heard 2 years afterward that Francis Bowen had been committed to a mental hospital, I wondered what type of aberration the resident physicians had discovered. I had built up some faith in

---

[5] "Again, the singers are not supposed to talk, but there is no restriction. Singing is enough. The conductor does not speak."— (He-strikes-the-rushes, June 1934.)

the strength of the societies to bolster self-respect and
pleasure for those who believe in their efficacy. Unfo
cis Bowen's difficulty required different treatment.

He "was admitted to (the) hospital in an advanc
chosis with syphilitic meningoencephalitis. In sp
treatment, he has shown no response and the outlook is considered
rather hopeless. It is too bad that he could not have had proper
treatment sufficiently early instead of his tribal rites which you describe. The majority of these cases can be much improved or recovered under proper treatment, if gotten early enough." [6]

THE ANNIVERSARY CELEBRATION OF RESTING-SKY'S CURE

During the first day of the 1934 Midwinter Festival at Coldspring,
Resting-sky, a Cayuga of the Turtle Clan, "put up" an anniversary
of his cure by the Eagle Society (pl. 2). He selected Leads-him
(ha'nodje·nę's), of the Snipe Clan, his wife's sister's husband, in the
other moiety, to conduct the rite. My informant, Sherman Redeye
(SRE), of the Snipe Clan (pl. 3), said it was the conductor's duty to
invite the ones whom Resting-sky intended should come. The invitations were privately issued at the longhouse on the first day of the New
Year's Dance (Jan. 1, 1934).

It is up to the conductor to provide singers and dancers. However,
SRE (Snipe) did not know he was going to be second singer until he
arrived.

Resting-sky, the recipient, the one for whom the ceremony was performed, asked Wood-eater (Bear) in his own moiety to give thanks to
the Spirit-forces and make the proper announcements.

The conductor secured the services of Great-night, of the Wolf Clan,
son of Hemlocks-lying-down (Turtle), as drummer or first singer, because his father had already been chosen for Earth-hiller's meeting
that night. The conductor depended on SRE of the Snipe Clan, in
the other moiety, to help Great-night sing, because he knew SRE
would be there.

The conductor also chose the dancers. The conductor had some
difficulty securing dancers representing both moieties, because of
Earth-hiller's meeting. "The dancers are of equal status. They were
both Bear Clan, but they are supposed to be of different moieties."
He could not find the proper people. Further, he should have had a
speech made borrowing one of them from his moiety and then later
returning him to his own clan, which he neglected to do.

Resting-sky left the cooking to his wife, It-dips-water (pl. 5), and her
sister, the conductor's wife, the sisters of Corn-husker.

---

[6] Earle V. Gray, M. D., Superintendent, Gowanda State Homeopathic Hospital (correspondence, April 9, 1937).

When they had finished their evening meal, the invited guests gathered up their tin pails and convened at the house of Resting-sky and It-dips-water. When they had all assembled, the conductor arranged the seating for the ritual (fig. 2).

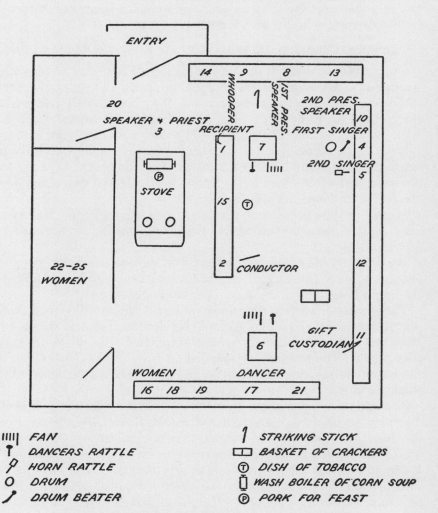

FIGURE 2.—Floor plan of Eagle Dance for Resting-sky.

The following people were present:

*Participation in the meeting**

	Moiety	Mem-bership
1. Resting-sky, Turtle Clan, *recipient and sponsor*	II	X
2. Leads-him (ha'nodje·nε's), Snipe Clan, *messenger and conductor*	I	X
3. Wood-eater, Bear Clan, *speaker and priest*	II	X
4. Great-night, Wolf Clan, *first singer*	II	X
5. SRE, Snipe Clan, *second singer*	I	X
6. Town-destroyer, Bear Clan, *dancer*	II	O
7. He-watches-water, Bear Clan (Snorer's son), *dancer*	II	X
8. Ten-mornings, Bear Clan, *first presentation speaker*	II	X
9. Corn-husker, Hawk Clan, *whooper*	I	X
10. Wm. Cooper, Snipe Clan, *second presentation speaker*	I	X
11. Stick-lodged-in-a-crotch, Deer Clan, *gift custodian*	I	X
12. Takes-in-a-woman, Snipe Clan	I	X
13. Snorer, Hawk Clan	I	X
14. Cold-voice, Beaver Clan	II	X
15. Falling-word, Cayuga of Turtle Clan	II	X
16. It-dips-water, Hawk Clan, *matron and cook*	I	X
17. Voice-above, Hawk Clan, my interpreter (pl. 4)	I	O
18. Full-of-thistles, Deer Clan, wife of 15	I	X
19. Sister of 16 and 9, Hawk Clan, *matron and cook*	I	X
20. Duck-on-water, Beaver Clan	II	O

21. W. N. F.
22–25. Sundry odd women and children in the bedroom with Duck-on-water's wife, daughter of 16, who is sick, but this ceremony is not for her. However, she may, as member, derive benefit from hearing the songs.

*X=member; O=nonmember.

Again, the following facts, bearing upon the problem of moiety alinement, emerge from an analysis of the floor plan. The recipient secures a "headman" or conductor from the opposite moiety, but the first singer and the speaker and priest are of his own moiety. My informants explained this as convenience, necessity overriding convention. The singers represent each moiety, but the dancers are of the same clan; however, one of them serves for the first moiety, and the presentation speakers are of each moiety, conforming to native theory. The whooper and gift custodian are of the opposite moiety to the recipient, but this is accidental, although desirable. Again there is no spatial separation of the moieties into a dual division. Once more, the greater part of the functionaries and participants are the close relatives of the host or his wife, and all who had any active part, with the possible exception of one dancer, who, I think, belongs, are members of the society. My interpreter definitely stated that she does not belong. She merely went along with her husband to her mother's house.

THANKSGIVING

The Speaker gave thanks to all the Spirit-forces from the earth to the Creator, and asked a blessing for all those present. He announced the purpose of the gathering to renew the association of Resting-sky, who has been feeling badly, and the Dew Eagle, as he thought that it would help him.

TOBACCO INVOCATION

The conductor took the wands with the rattles attached from the drying rack above the stove and handed them to the speaker, or priest, in this case, who then stood before the fire, holding this ritual equipment so that the Dew Eagle, the bird to whom this ritual is addressed, would know he is talking to him. He committed the tobacco to the fire a pinch at a time, employing the same prayer he had used for Francis Bowen, but he did not sing over the first song.

ASSIGNMENT OF ROLES AND PARAPHERNALIA

When he had finished, the priest returned the wands to the conductor, who in turn handed one set to Ten-mornings so that he might present them to He-watches-water (Bear), the dancer in his own moiety and, in this case, his clan.

The headman appointed Corn-husker (Hawk) whooper. It is his duty to whoop (pa·a·') just previous to, and as a signal for, the singing.[7] He appointed William Cooper, Snipe Clan, to present the other wand and rattle to the second dancer, his own son, who was dancing for that moiety. Lastly, he appointed old "Stick-lodged-in-a-crotch gift custodian, setting the basket of soda crackers before him. The former remarked that maybe the latter could stay awake if he had a job."

Here the dancers entered, coming downstairs in full costume with a round red spot painted on each cheek. Instead of wearing the old Seneca headdress with the single revolving feather, they wore quasi-Plains Indian headdresses, which they wear on the road with "Indian shows," and leggings similar to chaps. All the old Seneca costumes have long since either gone into graves or they have been sold to museums. Now, although the old people know what they should wear, the dancers wear makeshift "play" Indian costumes. The old people disliked my raising this question because it revealed a spurious element in the modern ceremonies which Wood-eater likes to regard as genuine.

THE RITUAL

(1) *Corn-husker whooped and Song I commenced.*—Ten-mornings beat the floor with the striking stick and returned it to the headman as

---

He-strikes-the-rushes says this is the war whoop, but SRE denies this is the same as the war whoop the singing ceased. He made the conventional speech about being invited to dance, and then he handed the wand and rattle to his clansman, the dancer.

(2) *Corn-husker whooped the second time and Song II followed.*— William Cooper (Snipe) of the other moiety, struck the floor and spoke. He said of his son, "He is not as good a dancer as I am; I can still beat him. However, he thinks he is pretty good." And then addressing his son: "Do the best you can to beat that other dancer." Then he handed him the fan and rattle. Then he passed the striking stick back to the conductor.

(3) *The Whooper uttered his third contribution and Song III commenced.*—Before the singing started the conductor had handed the cracker basket to Stick-lodged-in-a-crotch, when he made the other appointments. During the third song the conductor handed the stick to him. We will call him gift-custodian, but he has no official title, according to my informants. He merely talks and distributes crackers, first, to the dancers; second, to the singers (this time the second singer first); third, to the whooper; fourth, to the host; and fifth, to the conductor; but this last is not necessary.

(4) *Whoop and Song IV.*—The whooper always yelps before the songs.

The dance begins here.

In all of the songs for the Eagle Dance the drummer sings the song through once alone, accompanying himself on the water drum. The second time through, singing the same words, the second singer joins him, using the horn rattle. The dancers commence on the fourth song, just previous to the second round of speeches. They wait until both singers have been over the song together.

SRE says, "The dancers are supposed to sway on their chairs, then they jump down and crouch on the floor like Dew Eagles and advance by hopping, turning from side to side; when the song is repeated, they bend down weaving their shoulders in imitation of Dew Eagles picking food off the ground."

Then they retreat and the song ends with three quick, rapid beats, which the dancers duplicate with their feet and rattles. About this time the speaker strikes the floor or, anciently, a striped striking pole, and the music stops.

Now the second round of speeches begins.

According to informants, William Cooper spoke. "The stick went back to him, and then to Ten-mornings, and then to Stick-lodged-in-a-crotch." According to my notes above, the order was Ten-mornings, William, and Stick-lodged-in-a-crotch in the first round. William made a speech to the man who put up the feast, Resting-sky, telling him to behave himself and have good luck. He said, "Behave yourself. I wish you luck that you may be fortunate and keep well."

(5) *Whoop and Song V.*—According to informants, Ten-mornings said the same thing as William Cooper.

(6) *Whoop and Song VI.*—Stick-lodged-in-a-crotch said the same thing; the previous time he said he was giving out crackers. However, my informants were somewhat reluctant to tell all that each one said, preferring to give me the pattern of what they were supposed to say.

Up to this point crackers are distributed only to the dancers, singers, whooper, and the host, and possibly the conductor. This completes the second round of speeches.

(7) *Whoop and Song VII.*—Now the floor is open for anyone to talk.

Takes-in-a-woman (Snipe) made the same ritual speech as his predecessors and gave crackers to the same people.

SRE says, "We do not make fun of the other moiety here when we talk in the Eagle Dance, but I have heard that they do it over at Newtown [Cattaraugus Reservation]" (Parker, 1913 b, pp. 124–125).

(8) *Whoop and Song VIII.*—Snorer (Hawk), an old man who formerly lived at Newtown and is generally out of sorts with everyone wherever he lives, talked at length of his present social status.

I hear all kinds of stories about myself: that I am pretending that I am sick. I wish whoever said these things would suffer like I am suffering; then maybe they would not say them. I only laugh when I hear these stories. I like to come to doings like this, only sometimes I am unable; I am so lame that I am hardly able to get about any more.

(Afterward, to me my informant commented, "I did not listen to him. I do not like to hear things like that at a medicine society meeting. It makes bad feelings, this gossip. Snorer always says, 'Everybody talks too much'; he even says that in the longhouse.")

Snorer distributed crackers to the necessary functionaries, including the conductor with whom he is at times in good rapport, and the latter has much respect for the old tyrant's erudition, which is considerable.

(9) *Whoop and Song IX.*—The conductor passed the stick to Cornhusker, the whooper, who made the customary remarks which convention demanded. He distributed the crackers to those whom he should, and to me, a guest, saying that I had come a long way to be amongst them once more and I must be getting hungry. He further said "He is an Indian in spirit, even if his face is white." (The remark illustrates the pleasant raillery which pervades the whole affair.)

(10) *Whoop and Song X.*—Cold-voice (Beaver) struck for silence. This was his first speech and one is not supposed to extemporize until the second.

(11) *Whoop and Song XI.*—Wood-eater (Bear), who had made the

first prayer of thanksgiving and the tobacco-throwing invocation, addressed Resting-sky, the host.

"Each man speaks differently, but in the main he says about the same thing to the man for whom the feast is held" (SRE).

(12) *Whoop and Song XII.*—Falling-world, a Cayuga of the Turtle Clan, "did not do much preaching to his host, but he talked about his wife. His jokes are too strong to suit the public. My ears would burn if S. said things like that about me. He said, 'My wife is always kicking me in the shins so that I will be laid up with sore legs[8] and she will be able to attend the New Year's dance alone. She is cross and is always hitting me with something.' All the time he was saying that his wife was there. (However, she seemed amused.) He then told Resting-sky and my mother, It-dips-water, to remain together until either one of them dies" (CRE).

(13) *Whoop and Song XIII.*—SRE gave the signal and talked. He said what I have quoted above (see (4)). Later, being my informant, he added, "If he [Resting-sky] is sick, it (my wish)is supposed to make him well." SRE was the second singer, and did not have to speak. The first singer, Great-night, did not speak, but it is not required of the first singer. He is a peculiar chap, inclined to moroseness, and is of a vengeful disposition. He is a fine singer and, like his father, a fine craftsman. At times he is quite jovial. However, singing is enough and the first singer has fulfilled his duty without speaking.

(14) *Whoop and Song XIV.*—It-dips-water (Hawk), wife of the host, commenced to talk, but her sister started kidding her and she was unable to finish.

(15) *Whoop and Song XV.*—Stick-lodged-in-a-crotch (Deer) woke up in time to talk a third time. The headman was about to prod him with the stick. This elicited much amusement and laughter. He began to poke fun at Corn-husker (Hawk), the whooper, a man of his own moiety, by alluding to the "possum" which Corn-husker had claimed, at a previous Eagle Dance, that he met every time he went into the woods hunting. Corn-husker said that when the possum smiled at him he had good luck. (Corn-husker had told about his possum at a meeting, held the week before in the same house, for SRE and his father, Wood-eater. This is one of many stories Corn-husker is reputed to have told to amuse people. He always says his stories do not hurt anyone, since they are not true. They are merely intended as jokes.) Stick-lodged-in-a-crotch concluded by wishing Resting-sky would live to grow old.

---

[8] Sore legs is a symptom of being sick with the disease the Eagle causes. Whereas the content of his speech is different from that of Snorer, in character, it is the same. They both came from Cattaraugus, and he is more true to his local tradition than Snorer in ridiculing someone in the opposite moiety, who happens to be his wife. However, he does not exalt his own clan.

There were no crackers left by this time, so the speaker promised Resting-sky a 5-cent cigar the next time they were in the city together. Everyone laughed, knowing his reputation for stinginess.

"Everyone knew he was safe, for they will never be in the city together, not now anyway" (CRE).

(16) *Whoop and Song XVI.*—Corn-husker reached for the stick, as was expected, and made his second utterance by way of rebuttal. Naturally his subject was "my possum." "People make more of a story than what I said, because they know it is not true. You all know me. I am the worst liar around here. I wish you would not talk any more about my possum when anyone has another meeting like this." Then he addressed his blessing to the host.

The dancers, by this time, had most of the crackers and had stored them under their chairs in the original cracker boxes provided by the host. Nevertheless, Corn-husker had a good supply given to him, in the capacity of whooper, and he gave these to the dancers, singers, and host, saying, "I am afraid to carry them: a ghost might chase me." He donated two crackers apiece to the functionaries. Corn-husker is frequently troubled by ghosts coming up behind him on the road.[9]

(17) *Whoop and Song XVII.*—This was Bill Cooper's (Snipe) third speech. "I do not really wish that Resting-sky will grow too old, as Stick-lodged-in-a-crotch hopes. When people grow too old they are not able to help themselves or do anything." (My informants interpolated: Takes-in-a-woman (Snipe) had an Eagle Dance meeting once and Stick-lodged-in-a-crotch said, "When a man becomes old, every time he eats a good meal he gets sleepy and goes to sleep.") William Cooper concluded, "I think 'Flying' [the old man's boyhood name] must be pretty well off and full all the time, because every time I look at him he is always asleep. He must be filled up all the time, for he always goes to sleep."

I might add here that Stick-lodged-in-a-crotch or "Flying" is one of the head religious officers in his moiety. He is usually asleep in councils and during the preaching of the Handsome Lake Revelation, of which he is one of the custodians. It makes a good joke. He usually wakes up, however, in time to drowsily intone his contributions.

(18) *Whoop and Song XVIII.*—By this time the dancers were becoming tired. Ten-mornings (Bear) talked for the third time. His subject was the longhouse, and he urged the people to go there and help out the leaders, meaning the conductors, Levi Snow (Heron)

---

[9] See Case II, p 43. He referred here to the typical magic flight incident in Seneca folklore where the hero casts out gifts behind him to distract his pursuers. It is believed that if chased by ghosts, one may impede their speed by throwing bread to them.

and his own brother, Arrow (Bear), who are running the New Year's Festival. Ten-mornings is a Faith-keeper. Then he concluded, "Resting-sky is lucky in having so many people come here. One man came from way off in the East [a jibe at me]. I live just a little way this side of him. [He lives east of the longhouse, across the river in Crick's Run.] He came all the way to see these doings; it is a good idea. The conductor came from way up near Red House to help out Resting-sky, the host. I wish the meeting would last all night." [10]

(19) *Whoop and Song XIX.*—Cold-voice made his second speech. He preached to Resting-sky, joking him; then he said, "He has lost his brother (died last winter) and sister and is all alone. He should try and forget that and be good and go on with his work and live peaceably with his wife."

The conductor rose and said the following song would be the last, the one for laying down the wands or fans.

(20) *Whoop and Song XX.*—Following this last song the dancers left their rattles and fans on the floor and retired. At meetings like this one "when there are a good many speakers who fight for the striking stick, the dancers do not have to work hard. Otherwise, they must continue until someone strikes the pole or floor.

"The host should immediately stand and thank those who have said good things to him. Resting-sky did not do this. He should stand and thank the people of both moieties who have striven to beat each other at wishing him good luck."

Resting-sky, the host, turned to Wood-eater, the Speaker, asking him to talk once more. Wood-eater gave thanks to all the people who had helped: (1) the dancers, (2) the singers, (3) the conductor, (4) all the people who came to talk, (5) all the women (members), and (6) all those who came to look on. Then he asked the four "angels" to help them to arrive safely home, that no accidents befall them on their way. He gave thanks to the "maker" without calling him by name; and he hoped that everyone would be well by the next dawn. "Let everybody in this crowd give thanks to each other." It is finished.

THE DISTRIBUTION OF THE FEAST

The distribution of the feast by the conductor follows. First, he hands out seven pieces of meat: one apiece to the dancers; one each to the singers; one to the whooper; a woman put one in the conductor's pail; and he gave the last piece to the tobacco-thrower. Second, there was a pig's head, but in this case it was a roast shoulder

---

[10] "Jokes about long journeys were common in the old Newtown meetings." Snorer usually has this meeting early in the morning. Anciently the society met out-of-doors at dawn.

of pork, as a head was not available. The host has the first bite, then the dancers, singers, and last, the crowd. It is passed in a counterclockwise direction "to the right," that is, the conductor always has the benches on his right as he proceeds. "To go around to the left," clockwise, is considered incorrect and means death or evil.

Snorer follows the old tradition of picking up the head in his hands, turning it over and biting it; others, in the newer school, tear off a piece between their fingers. The older men most consistently grasp the whole head and tear off portions with their teeth. Everyone is supposed to say ga′·'ga′·' in imitation of the crow, and especially the great raven. My informant said that the first time he sang he took an ear and ripped it clear to the nose. Everyone laughed.

Anciently the head was served in a bark bowl, or the conductor merely passed it in his hands. People may say ga′·' to make someone stop. The young people object to Snorer's dirty hands and avaricious temperament. "He used to go outside during the meeting and then return. He never washed his hands, and when he handled the pig's head many objected. Everyone said he had dirty hands."

When Snorer has been conductor he has increased his evil reputation. "He used to pass the head around once and then put it aside for himself. He has earned the name gwi′sgwisgo·wa·' [the great hog]. Conductors are supposed to pass the feast around until it is entirely finished, or the company is satisfied."

When chided, Snorer has threatened to return to Newtown, Cattaraugus Reservation, "but the people over there say they do not want him back because then they could not have any medicine meetings, because he takes all the pig's head for himself."

The third part of the feast is always corn soup. This is the same type as cooked for False-faces. It is hulled-corn soup made from the white squaw corn. It is the duty of the host to ladle some from the wash boiler into the conductor's pail. The conductor then calls for the members to set down their pails and he fills all the pails brought by the members and guests, which they have shoved out on the floor. Some is dished out for the house. At a signal each person retrieves his pail and goes home.

Discussion.—Even at pain of some repetition, I have presented the raw data from two meetings which served to establish the frame on which, during later field work, I hung most of the meat of this paper. This particular meeting not only demonstrates how consistently the local pattern of a ritual is repeated from time to time, but there are also several interesting discrepancies in the matter of required moiety alinement which are at variance with native theory. This type of information should stand as a caution against the ethnologist's tendency to oversystematize his description of a native culture. There are rules, but they are not always adhered to. We have also shown how Corn-husker, Wood-eater, and Snorer found expression for their individuality in this Eagle Dance. Truly, the type of thing they did was patterned by tradition, by the history of the ceremony, but the content of their behavior as individuals had its roots in each one's individual history. What Goldenweiser has called "involution," or the telescoping of repeated behavior patterns, is well illustrated in this ritual. The same songs, the same type of speeches, the same old jokes are all heard again and again; but not so much what one does, but how one does it is the important thing to the individual participant in the culture. This constant repetition at times is even boring to the Indians. He-strikes-the-rushes told me that one of the reasons he moved away from Allegany was because he became "sick and tired" of the continual repetition of the same old jokes at successive Eagle Dances which that winter followed one another night after night.

LATER CELEBRATIONS AT ALLEGANY

The ritual of the Eagle Dance is gone through many times in the course of a year at Coldspring, so that participants come to sense the pattern of sequence which guides the program and to forget the details after a meeting. The same process affects the observer. At first he sees all the detail and misses the pattern. As he learns he looks for the fine points and forgets the details. My own observations of Eagle Dance at Coldspring have been supplemented by those of Charles E. Congdon, of Salamanca, N. Y.; M. H. Deardorff, of Warren, Pa.; and the late Dr. Frank G. Speck (Speck, 1950). We have all shared observations in correspondence and discussion, and Speck's first impressions are published and supplemented by the account of the Seneca.

Clayton C. White has been Deardorff's principal annalist at Coldspring, and his records of ceremonial events are quite accurate and clearly portray the "doings." His language is equally picturesque, but requires some editing for the general reader. His notes describe two meetings of the Eagle Society in February 1942: a family feast, and a cure for a neighbor's daughter.

Wednesday Evening, February 4, 1942, we have a gane"gwä'e·', or Eagle Dance. This [is] Big Bird Dance. We have [it] at our home. [Two leaders were appointed] William Cooper and Lendsay Doudy. These two are [supposed to] notify to the Bird Dancer members to come to the home of Mrs. A. E. White in the evening.

First Albert Jones made the Thanking Speech. And [continuing] on after that, he also [told] the Members who are to be Benefit [beneficiaries] of this dance. There are four [such] persons: Alice E. White, Clayton White, Sally George, Rudolph George. " . . . and now you members know where to be wishing for it [to whom to address your pleas] to have good luck."

And after this he also [tended] to throwing the Indian Tobacco in the Fire. And [the priest through his prayers is believed] to be notifying the Birds. These are

Big Birds and they are flying way above the clouds. (So this is not the Eagle. For this Bird don't come to the ground. The Birds are bright red and some are white as snow. The Red Bird is more powerful.)

And the singers are Richard J. John, and the helper, Jake Logan.

And there are four dancers: Avery Jimmerson, John Deer, Kenneth Fatty, and Wilton Cooper.

There was a good crowd and all were good speakers.

And the Flute Singer, Walter Jimmerson.

And the Halloa [Hollerer-Whooper], Cornelius Abram.

Some interesting facts on participation can be gleaned from Clayton White's record. It was a family feast for members of the Wolf clan, in the lineage of Alice White, including her son, her daughters' daughter, and the latter's son. She selected as conductor William Cooper (Snipe Clan), a man of the opposite moiety. Since it was to be a large affair with four dancers, the conductor had an assistant, or coconductor of the opposite moiety, L. Doudy (Beaver Clan), on the same side as the sponsor. The speaker and the priest, Albert Jones (Snipe Clan), is of the opposite moiety, but the relationship may be fortuitous, since he is a good speaker and possibly the only one available. But note that the singers are of opposite moieties—R. J. John (Beaver) and Jake Logan (Snipe)—the first being of the sponsor's side. But Dick John is a good singer (cf. Kurath's transcription of his records, and my text below).

The dancers were equally divided between moieties—two Bears and two Hawks. It would have been nice to have Clayton's account of the speeches, but that they were routine, I judge from his omitting them.

But note the presence of a "Flute Singer," Walter Jimmerson of Wolf Clan, who presumably blew the whistle in imitation of the birds.

The last role, whooper, fell to the Beaver Clan.

In general, it may be observed that custom has assigned the principal roles to persons of the opposite moiety to the sponsors, and dual roles are equally shared between moieties. But the success of the ceremony depends on a good singer.

Of perhaps greater interest are Clayton White's answers to some questions which Deardorff put to him concerning Eagle Dance. He traces the origin of the rite to the warpath, he relates how Handsome Lake, the Seneca prophet, received supernatural sanction for its continuance, and how it survives as a curing society. Membership comes through a dream about the mythical birds which he describes again, and he concludes by citing recent proof of the bird's power.

And now about the Gane"gwä'e", or the Eagle Dance. [It derives from] . . . the Indian War days. These Big Birds gave their full power and help to the Seneca Indian Men in their fighting. But [after the Indian wars were over] when [in 1799] the Four Angels (the messengers of the Creator) were teaching to the Handsome Lake, they tell him to tell his people that this Big Bird Dance shall be changed [into] the way they are doing it these days. And so they changed it.

And the Four Angels fully approved. Before the Four Angels [talked] to the Handsome Lake, the Seneca only talked [in meetings] of how to fight, of how to scalp, and they also [were] telling of how many scalps a man has. In those days he is a great Indian if he have a great many scalps. This is why the Four Angels . . . prohibited [boasting on scalp records], and they say, "This will stop, and it must be changed." And so the People take it [and do so] the Four Angels say.

And now at this time the people only [have Eagle Dance and speak] to wish [the sponsor] to have good luck, and to tell the Big Birds to take it away all the Bad Luck and the Bad Enemy coming to the Persons who are having a Bird Dance. And also they have a little Joke. So this is the way it is now. To this Big Bird Dance the Four Angels have given full approval. It is because they have great power. They have power to help in this world even if the person is very sick. The Big Birds have power to help the sick person to get well again if the person belongs to the Bird Society.

Mostly [membership in] this Society is come in by the Dream. And also some of them come by the Fortune Teller. And if this Big Bird is not very [satisfied with the behavior] of the Person who belongs to this Society, it is just as bad. Because this Big Bird has great power to bring the bad luck and bad Enemy to to the Person who is not doing right by them.

Now I am going to [tell] the truth. This Big Bird is not the Eagle. There is another kind of bird. This kind of bird does not come down to the ground but once in a great while, but when they do come down to the ground, they mostly come to the top of a High Hill or a Mountain. And this Bird is of a Bright Red Color, and there is another all White Color. There are two kinds. But they are the same Nation. This Bird in truth has a big power.

Our people have good evidence [of this] just last Wednesday night, February 18, 1942. Mr. Cornelius Abram and his little daughter had this Bird Dance to their home. And this little Baby Girl is very sick for about a week. So they got the Fortune Teller (Sara Snow of Quaker Bridge) to look of what is the trouble to this little baby girl. [This was a last resort] Because the [White] Doctor can not understand [the nature of] what is [troubling] this little girl. So [the parents resort to] the Fortune Teller. She says, "This little baby girl is not sick, but she will pass away very soon now if you do not have Bird Dance. There is a Big Bird [hovering] above her. Hear now [this] is on account [of the fact] that Cornelius Abram belongs to this Bird Society, and he didn't have the Bird Dance for a long time now. So this Big Bird got tired of waiting for him too long now. So the Big Bird got to this little Baby girl's."

So after this Fortune Teller tell them, and they hurry to have it the Bird Dance. And this time that the little baby girl is better. Now that is good proof of [the fact] about this Big Bird have a power. [Clayton C. White to M. H. Deardorff, 1942.]

If Handsome Lake foresaw that the Bird Dance would change from a ritual for boasting on scalp records to a medicine society of persons whom the Big Birds had accepted for membership by making them sick, he probably did not anticipate that the Society would include non-Indians. I can think of no better measure of acceptance than the ceremonial sanction of the Eagle Dance for three adopted White men. Adoption in the Turtle Clan has been followed by acceptance in the Eagle Society. Congdon, Deardorff, and Speck have all been accorded both honors. The first two gentlemen were taken in as "friends"; the last had a dream, was accorded a "cure," and a year later a renewal.

The only record I have of an Eagle Society meeting held at Chauncey Johnny John's in August 1942 to celebrate a "friendship" between "Big-canoe" and "He-is-carrying-an-ax," consists of a series of photographs taken at crucial stages of the ceremony. The photographs were made to illustrate this monograph. As illustrations they are not all successful, but the series covers the ritual pattern at the following points:

(1) Invocation. Wood-eater, speaker and priest, goes to the stove and puts tobacco in the fire and prays to the Dew Eagles to protect these friends with long life; Deep-night, the conductor, sits by during the invocation. Others listen. (Two strings of Indian tobacco (*Nicotiana rustica* L.) hang over the stove drying)(pl. 6, *1*).

(2) After the presentation of fans to the dancers, the second round of speeches is addressed to the Dew Eagles. Members sit with bowed heads listening intently to Chief Jesse Armstrong (Bear Clan); Leslie Bowen (Hawk Clan), dancer; C. E. Congdon; M. H. Deardorff; Richard Johnny John, first singer; and Ed. Coury, helper (pl. 7, *1*).

(3) The Eagle Dancers crouch and sway with the song. Singers, speaker, and host sit along the wall. Note the feathered fans and tiny horn rattles which here replace the usual gourd rattle at Coldspring. The striking stick lies on the floor (pl. 7, *2*).

(4) Each speaker puts down the striking stick, which is a cane, speaks, and distributes crackers from a splint market basket to the dancers.

(5) On the last song, the dancers lay down the feather fans and retire (pl. 6, *2*).

(6) The conductor passes the pig head counterclockwise, starting with speaker and singers, who cry like crows, and pick at the meat (pl. 8, *1*).

(7) At a cry from the conductor, the members put down their pails, which he fills with hulled-corn soup from a wash boiler, going counterclockwise, a dip to a pail, until all the pails are filled equally.

(8) The members pick up their pails and scatter like birds in every direction (pl. 8, *2*). Neighboring Whites often ask why Indians are continually carrying pails on the road at night.

Speck, following a convenient dream of "large birdlike bodies . . . across the sky in rapid flight," was feted by the Eagle Society on the night of March 10, 1949. Fast-talker of the Beaver Clan was his host. Speck's account, published in Primitive Man (1950), lists the participants, and gives their Indian and English names, their clan and moiety, and role in the ceremony. He also gives the seating arrangement. The arrangements seem to have preserved the proper balance between the sponsor or patient and the main role fulfillments. An exception to the rule of conductor being of the opposite moiety to the person honored may be noted, but singers and dancers were properly apportioned between moieties.

Speck's account of the performance of the ritual leaves nothing to be desired. As always he is the master of detail and catches the essence of behavior even when he may not understand the language. Speck was well prepared by having studied the Cayuga version of the rite. The preparations and ritual equipment are quite detailed even as to cost. What is impressive, moreover, is the detailed reporting of speeches in his honor. What participants said to Speck in Seneca and was afterward interpreted to him convey the close relationship between tutelary and patient. One speaker describes the birds as being of three colors, though not seen since White discovery. The birds appear only in dreams and may be reached with sacred tobacco. The bird would help him in his work. He is assured of the good will of the members.

Another speaker, who always seizes such opportunities to preach a sermon, admonishes the members on their sacred duty and reminds Big Porcupine (Speck) to renew his membership from time to time with a feast.

Speck encountered the same difficulty I have experienced in afterward getting speakers to recall their remarks. Once a ceremony is over, it is finished and participants do not want to go over it. There must be, however, as the records of meetings indicate, individuals who suffer from a retentive memory and lay up speeches for the next meeting. (See the case of Snorer, Corn-husker who wanted them to forget his possum, and He-strikes-the-rushes at Tonawanda.)

Apples as well as crackers were distributed after speeches. When the presents gave out, money was substituted. One woman speaker gave him a dime to treasure as "medicine." The meeting Speck attended was unusual in having two women who spoke. Although permitted to speak, it has been my experience that women almost never speak at the Eagle Dance.

Nothing else in Speck's account is extraordinary except his concluding comment: "Memories of the Eagle Dance given for my benefit . . . bring forth soft and pleasant thoughts marking a milestone in an ethnologist's background of experience . . . I can aver that their ceremonial ministrations gave me benefit . . ." (Speck, 1950, p. 59). Think how the Iroquois must feel, for they take their religion seriously.

Another Eagle Dance was held for Big Porcupine at the Midwinter Festival of 1950. Membership in a Seneca medicine society carries an annual obligation of renewal, else the person becomes sick. Speck and the Seneca felt that he had been improved by the first ceremony.

As a member of the Eagle Society, Speck was given a set of feather fans, and the next year he was to receive a set of rattles which were being made for him and which he was to put in use each time he sponsored a feast for the Society. Accordingly, he brought the Eagle bundle with him when he came up from Philadelphia to Red House on January 20, 1950, for the Midwinter Festival at Coldspring Longhouse.

Speck wore himself out in the preliminaries and collapsed on the first day of the Festival, January 22. When I arrived the following Friday for the sixth night, when the Husk Faces arrive to climax the ceremonies, the Longhouse officials were greatly concerned over Speck's condition.

Speck lay ill throughout the Festival. On the last day of the Festival, four of the ritual holders, two men and their wives, accompanied me to see Speck. His last request to me was a modest concern over an obligation to renew Eagle Dance. It is gratifying that his Seneca friends were impelled to go through with the ceremony while Speck was yet so near them. They sensed that he too felt it would be worth while. One of them quietly took the feather fans and the other couple accepted responsibility to arrange for the ceremony and prepare the feast—cook the corn and bean soup, boil the meat, provide apples and crackers for the dancers, and get Indian tobacco for the invocation. They knew that the sponsor was obviously near the end of his road, but, the old people say, "Eagle Dance has revived persons before, even on the brink of the grave." At least Speck was able to return to Philadelphia before he took the long trail a week later (Seneca of Coldspring Longhouse, 1950, pp. 60–61; Hallowell, 1951).

Perhaps our finest record of an Eagle Dance is the account by the Seneca of Coldspring Longhouse of the Eagle Dance held at the home of Albert and Geneva Jones, Wednesday night, February 1, 1950, in which the Society did its best—"all we could"—for a sick member. The account was transmitted afterward to Mrs. Speck by the Indians *ibid.*, pp. 61–64). A big crowd attended the "doings" and a record was kept of what was said. The pattern of the ritual stands out clearly in this account:

1. Greeting and Thanksgiving to Creator, and his workers.
2. Tobacco invocation to Dew Eagle, asking his help.
   Members smoke tobacco.
3. Introductory songs.
   First speaker presents fan and rattle to dancer.
   Same procedure for second dancer.
   Third speaker puts out crackers and apples for the members to use in striking.
   Urged not to waste the music and use a certain stick.

4. Dance starts on the fourth song.

Twelve speakers interrupt as many songs by striking.

Appeal to sponsor to keep on believing and express faith that Dew Eagles have power and will to help him. Sponsor will be up and around soon. Another puts his voice with the one who threw tobacco. A young man imparts the analogy of his own vigor. Even the timid speak. *"Sa-da-ga-ah* will help you because you believe in them. I ask them to remove all obstacles from your path, keep winds pure around you and keep you healthy. They helped you a year ago and they will again. They are powerful and they know you are thinking of them. (To the people.) You came to see the New Year's dance and to have *Ga-nay-gwa-ayk*—but was stricken with sickness. You are a firm believer in it so he is sure the doings here will help you as it did before." (Passes out crackers.)

5. Closing. The conductor thanks the members for coming out of respect for their friend. He adds his voice to the hope of others. The crackers and apples are now all distributed. The sponsor "is not here to receive your individual medicine."

6. The fourteenth song is for laying down the fans.

The speaker now thanks the participants: dancers, singers, all who took part.

The speaker thanks the Creator and the four messengers to see that all the people get home safely.

7. Feast.

Meat is passed.

Corn soup is given out.

THE SONGS [11]

The songs of the Eagle Dance as they are sung at Coldspring were recorded in 1941 for the Library of Congress by Richard Johnny John and his grandfather, Chauncey. Water drum and horn rattle are the respective instruments of the singer and his assistant. These are the old man's songs (Record No. 56, Fenton Collection of 1941, L. C.). They were shortened for purposes of recording to get them all on two sides of a record.

(1) yowehanee yowehanee
yo'owehane yo'owehane yo'owehane :][DC, repeat first word five times and repeat.]

(2) weya'a weya'a wahe'eya'a heyo· nǫ':]
ya'a'a heyo·nǫ'
weheya heyonǫ:] [DC] [End]

(3) yohonǫ'ǫ'ǫ yohonǫ yohonǫ
yohonǫ'ǫ'ǫ yohanondiyawe'i
honǫ'ǫ'ǫ : (6 times)] [DC]

(4) weya :] waheya wehenǫ :]
ya'a heyonǫ :]

(5) yahowe hane'i :] wehane:]]
yahowe hane'i wehane:][DC] [End]

---

[11] For the musical notation, see Kurath's supplement to this paper.

(6) ya'aha heyo'onǫ heyonǫ :]
weya heya heyo'onǫ :]]

(7) nigosa nigosa'a hanehe:]
yowega'nowe'e ya hanehe :] [DC] [End]

(8) yahaheyonǫ :] yahaheyonǫ
yahaheyonǫ yahaheyonǫ:] 4 times :]] [DC]

(9) yaheyonǫ'ǫ heyonǫ :]
waheya heyonǫ heyonǫ:]]

(10) wiya'a ha'a'a:] wiya ha'ne·he·
yo'o howiya ha'a'a
wiya'a ha'a'a:] wiya hane·he·:]]

(11) yaweyǫnǫ weyǫnǫ :]
waheya yaweyǫnǫ weyǫnǫ :] [DC]

(12) honǫdiyo ya'a he'e :] "Shortest song of all; different."
ya'a honǫdiyo ya'a :]]

(13) weyanenǫ weyanenǫ'ǫ he'e'e
ya'a he'e'eh weyanenǫ'ǫ
weyanenǫ'ǫ he'e'e [he'e] :]

(14) wigosa wigosa'a hanehe:]   (Record 56 A)
yowega'nowe'e ya hanehe :] [DC] End]

(15) neyanenɛ' goyaha'a nehe :]
neyanenɛ' goyaha'a nehe :]-yɛh :] [DC] [End]

(16) wahe'ya'a heyo'onǫ :]
wiyeʼɛʼɛ :] wahe'ya'a
wahe'ya'a heyo'onǫ :] [DC]

(17) ya'ne ya'ne
goya haweya goya'haweyonǫ'ǫ :]

(18) Last song for laying down the feather fans.   The third and last time, slower,
when they lay down the fans.
yowadjine gonǫ'ǫdiyawe
ya'ha'he·heyo'onǫ
yowadjine gonǫ'ǫdiyawe heyonǫ:] [DC 3 times]
End: yahowiha· ha he··
heyo'onǫ

THE PARTICIPATING PERSONALITIES AT COLDSPRING

THE EAGLE DANCE AS A VEHICLE FOR PERSONALITY EXPRESSION

When one knows the actual people who perform the Eagle Dance ritual, individual behavior variations within a more or less formalized ceremony are expected, and the form and content of two meetings will differ somewhat by their presence or absence. I have selected five men and a woman from Coldspring whom I know fairly well. Three of the men were present at both meetings I attended at Coldspring. Two, Wood-eater (pl. 9) and Corn-husker (pl. 10), performed the same offices twice. Stick-lodged-in-a-crotch (pl. 11) participated in both meetings, and Snorer (pl. 12) was present only at the second. Hemlocks-lying-down (pl. 13) was conductor and singer for the first meeting, but his son replaced him as head singer at Restingsky's "doings." He sang that night at Earth-hiller's (pl. 14), who attended neither of the two described meetings, but, because she also held a meeting on the second night of the new year, and because she leads another faction in the community, she limited Resting-sky's meeting by a prior choice of dancers.

The reader will find other personality references in the proceedings of the actual meetings.

No attempt is made here to analyze and classify these individuals according to any of the systems of psychiatry. In the first place, I am operating with an insufficient amount of biographical data. Furthermore, by training I am not an analyst. Second, the field work predated the several series of projective tests now in use. The purpose of these sketches is different. They serve to introduce six individuals whose past history of interpersonal relations affected their attitudes and behavior during two Eagle Dance meetings, which I attended. I have assembled observations and remarks around these selected individuals that in some way explain each one's position and status with reference to the group. Elsewhere in the text, particularly in the general chapter, I cite their experiences in joining the Eagle Society; I note gaps in their knowledge and quote their accounts as they gave them to me. My informants were the best available. In fact, at Coldspring they included all the leaders and many passive participants of the rituals. What these individuals actually did and said in meetings of the Eagle Society was determined first by the history of the ritual, a cultural phenomenon prescribing limits to their behavior, and secondly by their reactions to each other as determined by their own individual histories within the life at Coldspring community. The subjects of these cases have all since died and the cases afford a general perspective on Iroquois personality.

I endeavored to learn how Seneca culture has affected several individuals who manifest it differently. The culture passes the same songs and prayers along from generation to generation, but the individual professor is noted not because he knows this or that song, but because of how well he executes it. Naturally, some individuals have specialized in certain types of learning or arts, say, herbalism or basketry. Also, in a broken-down culture there is real compensation to be derived from knowing about the old things. There is fear of being scoffed at by the bewildered younger generation, but most everyone respects the wisdom of old people. A representative study of Iroquois personality should take into account several cases of insanity that have developed among younger people, who, having found nothing respectable in the old culture, have also been frustrated in an attempt to adjust themselves to White culture as the progressive Indians see it. They are caught between two spurious cultures. However, my studies have been confined to the devout followers of

Handsome Lake, who, I believe, in seizing upon the accumulated goods and traditions of their own culture, have unfolded their own personalities within its framework. Despite conflicts with one another, they share a common love of the old way. They forget the uncertainties of a changing world, and derive real pleasure from being "Indians," at least for the duration of the ceremonies. This statement is offered in an attempt to illustrate how individual variations in behavior can affect ethnology (cf. Wallace, A. F. C., 1952).

CASE I. WOOD-EATER, AN ELDERLY MAN OF THE BEAR CLAN

When I first heard of Wood-eater in June of 1933 it was through the recommendation of a white missionary who thought that the old man might possibly suit my interests as an anthropologist because he listed Wood-eater among those who caused most consternation in the work of Christian uplift. The missionary could boast some progress with the pagan Indians, as he called them, since they now let him speak first at their funerals before Wood-eater rose to deliver his address and tell the people not to believe what the white preacher had said.

During the summer I came to know old dji'wa', as the Indians fondly called him. In August he was making elm-bark bowls to exhibit at the New York State Fair. He showed me an elm-bark cradle of a type which preceded the wooden cradleboard. From a discussion of handicrafts and their uses in the old culture, our conversations drifted to herbal medicines, the content of the ceremonies, and ritualistic forms of address. Unlike others of the Seneca who were unsure of themselves in such matters, Wood-eater had full confidence in his knowledge, and he was always willing to impart accurately just what the old people told him.

He invited me to stay with him during the Midwinter Festival of 1934, and I returned to live in his household the next summer. With the old man as informant, his son clarifying what the old man had said while biting his pipestem, and his son's wife interpreting, we worked at ethnology at the dinner table, around the stove while wiping dishes, on summer evenings propped up in chairs facing the road. Sometimes to my regret but to his own interest, the old man would tire of my questions and retire to hoe his garden, or he would vanish into the bush to return with some medicinal plant for the herbarium.

Visitors came to see him frequently, or to see me. Sometimes the Coldspring Singers Society came to dance, or just to sing; and when these activities flagged we "put up" the False-faces or held a feast for some other medicine society.

I attended the public affairs at the Longhouse with the family. There we listened to the old man, there formally designated Twi'yendagǫ', Wood-eater, the principal speaker for the officers. As my ability to take Seneca texts phonetically improved, he would dictate "for the book" what he told the people. Thus he gave me the long address which he customarily delivered at funerals, and which he used a few days later over Chesley Snow (Fenton, 1946). It was on this occasion that I heard him contradict the missionary.

As we walked home from the cemetery, he said:

Chesley was there among his relatives. He knew what I say this morning. I told them it was no good for the missionary to talk because [English] is hard language to understand. Some do not know what he said. I told them today that somebody should chose one preacher. It no use to have two preachers. Poor Chesley will not know where to go. He will be all mixed up. There are two roads. The missionary directs one, I another. He can't go on both. Chesley stays on the middle and he does not know where he goes . . . I did the best I could.

He went on to tell me how he would like to have his own funeral.

They used to get a horse to take the body to the Longhouse . . . if a man had gone there during his lifetime. I want to be buried in a plain board coffin. Just the body uses it. The soul has gone out of it. He sees the body lay down. He don't know what is the trouble.

The Indian poormaster, appointed by the people, has no money to pay, but men at Coldspring can make a board coffin.

This is how it should be with us Indians.

Dji'wa' got his wish. They did not bury him in a cloth-covered coffin such as he abhorred. When his body was brought home from the Salamanca City Hospital where he died in 1946, his neighbors dressed him in Indian costume and buried him in a pine box which they made for him.

Wood-eater was about 70 years old when I first knew him. His mother was an Onondaga of the Heron Clan, one of a little band of Onondaga descendants of that lineage who had settled among the Allegany Seneca. His mother's mother had come from Onondaga many years ago. Seneca was his native tongue, and he had little English. A matron of the Wolf clan remarked:

His mother was really of the Heron Clan but he was adopted by Nancy Billy, mother of Arrow and Ten-mornings, matron of the Seneca Bear Clan. She changed his clan and name to the Bear roster. Adoption by a woman of another clan changes his clan but not his nation.

His name, however, belongs to the Bear Clan, in which he functioned. But his nickname (dji'wa') is not clan property, and was shared by a member of another clan at Tonawanda.

He remains an Onondaga on the annuity rolls. The councillors have to accept him before he can be put on the Seneca annuity roll, thus adopting him into the Seneca Nation.

Formerly they used to adopt aliens of other nations. The councillors have put a stop to the practice because abuses arose. Hemlocks-lying-down's mother was caught collecting annuities in both Canada and in New York.

After his mother got another man, Dji'wa' grew up at his grand-mother's house where he came under the tutelage of his foster mother's brother, Oscar Crow, from whom he learned the message of the Seneca Prophet, Handsome Lake, and how to speak in the Longhouse. Much participation as well as hard listening to the older speakers at the ceremonies etched in his mind the content of the entire Coldspring Seneca ceremonial cycle. He used to practice the learning of the Longhouse while walking in the woods and when felling timber. Old men must have liked this youth because they told him many things to remember, including the tobacco-burning prayers for Eagle Dance.

At times he had been a seasonal farmhand for my family, a railroad worker, a pretty fair carpenter. He had felled timber in the big woods, and during the last lumber boom along the Allegheny River he had ridden the rafts downriver to Pittsburgh. He had owned teams and cattle, and he had built the house where he lived.

He married twice, had several daughters and sons. Only his young-est son and a daughter's son lived with him. His wife had been a Longhouse official of the Snipe Clan. Other daughters by another husband lived nearby but were not friendly to the household. He feared other neighbors too.

The man was no physical coward. Broken knuckles in his later years attested to many summers of playing baseball without a glove. The Coldspring people, like all Seneca, are ardent fans. I have seen the old man stop a hard liner with one bare hand. He loved lacrosse and he had played it well on a team with Stick-lodged-in-a-crotch and others when they were youths. He never mentioned his prowess as a runner, but it is said at Quaker Bridge that he and Deerfoot, a noted Seneca runner, had gone across the ocean as youths to defeat the best runners on the Continent. With failing health, he gave up his games, and he sold his carpenter's tools to buy groceries for his last days.

As a ritual speaker and preacher of the Handsome Lake Revelation, Wood-eater heeded many calls on his services both at home and abroad on such occasions as the Green Corn and Midwinter Festivals and at the annual revivals of the Longhouse People which they call "Six Nations Meetings." At home, Stick-lodged-in-a-crotch and old Twenty-canoes accepted his version of the Good Message (Deardorff, 1951). Draped-over-a-log and Arrow, his adopted half-brother, asked him to conduct the stated festivals at the longhouse. It was usually he who appeared to "put tobacco in the fire" at meetings of Eagle Dance. Wood-eater was the one, moreover, whom the officials of other longhouses—Newtown, Cattaraugus, Tonawanda, Onondaga, and the three longhouses at Grand River, Canada—summoned in the fall with notched message sticks and a short string of white wampum to preach at their meetings. "We like to hear that old man from

Allegany speak Seneca," I was told at Ohsweken in 1945. What he said was most like the words spoken at Burnthouse (Cornplanter, Pa.), a century and a half ago.

The old man had his qualms about appearing before a crowd, particularly in Coldspring. Actually, members of the other faction—Snorer, Earth-hiller, his son's half-sisters—annoyed him. He feared them. I have observed him taking a potion to ward away witchcraft, which he thought his rivals were attempting, before going up to the longhouse to speak. When he was called to Tonawanda for the Six Nations Meeting of 1933, Snorer got his chance to conduct the Green Corn Festival. Earth-hiller and her son Sunshine immediately came into prominence; the mother was very active in the longhouse and the son outside parking cars. Both knew that Snorer was an outlander, and that his version of the ceremonies countered local tradition. To all this Wood-eater feigned amusement which was not convincing.

Wood-eater was a splendid informant. His pride and reserve melted before the wishes of a grandson. He told stories on winter nights. He had confidence in his knowledge, and his honesty asserted itself when in doubt. "I only know what the old folks tell me," he would say, and not claim knowledge of what happened long ago.

It perplexed him that Hemlocks-lying-down should give way to tears while singing Handsome Lake's song to the Wind and Thunder at the Midwinter Festival of 1934. He himself seemed emotionally stable, unhurried, and confident that he fulfilled the Prophet's canons of good behavior. For this he was respected.

Because his son's wife is the daughter of Resting-sky's wife, It-dips-water, his presence at the Eagle Dance for Resting-sky was expected.

CASE 2. CORN-HUSKER, A MIDDLE-AGED COMMONER OF THE HAWK CLAN

Corn-husker (nǫwiya''gǫ')—or Parts-the-riffles—is brother of Resting-sky's wife, and they both are of the Hawk Clan like their mother who bore him 57 years ago at Coldspring. She was a reputed basket maker, and his father was a Faith-keeper in the Wolf Clan. The latter, a sharpshooter in Grant's army during the Civil War, knew many White families in the Conewango Valley, between Allegany and Cattaraugus Reservations. Amos was jovial and fat, but his son is muscular and slight, though good-natured.

The father's greatness is much impressed upon the son, who provisionally carried on his father's duties at the longhouse for a time in lieu of a successor in the Wolf Clan. Finally, constant duty as a section hand on the Erie Railroad during 30 years prevented his attending the "doings" at the longhouse. So he gave up his office. Illiteracy and drink, the latter perhaps an expression of conflict, prevented his getting a foremanship on the railroad. He could set a good curve, even after being drunk, but he could not write reports.

He belongs to the Coldspring Singers, an organization for mutual aid composed of younger men and certain old women whom they befriend, and he regularly attends their meetings and excels in singing the Pigeon and Sharpening-a-Stick Dances. He is well liked by his fellows who always inquire his whereabouts when he fails to appear of an evening. His clownishness insures a laugh from the Feather dancers, even during religious festivals.

If deficient in ritualistic pedantry, Corn-husker compensates by wit and a genius for material culture. He is a good gambler and famed maker of "snow-snakes." He "fixes" water drums for his fellow singers by converting discarded paint kegs into resonators over which he stretches a soaked hide. He makes turtle rattles and carves false-faces (masks), in all of which he has a reputation for brilliant and feverish execution, usually induced by procrastination. His wife told me that once he took plenty of time and carved a beautiful drum-stick adorned with a human head on the handle. He is generous and helps her at night in the gardens.

His wife attended Carlisle, and after they began to live together he told his sisters that when she first returned she could not cook. When meals are late, he frequently remarks that he has just seen skeletons of men starved by their wives passing westward along the road to the hereafter. He admits his wife keeps a good garden and that she picks berries enough for the winter. They have lived together over 30 years. Like her, all the children are shy, and his relatives often remark about this. One was recently killed accidentally, but Corn-husker, wishing to avoid trouble, insisted no foul play was involved. He is quite susceptible to public opinion.

Corn-husker has an inordinate fear of ghosts, according to his relatives, and a penchant for fabricating and enlarging upon his adventures—particularly his relationship with Whites. My long residence on his premises was welcome substantiation of a long-boasted friendship with my grandfather. I must confess the advantages of this situation were manifold. His hospitality includes harboring a great number of pets: young hawks, skunks, and a crow which he claims speaks Seneca.

When Corn-husker was younger he had aspirations of becoming a great athlete; he especially aspired to pugilistic prowess. Wearing shorts, he ran about a triangle of roads in Coldspring every evening hoping to improve his wind. Some confreres, wishing to scare him, wrapped themselves in sheeting and stood on a fallen pine tree near the council house as he passed. Seeing them and thinking them ghosts (dji·sgɛ.), he threw stones at them; and one fell and sprained a shoulder.

Corn-husker is usually appointed "whooper" at medicine society meetings. He is normally invited everywhere, but his wife seldom accompanies him, being both shy and somewhat incredulous of the medicine societies, as well as uninformed. She told me that once her children were sent away from a neighbor's, where they were having a False-face anniversary rite, because their mother is not a real pagan.

Possibly this has something to do with his frequent visits at his sisters' homes. They often hold medicine rites for him. He was expected to come to Resting-sky's meeting. He finds in the Eagle Dance a legitimate outlet for his stories and good-natured wit.

CASE 3. STICK-LODGED-IN-A-CROTCH, GUARDIAN OF THE GOOD MESSAGE IN THE DEER CLAN

Stick-lodged-in-a-crotch (hawi'theọ·k) is now an old man, and his people before him lived at Coldspring. He is of the Deer Clan and custodian of Handsome Lake's good message, the senior religious office for his moiety, which includes the Deer, Snipe, Heron, and Hawk Clans. That office necessitates his spending many weeks traveling while visiting other longhouses with "Twenty," the corresponding officer of the Bear Clan in the other moiety, and Wood-eater, the preacher. Besides, he is the Big Crow of the "Little Water Company," which holds its periodic meetings at his home. The members leave their ritual paraphernalia there and he is custodian of the tribal medicine. Corn-husker left his bundle there, and he says that when he went after it, it had disappeared because Stick-lodged-in-a-crotch sold it at one of the Canadian longhouses.

Still a hard-working and thrifty farmer, Stick-lodged-in-a-crotch has by far the most substantial buildings and means of the people who follow the "old way." He still keeps a horse and a few cows. Besides he has raised a large family. His wife is now dead, but some of a daughter's family live at home.

His proclivity for falling asleep during rituals and longhouse meetings is noted. He suffers some shyness in talking and is not readily understood, partly because he mumbles sleepily and because he has a number of nervous habits. He is apt to rub the back of his left hand, or his forehead, or scratch his head above his right ear. When he rises to talk he characteristically removes his felt hat by grasping it from the rear and bringing it forward, instead of doffing it from front to back. It is said that once he tore off a collar while talking, and another time the rim of his hat; and again while reciting his mission, he twisted a button from his overcoat, and the button flew across the room.

He is reputed never to have learned the origin legends for the rituals, because he has always gone to sleep while others were talking. As I suspected, this is not entirely true. He has been my informant, and his long life in ritual has made him conversant with all the forms, but I did not find him a ready teacher. No Eagle Dance is quite complete without him (and a great butt of jokes and conversation was lost when he departed).

At the longhouse social dances, young men who are scheduling the events usually hand him a horn rattle to lead the Linking-arms or Hand-in-hand Dance, which he is fond of singing. If his partner, "Twenty," the chief of the opposite moiety, is present, floormen organize the Trotting Dance and ask them to lead it. They also join as partners in the Fish Dance. The partners are famous in other longhouses where they visit. At Tonawanda, they call it "Great Quiver Dance," when these two old men lead. In passing, it might be said that such friendships frequently emerge from standing in particular ceremonial relationships to another person in the other moiety as ritual singing partners, dance leaders, and chiefs. However, dancing partners are usually friends, and may be of the same phratry. Each longhouse officer has a correspondent on the other side, and the two are supposed to work together.

Such situations of paired roles may lead to rivalry. For example, a funeral requires that the preacher be from the opposite moiety to the deceased. In Coldspring, where there are only two speakers who now perform this office, the rival factions sometimes have to call upon an adversary, and the family which is affiliated with the other faction, so as to draw the unwanted one, may be at a loss. The two might be cronies, but they are rivals.

To return, Stick-lodged-in-a-crotch's role in the culture of the local group is rather that of a participant than a shaper. He exerts a negative rather than a positive force, which might be characterized as an anchor to windward for the "longhousers."

CASE 4. SNORER, A FAITH-KEEPER OF THE HAWK CLAN, A CONSCIENTIOUS OBJECTOR

Snorer (shogǫ'gwa·s), of the Hawk Clan, lives up on "High Bank" overlooking Wolf Run and the Allegheny River to the east. His youngest son, of the Bear Clan, who lives with him, will inherit part of his father's knowledge, having been home during the years of Snorer's greatest erudition. The mother and many of Snorer's children preceded him along the westward road to the hereafter, leaving him somewhat lonely. A son lives at Coldspring, and still another works on the Erie Railroad near Jamestown.

Born and nurtured at Plank Road, Cattaraugus Reservation,

Snorer learned English and Asher Wright's missionary orthography for Seneca. He sold baskets in Buffalo and sought fraternity in waterfront saloons. He is reputed to have drunk and fought at Newtown Longhouse, instead of listening to the older men. Nevertheless, he soon distinguished himself as a craftsman and as a ritual singer. He still has a stentorian baritone voice and a phenomenally inconsistent memory which contradicts versions of songs he has previously taught his pupils.

He-strikes-the-rushes says that his father, a noted ritual custodian, went to Snorer once for the medicine songs. He soon gave up trying to learn Snorer's version and went to someone else, because his tutor sang them differently at each sitting.

Snorer moved to Allegany, his wife's community, and his younger children were born there. Although now a long-time resident and even a Faith-keeper in the longhouse, he is still regarded as an interloper. To fortify his position he has established himself as an authority on ancient lore and learned everything possible. His inordinate pride and anxiety lest he be outstripped by Wood-eater has prompted him to pretend knowledge of Handsome Lake's Revelation, saying his father before him was a preacher and taught him; but his recitation was not approved by the committee appointed to hear him.

Nevertheless, he is an impressive orator, and commands the respect of his listeners which at other times he demands but cannot control. He modulates his voice, speaking some parts softly. He says, "You notice how they are all quiet when I talk in the longhouse. There is no whispering as there is when Wood-eater speaks."

In 1933 when Wood-eater was called to the Six Nations Meeting at Tonawanda, the two male longhouse officers asked Snorer to conduct the Green Corn Festival. On the third day, before addressing the Creator between songs of the Thanksgiving Dance, a role usually performed by Wood-eater, Snorer explained it as his first attempt, confessing a sketchy knowledge of the forms; but he did not call on another Faith-keeper who was present and knew the invocatory chants.

Snorer is an excellent informant. Having been derided, he has pumped his rivals, endeavoring to learn all they know and at the same time render himself indispensable. His thirst for knowledge in part accounts for his inconsistencies. His store is vast and necessarily his selections differ periodically. He has acquired a world of information, which, of necessity he has thought through. He becomes the preacher when Wood-eater is ill or unable to preach. This happened when Wood-eater's wife died a year ago.

Snorer hoped that he and his young son might attend the Six Nations Meetings, that they might learn of extra local affairs. He would like to be recognized among all the Iroquois peoples. "Once he went to

Canada, saying he had been called, but no one had heard of him there."

When delegates are summoned to Six Nations Religious Councils, the messenger summons only the chiefs by name. Then all the Faith-keepers are summoned in a body, before the common people. It irks both Snorer and Hemlocks-lying-down considerably to be bracketed, for they feel their names should be mentioned individually.[12] It is only unfortunate that they have no living mothers or sisters of naming rank who could nominate them for high office. Further, Hemlocks-lying-down is only Seneca by sufferance, being an outlander by birth.

It must not be construed that Snorer is without power or friends. His singing ability promoted him to head singer for the "Little Water Company," although he no longer holds the medicine. Chauncey Warrior of the Turtle Clan, a Cattaraugus Cayuga in the other moiety, is his "partner." Earth-hiller, the old woman of the Wolf Clan, leads the faction which opposes Wood-eater, and she employs Snorer as her spokesman.

Snorer exhibits a blunt exterior and is easily offended; and he is given to sudden and sustained anger when crossed, but to "Rabelasian" humor if encouraged. Recently, Snorer's son brought home a Canadian Iroquois mistress, but another Coldspring youth enticed her away. Snorer remarked, "I guess my son just rented it. He and his friend are too weak to dance Eagle Dance any more."

Like many of his tribesmen, Snorer has been a "show" Indian, and once visited Glen Island beyond New York City. He is proud of his knowledge of White culture. When away from home, he becomes Chief "White Eagle," a fictitious person, and a vendor of fabricated ethnography. Loyalty to his own culture does not permit his singing anything but "show songs" away from home.

Even as an old man, he bragged that White women wished to marry him, but old Seneca women remark that he is even too lame to get firewood. They call him "curly-headed-John," a somewhat sinistral compliment, since Indian hair is traditionally straight. However, he claims descent from Mary Jemison, the "White woman of the Genesee," who is a coveted ancestor of many mixed-bloods.

One may readily understand that bitterness as well as increasing lameness kept him from the longhouse in 1934 while Wood-eater conducted the New Year's Dance. Referring to his excessive lameness and attributing it to the sorcery of his rival, he said:

"I am tired of the trouble I am having. I am going to turn it around. Clairvoyants say that they are jealous because I was a great dancer of social dances. I mean the ones that are on this earth for our enjoyment, not the four sacred rituals, which alone are in heaven."

---

[12] Since this was written he was called to preach in Canada and at Cattaraugus, his old home. His ambitions were not unavailing.

Nevertheless, the proximity of Resting-sky's home to "High Bank" and the lure of hog's head and a pail of corn soup, permitted his hobbling down to the Eagle Society meeting and participating. Life at Coldspring is different without him.

CASE 5. HEMLOCKS-LYING-DOWN, A SO-CALLED "CAYUGA" OF THE TURTLE CLAN

Hemlocks-lying-down was a grown man when he came to Coldspring about 1889 from Cattaraugus Reservation. Though a functioning member of the Turtle Clan at Coldspring, local Seneca call him a "Cayuga," which, like "Delaware," is a smear word for one of uncertain social position, to underscore the fact that he is an outlander. The man who marries into the Seneca Nation, or who removes from Cattaraugus to Allegany or to Tonawanda, is never allowed to forget that he does not really belong to the community where he may spend his adult life.

Born at Cattaraugus at a place called Plank Road before 1870, his father was a recognized Seneca of the Beaver Clan from Buffalo Creek, named Split-house. His mother was really a Seneca of the Turtle Clan with the name of "Big leaf," but she went off to Grand River, Canada, to make a second marriage with a Cayuga with whom she resided so long that they added her name to the Cayuga tribal roll. Therefore, old Seneca women around Coldspring came to wonder whether his mother was not really a Cayuga, or of some other, perhaps Algonquian, tribe, saying, "They came from way beyond Canada," meaning the Grand River Reserve.

His first recollections are of life along Clear Creek in a predominantly Turtle Clan house. Later he lived on the ball ground or common at Newtown Longhouse where the life of a growing boy is full of sport and where the ceremonies take place. The boys of Newtown gave up their ball game only when an official called from the door for them to come inside as the ceremonies were to start. They listened, and danced at the end of the line. Unlike his grandsons, who are famed dancers, he learned late, at 18, under tutelage of his father. Boys were helped at home before joining public ceremonies.

Likewise he was 21 before he sang Great Feather Dance in public. He and a singing partner listened to his father and practiced, and their great day came when the regular singer got drunk on hard cider en route to the Green Corn Dance. "Word came that the regular singer was lying under a tree. The officials put us in. I was nervous the first time we sat down on the bench in the longhouse. After that we used to sing at every ceremony."

Hemlocks-lying-down was thus an accomplished singer at the longhouse before he ever came to Allegany. As he learned, the old men coached him. But he did not sing for the Medicine Society until after he came to Coldspring. An old lady, mother of Earth-hiller, taught him the legend and songs.

He settled first at Wolf Run close to his work, which was first in a lumber mill, then on the section gang of the Pennsylvania Railroad, a job he was to hold 35 years. He worked 9 years for the Erie. From the time he first went out to work in the basket factory and the cannery near Cattaraugus until his retirement from work on the section, he has been a steady worker. He was still a man of tremendous physical strength in his sixties when I first knew him. He was then living at Coldspring, just south of where the creek enters Allegheny River, in a cluster of three houses occupied by his offspring. His wife, with whom he stayed for 40 years, had died but a few years previously.

Actually, the latter was his third marriage, not counting an affair when he first came to Allegany with a young girl, the sister of Corn-husker and later wife of Resting-sky. At 16 he had married a Canadian Iroquois girl, whose picture he still carried in 1948. They had met at a dance at Sour Springs; he brought her home, but she was taken sick and died within 18 months of a rheumatic heart. A son died in the Canadian army in 1919. A second marriage was with a Newtown girl, but some trouble developed, and he came to Allegany.

Here developed the trysts at the river crossing with It-dips-water, whom he never considered a wife, but this attitude in itself reflects distance between him and her kindred, which is of significance for this study. He does not go to Resting-sky's, so his not appearing at that Eagle Dance is not perplexing.

When I first knew him he claimed not to know many people because he always remained at home making baskets.

"I make the best baskets in Coldspring and White people come from all over to get them. No one around here knows as much about the medicines. Life at Cattaraugus is nearer the old way."

His household in Coldspring includes his son's son, a Beaver, and the latter's current wife. His only son, a Wolf, lives across the road with a second grandson. When questioned about this offspring, he said,

"I had only Great-night; I guess I was no good for that sort of business." Actually he and his son are not close; his two grandsons, whom he raised, are his closest kin.

His deceased wife's brother, djidógwas, also lived across the road in the only log house extant in Coldspring. This little cluster of households forms the basis of a family clique in Coldspring society.

Corn-husker's remarks reflect the opinion of a faction toward a smaller feud group encysted in the community: "I told my wife that if you go down to his place all the time, you get all twisted up. I am not going to tell you anything more. I always tell the truth when you write it down."

I had noticed that Corn-husker was a bit offish at Great-night's house one evening, when the Coldspring Singers Society met there. He remained outside and went home early. Later he mentioned that there had been trouble between the families. Corn-husker does not like to believe that Great-night's group know anything about his son's death, although others have told him.

That man is a trouble-maker. He is mad at the longhouse people because he insists ritual songs and the Handsome Lake religion should be different from the way they are conducted here. They [the longhouse officers] do not have him sing Feather Dance any longer.

Those two families down there are by themselves. There will be trouble if you go there. Draped-over-log and Arrow, the two longhouse headmen, and Stick-lodged-in-a-crotch and the Snows will not like it. They are like children; they run about [as if] they did not know where they were at.

The men of Cattaraugus, like Hemlocks-lying-down and Chauncey Warrior, his clansman, are truly foreigners within the community. One is a fine singer and a capable orator, but he holds no office; a feigned lack of interest in not being a Faith-keeper is but a mask for a sense of social inferiority. Undoubtedly Hemlocks-lying-down excels many of those in office. His singing ability is a hold on fame. He renders the sacred songs particularly well and when not "mad" at the longhouse officers, they usually request him to sing. The officials were in his good graces at the 1934 "New Year's," but on two important occasions he failed to appear. Someone said he liked to be coaxed. He told me, "I am the only singer who knows all of the Big-Women's Dance. Once Fannie Stevens [an Onondaga of the Heron Clan] had to come after me so they could have it." Then he chuckled.

He-strikes-the-rushes relates how he and Hemlocks-lying-down were invited to sing Feather Dance together at a Six Nations meeting at Coldspring. The former had a new turtle rattle which the latter borrowed and in singing beat it so hard on the bench to keep time that the handle broke. "Afterward, Old Yéndi told me that he was jealous of my singing ability, and he beat that rattle hard enough to break it."

Although Snorer and Chauncey Warrior find solace in each other's company, Hemlocks-lying-down maintains only a "kidding" relationship with the former. He had a serious falling out with Snorer one winter, because the latter borrowed six strings of corn and two bushels of potatoes, when facing starvation, and did not later repay them. Later, when Snorer had a horse and buggy, he took Hemlocks-lying-down to Randolph and wanted money and more corn to boot for his services. Hemlocks-lying-down alleges he has to feed half the neighborhood every winter.

Pride in the productivity of his garden is warranted. He regretted that his deceased wife's brother, djidǫ́gwas, should raise better corn in 1933, and that Draped-over-log should raise the best cabbages, but he contends that his seed is ancient and usually grows. His gardening ability is only surpassed by his craftsmanship.

His and Snorer's relative merits as woodworkers approximate their rivalry as singers and folklorists. He claims that whenever he has developed a new lacrosse stick or baseball bat, Snorer has endeavored to copy it. But every time Hemlocks-lying-down has scooped the market and left his rival with a frozen stock. In the meanwhile he develops a new idea.

Of the two, one is impressed that Hemlocks-lying-down fashions for the love of it. His baskets and musical instruments have a dignity which results from a mastery of technique and patient leisurely handling. In contradistinction, one notes the bold regular facets of a ponderously intuitive style of carving which is his rival's, and which one feels may be susceptible to greater refinement. Hemlocks-lying-down reluctantly admits that the Snorer is the only man at Coldspring who knows how to make a flageolet.

Hemlocks-lying-down frequently goes into the woods to gather medicines. His knowledge of ethnobotany, though characteristic of elderly Seneca, is considered extraordinary even among his own people. I have rarely suggested a plant for which he did not know many uses. His preoccupation with botany and carving has influenced many to suspect him of sorcery.

Hemlocks-lying-down kept an angora cat named "Mickey" and a mangy nondescript pup called "Zero," because, as he said, he "amounts to nothing." He was nearly as sentimental about a small pig.

He is inclined to whimsey. During the New Year Dance of 1934 he was appointed conductor by several medicine society ritual sponsors. While requesting a man who was seated on the second row of longhouse benches to sing, he would lean over and pinch a youth's leg—the while he was whispering earnestly to the singer—and then stand back, look surprised at the boy and laugh. This behavior, coupled with amused chuckling, especially at his own bon mots, which usually have humorous sexual reference, is perhaps an expression of his own sexual preoccupation, a business at which he admits he was unproductive. Further, it expresses a peculiarly Seneca love for the "little ones," which emerges in one form or another among all the older people.

All of our friends, cited in these case studies, are among the truly devout followers of the "old way," but each of them manifests his culture differently. As a savant, Snorer would have the community support him. Hemlocks-lying-down, essentially anarchical, is more interested in himself and his art than in what others think of him, except that his singing remains indispensable to the longhouse people. Rather than thrust himself forward he patiently waits to be coaxed, and sometimes goes home in a peeve when slighted. But when active he is sincerely emotional and deeply moved by his own singing and its symbolism within the ritual. More than once I have seen the tears course down his cheeks as he sang Feather Dance or the Dawn Song which his father sang before him. More than any other person I know, he has identified himself completely with his cultural environment.

He conducted the first meeting of the Eagle Society but was absent at Resting-sky's anniversary, both for reasons explained above and because he was singing at Earth-hiller's "doings" in Coldspring. He happened to be in her good favor that winter.

CASE 6. EARTH-HILLER, MATRON OF THE WOLF CLAN

A woman named Earth-hiller (gain′dahgwa′) (pl. 14) is the old woman Faith-keeper of the Wolf Clan. She lives at Coldspring near the longhouse with Sunshine, her son, and a granddaughter, now grown up. She harbored (djǐdo·t) the reservation vagrant, whom everyone else feared. Although now lean and dependent on a crutch, she was once a fine-looking woman and still presents an imposing figure in the councils of the longhouse officers.

Like her son, who habitually affects a cane and doesn't need it, she too is able to dispense with her crutch, and not to be outdone by other spry old women, cavorts with great birdlike jumps in the women's dances, her crutch tucked beneath her left arm pit and the free end waving dangerously aft. She seems to enjoy the amusement she elicits and frequently whoops shrilly to incite it.

Sometimes her enthusiasm has led to subsequent ridicule. During the seventh day of the Midwinter Festival she was moved to express her thanks to the Great Spirit en marche between songs of the Traditional-woman's Dance. Suddenly she piped in all sincerity, "I am thankful I am living at this season." Everyone laughed, although her behavior was well within the proprieties of the occasion.

She, as well as any woman, illustrates the classic power of Iroquois woman. She objects to Wood-eater, not liking him, and employs Snorer as her spokesman. She would exalt her son to a status office, insisting his name is of chiefly rank. At times impatient, she shrieks her objections from her station near the women's door. She loaned her land to the baseball team for a diamond, but offered it to a second club a succeeding year, because the first was presumptive enough to assume a second season's use without asking for it. She entertains whom she wishes.

Usually anyone is welcome at Medicine Society meetings, especially if he pays the price of admittance, a pinch of Indian tobacco for the offering and for the members to smoke. It rests with the conductor whom the host has appointed to invite the members. Nevertheless, Earth-hiller makes out a list, hands it to the conductor, and designates who shall not be invited.

Hence, it is interesting that since she held an anniversary of the Eagle Dance on the same night as Resting-sky, which was legitimate, since midwinter is the appropriate season for feasts, her choice of guests included Hemlocks-lying-down as conductor, and limited Resting-sky's conductor's selection of dancers to two boys from the Bear Clan, for she had previously secured the two other boys who represented both moieties and knew how to dance. I suppose that no such conflict would arise in an aboriginal community in which normally most of the youths would know the Eagle Dance. The conflict naturally meant that certain people were invited to both meetings and had to exercise a preference which, in itself, is significant. The fact that some people came greater distances to Resting-sky's party indicates that proximity did not entirely rule their choice. It was, however, expected that Snorer and his son would go to Earth-hiller's party, but Resting-sky's was nearer and, moreover, Hemlocks-lying-down had already been chosen to conduct Earth-hiller's party.

THE SENECA EAGLE DANCE AT TONAWANDA

THE CEREMONY

The Tonawanda Eagle Dance exhibits minor local differences in the ritual which, however, Tonawanda residents feel set them apart from the other Seneca at Coldspring and Newtown. My observations and inquiries are centered about one meeting, an anniversary of the cure of Helper, an old Sachem of the Bear Clan (pl. 15), and the renewal of his ceremonial friendship with his young friend, He-is-coming, of the Snipe clan in the other moiety (p. 126). This meeting called forth the best wits in the community, and they were afterward my informants. Therefore, rather than set forth a detailed description of my own observations, I shall note obvious ritual differences and then relate two detailed accounts of the ritual by two exceptional informants, both sachem chiefs of the Snipe clan—Falling-day, a famed singer, and Hair-burned-off, a ritual speaker. Space does not permit a description of all the personalities involved in this situation. Nevertheless, certain personality references are made by my informants.

The Tonawanda version of the Eagle Dance is unique in the following respects: There seems to be an emphasis on ceremonial friendship.

The meeting requires the usual functionaries: messenger, conductors, first singer, and assistants; but the man who asks the blessing and returns thanks for all the stations of the pantheon is distinct from the tobacco-burning priest. Hair-burned-off performed the former office and Twenty-kettles (Hawk Clan) the latter. There is frequent mention of "your medicine society (swatcinǫ'gɛ'shǫ')," and the prayers are more elaborate. Before the ceremony, the conductor passes tiny pieces of raw meat among the members.

In the ritual, there were no songs sung by the priest when he burned the tobacco, but there was a presentation of rattles and drums to the singers. Twenty-kettles said that he was renting the rattles for the occasion. One speaker, Awl-breaker (Wolf Clan), in the other moiety, presented all the horn rattles instead of gourd rattles to the dancers. The dancers were three in number, and they did not employ fans; Edward Black (Hawk Clan) admits that fans should be used but were forgotten. There was no whooper; one of the dancers performed this duty. The striking stick and striking pole were not employed, but an informant says they should be employed and were used anciently; instead, the speaker stamps to interrupt the singers.

The speeches illustrated for the first time in my experience the ridicule of someone in the other clan. He-strikes-the-rushes of the Snipe Clan (pl. 16, 1) made fun of Awl-breaker in the other moiety, his father's clansman, saying the Wolves are awful liars, and the latter replied in kind. Great-root (Turtle Clan) says that Hair-burned-off (Speaker) said that the Creator had left everything to be used for medicine, that even the paper which wrapped the crackers might be used to allay blisters on the feet. This amused people.

Peculiar to Tonawanda is the donation of packages of chewing tobacco to the dancers. Crackers are also used as elsewhere. However, speakers do not make gifts to the singers and the persons ridiculed. Nevertheless, at the end of the ritual, when all of the store of gifts had been allotted to the dancers and the conductor had taken them outside, He-strikes-the-rushes and one other chap made speeches of praise and good wishes to the ritual celebrant, Helper, presenting him with a few pennies to buy medicine.

The feast consists of a boiled chicken, instead of pig's head, which is passed counterclockwise. Hominy soup was ladled out by the headman first to the two ritual celebrants, Helper and He-is-coming; then the sponsor, Helper's wife, filled the conductor's pail, after which he called for the members and guests to shove their pails toward the wash boiler of soup from which he filled them equally in a counterclockwise direction. Then he told them to retrieve them.

Great-root says that one does not necessarily have to belong to the society to speak.   He is sure that he is not a member, although he acted as first singer.

One time they had it in the longhouse during the Midwinter Festival and they came to me and asked me to sing.   I told them I did not know the songs.   Well, then the conductor said, "You help."   So I took a rattle and helped the head singer and although I did not know the rhythm at first, I soon learned it and got used to the songs.   Later, they asked me to be head singer.   I don't know whose songs I sing, because I learned them of several people whom I assisted at different times.   The songs have no words.   The number seems indefinite.

Following this meeting, He-strikes-the-rushes explained why he took the liberty to ridicule Awl-breaker; it was because Awl-breaker is his father's clansman.   However, this joking relationship is unknown at Tonawanda, and two other informants misunderstood him.

The Turtle Clan are fibbers.

The Wolf Clan, they say, are know-it-alls. They used to say that at Newtown in the Eagle Dance.   The Wolf Clan would brag.   Then someone would reply, "I am not of the Wolf Clan.   Therefore, I cannot boast.   My clan has never been noted for anything."

One jokes with one's father's clansman.—Awl-breaker is of my father's clan, the Wolf.   We always pick on each other.   But we do not take it seriously.   He talked first at Helper's.   When he gave out the rattles to the dancers, he said that they were his.   So I replied that he would soon own them, that he boasted.   I started it after he presented the rattles.   I said he was full of lies.   You can't tell a Wolf anything.

The opening speaker should tell what there is to distribute.   He also said that jokes are permitted.   Some are supposed to speak in praise of the ritual sponsor. However, I think that my words are superfluous, inasmuch as this was an anniversary; it is different when someone is sick, so it is better to joke and have a good time.   They talk [encouragement] when it is really a serious case of illness.   Otherwise, the sponsor's health is taken care of in the tobacco invocation.   Hair-burned-off, the orator, said that there would be no limit to the joking.   The jokes were to be only lasting for the duration of the ritual.   The jokes are permitted so long as the sponsor is not too sick.   No one must take offense.   Awl-breaker got mad and went home.

The origin and early history of the Eagle Dance Medicine Society are unfamiliar to Falling-day, although he is 67, a sachem chief, singer for the ritual, and generally considered well posted on other matters. The idea that the ritual may have been formerly associated with peace or war is also unfamiliar to him; the ritual and its significance as a medicinal curing society have remained constant within his memory.

MEMBERSHIP

In answer to the query as to how memberships were created, Falling-day answered:

You get sick and your folks might think it might help you, and they put you in that society.   They dance gané'gwä'e''.

Of course, a fortuneteller, one who tells what you don't know, might tell your people that you should join.

They do different ways but they have the same name. Some use tea, some cards, some employ medicinal herbs. They gather certain herbs and put them under their pillows when they sleep.

Dreams are a third mode of entrance. "They sometimes dream to help such, but I have never seen one." He refers to the practice of a person's dreaming of a sick person in association with the ritual of some medicine society. Then the society holds the ritual and cures the sick person.

The frequency with which Falling-day answered my queries (and I believe honestly), "I don't know; I never heard; they never told me about that," is in itself indicative of the importance of recognizing individual differences and their bearing on the problem of culture for understanding Seneca ceremonies. Unlike so many lesser members of his group, he was well on in years before he joined the Eagle Society. Nevertheless, he was a singer for many years.

I was lame and some people thought that it would help me, so I tried it. This was not many, perhaps 15, years ago.

If I want to get up such a dance, I go to any member and ask him to give the invitations. The messenger (hadjáswas) is supposed to be a member, but sometimes when a member is away, a nonmember acts as messenger. Anyone can do it.

Quite a number of years that I was singer, I was not a member of the society. They give you the invitation to go sing, if you know how. If you have a drum, the messenger tells you to bring it along; if you lack a drum they will get that of someone else and the rattle boxes. I never had a drum; always someone else furnished the drum.

If I were going to have a meeting I would get anyone to do the cooking. Hominy is required for soup; and once in a while they hulled white corn soup but the soup must have meat in it because Shada'gé·a·' eats meat. One whole chicken is required. It must be white, but that is hard to get, so we use any kind of chicken.

Falling-day says he thinks pig's head was formerly used for the feast, as now at Allegany, but not often; "it has got to be chicken."

The cooking proceeds any time during the day or afternoon—"anytime before the dance goes on."

Several things are required for the meeting [yene'gwä"istha']: crackers and chewing tobacco to give to the dancers; Indian tobacco for the prayer; yene'gwä'istha' ga'nya'—a stick to strike the floor before speaking; and my uncle and predecessor Chief Chauncey Abrams [Snipe], and Old Jim Scrogg, who lived across the road, told me that at Tonawanda they used to have a post that was striped red like a barber pole where they hit the stick when they started dancing. It was used in the house where they were dancing.

SETTING THE BUNDLE UP BEFORE A MEETING PLACE

Falling-day volunteered that, "Years ago, but I have not seen that, when they were going to have such a dance, they would give the invitations just the same, but they set up a pole nearby the house and hung up one rattle box, the drum, and one fan." Falling-day thinks that they did not hang up the tobacco, nor has he heard that they crossed the two fans as at Newtown, but he has never seen the ritual paraphernalia displayed on the forked striped pole. "Now this is an invitation 2 days before they are going to have the ritual." They do not burn tobacco when they erect the pole, "not until they are ready to dance."

The messenger goes from house to house inviting the members to the meeting.

He selects, that's his duty to select, singers and dancers. He gets two dancers, three if he can get three, two anyway. Sometimes four. No difference. Dancers do not have to be of opposite moieties. Not here at Tonawanda. The four-dancer pattern of Coldspring is absent at Tonawanda. [See below.] Notched invitation sticks are not used, and corn is not distributed to the members to present at the meeting as a sign of membership and receipt of invitation. The same invitations are given for a celebrant as for a sick person.

The messenger sets the time. He tells them that such and such a time they are to come to the house. He might say early, just before dark. Or niyóntcis·do·tha'— such a time when you light the lamp.

THANKSGIVING

Before they are seated at the meeting, then the announcer (hatha'ha') begins the thanksgiving (ganọ'·nyọk). When he starts speaking [it is not necessary for him to run the whole fixed gamut of the pantheon], he must think of (1) the people, (2) the four persons [who are] the messenger[s] of the Creator, and (3) the Creator. This is the beginning.

ANNOUNCEMENT

Then the speaker tells who got up such a dance; he tells what ails the person— that he is not feeling well and that he thought that the ceremony might help him. Another way, people tended the sick man. They try all the herbal medicines, but they don't do any good, so they thought it might help this kind [that type of ceremony might help him]. If you have been attending the sick man and you think it may help such [that gane'gwä'e·' may help him] and you expressed the thought that it might help him, then the speaker tells what you thought.

The speaker tells who is going to sing and who will help. [At Tonawanda, singers do not have to be of opposite moieties.] He mentions the names of the dancers and how many will dance and that he himself was invited to speak.

A speaker may have many ways to speak; then he may elaborate and talk for a long time, otherwise "a man who can't says but a few words." Hair-burned-off is among the best. When he finishes, then they are seated.

The messenger becomes the ritual manager or the conductor at the meeting. When they all get there, the conductor tells the dancers to put on their costumes. He seats the singers and functionaries, leaving an adequate space for the dancers.

[At this point Falling-day forgot the outline, omitting to mention the general thanksgiving speech, announcements, and the invocation.]

TOBACCO INVOCATION

Twenty-kettles usually does this, but anyone who knows how may make the tobacco-burning invocation. Nowadays few know how. Falling-day never burned tobacco at this ceremony.

Falling-day heard that when the priest starts to burn the tobacco he makes a war whoop and sings part of the first song, but he never saw this done. The fan, rattle, drum, and the gifts to distribute after the speeches lie on the floor near the stove (fire). The priest does not hold them in his hand.

The tobacco-burning invocation to the Dew Eagle by Twenty-kettles.— Twenty-kettles, an old man of the Hawk Clan, senior officer of Tonawanda Longhouse, invariably makes the tobacco-burning invocation at meetings of the Eagle Society.

Someone told the conductor [hadja'swas] to gather the medicine society [honǫ'tcino''gɛ'], and somebody speaks giving thanks when they come in to the meeting. He tells them who will sing when they dance. When they are ready the singers sit on the benches. There must be two singers and they must be of different moieties. Someone puts tobacco and then the song commences. This is gane''gwä'e·'.

Now you will partake of tobacco, you who are wheeling in flight at the elevation the clouds are scudding, you who are of the mists—the Dew Eagles.

Now the smoke is rising from the real tobacco and through it you cloud dwellers shall hear.

Rightly our ruler ordained as he intended [or said], "I will create mankind on the earth, that there shall travel to and fro human beings to whom, no matter where they are, aid shall come from time to time."

And they tobacco shall partake, they whom he created, the wild animals; and they [humans] shall continue to derive benefit from a bond of friendship between themselves and the game animals.

So now it is fulfilled you [all] shall partake of the tobacco.

So now then, as it should be, her illness will cease.

Now then it is well that it has happened so, that she shall continue to travel about here on the earth.

Now then you, our ruler, you reside in the sky place; you should grant strength or power when it is fulfilled; the Dew Eagles have partaken of tobacco.[13]

Now then the fan has partaken of the tobacco, that which is derived from your being of which it is symbolic [represents].[14]

Now the ceremony is about to commence.

Now then your drum receives tobacco.[15]

Now the very songs partake of the tobacco.

---

[13] The invoker addresses the Great Spirit because he originally endowed the Dew Eagles with healing power. He has supreme power and should give strength to everything when it is fulfilled. The people have already done their duty to the Dew Eagles by giving them tobacco. One always returns thanks to the Great Spirit.

[14] The feathers of the fan are plucked from the Eagle. The fan represents the eagle's wing and is symbolic of his body [heya'da·de'—his being].

[15] Now they are mentioning the items in the ritual and the feast, which is a chicken at Tonawanda, having dispensed with the principal functionary, the Dew Eagle; so they may now touch on the minor elements of the ritual such as the equipment and the feast.

Now this very feast has received tobacco which they are going to pick at when they complete the ceremony—they of the medicine society.

So now also this very striking pole has received tobacco, which they will strike and make speeches.

It is finished (da''ne'ho).

DISTRIBUTION OF TINY PIECES OF MEAT

"After the announcements and the invocation, when everything is ready, the conductor comes around counterclockwise with little pieces of cut-up pork meat. He distributes this to all the members. This meat must be raw. Shada'ge' a·' don't eat cooked meat."

All ceremonial circuits and distributions which I have observed during years of witnessing Seneca ceremonies have been counterclockwise. Falling-days says, "The conductor goes 'to the left' in a circle [shatgwadi·gwa 'e'ǫt'wada·se·]"; clockwise is called a circle to the right-hand side (heyeǫstǫ·gwa 'e'ǫt'wada·se·).

ASSIGNMENT OF ROLES AND PRESENTATION OF PARAPHERNALIA

Frequently now, the conductor has handed the drum to someone, other than the singers, and the rattles and fans to a different man. He does not appoint a special whooper; he merely asks someone to make the whoop.

Whoop.—No song is sung at Tonawanda until the drum has been presented to the head singer.

Striking for silence.—Somebody has to hit his foot on the floor or strike the stick; they are supposed to have a stick. Then the man who has the drum says, "I was supposed to sing. The messenger invited me to sing, that's why I have the drum. But now I see there is somebody else who is going to sing, so I will let him use the drum. You see that that fellow who thinks he is going to sing has no drum and his assistants have no rattle boxes so I will let them use or borrow these tonight." Sometimes he says, "I will give it to them." Speaker gives drum and rattles to the first and second singers. Infrequently a second speaker presents the horn rattles to the second singer.

THE RITUAL

(1) *Whoop and Song I.*—Another man, to whom the conductor has entrusted the rattles (for fans have gone out of use recently at Tonawanda), hits the stick and presents the rattle boxes to the dancers. "In the invitation I received, I understood that I was to dance, but now that I have arrived I see that someone else has been selected to dance, and I will let them use what I ordinarily employ when I dance." This one speaker presents the rattles to all the dancers, who do not seem to be alined according to phratries. Speeches by members of

alternate moieties seemed foreign to Falling-day. Moiety ridicule of the other dancer or encouragement to surpass the dancer of the other moiety seemed equally strange. "Not here. Dancers do not have to be of opposite sides."

The four-dancer pattern, with dancers of opposite moieties as at Coldspring, is unfamiliar to Falling-day; it is absent at Tonawanda.

(2) *Whoop and Song II.*—The Speaker or announcer gives the crackers and tobacco to the crowd. He sets it conveniently on the floor at one side of the open space among the speakers for the convenience of anyone who wants to make presents to the dancers. He delivers the stuff that the host has made ready for the speakers.

Hair-burned-off, speaker at Helper's, said that even the wax paper is medicine.

(3) *Whoop and Song III.*—

They sing and here the dancers commence to dance.

Somebody strikes the floor and speaks. Anyone now—you can say what you want to say. Most of them urge the dancers to keep up their willingness to dance. It is well to begin this way; you can urge the dancers, but if you have anything special in your mind to say, you may go ahead as you did that time last year. You had a joke between yourself and another fellow present. It is alright to tell that.

After the third song anyone is priviledged to talk. Women may speak. William Gordon's wife [skadi] used to speak. Anybody: women, children, may speak.

In joking, they don't mean what they say. It is a joke to make the sick one feel good and forget his ailments. It encourages him to think that he amounts to something when all these people have gathered to wish him good luck, health, and friendship, and deride each other.

Moiety separation does not occur at Tonawanda. "We do not separate according to sides here at Tonawanda."

Any joking relationship is unfamiliar to Falling-day. "If you find a chance to joke with anyone, do it—we do that here." I asked about He-strikes-the-rushes' alleged joking relationship with Awl-breaker, his father's clansman, because they stood in that relationship, and Falling-day replied, "Jesse makes fun of da'hǫ because they are well acquainted, not because da'hǫ is Jesse's father's clansman. People who know each other well don't get mad. A few people here can't stand a joke on them. They will make fun of you and enjoy it, but when you joke back, they can't stand it. Dji'wa' is that way. He is the only one I can recall, who is like that."

(4) They continue dancing and speaking until all that has been prepared to give away is distributed—that is, it is given over to the conductor to divide equally among the dancers at the end of the ceremony. Then the Speaker [hatha''ha'] has to announce that all that was prepared to give away is exhausted. Then he says, "If anyone wants to continue, then he must furnish his own presents"— perhaps pennies, or an apple which he may have in his pocket. Sometimes they give these presents to the one who has got up the dance; they claim they make medicine that way [the idea being that the patient may buy medicine].

The singer does not have to speak.

Money stood up in floor cracks to test agility of dancers.—As at Onondaga, pennies are frequently stood up in a crack in the floor to test the agility of dancers.

If you pick it up it is yours. The dancer bends over first, trying to pick it up in his mouth. A dancer may try several times and finally pick it up with his hand. I once saw a fellow who could not bend down on his knee, so they set it up elevated on a stick above the floor (6 inches). If a dancer succeeds in picking up in his mouth a coin which a Speaker stands on edge, next time they will lay it flat. There used to be dancers around here who could pick up a flat penny—the trick is to lay your ear flat on the floor. I could never do it although I used to dance quite a lot. [Falling-day did not say that this behavior was at all symbolic of the feeding birds.]

(5) "The singers continue to sing as long as anyone continues speaking. If no one speaks after the gifts are gone, that is the end of the dancing."

There is a special song at the end, but Falling-day has never heard it called at Tonawanda "to lay down the fans."

After the last song when they have finished dancing, they lay down the fans and rattles. They get up and retire to change their clothes.

Now, the conductor divides the crackers and packages of chewing tobacco in as many equal piles as there are dancers. It is ready when they return. Then he distributes to each one his share of crackers and tobacco.

THE DISTRIBUTION OF THE FEAST

"After that, they bite the meat that is passed like crows (wa·diga′hga·′). It is chicken. The conductor, for he is always a man, passes the chicken counterclockwise." Falling-day never saw a pig's head—has heard of its being used occasionally. "Dew Eagle will eat any kind of meat."

Falling-day is anxious to know what kind of a bird shada'ge·a·′ is in English. He thinks it is a pretty bird like the eagle that lives above or in the clouds somewhere—not a dirty or ugly bird like the condor. "They say this is a pretty bird. I think it is lamajery (??)—like the eagle and about the same size." He knows only one kind.

Now the Speaker has to announce that they are through. He speaks for the host [hodɛ′ša·ni·], and his words are as if they were the host's words. He is thankful that so many people are willing to come to the meeting, and he thanks the messenger who brought them there and conducted the ritual. Then he thanks everybody, the singers and dancers, etc. Then he says he hopes that this ceremony will help the sick one, no matter what ails him. He asks the Creator to make strength for this one. After that, he says "let's all hope that we have helped her [the one who got up the dance]. After that, then thanks (ganọ′nyọk) again. Then he says we must wait for the corn soup, or hominy—anyway the feast (′tgaya′swa·yɛ·′).

The conductor has to divide up the corn soup. There are no chunks of meat. (1) The host has to fill the pail of the conductor; (2) now the conductor has to get a pail from the Speaker (hatha'·ha') and give him his soup first after himself; (3) at the command from the conductor, "Ready now, set down your pails [kettles], [ha' o·nɛh djinǫ'dza'ge'ǫ'), and they set their pails down near the kettle;" (4) when the manager has filled the pails, going ladle by ladle from pail to pail in a counterclockwise circuit about the kettle, he cries, "ready now again pick them up" (ha'o nɛh nai' dǫsadje·'k) and the members retrieve their pails, and as he says, "Now scatter and fly whither you will" (o'nɛh nɛ·' ganyo' gɛ's hɛ'sga·die'·'ɛ), they file out the door and disperse in the darkness.

To supplement Falling-day's account of the Eagle Society ritual, I consulted Hair-burned-off, Speaker of Tonawanda Longhouse and Speaker for the Eagle Society at Helper's and He-is-coming's meeting. Of course, he knew that I had attended several rituals.

(1) When the medicine company has gathered at the designated place, the Speaker arises, removes his hat and says:

Now you all listen—members of the medicine company (honǫtcino''gɛ'shǫ).
We have come to this house [honǫ'sgwadenyǫ']. We came because a man was appointed to go from house to house to tell the members of the society to come to this place.
That is all for the moment.
Now we must say what the Creator has ordained we should say whenever we start our ceremonies. (Here we return thanks to all the spirits up to the Creator. Sometimes I only say a few words, but this depends on how I feel, how serious is the occasion, the time we commence, and if it is late I only say a few.)
Now the speaker mentions the name of the person who has invited all who belong to the society. Now this person that is putting up the ceremony of striking [gane''gwä'e·'] belongs to the society, and he has sponsored it before when he was pretty ill, and it has helped him. After the ceremony he became better, but since that time he has never had any subsequent ceremony. So now he is sick again. He has used some medicine: the roots, bark, and leaves of the various plants which our Creator has given us to use, but it does not seem to help him. Now he is recalling that he belongs to the Eagle Society. He thinks that perhaps if he puts up the ceremony of Striking-the-stick or Shaking-a-fan, he might get better again. He has been considering for several days how he will sponsor the dance. It is difficult because he is helpless. His folks [relatives and housemates] have discovered what he wants, and so they have decided to help him. They have decided to procure all the things that we use when we hold the Eagle Dance.
Now all of you have come to help him, and we must use our power [gaha'sdɛshɛ'] to help him. Now his folks are ready now to have the striking ritual to help him recover from the sickness. They have provided a feast, and it is ready: hominy corn ['onondɛ·'] and pig's (bear's) meat [gwisgwis owa·'] for the soup, since after the ceremony we must have that in which to dip our bills [ɛdwadenyonda'so'] [16] (for this is the feast which we eat after the Eagle Dance); his folks have ready also presents to distribute on striking the stick [yene'ɛgwa''istha']; and they have provided that which you like to eat [eǫdiga'hga·'] and it will go around after the cer-

---

[16] Any member of the medicine company—any bird—has a bill, especially Eagle.

emony when we say ₣swa'tcinǫ'g₣''shǫ?₣swe·he·k o·n₣ wa'agwaga'hga·'—you of the medicine society, all of you now, we are about to feast like ravens.[17]

Now then they appointed a man to notify the members of the Eagle Society. Now he is already to commence. He has a man to sing [name mentioned] and two to help him. [There may be only one helper, but there should always be two.] Now when we sponsor certain kinds of dances, a ritual of any kind of animal society, when we wish them to help us we must use the genuine tobacco which our Creator has given us. We must throw it in the fire. Now he [the conductor] hasappointedamanwhowilldoit[mentionsthenameofthe man]. That is all.

(2) *Tobacco invocation.*—Then comes the tobacco invocation.

I have heard them sing the first phrase of the song when offering the tobacco at Canada. Alex Clute [Seneca of Tonawanda] used to do that here, but he got that somewhere else. He brought that here from Cattaraugus. Sanǫ''gai·s (long-horns) burned the tobacco at an Eagle Dance at my daughter's at Newtown, Cattaraugus, when I was visiting there and he sang a little ways through the first song. This is not a Tonawanda custom.

Hair-burned-off heard about an old man here at Tonawanda who, when he offered the tobacco and said, "You of the medicine company, you have this to pick at, now he says 'here is your tobacco that you may hear our words, now here is your bird for eating,' " went so far as to pick up the bird and throw it in the fire, saying, "You have got the bird, now it is up to you to eat it." "Now the dancers and singers and speakers had nothing to eat. That is how he did when they asked him to make the tobacco offering."

(3) Then they have a little meat which is cut in small slices; the conductor gives that to each member.

(4) Now after that the conductor gives the drum to someone. A man hollers hu' hu' and the man who was given the drum strikes and makes a speech, presenting the drum to the appointed singer. He says:

Well, I was appointed first by the conductor to sing and so I have the drum and the rattles, and I have brought them here to the place he designated, and I was ready to sing. But after I heard the Speaker mention the name of another, I notice that he has nothing. Now he must use the drum and rattles. I will lend it to him for the night, but I will not give it to him.

(5) *Whoop and Song I.*—Now the singer takes the drum and the dancer yells and Song I commences. ·

The conductor gives someone the rattle and feather fan.

He strikes the stick and says about the same things as the preceding speaker. The striker announces that he has the fan and rattle because he is a member of the society, but that he sees the appointed dancers lack fans and rattles, so he decides to lend one set in lieu of dancing himself as he pretended to have been invited.

---

[17] "The medicine company [honǫtcino'g₣'] are ravens [ga'hga'shǫ']. The head ones are the giant ravens—singers [ga'hga'go·wa·']; crow [ga' ga·]. We tear off meat in our bills like the great birds whom we imitate, crying ga'·'. Raven is also messenger [hadja'swas] for the Eagle Society and the Great Medicine Company. Whenever he sees anything, he hesitates and cries out the news."

(6) Dancer whoops and Song II.—Then the Speaker (hatha′·ha′) gets up and announces;

We have already heard in the announcements that they have provided presents for the strikers. Now I have them here.[18] Now the conductor gave me orders to say that whoever strikes may have his own way to say whatever he wishes when he *strikes*, but he must not use any bad language that will hurt people. We have some foolish words [gawęnowe′hda·shε′], but we know just how far to go and yet not hurt anyone's feelings. One should hope that the sick one will get better. Perhaps someone will wish the sick one may recover, and he may return thanks to our Creator who has given us our lives and this earth to roam on, and he may consider that he may get help by asking the four messengers or the Creator to help the sick one to go about again on the earth.

(7) Whoop and Song III.—

"Now it is open for anyone to speak.

"Sometimes two strike at once, as they did at Helper's and they both continue to speak at once until one quits."

He recalled how He-strikes-the-rushes had ridiculed Awl-breaker at Helper's meeting, and explained why Awl-breaker went home early.

"Jesse was too hard on da′hǫ and he left. Jesse went too far. Da′hǫ did not show up at the next few meetings of the society, and then he finally returned."

Hair-burned-off seems entirely unfamiliar with Jesse's concept of a joking privilege with one's father's clansman. I went on to explain what I understood the old Newtown pattern to be—spatial separation of the moieties and joking across the room. He insists that this did not occur at the Newtown meetings which he attended.

You can joke anybody so long as you don't hurt him. Jesse went too far. Da′hǫ is a much better speaker than Jesse. He is witty and Jesse was getting beat. Jesse finally arose and said, "If he wants to fight with me, I'll get the better of him." Da′hǫ did not reply. After another song, Jesse got up a second time and said, "I frequently see him returning from Akron. Next time I will stop him and talk with him." Now I myself would be afraid. No one quite understood what Jesse meant. Anyone would feel anxious. Jesse could not take it because he was getting beat.

The general idea seems to be that Jesse should have had more respect for an older man, particularly one of the chiefs and ritual speakers, who is usually good natured and quite defenseless.

(8) The Speaker makes this announcement:

After they have used up the presents provided by the host, then the conductor tells the Speaker [to announce] that this is the last strike to be made on the host, but that this should not end the dance, merely because the presents provided for the strikers to distribute are all gone. Whoever would strike again must dig in his pocket and furnish for himself presents to give away with his striking, his shoes, perhaps his pants, a cow [this is considered a joke] because it is always

---

[18] In making this announcement at Helper's he said that even the wax paper on the soda crackers was medicine—good for blisters. "The idea is to make the sick one laugh and in that way forget his pains."

money. In the older days whatever they gave was considered medicine for the sick one. Whoever has money may strike, etc. That's all.

(9) The dance continues as long as anyone continues to speak.

Then they sing a special song which is slower than the others, slowing up toward the end. This is called "laying down the fans" [yene'ɛyɛ'ndahgwa']. Here the dancers lay down their fans and rattles, and the singers lay the drum and rattles on the floor. "Then the conductor picks up the drum and rattles and the fans which they have laid on the floor, and he puts them away.

"Now he divides up the gifts: the crackers and tobacco. He gives it to the singer, his helper, the dancers, the Speaker, and the tobacco thrower, and himself, dividing it equally."

(10) Then he grabs the bird and says, "You of the society have in mind now to eat [swatcino'gɛ'shǫ' ɛswehe·k o''nɛ wa'a·gwaga'hga·']."

The society say ga'' [high tone] like crows.

He goes over to the host. He passes the bird to the sick man first. [When conductor] I go next to the head singer and his helpers and then the dancers, and then I go around to everyone who belongs to the society so that they can have a bite . . . until they get tired . . . Then I take home what is left . . . the bones [he shrugged his shoulders and grinned]. The conductor gets whatever is left of the feast. Sometimes there is a bit left for soup.

Then he tells the Speaker [and the speaker announces this—he is speaking for the host]:

Now, we have done. People have in mind that we have done. And therefore, I give thanks to the singers and also the dancers and the people who have come to this dance. Tell them that I give thanks.

Then the Speaker arises.

Now we have in mind that we have finished the ritual. In the first part we heard that the sick one has been ill for sometime. Now he wants the Medicine Company to help him because he belongs to that society. It has helped him before. He hopes that it will help him again, but we also must hope that this dance will help him. So we all came here to help him. We hope that the Four Messengers and the Creator will give us the power to help him with this dance [ceremony] so that he will recover and his people will feel better; it will elevate their minds. We must keep that in our minds after we get up and we have all gone out.

So now his folks have hominy for the feast. The conductor will divide it for us.

Now we have done, but we must go through again that which the Creator has given us to return thanks to the Four Messengers, our great leader [Handsome Lake, the prophet] and our Creator where he resides [and he repeats the ganǫ''nyǫk]. Now we have finished.

The conductor divides the feast. He cries, "Come now set down your pails! [ha' o·nɛ djinǫ'dza'ge'ǫ']."

When he finishes, he tells the Speaker that he is done.

Then the Speaker says, "pick up your pails and fly away—go where you are wont to fly [ha' o·nɛh nai' dǫsa·dje·'·k o'nɛ ganyo·' gɛ·'s hɛ''sga·die''ɛ]."

THE SONGS

The present name for the Eagle Dance at Tonawanda is gane''
gwä'e·', "to strike a fan," but Robert Shanks, who recorded it for
M. C. Randle and the writer in 1936, declared, "The real name of this
dance is gane''ǫda·dǫ', to shake the feather fan." (Thus it appears
in Morgan's list as Scalp Dance.) The speeches referred to war
records. They used to wear a feather bustle on the rump and between
the shoulders, Shanks thought, but he alone made this statement.

(1) Before every song an appointed whooper shouts: "pa·haî·he·."

Leader: "yowehane."
Chorus: "yowehane." [19]

Here someone presents the drum to the first singer or, later, a fan
and rattle to a dancer. Every time there is a song, one at a time they
present: (1) drum, (2) horn rattle to first singer's helper, (3) a fan
and rattle to a dancer, (4) (or (5)) someone takes over distribution of
presents. The order is whoop "pa hai'," then song, speech,
present drum or what else, dance. Dancers must have horn or tiny
gourd rattles.

(2) Second introductory song:

waheya waheyonǫ heyo'onǫ:

(3) In the middle of this song the dance begins, recognizable by
change in tempo.

waheya waheya heyonǫ'
goyaheya heyonǫ'
waheya waheya heyonǫ'[20]
(4) (7)   wiyeha wiyeha wiyeha néhe'eh
we'ha'yo wiyeha ne'he·'yeh ('eh)

(5) In the first rendition of the text the leader with his drum
sings alone.

yonǫwiyo· honǫwiyo'oh:]
yonǫ'wiyo nǫwi'yo
waheya nǫ'wiyo-o-o nǫ'wiyo
goyaheya heya'a'
(6)   goyoheya heya'a':]
      (ya)
(8)   weyaha wiyahaô
    wiye yane(ni) nǫ hanehe:]
    :weyaha: ninǫ hanehe:
(9)   weha hiyo'onǫ'ǫ heyo'onǫ':
    weha yo·nǫ heyo'ǫnǫ':]

---

[19] This song resembles one of the Little Water Medicine renewal songs, to which rite Eagle Dance is linked.
(Shanks says the priest doesn't sing. After tobacco invocation at Cattaraugus and Allegany, the priest
hums over the first song before the ritual commences.)—W. N. F.

[20] Shanks says "repeat this song twice." This song and the other would be used twice in its (their)
entirety, stopping for a speech and then repeating it before singing the next song.—W.N.F.

After this came several optional songs, omitted by Shanks.

(10) This is the final song, when they lay down the fans. The dancers know this is the end of the dance. It is usually sung when the speeches have begun to pall—humor has run out of the meeting.

yowadjinę'he gonǫdiya'awe(wi)

heyonǫ yowadjine

ya'ahe heyo'onǫ':]

End of song, not complete on record, should end with short "heyo''onǫ'."

THE ONONDAGA CONDOR DANCE

At Onondaga Reservation, south of Syracuse, N. Y., I readily found two boys who had danced in recent Eagle Dance meetings. Floyd Henhawk, Eel Clan, a slight likable young lad beyond 20, who had lost an eye at jacksticks or lacrosse, said he had danced at the last meeting. He promptly recited a fair outline of the ritual, but he recommended his friend, George Allison Thomas, an Onondaga of the same clan, then age 25, who proved reticent but well-informed. I had met his father, Chief George Thomas, who the boys told me is a speaker at longhouse meetings. We worked at the Thomas house, and Mrs. Thomas' remarks, interjected from her station near the cook stove, comprise much the best of the following information. Where possible it is credited to the informant. Toward noon, Chief George Thomas arrived home to confirm and supplement our morning's progress.

At Onondaga, as on the Seneca Reservations, the Eagle Dance Society membership is composed of followers of the Handsome Lake Religion—"the real and genuine people" [(henǫ'gwe hǫweka'·") (ǫgwe'' ǫweka·' (S.))].

The ritual (gane''gwa·e·') (gane''gwä' e·' (S.)) and the membership (hadine'gwa''is) are derived from one stem with the Seneca.

Informants seemed unfamiliar with the history of the society except that "it has been carried on for a long time." "Before Handsome Lake came here (1815) the Onondagas used liquor at the dances; since then they have food to eat." Mrs. Thomas had heard her grandfather relate the legend of the boy who was carried away in a hollow log by the bird, but she did not offer it as an origin legend. Chief Thomas said it has been handed down for a long time, although his wife thought he might know the history.

Onondaga do not associate Eagle (skadjie'·na') with the dance but a bird like the condor whom they call ha''guks.[21]   This bird lives beyond sight; Chief George Thomas knew of but one kind (species).

EQUIPMENT

The society meets when anyone is taken ill.   Prerequisites for a meeting are: (1) Indian tobacco (oyɛ'gwa hǫ' we) for the invocation; (2) about 12 packages of chewing tobacco for speakers to distribute among the dancers; (3) soup (ono nda'),[22] or specifically hulled white corn soup (onɛho' hgwa');[23] (4) a chicken to boil in the soup; and (5) a feather fan.   The Onondaga fan has 4 to 5 feathers suspended vertically from the quills, instead of horizontally.

"My younger boy belongs to the society.   At the [recent] New Year's dance, somebody promised that they would give him one. They have to make it" [24] (Mrs. T.).

The dancer uses any rattle (gasda'wɛ'shɛ') from the stock of cow-horn rattles.   He holds the fan in his left hand and the rattle in the right, depending on whether the dancer is right- or left-handed. If he is left-handed he holds the rattle in his *left hand* (say ɛno'ga di'). "*Right hand* is ha yɛ ne'hgwi" (F. H.).   Onondaga to shake a fan (gane'ɛdakdi') is cognate for the old Seneca (gane''ǫda dǫ').

"Sometimes they still stand money up in a crack in the floor. If a dancer can get it in his mouth while dancing, it is his.   My son there could do that" (Mrs. T.).   Each dancer has one fan and one rattle according to the number of dancers.   Sometimes there is one dancer, but "if you can get four or five, that is preferable"(Mrs. T.).

Chicken feathers are used for the fans, but hawk feathers are preferable, or better still eagle feathers (G. T.).

Mrs. Thomas has seen bark cylinder rattles, but white men have been continually buying things at Onondaga for years.   She never heard of a whistle in the Condor Dance.

A query concerning setting a twined corn-husk tray filled with Indian tobacco on the floor for the members elicited the reply, "They only put tobacco in the stove [invocation].   They do not smoke a pipe.   I have only seen the pipe used at Condolences"(Mrs. T.).

Instead of the regular striped crotched pole and beater, "they use any stick for a beater (ɛne'gwa''ist'a')."

---

[21] Chief Howard Pierce, Tonawanda Seneca, Bear Clan, claims that once while he was a tribal delegate to a Senate Indian hearing, he saw the bird, a condor, in the Washington Zoo.   The Seneca call it "cloud dweller."   Howard has dreamed of the bird flying down and dancing before him.   He burned a little Indian sacred tobacco which he carried and it flew back.   The Cayuga and Onondaga in Canada know it as ha''guks.

[22] 'ononda'—hominy (S.).

[23] ono'hgwa' (S.).

[24] During the dream guessing, whoever guesses what the person needs—some object symbolic of the ritual, a friend, etc.—has to furnish that object and sponsor the ritual implied in the proposition.   This is also an old Seneca custom.   (He-strikes-the-rushes.)

"We get chickens and put them in the corn soup. Long ago we always had that [chickens for the corn soup]. We put two chickens in one boiler" (Mrs. T.). So apparently the wash boiler has become the cooking vessel for feast soups at Onondaga as among the modern Seneca.

MEMBERSHIP

Membership in the society comes through sickness and a cure by the ritual. Mrs. T. considers dreams an infrequent mode of entrance. Usually some fortuneteller (haksa'kdǫk) tells the person to join. He uses tea for divination.

To a query about Seneca hɛne'·yǫ, Mrs. T. distinguished for Onondaga, "hɛne'·yǫk is a prophet and he can tell what happened way back. An old man [here at Onondaga] was called this as a personal name; but he did make prophecies."

"My son [George, Jr.] would have been one had they taken care of it [the caul over his head].

"They should have preserved that, instead they let it go down the river [Onondaga Creek]. I wish they had kept it. Yes, I wish they did; anyway, I can tell [prophesy] pretty good sometimes" (George A. Thomas).

On questioning, there seems to be no special training for clairvoyants. It is born in them. There is no ceremony to make those who were born with a caul more potent.[25] Mrs. Thomas' little younger son was sick, and the fortuneteller used tea. The fortuneteller said he needed Condor Dance to be performed for him. George Alanson Thomas does not belong to the society. However, Floyd Henhawk is a member. Floyd was sick, but he does not remember how and why he joined when he was quite young.

Preparation for a meeting.—Mrs. T. said,

They used to hang the fan out near the fence on a pole all day before the meeting. There was only one fan on the pole, just one.

Then a man goes from house to house to notify the people. He is called "news carrier" [ɛhǫt'ǫgáindi']. He tells what kind of a dance, the place where it will occur, he instructs the person to take a pail, and says, "You go there and strike the stick and talk [ɛswane'gwa'e's'a']." It is a long message. They generally have it at night. He chooses the singers and dancers and notifies them. He tells the singer to be sure and go there and sing.

At night they all go straight to the meeting. Having arrived, they go in. One sits anywhere. Then the conductor arranges the seating when the dance [ritual] begins. The messenger becomes the ritual manager or conductor, "he takes charge' [hoste'i·s·di'; hosdeisdǫ' (S.)].

---

[25] At Tonawanda, Robert Tahamont's son, Dave, was born with a caul, and Harrison Ground suggested putting him through some ceremony to increase his potency. Nevertheless, he is reputedly clever at finding things. The belief is strong.

MOIETY PATTERNING

The dual division seems an important aspect of Onondaga ceremonial life. Mrs. T. remarked, "I am Eel Clan; Turtle Clan has to help me with everything." The phratries take their names from the place they meet during their separation for dream guessing at Midwinter Festival.

They of the mudhouse (dehodidaige'):	They of the longhouse, "Four house corners" (gaye·hodinǫhske·):
Eel	Turtle
Bear (now extinct)	Beaver
Deer	Wolf
Hawk	Snipe

Moiety patterning is preferable at the Condor Dance but apparently not strictly followed. They do not sit opposite facing each other according to phratries.

RITUAL PATTERN

An appointed speaker returns thanks.

A priest burns tobacco; and the song commences during the prayer. Mrs. Thomas remarked, "It always gives me shivers when they sing the first song while he is still burning the tobacco." [26]

When he finishes speaking, the tempo increases and the dancing commences. The drummer (tainagetskwa·s, "he raises the song") sings the first song without the drum.

Speeches.—There is a whooper. Notes do not indicate that he whoops during tobacco invocation, before the song.

An appointed speaker interrupts the song by beating the stick and presents the drum and rattles together to the first and second singers (hadɛnawą'sɛ'·k). Everyone knows who is going to speak. He says they have designated a certain fellow to sing, but he himself is a good singer, well able to do so, but that he will accede to their wishes (F. H. H.).

Whoop and Song II.—There is a man appointed to present the fan. Usually the fan belongs to the sick person, and the speaker is to give it to the dancer. Moiety alinement is said to be unimportant.

The second speaker in presenting the "flag" [27] tells that he, himself, was invited to this place and he has brought along the fan that he has been using many years since the time when he was still young and able to dance. You see old men can't bend; they are too stiff to dance. They are no longer flexible. Then he gives the fan to the dancer. [F. H. H.; gives fan and rattle.]

---

[26] The song which the priest sings while burning tobacco ascends on the tobacco fumes to the Dew Eagle. The Seneca say this is the only part of the ritual that he hears. The priest waves the fans on the smoke. (He-strikes-the-rushes.)

[27] The calumet brought north to Albany by the peace-making Catawba in the mideighteenth century was first likened to a flag (p. 166).

Whoop and Song III.—A man has been appointed to present rattles to the extra dancers. There are ordinarily as many speakers as there are dancers, and they speak one at a time. For the next dancer the speaker repeats that he is no longer flexible enough to dance but that he will give the rattle to the dancer. "Yes, sometimes he tells the dancer to try and beat the other dancer."

The dancer is called gane''gwa·'e' deha'tk'wa', "striking-fan dancer."

Whoop and Song IV.—A man (at Tonawanda it is the Speaker) makes a speech about the tobacco which he says is to be distributed by the speakers. He says, "All of you are [swadwenonya''da'] to talk and transfer the tobacco to a pile for the dancers and singers." After the ceremony ("Gives one tobacco"), the headman distributes it among the dancers and singers.

Whoop and Song V, etc.—"Every successive speaker transfers a package of tobacco [from the pile] over to the conductor, and he puts it aside for the dancers and singers" (F. H. H.).

Whoop and Song VI, etc.—"When the tobacco which the sick person has bought for the ritual is gone, the speakers may use money and present it to the sick person at the same time wishing him early recovery from his ailments. The speaker tells him to buy medicine" (Mrs. T.).

"Now when they use money, they joke and make fun of each other to stimulate the sick person so that he will forget his illness" (Mrs. T.).

All the speakers are men. Jokes are exchanged back and forth, but a speaker can tease anyone present: any relative, his own brother, or his father (Mrs. T. and boys).

"When the tobacco is gone, the joking helps to heal the patient; but previously while giving tobacco, they do not joke, but ask the Creator to grant favors and help the sick person" (Chief G. Thomas).

With reference to joking, "We are divided into clans and there are two divisions. When we gather at public places people of one division should get together for they are brothers." Moiety joking is common, it is reciprocal, and it is preferred; "but if your brother jokes you, you may answer. No matter who jokes, it is approprate to answer."

Regarding a joking relationship between children of clansmen, I merely learned that people who are related joke; it depends on the people, and the whole practice is not seemingly rigidly patterned. As among the Seneca, this whole pattern of striking and joking occurs also in the war dances.

The balance of the ritual is quite similar to the Tonawanda variant, and one notes the linguistic similarities to the Onondaga and Cayuga variants at Grand River, Ontario, which may mean that the ceremony prevailed among the Onondaga and Cayuga before the present Canadian Iroquois migrated to Grand River.

THE EAGLE DANCE ON GRAND RIVER (SIX NATIONS RESERVE), CANADA

The Eagle Dance ritual at the Six Nations Reserve has been described for the Cayuga by Speck (1949, pp. 111–113), the Onondaga Longhouse version of the songs is available on a record with a brief notice of the Eagle Society (Fenton, 1942, pp. 29–30), and both the Onondaga and Cayuga rituals are described and analyzed by Kurath in her contribution to this volume. Only new material will be added here.

THE ONONDAGA CEREMONY

At Onondaga Longhouse, the second day of the Midwinter Festival is given over to rites performed in response to dreams. Participation is restricted to members, and the sixth listed is Eagle Dance Society (gane'gwa''e'', "Striking a dried skin.") (I have often wondered whether a scalp was formerly struck or waved in this ceremony? Had Simeon Gibson (pl. 16, 2) lived we might have made a book of his notes begun in the summer of 1940.)

In the private rite described by Mrs. Kurath, the Logan family dominated the roles. My impression is that the rite is less formal here than among the Seneca. It is also less elaborate.

I have long suspected that the Eagle Dance of the Iroquois on Grand River is derived from that of the Seneca. Kurath has now demonstrated identical and related songs in three cycles: Seneca, Onondaga, and Cayuga. But there are also close resemblances between the lore of the ceremony at Onondaga, New York, and Grand River. There was a strong strain of Seneca participation in the Onondaga Longhouse on Grand River. The Seneca band was small and the Seneca Longhouse stands close by. They exchange singers. The Onondaga and Seneca have intermarried, and Seneca chiefs have been speakers of Onondaga Longhouse. The maternal antecedents of Chief John A. Gibson, the most renowned speaker of Onondaga Longhouse, came out to Grand River from the Seneca Reservation at Buffalo Creek. It was Tom Smoke, a Seneca chief, who always participated at Onondaga Longhouse, who taught the Eagle Dance to Onondaga Chief Joseph Logan (Fenton, 1942, p. 30).

THE SONGS

Since about half of the 16 songs recorded are included on the published record and the texts are printed in the program notes, they are not reprinted. I leave the description of the dance to Kurath who has transcribed the Logan version, analyzed it, and compared it with other local and tribal variants.

Chief Logan (pl. 16, 2), in the course of our recording, related a variant of the roc or bird abductor legend, which will be included in the appropriate place (p. 90).

THE CAYUGA EAGLE SOCIETY CEREMONY AT SOUR SPRINGS LONGHOUSE

The Cayuga Eagle Society ceremony originally was contributed to the dissertation by Speck. That chapter has now been published verbatim (Speck, 1949, pp. 111–112), with substantial additions which Speck added after reading my 1937 dissertation in manuscript and making further inquiries of his informants (Speck, 1949, pp. 112–114). Speck's account and his observations have now been checked and substantially added to by Kurath, who describes the public ceremony of the Eagle Society which she witnessed at Sour Springs in 1948. The reader is referred to her description (p. 232). She also has recorded and transcribed the songs. The dance at Cayuga resembles the Canadian Onondaga variant; the ritual is less elaborate than the Seneca; but moiety patterning is shared with the Seneca.

Discussion.—The researches of Goldenweiser, Waugh, Speck, and now Kurath at Grand River establish the Canadian Iroquois version of the Eagle Dance as essentially similar to the Onondaga variant in New York. We find the same terminology and the same type of feather fan. As at Tonawanda and Onondaga, chicken is the feast animal. The Seneca of Cattaraugas and Allegany Reservations had the ceremony in its most elaborate form (Parker, 1913 b, p. 124). There is no question that the Iroquois variants are historically one complex whole. Further, Speck's other researches at Sour Springs Longhouse disclose that the "striking" pattern occurs in the same series of war dances as among the Seneca. We are treating with local variants of the same ceremonial complex. However, we must not forget how real the local differences are to the Iroquois hailing from different local ceremonial groups. To the individuals, these differences of ceremonial detail determine whether or not he feels comfortable in a strange community where the ritualistic setting is quite like the one at home, but the mode of procedure differs, say, as between "high" and "low" church. Etiquette and rearing demand that the individual conform to the new way, but after he has lived in the community for a time, his own local tradition asserts itself and he essays changes which he feels are justified. Frequently, he is misunderstood. Then returning home, the process works the other way. He-strikes-the-rushes has frequently remarked how different things are from place to place, that having lived at Newtown, Coldspring, and Tonawanda he notices these variants, but that his father told him as a small boy, "Wherever you go, my son, do not be forward. Conform to their ways!" Nevertheless, he leans to the old Newtown ways, and we have observed how in one Eagle Dance for Helper and He-is-coming at Tonawanda his behavior was quite misunderstood.

THE IROQUOIS EAGLE DANCE AS A CULTURAL PHENOMENON

SALIENT FEATURES

The Iroquois Eagle Dance illustrates the pattern phenomenon in ritual and it permits the free expression of personality within set forms. It is one of several medicine societies which have been termed "secret" (Parker, 1913 b), but they are quite well known to all non-members living within the so-called "pagan" or "longhouse" communities at Coldspring on the Allegheny River, Newtown on Cattaraugus Reservation, and at Tonawanda Reservation. Similar societies prevail at Onondaga, near Syracuse, and among the Onondaga and Cayuga communities at Six Nations Reserve, Ontario. Their present distribution coincides with that of the Handsome Lake Religion (Parker, 1913 a; Fenton, 1936 b; Deardorff, 1951). Membership includes both sexes and is gained by having had a dream of a specific type, or by having been cured by the society. The society holds private curing rites in family homes, but at anniversaries visitors are more welcome to "come hear the songs," as they are when the society convenes publicly at the longhouse.

The society calls itself "the strikers" (hadine'gwä''is) or "the medicine company" (honǫ'tcino''gę') meaning an association of men and of mystic animals who have the power of transforming themselves into men to participate with their human associates during the ritual. The ritual is addressed to a species of eagles that wheel in flight high in the heavens amid clouds; the Seneca call them variously the "cloud-dwellers, they of the vapors" ('o·'shada'gé a·') or (shada' ge'a·') or the Dew Eagles; Onondaga (ha''gaks); and they have the power of restoring life to wilting things. In Seneca, the song is called "striking-a-fan song" (gane''gwä'e·' oenǫ') or "shaking-a-fan" (gane''-ǫda·dǫ') at Tonawanda; gane'gwä'e·' in Onondaga is thought to mean "striking a dried skin." Locally individual singers include songs that may not be part of the common repertoire of all the singers. A song leader with a water drum and his helpers with horn rattles accompany a singular dance in which pairs of youths or men, holding a rattle in the right hand and a feather fan in the left, crouch swaying and advance to pick up objects in their mouths, and retreat hopping, in imitation of birds feeding on the gound.   Near the end of the song, a speaker, almost invariably a man, strikes a pole and interrupts the ritual long enough to praise his host or the dancers, to recite some record of personal achievement, relate a humorous anecdote, or ridicule himself or another.   Then he distributes presents to his victims.   After the dance, the master of ceremonies, or conductor, passes an animal head or a chicken among the guests, who cry like crows and bite at it.   These are the salient features.

A CENTURY OF ETHNOLOGY

L. H. Morgan published in 1851 the first scientific study of a primitive people after 10 years of field work among the descendants of the tribes that formed the Iroquois Confederacy.   His now classic League of the Ho-de-no-sau-nee, or Iroquois, contains an account of ceremonies then current at Tonawanda Longhouse, yet he devotes little space to the almost nightly winter meetings of medicine societies and refers to them only as "concerts," saying nothing of their imputed medicinal power (Morgan, 1901, vol. 1, pp. 276–277).   We recognize in his list of thirty dances, number "27 Ga-na-un-da-do, Scalp Dance, For Males," which he marks as both costumed and obsolete (ibid., vol. 1, pp. 278–279).   Shaking-a-fan is the Tonawanda name for the Eagle or Bird Dance, and it is by no means obsolete.   Examining Morgan's field notes partly resolves this puzzle.

Morgan obtained most of his information at Tonawanda and by correspondence with his extraordinary interpreter and collaborator, Ely S. Parker.   A list of dances among the Senecas of New York, by Ely S. Parker, dated May 1848, was in the manuscript collections of Dr. Arthur C. Parker, apparently the same list which Ely furnished Morgan for writing the League.   Of the 39 dances, "33. Ga-na-un-da-doh, Shaking a bird's tail, or Scalp Dance" is marked obsolete; and "Calumet Dance" appears as 39 without its Seneca name or any additional comment.   One wonders whether the Seneca may have known the Pipe Dance of the northern plains, or whether this is the same as 33.   "Squat Dance, For Males (26. Ne-ho-sa-den-dat)" appears in Morgan's list (Morgan, 1901, vol. 1, p. 278), but Ely marked it obsolete.   If "squat" refers to the crouching posture of the dancers, none of my informants has recognized it.   Lloyd appended a list of 21 dances to recent editions of the League from a manuscript then in the possession of Mrs. Harriet Maxwell Converse, written by Nicholson Parker, Ely's brother, but the Eagle Dance is missing (ibid., vol. 2, p. 287).

Morgan methodically bound his correspondence and field notes into eight journal volumes which passed at his death to the University of Rochester (Gilchrist, 1936).   These journals disclose that Morgan's expeditions to the Seneca fell in the late fall and winter; there are notes for at least 11 field trips, comprising in all about 18 weeks in the field, before he published the League in 1851. The journals contain the finest materials in his publications. I have established that Morgan missed the Bean Festival in August (Fenton, 1942); and the quality of his detailed notes on the War Dance which he twice observed, published in part in the League (Morgan, MS., Journals, vol. 2, pp. 36, 123–143; 1901, vol. 1, pp. 250 ff.), and his passing remarks on the Eagle Dance, which appear in an enumeration of dances and ceremonies, taken in October 1846, indicate to me that the dance was current but that Morgan never saw it.

14. Ga na un da doh (gané''ǫda'dǫ'). This dance has nearly become obsolete on account of its being so difficult. It was considered the most difficult known among the Indians. The name signifies the shaking of a birds [sic] tail, called no doubt from the fact that that [sic] the dancer in the dance shook his rattle back and forth in the form of a birds tail spread . . . . (Morgan, MS., Journals, vol. 2, p. 35).

War Dance appears in the same list, with a hope of its being performed for his benefit, but it did not occur until December 3, 1849.

Morgan does not mention the feather fan, although his informant alludes to it, and Morgan confused the fan and the rattle. I cannot explain how he missed seeing the Eagle Society bundles with wands protruding from the ends hung aloft in the rafters or hanging on the walls in Tonawanda houses. I am convinced that the society did not meet during one of his brief visits, because Morgan, always the competent observer, carefully notes other private and public rituals which occurred.

Morgan understood the importance of medicine societies in Iroquois life, if he did not describe them. Visitors who remain among the Indians over protracted periods are invited to attend meetings. Many witnesses and a few Indians are not aware that these performances are different from ordinary dances, or that certain rites belong to particular societies. The Indians do not volunteer information to strangers. Morgan's journals and Ely Parker's letters make unmistakable reference to the medicine societies. In 1877, in a great book "Ancient Society," Morgan wrote of them as something already obsolete.

The Senecas have now lost their Medicine Lodges which fell out in modern times; but they formerly existed and formed an important part of their religious system. To hold a Medicine Lodge was to observe their highest religious rites, and to practice their highest religious mysteries. They had two such organizations, one in each phratry, which shows still further the natural connection of the phratry with religious observances. Very little is known concerning these lodges or their ceremonies. Each was a brotherhood into which new members were admitted by a formal initiation. [Morgan, 1877, pp. 97–98.]

In another place, speaking of the widespread distribution of dances among American Indians, he probably refers to Seneca ceremonial associations.

Particular dances are special property, belonging either to a gens, or to a society organized for its maintenance, into which new members were from time to time initiated. [Morgan, 1877, p. 118.]

Possibly Morgan's informants were loath to admit the presence of orders which were at that time infra dig, because of the popular ascendancy of the "New Religion." Handsome Lake, the Seneca Prophet driven from the Allegany settlements, lived at Tonawanda 4 years before 1815, when he undertook his journey to Onondaga where he died on arrival. To the end, he was plagued by the jealousy of rival village chiefs. Tonawanda sources say that the Prophet's revelations were in suspense 10 years following his death until, persuaded by the Tonawanda women, his grandson Johnson, Morgan's informant, commenced reciting their Prophet's message, and Tonawanda became the central fire for the Handsome Lake Religion. The Prophet drew his precepts from the old culture, and incorporated certain doctrines from the Quakers (Deardorff, 1951).

Finding that he made little headway in his teachings, he sought to destroy the societies and orders that conserved the older religious rites, by proclaiming a revelation from the Creator. The divine decree was a command that all the animal societies hold a final meeting at a certain time, throw tobacco in the ceremonial fires, and dissolve. [Parker, 1913 a, pp. 38 ff., 114.]

Some of these rituals came from foreign tribes, and it is reasonable to assume that the sources were captured Huron, southeastern Indians, and the neighboring Delaware and Nanticoke, notable sorcerers who were then living near the Seneca in the Allegany and Ohio settlements.

The prophet said:

It is not right for you to have so many dances and dance songs.
A man calls a dance in honor of some totem animal from which he desires favor or power. This is very wrong, for you do not know what injury it may work upon other people. [Parker, 1913 a, p. 39.]

Another version enumerates four great sins which he sought to eliminate, and complains specifically of foreign influences.

4. You sing tunes from other nations at your dances. These are poison. You may dance again and have the kettles boiled, but repent of this. [Caswell, 1892, p. 209.]

A council of friendly chiefs and those who feared him held a last meeting; they decided to disband the societies forever, but they neglected to cast sacred tobacco in the fire. Cornplanter, Blacksnake, and other rival leaders at Cornplanter and Coldspring settlements asserted that the efficacy of the old orders had therefore not been impaired. Though persecuted, members continued the rites sub rosa, until gradually tension ended and certain societies commenced appearing publicly at annual festivals. The function of compelling animal spirits changed gradually to curing, and the societies assimilated adherents of the New Religion who perpetuated them. There is no evidence that the old dream societies ceased at Tonawanda. Possibly Johnson, out of respect for his grandfather's opposition, did not elaborate on the function of what Morgan calls "concerts," and this had led to their supposed extermination.

The year after the founding of the Bureau of American Ethnology in 1879, Erminnie A. Smith went among the Seneca of western New York. She is the first to mention the Eagle Dance.

Private dances are held by the medicine men, in which are introduced Ka-nai-kwa-ai, or eagle dance . . . On the death of a medicine man a special meeting is held by his fraternity, and during the giving of certain medicines, medicine tunes are chanted. [Smith, 1883, p. 116.]

She also mentions the rite of creating Ceremonial Friends.

Private dances are not infrequently given by individual members of the tribe who, having conceived a great affection for each other, publicly cement it by a friendship dance. [Ibid. Cf. Stone, 1838, vol. 1, p. 28.]

Rev. William M. Beauchamp, for many years Episcopal missionary at Onondaga, described the ceremonies and devoted a great deal of energy to the historical sources. From his description I judge that the rite was well developed among the Onondaga at Syracuse:

Eagle dance (striking stick dance). Two men dance side by side in precisely the same way. Each holds a stick, with feathers spread out on each side. They bend down, bending one leg under the dancer, and stretching the other out on the side. A cent is placed on the floor and picked up with the mouth. Some strike on the floor with a stick, and this gives it the name (Ga-na-gah-a). A dancer makes a speech and presents tobacco. [Beauchamp, 1895 a, p. 212; 1922, p. 218.]

He also informs us that some old Onondaga tunes survive, but that the songs and dances are now all Seneca, having been introduced by Handsome Lake, and that they are composed of burden syllables. Were the Seneca the source of Eagle Dance?

It is doubtful that the Mohawk had the Eagle Dance. There is apparently no word for it in Father Bruyas' dictionary, which was compiled prior to 1700 (Beauchamp, 1895 b, pp. 217–221; Bruyas, 1863). The nearest approximation in Cuoq's later grammar is *"Kana-kare*—perche, baton long; petits arbres coupés pour faire des cercles" (Cuoq, 1882). The late J. N. B. Hewitt told me that the generic term for the ritual meant, in Mohawk, "to strike a skin." A warrior pledged his word on the hide of a deceased enemy (J. N. B. Hewitt, conversation, November 1935). "To strike a drum" (ga'nahgwa"e') was the nearest a Mohawk source could reach.

Parker wrote the first consistent account of the Seneca Medicine

Societies, which served as a constant guide in gathering additional information. Writing of the Eagle Dance among the Seneca at Newtown, Cattaraugus Reservation, he says:

The ritual of the Eagle Society consists of ten songs and a dance. . . . Every member participating in the ceremony paints on each cheek a round red spot. No one but members may engage in its ceremonies, even though these be performed publicly. The Eagle Society's ceremony is regarded the most sacred, in this respect next to the Great Feather Dance. . . . [Parker, 1913 b, pp. 124–125.]

All my information differs with Parker; nonmembers, as we shall see below, do utter Eagle Dance speeches. He-strikes-the-rushes says, "Outsiders may participate if the meeting is open to all." However sacred the ritual may be as compared with the Feather Dance, which is open to anyone who wishes to pledge his allegiance to the "old way," participation in practice does not conform to theory which may have anciently restricted participation in Eagle Society meetings to members only. Dr. Speck's and Alex General's investigations at Six Nations Reserve bear out my contention that nonmembers do participate.

Parker continues:

It is believed that the society holds in its songs the most potent charms known. It is said that the dying, especially those afflicted with wasting diseases, and old people, have been completely restored by its ceremonies. This is because the Dew Eagle, to which the society is dedicated, is the reviver of wilting things. [And here he adds in a footnote:] The Dew Eagle refreshed the scalp of the Good Hunter by plucking a feather from its breast and sprinkling the scalp with the dew from the lake in the hollow of its back. [Parker, 1913 b, p. 124; 1923, p. 389; Converse and Parker, 1908, p. 152.] [28]

ORIGIN LEGENDS

THE LEGEND OF BLOODY HAND

Origin legends describing the adventures of a good hunter or an orphan boy who is befriended by mythological creatures are prevalent in Iroquois folklore. The adventures of a good hunter, called Bloody Hand, embrace the beginnings of the Medicine Company of which the Eagle Dance Society is a dependent order. This legend, which has Onondaga and Seneca variants, describes the adventures of a war captain and his party in the southwest country where the Iroquois went to learn new things and take captives. Bloody Hand, killed and scalped, is discovered by the flesh-eating birds and quadrupeds whom he had always remembered with sacrifices of his first killed game. Dew Eagle participates in a council of birds and animals

---

[28] The legend of the Good Hunter and the Mystic Animals appears in a number of sources: Canfield, 1902, pp. 129–135, 206–208; Beauchamp, 1901, pp. 153–159. This includes Seneca and Tuscarora versions. Converse and Parker, 1908, pp. 150–156. The same version is reprinted with minor phonetic corrections in Parker, 1923, pp. 386-393; Caswell, 1892, pp.221 ff.; Curtin and Hewitt, 1918, pp. 273–276; and a Huron version appears in Barbeau, 1915, p. 333.

who concoct a medicine, taking their flesh and procuring the roots of herbs. After several failures, a bird retrieves the scalp from the smoke hole of an enemy lodge.

It was smoky and dried and would not fit the head of the man. Then Big Crow (buzzard) emptied his stomach on it to clean it of smoke and make it stick fast and O'sh'ada'gea' plucked a feather from his wing and dipped it in the pool of dew that rests in the hollow of his back and sprinkled the water upon it. The dew came down in round drops and refreshed the dry scalp as it does a withered leaf. [Parker, 1923, p. 389.]

The birds sang and the rattlesnakes rattled to increase their medicine.

Above the clouds and mists of the sky dwells a bird who is the chief of all the birds. His name is S'hadahgeah. This assembly of bird and animal sorcerers chose the chief of the crows to notify him of all that was taking place. This is the reason, according to the tradition, the crow today sings the note "caw caw." The eagle is another chief who is under the great bird that dwells above the clouds and mists of the firmament. [Curtin and Hewitt, 1918, p. 275.]

The long legend describes the founding of the Small Dose or Little Water Medicine Company, its rites of renewal and celebration. Thus, Dew Eagle and his messenger, the Raven, are of the sacred company of mystic animals, but they also have a separate society of their own. The Eagle Dance and the Eagle Society have been reinterpreted from incidents elaborated in this type of legend.

Newtown Seneca informants consider the Eagle Society a subsidiary of the Medicine Company. "Dew Eagle is the highest of the eagle species. His feathers are not used for the dancers' fans but ordinary American eagle feathers are used. The fan stands for Dew Eagle."

Stick-lodged-in-a-crotch's grandfather told Long-horns, my informant, that Eagle Society grew out of a pact between Dew Eagle and a man who was seeking meat for an ingredient in the Little Water Medicine. During Eagle Society meetings at Allegany they anciently employed a whistle (ga''gända') made from the wing bone of an eagle to give the pitch to the singers, but now they use a cane or bamboo whistle as in the sessions to renew the strength of the Little Water Medicine, which makes a further connection between the two orders.

Dew Eagle was caught by a man who purged himself for 10 days. A man wanted meat of Dew Eagle to complete the potion for the Little Water Medicine. He fasted for 10 days and purged himself. He burned sacred tobacco daily for 10 days, imploring the bird to come down to a certain spot. Finally, on the tenth day two eagles came down. The man was able to converse with Dew Eagle. He requested a piece of his thigh meat as an ingredient for a medicine. Dew Eagle instructed him to make a poultice, employing the saliva which Dew Eagle supplied from his bill, in order to heal the wound. Dew Eagle suggested that they form a pact of friendship, and out of this pact, the Eagle Society, its songs, and ceremonies were formed. Thus at Newtown, after the priest has finished burning tobacco, he sings over the first song, a short song for the benefit of Dew Eagle, to whom the song arises on the tobacco smoke.

THE TWO BROTHERS LEARN SONGS FROM BIRDS

There is also the story of the Two Brothers living alone in the forest. The younger does the thinking and planning for both. He directs his older brother to shoot a turkey, and he devises the two-feather headdress with revolving socket and chin band. He repairs to the forest, learns songs from birds whom he does not shoot, and directs his brother to practice them. He makes a rule that people of his tribe should wear feathers as insignia, and he invents the war song.

From the time that the youth had commenced to study the singing of the birds he had begun to grow wise. . . . He kept saying, "These are songs which the people shall sing, and they, too, shall wear feathers on their heads." The people had never heard anyone sing. . . . He declared to his brother the dangers connected with singing the songs, saying, "You must be careful about singing this song; if you are not, it will bring you senseless to the ground. . . . I am singing praises, for I have learned to sing from the birds. I give thanks as I have learned to give them in my hunting expeditions. I dance to my songs because I hear the birds sing, and I see them dance. You and I must do the same, for it will rouse a feeling of joy in our hearts." [Curtin and Hewitt, 1918, pp. 277, 279, 282.]

Although this dance is derived from birds, its character is reminiscent of Feather Dance, rather than the Eagle Dance proper.

The widespread North American Indian tale of a lost boy who is carried away by a giant bird, either willingly on its back or in a hollow log into which he has crawled, occurs in many variants as the origin legend for the Eagle Dance. The boy lives for a time among the Eagle people in the rocky crags above the clouds. He learns their songs and dances. Either through a strategem of beating the head of an eaglet on whose back he has mounted for trial flights, or at the end of his visit, he is returned graciously to the scene of his abduction.

CHIPPING SPARROW'S ADVENTURE AMONG EAGLES

Harriet Maxwell Converse recorded an exotic variant at Cattaraugus years ago, which in substance follows:

Golden Eagle is the head chief of all the birds. He employs assistants to visit the earth. Bald Eagle, a subchief, who has keen sight and rapid flight, is assigned to the earthly mountain tops. He assigns the task of keeping the earth free of carrion to Hunting Vulture, but he permits them access to the clean upper spaces and the clear waters of earth because they have pure hearts. All earthly refuse is theirs. Hunting Vulture soars amid the clouds, to and fro ceaselessly searching for spoil, and he occasionally passes swift-flying Bald Eagle.

A young lad named Chipping-sparrow becomes lost in the woods during a rain and weeps bitterly. Bald Eagle discovers him, lifts him on his back, and deposits him near an Indian village, but he is not found. Hunting Vulture, in search of night prey, finds him nearly dead and, failing to find his home, bears him aloft in his talons to the sky land. There the birds are celebrating the New Year Dance. He learns their dances. Chipping-sparrow promises to protect their nests in early spring, they show him the grains which they prefer, and he promises to instruct his people.

The seven dancing brothers (the Pleiades) are dancing the New Year Dance over the council house, when the Golden Eagle directs the Hunting Vulture to return him to his people.[29] It is winter and the snow is on the ground. He finds his people gathered in the council house feasting. He relates his journey and teaches them the new dances and the songs. The name Hunting Vulture is added to the list of clan chiefs and conferred upon him, to whom the vulture had been a good friend.

Except for using the Seneca term for the Buffalo Dance, the description fits the Eagle Dance, the musical score is printed without text, a plate illustrates a set of superb six-feather fans, and a meeting of the Newtown Eagle Dance Lodge is illustrated by Jesse Cornplanter, then a rising boy artist.

By this legend the Iroquois know the origin of . . . the Bird Dance; which was brought by Jo-wiis [the founder of the Eagle Society] from the land of the sky birds, and is the most prominent dance of the Iroquois. It is celebrated at their New Year feast, and during its performance the dancers imitate the motions of a bird, squatting low and moving their bodies and heads as if picking the grains of corn which have been scattered on the floor.

This dance reminds the people of the law of Ga-do-jih, that the Indian must nourish and care for the birds in the winter as well as in the summer time. [Converse and Parker, 1908, pp. 69–73.]

BOY ABDUCTED BY DEW EAGLE

Coldspring informants agree that the ritual songs for Eagle Dance originated in the adventures or from a subsequent dream of the man whom Dew Eagle kidnapped and kept in her nest in the rocky crags. However, each imformant's version differs in detail or in method of elaboration.

VERSION OF DJIDQ''GWAS

The late Djidǫ'·gwas of the Seneca Wolf Clan (pl. 17) related the following tale, elaborating the plot in the form of a dialogue which was his characteristic style of recitation (Radin, 1915, p. 9).

Dew Eagle picks up a little boy from his village and takes him to

---

[29] When the Pleiades, "the dancing children" (hadí''tgwa'da·'), are on the zenith at dusk (about January 15), it is time for the New Year Dance. The correlation of lunar and sidereal years is thus regulated.

her nest to the west in the Rocky Mountains. There she has two little eaglets and they play together with the boy, dancing gane''gwä'e·' with him. They sing the songs as they dance. The boy stays there a long time.

The Dew Eagle finally says to him, "Do you want to go back now?" And the Boy says, "Yes."

She flies far to the east and circles, descending slowly. As soon as he gets down from her back she disappears. He goes to his house, and his old folks say, "Where have you been?"

"I have been way to the Rocky Mountains. While I was there I played with two little birds. We danced all the time I was there and we sang songs which they call gane''gwä'e·'."

Then the old folks say, "Who was singing?"

And the little boy replies, "The birds were singing themselves."

So the boy sang the songs, and the old folks learned them.

While the boy was living with the eagles, he and the birds ate hulled-corn soup and fresh meat.

His people then asked him, "What did you eat while you were living among the birds?"

"I ate fresh meat all the time," he replied.

"And at night did you go to sleep?" they continued.

"Yes, I slept pretty well."

"Did you keep warm?" they queried.

"Yes, I kept warm."

"Who slept with you then?" they wanted to know.

"When night came I slept together with the two little birds (shada'-ge'a·'), and the old mother bird in her nest."

So this is the way the ritual called gane''gwä'e·' started, and this is how it reached the Seneca people.

VERSION OF CHAUNCEY WARRIOR

Chauncey Warrior, a Cayuga of the Turtle Clan, narrated the same legend, but in his version Dew Eagle disproves the magic qualities of a hollow log which, it is believed, ghosts cannot enter (Parker, 1923, p. 283), by carrying him off in the log. Later, Dew Eagle appears in the youth's dreams to foretell the episodes which are subsequently elaborated in the myth. He returns home riding on the Eagle's back.

The old folks say that long ago a group of young boys went out hunting in the fall. They went down into the southwest country in search of game. One day one of them became separated from the rest. As he journeyed through the forests carrying his rifle, he noticed that a small bird kept continually flying around his head as he walked. This bothered him.

Hearing something, he looked up and saw some great black patches bearing down upon him from the heavens. This frightened him and he commenced running. The little bird led him near a hemlock tree to a fallen log which was hollow.   The bird flew in one end of the log and out the other and then back to the hunter, and again.   The hunter leaned his rifle against the hemlock tree and followed the bird into the hollow log.   A great bird swooped down upon the spot where he had stood a moment before.

Thinking himself safe within the hollow log, he lay quiet, but presently he experienced a sensation of being elevated, as if the log and all its contents were being raised aloft.   Crawling forward he peered out the open end before him.   He felt a rush of wind and saw the earth receding far below.   Presently, he looked out again and the earth was no longer visible; he was above the clouds, which appeared to be moving rapidly eastward.   He glanced aloft to see a great female Dew Eagle carrying the log in her talons.

They traveled westward during several days and finally arrived at the Rocky Mountains where the Dew Eagle had her nest high on a rocky promontory.   The nest was constructed of huge timbers like the hollow log she was carrying.   She set it down beside the nest, which contained four little eaglets.

The hunter stayed inside the log, hiding.

That night he had a dream.   The old mother eagle appeared to him saying that if he would feed her little ones in her absence, she would bring him all the game he could eat, and that he would always have good hunting luck in the future.

The next morning he awoke and there in front of the log lay a freshly killed deer with her talon marks in its back.   The hunter emerged from the log, took out his scalping knife and cut up the deer in little pieces, which he thrust down the gaping gullets of the awkward eaglets.   Then he struck a fire with flint and steel which he carried, spitted a venison steak and roasted it for himself.   This went on from day to day.

Each night he crawled back inside the hollow log to sleep.

Later he had another dream in which the old eagle appeared to him again, telling him that when her little ones grew up and flew away from the nest she would take him back to his people.   In return he must promise several things: To sing songs which she would teach him, to teach his people the Eagle Dance, which is a dramatization of eagles scratching and feeding, and always to remember them with tobacco and a feast.   He promised.

As the days went on the hunter was growing older and the young eaglets were feathering and daily growing hungrier.   They had commenced hopping about on the edge of the butte, and flying short distances between the crags.   Finally one day, one took off and disappeared in the east, then another.   By afternoon two were left, and by sunset they also had followed their siblings.

The hunter was now downcast, fearing he would be left there indefinitely to starve.   He was now a full-grown man.   Finally the old mother eagle returned, alighted, and said, "Now I am taking you back where I found you.   Climb on my back and we shall go home."

The hunter climbed on her back and she flew eastward into the gathering night.   He looked below and he could now discern the place where he had once stood on the earth.   At last she alighted, saying, "Now you have got back. Remember me with the ceremony which I taught you and you will always have good luck."

The hunter looked about.   The brush had grown up where the log had lain. The hemlock tree had enlarged and grown around the place where the muzzle of his musket still rested.   Raising the musket with some difficulty, he discovered that the barrel left a smooth worn mark on the tree.

Now he went home and found his village with some difficulty.   His people finally recognized him as the youth who had gone off hunting one fall and got lost in the forests. He had since grown to manhood. He gathered them about him and related his adventures, and he taught them the songs and the dance.

Later the man had a dream and the Dew Eagle revealed the necessity for his sponsoring these songs. In the future all those who became ill and dreamed of the birds would be the ones the Eagle had accepted for his society. By putting up the ritual they would be cured. That is how the Eagle Dance commenced.

VERSION OF SNORER

Snorer of the Hawk Clan, at first reluctant to discuss the origin of the Eagle Dance, said, "It (gane"gwä'e") is Eagle Dance for Dew Eagle (shada'ge'a"). I never heard about that. There is no use any longer remembering those things."

Snorer was also familiar with the myth of Boy carried away by Eagle, but declared that the bird did not carry the boy away in a hollow log. Boy rode willingly on the bird's back. However, Snorer does not consider this tale an origin legend for Eagle Dance.

"There was a settlement of Senecas and they lost a boy. He disappeared. When he finally returned afterward he narrated his story," which Snorer related somewhat sketchily, as follows:

The boy was playing on the sand along the margin of a river. A great bird came down and spoke to him, "Now boy, you jump on my back and we will have fun. I will carry you about." After several invitations the boy accepted. They flew away up next to the sky where the Eagles frequent. He stayed there and learned everything that they do. He learned that the Eagle has great power. The various tribes of Eagles told him all they know. They told him that Indians should keep up their religion. They told him that the people on earth should thank our Creator at Strawberry time, and at the other stated festivals, as we did in the olden times.

After a while the big bird says, "It is time to go home. Climb on my back," and the bird flew down to where he had taken him. The boy's parents were greatly surprised to see him return.

(Obviously, Snorer is omitting the best literary figures. Whether he is bored, unwell, or withholding information, I am not sure, but I always found him a difficult informant.)

The following fragment that War Dance and Feather Dance were learned by some young boys suggests the legend of the Two Brothers, already cited from Curtin and Hewitt.

War Dance (wasá'se") came from the Eagle! Some young boys learned the War Dance and all its songs. Finally they learn Feather Dance. This too came from the sky-world.

Gane"gwä'e"—Eagle Dance—came later from shada'ge'a", the Cloud-dweller or Dew Eagle. It was Eagle who carried the boy off on his back.

The Seneca learned Eagle Dance from a man, in reality an Eagle, who visited among them and taught the dance to the Indians. That is why the Seneca have such power, because they and the Eagles talked among themselves and the Seneca learned how to do it from them. The Seneca talked with the Eagle just as you and I sit here and discuss these things.

Long ago they used to have trouble and the Seneca were continually fighting.

There was a man whom they saw who came among them and he was one of the great eagles that we call Cloud-dwellers.

The birds had the power to transform themselves to human beings. One could not tell whether he was man or bird. The Cloud-dwellers taught men to dance gane"gwä'e·' on earth; it is the dance of the Cloud-dwellers. That is where the Seneca got it. They talked with this one who was leader of the great birds. He spoke to the Seneca. That is why the Seneca are great fighters, because those birds are powerful. Long ago there was a League of the Iroquois. They had a fight among the other tribes. The Iroquois were more powerful because they had their power from these great birds.

A TONAWANDA VARIANT, BY ERNEST SMITH

Older Tonawanda informants (and I think that they were honest) said that they did not know origin legends for Eagle Dance. Quite possibly they know the bird abductor legend and have never associated it with the genesis of the ritual. It came to me from a younger informant then in his twenties, Ernest Smith of the Heron Clan, a talented artist. Like a variant current among the Shawnee, Boy returns to earth via the strategem of beating the head of an eaglet on which he has mounted for a trial flight. Ernest said, "Mother used to tell a story of a little boy who was carried up. My memory is shady, but I do not think he was pursued into a hollow log. I remember this:"

A boy became lost in the woods. He was sleepy and he crawled into a hollow log to sleep. Dew Eagle picked up the log and carried it aloft to the crags where it nests. The boy awoke and peered out of the log and saw the earth receding far below.

Dew Eagle used the log for her nest. The boy would crawl out and play with the eaglets while the great bird was out hunting. I have forgotten the details.

The eaglets grew up. One grew big enough for him to mount on its back. It flew out and returned. It was so strong that he had to have a club to hit it on the head to weaken it. He had something for a club. As the bird flew higher, he would strike it. It fell toward earth. As it recovered, it flew higher. Now and again he whacked it. It would fall.

These birds were supposed to roam above the clouds and never come down toward the earth. The boy returned to earth by beating the young eagle on the head, and he related his adventure among the birds who dwell above the clouds amid high crags in the heavens, how among them he learned the Eagle Dance.

Ernest was never threatened by his mother that the bird might carry him off if he misbehaved. However, Hanover Spring, Beaver Clan, remembers being threatened as a child against going out after dark or beyond the clearing lest "it" carry him away. The old people did not explain what "it" might be.

A HISTORIC RECORD

There is some historical basis for anxiety lest Eagles carry off lone children. Jerome Lalemant, writing of the French and Indian communities along the St. Lawrence, describes the near abduction of a boy near Quebec in 1647. The eagle swooped down on a little boy nine years old, placing one foot on his shoulder and seizing the opposite ear. The father finally decapitated it with a sickle. "The Savages say that Eagles very often swoop down on men; that they sometimes carry off Beavers, and Sturgeon heavier than sheep" (Lalemant, Relation of 1647–48 in Thwaites, 1896–1901, vol. 33, pp. 45–47).

William Finley, the ornithologist, declares that the majority of such cases prove false on investigation and avers that he has robbed the nests of over one hundred golden eagles without once being attacked (Pearson, T. Gilbert, 1936, vol. 2, pp. 82–84). Such reports, nevertheless, appear repeatedly in the public press. In 1937, for example, an eagle with a wing spread of nearly seven feet is reported to have fastened its talons in the body of a 13-year-old Negro girl who was picking cotton on a farm north of Austin, Tex., and attempted to carry her off. The bird continued attacking her until finally dispatched with a gun (The New York Times, October 24, 1937). Responsible ornithologists dismiss such reports and the old tales of eagles carrying off young children as "pure fabrication by sensational reporters" (Bent, 1937, p. 311).

GRAND RIVER VARIANTS, BY F. W. WAUGH

Among the five tribes of the Iroquois Confederacy, innovations that occurred within a member nation spread rapidly. Dialectical differences have never prevented dissemination of folk tales, because, even where the languages are not always mutually intelligible, many persons, as in the case of the Iroquois, speak or comprehend several dialects. Young men and very old men visit from village to village. We are not surprised, therefore, at finding the bird abductor myth as the origin legend for the Eagle Dance among the Onondaga below Syracuse, and among the Cayuga and Onondaga at Grand River Reserve. The same theme prevails, although details and method of elaboration, owing partly to individual literary peculiarities, vary as much among Seneca informants as they differ between Seneca and Cayuga.

F. W. Waugh obtained the following tale at Grand River, in 1915, from David Jack (Cayuga); except for the Onondaga-Cayuga term (ha''guks) for Dew Eagle, it might be a Seneca legend. Again, the theme is of a hunter carried away by Ha''guks, with whom he lived for a time. The man is adopted by an animal foster parent. We find the thought, common is such situations, that food sharing pleases mythologic beings, and celebrating their ceremonies is a method of insuring their favor. Eagle Dance (gane'gwa''e') (Cayuga) must be held by a member or else he will be killed by ha''guks. The story is offered as an explanation of the origin of the Eagle Dance Society.

The Hunter and the Ha"guks

A man (once) used to go hunting alone. Some of the older people had told him not to go toward the west, so he said to himself, "I wonder why this is. I think I shall go to see."

He went a long distance and found no game; so he turned about and was a little more than halfway back when he heard a rattling against the tallest trees, as if something were following. He turned immediately and saw a large creature swoop down among the tops. He ran as quickly as he could and crept into a hollow log, taking with him his knife and tomahawk. The creature, which was a ha"guks, now picked up the log and carried it away home. It was a large pine log, and the ha"guks carried it to its nest, a good many miles away.

It usually went away two or three times a day and each time brought back a whole deer to divide among its six young ones.

The man took a look around and could see nothing but rocks which were so high that he couldn't see to the bottom. There was no opportunity to get away so he decided to accept his fate and crawled into the nest with the young ones. When the old bird came back again with deer, she gave the man a share, too.

The young ones were growing all the time and were always wrestling and playing with one another.

When the old bird was away, the man would chop off some of the log to cook the meat which had been given to him.

When the ha"guks next brought a deer, it gave the man a nice piece off the hind quarter, upon which he took his ax, chopped a portion up, and gave each of the young ones another share, keeping only a small piece for himself. The old bird was pleased at this.

Presently the young birds were nearly fledged and were making short flights and uttering their calls. One day, when they were all flying about, they came back for their share of the deer, and the man again used his ax to cut up the portions.

One day he said to one of the young birds, "I want you to take me home again." The bird looked at him.

Next morning early, when it was time to eat, the young ones brought some deer, too. The old one then went away. A young bird came close to the man who quickly gathered up his belongings, sprang on its back, and clasped it around the neck. It then took him back to the very place from which he had been taken, just one day and a night being consumed in the journey.

He went to where his shanty had been and where he had left a quantity of meat, but everything was gone. He thought that his people had probably taken it, supposing that he had been killed.

Next day he set out for home and arrived there just as his relatives were about to hold a feast for him, as they thought he was dead.

Waugh's informant adds:

Some people "belong to" or are under the protection of various sorts of animals. In this way a number of societies have originated, the members having joined when sick.

One society of the kind is called Gane'gwa"e', or Eagle Dance. A member of this will surely die if he doesn't hold the ceremony at appropriate intervals, as the eagle (ha"guks) is considered to be a very powerful utgǫ" (wizzard or witch). [Waugh, MS. vol. 1, p. 37.]

In 1915 Waugh also obtained from the same informant a legend of The Bad Boy and the Giant Crow. The theme is of a bad boy who is carried away by a giant crow (gahgago'wa), who replaces ha''guks in the role of Roc, and becomes the boy's animal foster parent. A moral is pointed against the prevalent Iroquois custom of parents frightening their children by telling them that the crow or other animals will hear them and will take them away when they are lazy or disobedient.

The Bad Boy and the Giant Crow

A man, his wife, and two children were (once) hunting in the bush. There was one boy who was large enough to help, but wouldn't. He was a very bad boy and wanted everything his own way. The parents scolded him and warned him that some sort of animal would take him away. The boy said he didn't care, which alarmed the parents, as the animals would hear what he said and would kill him.

Every time he got a chance he would go to sleep somewhere. One day he was walking along a little path when he saw a big log and went and laid down on the top of it to sleep. He woke after a while and found that a great crow had picked him up and was carrying him to its nest.

His mother called him, but he did not answer, of course, because he had been carried far away.

The boy found that there were three little crows in the nest. The old one left the boy there and went away; so the boy crawled in with the three little ones. He had in his shirt some mushrooms that he had been gathering, and he put one in each of the open mouths, so that they were shut when the old crow came back. The latter brought back some deer fawn, which she gave to the young ones, the boy gladly taking some of it, too.

After a while the old one went away and brought back some corn. There were four cobs, one for each of them, including the boy.

The young ones grew very fast, and, while the old one was away, the boy would take one of them and play with it and would try to get it to walk. He was always playing with them in this way.

After a while he began to play at riding on their backs, the young ones doing the same with each other. When the old one returned, the young ones called out and jumped on her back. The boy called like the little crows, too.

Very soon one of the nestlings could fly just like the old one. The boy got on its back and it flew around and came back. After a while the old one returned. The boy got on her back and she flew away with him until they arrived at the log where he had gone to sleep. He got off there and called like a crow. The old one flew off expecting him to follow her as the young ones did; but he stayed behind and ran and hid in a hollow pine. The old crow came back to look for him and kept calling, but he did not answer. When she flew away he ran home.

After this the old folks quit telling their children that the crow or other animals would hear them and take them away when they were lazy or bad. [Waugh, MS., vol. 2, p. 7.]

VERSION OF CHIEF LOGAN

The guardian spirit of the Eagle Society among the Canadian Onondaga, as well as the Cayuga, is ha''guks ("cannibal"), a giant bird. Chief Logan, in recording the Eagle Dance for me in 1941, related a variant of the Roc legend in which the Great Crow (Gah'-

gago·na) is the main character, and not ha''guks, so Chief Logan did not associate the tale with the origin of the Eagle Society.

Gahgago·na Abducts a Hunter

Gahgago·na carried away a young hunter. He swooped down and picked him up and took him so high in the air that he could no longer see the earth. They ascended through the clouds to where there is a great hole in the sky through which they passed. Beyond the sky is another world with woods, etc. At last it reached its nest and released hunter. Nest is in bush (forest). Hunter discovers little birds in nest.

The old bird went away daily in the morning to forage. Toward night old bird returned bearing whole carcass of freshly killed deer. Old bird laid burden down beside nest. Then young man took his knife, which was of sharp stone, and flayed and gutted the deer and cut up the meat, saving a piece for himself, distributed few pieces to each of the young ones. Repeated daily.

Daily he noticed that the young ones were growing. They were becoming accustomed to him. They were no longer afraid of him. As they grew bigger they commenced to fly a little. Then he was worrying how he would ever get back. One day he decided in his mind how he would do it—he would jump on the back of one of the young birds and make it carry him back to his village.

There is a hole in the floor of the sky world. There the young lad drove one of the young birds. At the edge he shoved the young bird into the hole and jumped on its back and grabbed its neck with his arms. When they were through the hole, the bird opened its wings and descended slowly—down, down—at first they could see nothing. Presently they could see just a black streak at the bottom. He recognized the bush (forest). Slowly they descended. Soon he could discern the bush. The bird alighted in the top of a big tree where they got hung up in the branches. Then the man released the bird and descended from limb to trunk and came down to the ground. Then, having reached the ground, he knew where he was. He returned to his village and told the people his adventure. As far as they knew he had been lost. He related his experience and told them that there is another world above the clouds.

SACRIFICES AND EAGLE TRAPPING

There is a close relationship between the old Seneca custom of sacrificing the first-killed deer to the meat-eating birds of prey and the widespread American Indian technique of luring down birds to shoot them or take them by pit trapping. We have already seen how folklore lauds the virtues of the good hunter who always remembered to leave meat for the birds and animals. In subsequent legends, youths purified themselves and prayed with tobacco, imploring the Dew Eagle to descend and donate meat for a sacred tribal medicine. In other accounts individuals lured down the rare birds for feathers, which they believed to have great power, because it is said the birds are rarely seen beneath the clouds. Gradually, these accounts pass from myth to legend to historical tradition of actual eagle trapping to procure feathers for a peace embassy to the Cherokee about 1770.

Such traditions are our only source for the customs associated with eagle trapping, because there are no longer individuals living who have practiced the art; but my informants cite the traditions both in rationalizing the symbolism involved in the dance itself and in explanation of how eagle feathers were anciently obtained. These individual traditions are woven through the warp of a tribal pattern imposed by the mythology itself, which posits a more or less hierarchical classification of the eagle species in the minds of the Iroquois who exalt them in direct proportion to altitude above the earth. The touchstone of Iroquois religion is this whole concept of augmented reverence progressing through the various stations of the pantheon, from the earth upward to the sky world, as opposed to fear and dread of malefic beings on and beneath the earth (Fenton, 1936 b, 14–18; Hewitt, 1928).

SACRIFICE OF THE FIRST KILL

The legends attached to several Seneca medicine societies describe adventures incurred on the fall hunt. According to Wood-eater, it was customary to revere all institutions associated by experience with successful hunting. One must sacrifice the first kill. The Eagle Dance derived from the experience of one legendary hunter whose observations are cited.

Hunters anciently sacrificed their first kill to the meat eaters. A man went up into the woods hunting and killed a deer. He took it to a high hill, and having cleared away the brush from a small area, he laid the deer down. He built a little fire and made a tobacco offering, saying the deer belonged to the Dew Eagle and that he was offering it to him. Then he hid in the brush.

Presently a huge bird came spiralling downward toward the place whence the smoke had arisen. Then another. More followed until there were many.

They warily approached the carcass to eat the meat, clutching a piece of meat, and then retreating at a distance to eat it.

Now this hunter was frightened, for the old folks say that these birds are about the stature of a man when they are on the ground. It seemed to him that they were dancing as they fed about the deer. Apparently they were eating peaceably and their sallies and retreats were but parts of the dance they performed. Four or five opposed each other.

(How similar to the arrangement of the dancers in the ritual!)

People used to make these sacrifices continually. Then they always had good luck hunting.

The songs came to him later in a dream.

For all his erudition Wood-eater seemed quite unfamiliar with any form of eagle trapping. He did not voluntarily connect the observations of his legendary hunter with an effort to procure eagle feathers. He thought birds were lured down and shot.

Eagle trapping likely came late among the Iroquois. Shooting at eagles occurs both in folklore and in the historical sources. For instance, Bressani's Relation of April 27, 1653, describes a memorable canoe upset en route from Three Rivers to the Huron country, when a Huron shot at an eagle. Evidently, the Huron revered the eagle.

The first evening, the Huron who was guiding our canoe, wishing to shoot at an Eagle, was the occasion of our wreck in the lake named for St. Peter; . . . The Hurons took this accident for a bad omen, and counseled me to return whence we had started as we were not yet more than 8 or 10 miles distant thence. [Thwaites, 1896–1901, vol. 39, p. 57.]

Seneca folklore is replete with incidents of shooting at eagles with bow and arrows. Among other ordeals at puberty, a youth named "Listener" heeds his uncle's counsel, and proves his magic power and supremacy over sorcerers by successfully shooting an eagle from the top of a large hickory tree, thereby winning the sorcerer's daughter in marriage (Curtin and Hewitt, 1918, pp. 139–143). In another variant Hat'honda's shot the eagle by aiming through the smoke hole (ibid., p. 793). In a third episode the wily nephew outwits the great eagle atop a tall tree in a clearing where it guards the sacred chestnuts belonging to the seven sisters, who are great sorcerers. Transforming into a mole, nephew emerges beneath the tree, scatters venison over the ground, and stuffs the sacred chestnuts into a bag while the eagle stuffs himself. In revenge, the seven sisters beat the eagle (ibid., pp. 149–150). Doonongaes wins the daughter of a chief by shooting through the smoke hole and felling the black eagle perched on the top of a pole which reaches to the clouds (ibid., pp. 318, 405). Hewitt says that shooting at an eagle is a common incident in other stories, and that such poles were frequently set up on holidays and during festivals (ibid., pp. 801, 749, 405). One adventurous youth brings down a hen harrier hawk and wins the chief's daughter in marriage (ibid., p. 569). All these legends describe an avuncular relationship between a youth at puberty who derives great power from heeding the instructions of his mother's brother. In the legend of Roots and his uncle Theplanter, the youth fulfills his evil mother-in-law's dream request by shooting s'hadahgeah (sic) who is perched on a cloud, and gets home before the door flap, which his wife has conspired to keep in motion with an invisible hair line, ceases swinging. The old witch begs one of the bird's wings for a fan, but he throws the bird in the fire to singe off the feathers, dismembers it, and boils the pieces in a kettle. He shouts an invitation to all her people, the whirlwinds, and they devour what proves to be her husband's body (ibid., pp. 394–395).

The Cayuga and Onondaga share a similar cycle of tales. In the adventures of sodię'sgǫ, a variety of suitors' tests are passed successfully by the gifted companions. They enlist a fellow who with an arrow shoots down a black sky-eagle (ha"guks) which is beyond sight (Waugh, Ms., vol. 7, p. 42). Again wings are used for sweeping (Waugh, Ms., vol. 10, p. 38).

The Sky or Dew Eagle is sometimes described as killing dangerous serpents. Waugh obtained the following tale, supposedly a historical tradition, from John Echo (Onondaga) at Grand River Reserve. A sky-eagle (ha"guks) is shot and a dangerous serpent, which it was carrying, is liberated.

The Slaying of Sky-Eagle and Serpent's Escape

A mythical bird resembling a very large eagle is said to live away up somewhere in the sky and seldom to come down into sight.

A very long time ago some Cayugas were holding a feast and making the customary division of the corn soup and other food. It was a bright day, but it began presently to get cloudy. One of those present looked up and saw something descending. He told the others and they looked too. The object kept coming closer and, when it got near, they saw that it was a ha"guks with an immense snake in its claws. Some ran quickly for their rifles and, when the ha"guks got near enough, they shot and killed both the bird and snake. They dropped to the ground, but the people all kept back, as the snake was the kind which causes vomiting of blood.

Some white people, having heard about this, came and offered the Cayugas quite a bit for the bird, and it was finally sold to them.

Next morning the snake had disappeared, no one knew where, and left no track. [Waugh, Ms., Notebook, "General," 1914.]

Shooting eagles then is the only method recorded of obtaining eagle feathers among the Cayuga. Dr. Frank G. Speck had the following account from Jerry Aaron at Sour Springs Longhouse, Grand River Reserve, Ontario.

The story of how eagle feathers were obtained in olden times describes a most particular process. The eagle hunter would smoke Indian tobacco and pray. Then he carries meat to the tallest dead tree in the district where he builds himself a hiding place about a hundred feet distant, within range of his weapon. He hangs the meat on a branch within sure range. Concealing himself he begins to call the eagle by whistling, pausing between calls. At last the eagle senses meat and lights on the highest branch of the tree, cautiously looking around for more than an hour. Then he drops to a lower branch and does the same until, finally reaching the meat, begins to eat, looking about for danger between bites. Sometimes the hunter would be a whole day in his blind getting the bird within range.

When the bird fell, the body was not touched until more than twenty-four hours had passed, because it was infested with dangerous "little bugs" which would cause the death of anyone should they get on his body. After this the feathers could be taken [Speck, Ms., Cayuga Field Notes, 1933; 1949, pp. 112–113].

Perhaps the best account of eagle baiting from the Canadian Iroquois is a manuscript in the handwriting of Hewitt in the Bureau of American Ethnology archive. From the handwriting and paper

I judge it was collected in 1889 on Six Nations Reserve from an Onondaga. Note the association of bird lice and disease.

The Method of Capturing the Mythic Akŭks

This gigantic bird in the majority of cases is described as being white, but in one instance a blue species is mentioned. The tail feathers of this bird were endowed with life, such a feature was thought to be a mark of the great craft and subtlety of this majestic bird, king of all others, and dwelling in the unfathomed depths of the empyrean. The parasites on its body, the ka'-nĕⁿ-hĕñ'-twa't, were preserved as charms and used as "medicine."

The method of capturing this bird is said to be as follows: A yearling buck deer called Tyoñ-oñ-wä'-ε-tă' was killed and cut up into very small pieces and spread out on soft maple bark upturned, in the place where this bird had been last seen. Then the hunter would secrete himself nearby to await the coming of Akŭks. Its habitat was in a vast mountain whose top was said to be lost in the clouds. At the base of this mountain the bait was spread. The great bird would gradually approach by alighting very far away and looking about for enemies very rigorously, and then by a short flight nearer and by a more rigid scouting of the surroundings; after a half dozen of such approaches, it would alight beside the meat and gorge himself so full that he could not fly to make his escape and so fall an easy prey to the wily hunter. Their plumes were almost invaluable and considered of great efficacy in a war dress.

EAGLE BAITING

Two seasons of diligent inquiry at Coldspring uncovered nothing concerning eagle trapping. My informants seemed unfamiliar with the practice. Even Yankee Spring (pl. 18) and Twenty-kettles at Tonawanda had nothing to offer. Yankee, who was very hazy as to how eagles were caught, in his peculiarly legalistic style explained how eagles might be procured.

In receiving the great mutual law the Iroquois accepted it as the Creator handed it down. He ordained that whenever they wanted anything, they should make a burnt tobacco offering and make their request through it to him. In this way they would never suffer any hardships whatever. Thus, by fiat of this contract, this was arranged so that his people would never be really in want, because they have tobacco. Moreover, he decreed that they must be in earnest when they make requests. Thus this great mutual law covers the past, present, and future.

For example, they might request via the tobacco, that he permit them to catch an eagle and lo, they do it as easily as a little child reaches and grabs a thistle from the air. This was because then the people had faith and, having it, nothing was impossible. Now these things are impossible.

I do not think my people ever had the pit trap. The only way I know of eagles being procured was by the bow and arrow.

He-is-coming remembers that Ike Seneca, an old man at Cattaraugus, told how they used to get eagles along the bluffs of Cattaraugus Creek from Versailles east toward Gowanda.

Possibly eagles were also trapped on the bluffs of the Genesee River below Portageville, and along the Niagara gorge.

Awl-breaker, a subchief of the Wolf Clan at Tonawanda, once a medicine-bundle holder for the Little Water Medicine Company, had belonged to the Eagle Society since childhood; he was not sure whether his people had practiced pit trapping of eagles, although he considered it reasonable. He knew that the Dew Eagles had been brought to earth to obtain meat for medicine and to procure feathers for fans. Purity was essential.

A real good man would get the feathers. Not a drunkard. So many days he would use medicine, purging himself and rendering himself odorless, and he would stay alone fasting. He would cleanse himself of all smell inside and out. After that, he got this eagle. Now today no one can get it.

Awl-breaker said only good men who, like the originator of the Medicine Company, always remembered the meat eaters when he first killed a deer in the fall, could lure down eagles. He implied that there are no longer any pure men, undefiled by liquor and other transgressions.

It was Falling-day, sachem chief of the Snipe Clan at Tonawanda, who finally, in April 1935, rewarded my search for an informant who knows of eagle catching. I had previously concluded that a Seneca tradition of pit trapping eagles to make calumet fans which were carried by a Seneca peace embassy to the Cherokee, which Curtin recorded 50 years ago at Cattaraugus and Mooney published, was the single record of an infrequent practice in the Northeast (Mooney, 1900, pp. 367, 492; Curtin and Hewitt, 1918, pp. 428–432). However, when I went back to Coldspring in 1937, fortified with Tonawanda learning, I discovered that Snorer, the old hold-out, knew all about eagle hunting; I had never found him previously in the mood to discuss the subject.

EAGLE CATCHING, BY FALLING-DAY, SNIPE CLAN, TONAWANDA

The old people told me that their old people used to skin an animal like a deer. The hunter would expose the carcass, and burning tobacco, he would summon all the Meat-eaters to come and partake of the feast. Then the hunter would hide in the brush or under a blind of brush and lie still waiting.

First the little fellows would come. They would be the crows, then the ravens, and the various hawks. They would eat, but the hunter would ignore them, casting his eyes upward expectantly awaiting the bird of his quest. After a while the little fellows would exhibit signs of uneasiness. They would be frightened and suddenly they would leave in a hurry reluctantly. He kept still, knowing that the big bird was coming. That is why the little birds are afraid.

After a while the Eagle (do'nyonda·') would come down, and after him the greatest of all the birds who dwell in the vapors (shada'ge'·a·'). He would remain quiet. At first the great bird would be wary; he does not eat right away. He would merely sit there, looking about. At last the bird would take a bit.

The trappers used to know how long to wait. They knew that when the birds became heavy from overeating, they could not rise quickly. When the great eagle became too full to fly, the trapper would jump out and chase him. The old folks used to tell it that way.

These were the feathers that they used in making fans for the Striking-a-pole (gane''gwä'e·') or Eagle Dance.

The accompanying water color (pl. 1, frontispiece) by Ernest Smith of the Heron Clan at Tonawanda illustrates a legend describing an ancient method of obtaining Dew Eagle feathers, which his mother used to relate to him when he was a small boy. It explains a method of obtaining feathers and gives a derivation for the imitative dance.

We were small children living with our parents on the Tonawanda Reservation. I used to ask Mother to tell us old stories as we sat about the fireside winter nights. This was before we went to the city of Buffalo to live. She used to tell of ghosts and we believed it. After we lived in Buffalo, she did not tell these things, and as I grew up I ceased believing. Now I wish I had listened.

Mother used to tell this legend. I don't know where she got it, but it belonged to the ancient stock of legends among the Tonawanda Senecas.

DEW EAGLE DANCES ON THE DEER, BY ERNEST SMITH, HERON CLAN, TONAWANDA

Feathers from the Dew Eagle were quite rare. They brought good luck. They did this to obtain feathers. A man went into the woods and shot a deer. He laid it out in an open place where the Dew Eagle could see it, because he wanted feathers.

The Dew Eagle was wheeling in flight high near the clouds. This man laid the deer out there for bait and hid behind a clump of bushes. The great eagle circled around. Finally the eagle flew down and landed at a distance from the deer, but he was wary. It flew up.

Then the eagle landed on the deer, and the hunter commenced singing gane''gwä'e·'. [There is no tobacco invocation mentioned. The hunter simply hid behind the clump of bushes and sang gane''gwä'e·'.] The eagle commenced to dance on the deer. He continued singing and it kept on dancing. It was so engrossed in its dancing that he approached singing and took the feathers from its tail. He took one feather and a little dew from the hollow in its back. He derived the medicine from it, and he learned the Eagle Dance.

The old people claim that they are white birds. The dew was always on its back. The Dew Eagle roams the crags above the clouds, hence his name—Cloud-dweller (shada'ge'·a·').

He sang this song, which he may have invented at the time, and after that they kept it up. From that time on, these songs were associated with gane''gwä'e·', the Eagle Dance.

Ernest remembers having heard of a second method which suggests the more orthodox pit-trapping method of the Plains Indians. In insisting that Seneca did not flay the bait, he confirms the Plains method, but disputes other Seneca informants.

Some stories tell that the hunter laid the deer for bait on a brush pile. The man hid beneath the pile. He sang songs and the bird danced on the deer. Then he grabbed the bird's legs as it danced and he pulled out the feather. Mother used to tell that.

No, they did not flay the deer. The Dew Eagle is wary. It would be suspicious of flayed meat. The bird was always suspicious. It flew around for a while before it finally landed on the deer. It took patience.

Hair-burned-off is principal sachem of the Snipe Clan at Tonawanda. The individual who bears this hereditary title shares the responsibility of tending the western door of the Confederacy with a correspondent of the Wolf Clan in the other moiety. He is guardian for the Tuscaroras, "keeping them under his wing," and presents the pleas of all western ambassadors at Onondaga. His rather considerable duties demand deep study with custodians of the tribal lore. The present incumbent, like so many of his Iroquois brethren, carried competitive athletics up to middle age, and only demonstrated a singular erudition and oratory after he had been appointed to office. The role of speaker belongs to a chief; his apprenticeship is a lifetime of patient unanxious listening and is supposed to exemplify good behavior. The present sachem is principal speaker at Tonawanda Longhouse, and his knowledge surpasses that of many of his older contemporaries. Thanks to such individuals, who have questioned the old men, Iroquois culture has lived several generations beyond its active functioning, at least, in the minds of a few individuals.

Hair-burned-off describes the same method of obtaining eagle feathers which I had from his cousin Falling-Day, which they probably heard from the same source, a mutual grandfather, but Hair-burned-off makes the old tradition explain the symbolisms involved in the imitative Eagle Dance which has survived eagle hunting. Again, we hear that eagles could only be attracted by uncontaminated persons.

OBTAINING EAGLE FEATHERS, BY HAIR-BURNED-OFF, SNIPE CLAN, TONAWANDA

The Eagles are tame now and so are the deer. Any day now we can see a deer running by. They used to be harder to get. My grandfather, Alex Snyder, used to say that deer and Eagle were very hard to attract.

They used to kill a deer or a bear or some other animal, having flayed it, they used this tobacco. They sent their words to shada'ge'·a·' (cloud dweller) or Eagle (do'nyonda'). They sent their words up on the tobacco smoke to tell him there is a big feast here on the ground, and they invited them to come down and eat the meat.

So the speaker would hide himself a little way away and he kept looking up expecting. When he sees something dark descending he thinks it must be the Eagle coming nearer to the ground. After a while he notices that it is a big bird. After much circling, it alights in the top of a nearby tree. It perches there looking around. It is wary.

The man watches it. Finally it alights on the ground and looks first one way and then the other way to see if anyone is about. Then the bird approaches the meat slowly, hopping, still looking from side to side.

[He asked me not to include these explanatory elements in the narrative.] *That is why in dancing the Eagle Dance, at first they hop looking from side to side, because the Eagle is shy and looks around as he approaches the meat. You understand, when he bends over to eat, he can no longer see.*

When the Eagle is near the meat he dances, turning from side to side to see whether anyone lurks around. When he fails to discover anyone, he stoops down and takes a chunk of meat. Now he looks around and eats the meat at the same time hopping, turning from side to side. When he fails to see anyone, he stoops over again and takes another chunk.

Halfway in the Eagle Song, the dancer stoops and eats fast—he picks things off the floor. In Canada I have seen meat on the floor for the dancers "to stoop and bite." This time the bird stoops a long time and eats fast. Then he looks around again. *Here the dancer returns hopping backward to his seat, which is the perch. Dji'wa' (William Gordon) dances pretty well. At the next song, the bird, now the dancer, alights from his perch and advances in hops looking around. When the Eagle lands that is the way it looks around.*

When the Eagle stoops over it to eat, he can no longer see and he eats fast. The man runs out behind him and takes the feathers [he thought the wing feathers]. This is better than killing him. Some fans are tail feathers. One had to be careful because an Eagle can carry a deer away.

Informant has heard of luring an eagle to a platform on a tree and shooting it.

Pit trapping, however, seemed unfamiliar. He had heard of tribes to the west doing that way.

PIT TRAPPING

SNORER'S ACCOUNT

Snorer, the sage of "High Bank" above the Allegheny River, knows a method for obtaining eagle feathers by pit trapping.

There are no eagle feathers now. In olden times, they got them from the eagle in some way. It is a long story. [Here Snorer held out for a fee which I agreed to pay.]

In the olden times men and warriors had little difficulty getting near animals. They were pure (hodi'ya'dawa·dǫ')—an uncontaminated man can approach without being detected by animals.

At that time, they wanted to procure eagle feathers to make fans (gane"e'). Now two or three went into the woods to a place where there was an opening and there they killed a deer; and one opened it and ripped it. Then he hollered, "I give you this, all you who like meat," and then he stepped back and secluded himself in the brush.

Soon then the Eagles fly down and eat of the meat where it is flayed, but the Eagle suspects something. He takes a few bites, then looks around. He eats again. Finally, he flies away. This was do'nyonda' (Eagle).

Then another species comes down. It is of more enormous size—a big bird. He eats of the meat. So just like the others, he suspects something. Finally he becomes scared and flies away. This was still do'nyonda', only larger. Another bird approaches.

Now another bird descends. He does the same. He eats a little, but he suspects something is coming. He is a great buzzard (ga'hga'go·wa·') (messenger of the sky birds), but he flies away, frightened.

Another bird comes down. Now this one keeps eating, eating and not looking. Well, he is finally filled up with all he wants. He flies away. This was Dew Eagle or cloud-dweller (shada'ge'·a·').[30]

This is how they procured feathers: After that he fixed some way to hide himself beneath the place where he spreads the meat. He places sticks athwart the pit

---

[30] Four is the ceremonial sequence; the fourth bird is the one desired.

to hold the meat, and covers the struts with brush.   Now when they come down, he waits for the bird he wants and then when it is busy eating, he grabs it by the legs, and pulls out all the feathers he wants.   He takes a few from the wings and from the tail.   Then he lets the bird go.   That is the way they get the feathers.

Seneca eagle trapping apparently occurred in the 'fall.   The accounts from Cherkoee, Shawnee, and Hidatsa suggest many points for inquiry (Mooney, 1900; Speck, Cherokee Ms.; Voegelin, Ms.; Wilson, 1928, p. 179).   However, Snorer does not specify that spring trapping is to be avoided.

Snorer had heard of great danger to be avoided in taking eagle feathers because of the "little bugs" on the feathers.   "They are like a flea or a louse.   The eagle is awful poison.   It has great power.   So the fleas must be very poisonous (powerful) to stay on the eagle which flies so high above sight.   These birds grow up next to heaven."

Snorer did not specify how long one should wait before taking feathers, only that the lice are very poisonous.

The Seneca unlike the Shawnee do not extract the pith from the feathers.   The feather has great power of strength.   The pith makes it healthy and wearing it makes the owner healthy because he burned tobacco to make easy taking the feathers.

Feathers are to make a headdress.   Anyone may wear it.   Any male could wear the feather cap.   The feather whirls, looks about.   Tie on red ribbons for decoration.

Snorer laughed at Henan Scrogg's remark about a torn cluster of feathers looking angry.   "A war chief would wear two feathers; warriors have only one feather.[31]   Sometimes, a warrior would merely hang it on his hair."

The information which I have cited leads to the following conclusions concerning Seneca eagle hunting: The Huron, Cayuga, and early Seneca shot eagles with bow and arrow.   The Seneca custom of sacrificing the first deer on the fall hunt to the meat-eating birds of prey presented a well-established pattern on which the Plains eagle-trapping technique was readily grafted.   The myths and legends associated with the origin and procuring of the Little Water Medicine are secondary rationalizations belonging to the period of Iroquois conquest, about 1680–1750, when eagle trapping was most probably introduced from the Southeast or Middle West.   Association with the fall hunt and fear of bird lice which appear in spring would indicate that eagle hunting as in the West was an autumn activity (Wilson, 1928, p. 179).   Sometimes only a single feather was taken and the bird released.   Mooney remarks that the Plains Indians are not customarily satisfied with a single feather (Mooney, 1900, p. 492), and Seneca accounts say nothing about strangling the birds.   Nor are they kept in cages as among the Pueblos.

[31] Champlain, 1922–36, vol. 2, pp. 97 89; the three Mohawk war chiefs at the Battle of Lake George in 1609 wore three plumes.

A full eagle tail contains 12 feathers. Frequently Seneca fans have 6 feathers apiece, but 4 is also common, 4 being the ceremonial number. The feathers are suspended parallel to the shaft, a method reminiscent of the Hidatsa method of twining the 12 tail-feather quills into a fan or mat (Wilson, 1928, p. 170 and fig. 11, b).

Snorer's account supports Curtin, who worked among the Cattaraugus Seneca between 1883 and 1887; the tradition of Seneca eagle trapping which appears in Mooney's Cherokee has been until now the solitary source for its occurrence among the Seneca (Mooney, 1900, p. 367).[32] Furthermore, the traditional association of the custom with a peace mission to the Cherokee about 1770 gives a basic date when the Seneca were actively employing the widespread Calumet Dance as an approach to a peace treaty.

THE CHEROKEE PEACE

A Seneca war chief named "Arrow" (ga''nǫ) decided to lead a peace mission to the Cherokee.[33] The legend describes mustering the war party and their retirement from the women to the deep forest to take emetics, bathe, swim, and wash their bodies during 10 days.

At the end of the ten days the chief said, "We shall go now on a high hill and there make a trench the length of a man's body. Then we will put a man into it, placing bows across so he cannot be seen and on top of all the whole carcass of a deer."

Now they had invited s'hadahgeah to come down, and the people stayed near the trench. The man under the bush heard a noise, and saw a common eagle come, eat a little, and then go off; then the eagle came back again, ate, and went away in another direction. It seemed as if it notified the other birds, for they also came. The man who was lying underneath the brush scared them away, for they did not want common birds to eat the meat. After a while the concealed man heard a tremendous noise, which he knew was made by s'hadahgeah, the bird they wanted. S'hadahgeah is a very cautious bird; it looked everywhere before beginning to eat the meat. The man got his hand carefully around the bird's tail, which he held firmly, and when the bird flew away he pulled out *one feather*. It took two years to get a full tail of feathers; hence they had to entice down a good many birds in this way before they got enough for their purpose. When secured, the party was ready to start for the Cherokee country. [Curtin and Hewitt, 1918, p. 429. (Italics mine—W. N. F.)]

The legend continues that after many days' travel they found the first Cherokee village stockaded. At dawn two Seneca warriors went forward dancing, adorned with eagle feathers, and shouted the signal yell. The Cherokee recognized the customary approach characteristic of the Calumet Dance and convened at the town house.

---

[32] Hewitt does not refer to the earlier publication of Seneca legends bearing on the Cherokee Wars (Curtin and Hewitt, 1918, p. 428).

[33] The name Arrow belongs to the Seneca Bear Clan at Allegany; Reuben White, an old longhouse officer, had this name as a boy, and people still call him ga''nǫ as a nickname.

The Seneca ambassadors followed the two dancers into the town house where they danced until tired. The Cherokee did not dance.

Then the Seneca leader outlined their mission and offered a wampum belt in token of good faith. The Cherokee chief accepted it, bidding his people gather food for the morrow's feast and council. The abundance of food was greater than their capacities and they ate a second day while the chiefs made addresses of mutual faith.

We have decided . . . to accept this wampum . . . and to be friendly and to bury all the weapons of war so no man may reach them again.

To which the Seneca chief replied:

"We are very glad that you have accepted our offer, and now all of us have put our weapons together, and the white wampum shall hang between us, and the belt shall be as long as a man, reaching down to the ground."

Then the Cherokee chief said to his people:

"Now is the time for any of you that wishes to do so to pick out relatives from among the Seneca to be adopted."

When the notice was given the Cherokee women picked out one man saying, "You are to be our Uncle, or Mother's brother." Some other woman took another for a brother; and finally all were taken except Ganon, the chief. Then Ganon, being alone, a Cherokee said, "No one has a right to take Ganon away, for a young man is here who will claim him as his father."—Everyone was pleased with the place and the relationship. [Curtin and Hewitt, 1918, p. 430.]

THE ROOTS OF THE EAGLE DANCE

The origin myths, cultural memories of eagle hunting, and contemporary traditions of earlier meetings all specify that the modern Eagle Dance ritual has evolved as a medicine society from an ancient war and peace ritual which antedated the preaching of Handsome Lake (1800). Many of the sacred and secular dances that have survived among the modern Seneca were once associated with war. The dance marked the organization and preparation of a war party and preceded its departure on the war path; likewise it celebrated their return after a victorious expedition. A few dances were definitely associated with peace. Since the last war whoop faded along the Niagara frontier after the War of 1812, the war dances no longer have their old significance. However, as Morgan observed, there is no cycle of dances from which the Seneca derive more pleasure. Their original function has disappeared, but they have survived for inducing rain, celebrating friendships, and elevating the mentally depressed, "curing" humans suffering from paralytic or enervating ailments. Dancers compete in these dances out of sheer local pride at all field days. Two war dances have become sacred religious rites of Thanksgiving.

Striking for quiet so that the speakers may talk in turn is the common feature of all war dances. An individual signals for quiet by beating a post so that he may list his services or recite his war record.

Early travelers and missionaries tell how many tribes from the St. Lawrence Valley to the edge of the Plains beyond the Great Lakes and down the Mississippi to the Gulf shared this custom. To the Iroquois, the feature of "striking" combines in one class the Rite of Personal Chant (adǫ'·wɛ'), the Thanksgiving or Drum Dance (gane'o'ǫ), Sioux or War Dance (wasa''se'), Striking-a-stick Dance (wa·'ɛ'no'e·'), and the Eagle Dance (gane''ǫda·dǫ'). All these dances provide the ritualistic setting for an individual to give vent to his personal feelings; they offer an escape for emotions, which are released in the traditional manner prescribed by the culture which assigns them all to the general category of "striking songs" (gane''gwä'e·' oɛnǫ'ǫ).

The rite of Personal Chant is ancient with the Iroquois. Each individual has his own set of songs which are to some extent the property of his family and possibly his clan. They range in character from war chants, through a motley series of ridiculous songs frequently having sexual reference, to personal thanksgiving for members of one's family or a "friend." It is the song of adoption by the clan. It is the last song sung by a warrior in torture or on the point of death, and each individual takes one with him "on the long trail" to the hereafter. The individual stands and sings part of his song and then, hesitatingly placing one heel forward, rocks his weight onto his toes as his other foot lags, and then advances in the rhythm of his chant. Thus he traverses the length of the room and returns. Men chant in unison and women clap hands. It is one of the Four Ceremonies which the Seneca believe were given to them by the Creator, and which were exalted by Handsome Lake (Fenton, 1936 b, p. 16; 1942, pp. 18–20). Of the many accounts coming down to us in the earlier literature, attesting its long use, Lafitau comes closest to conveying the real spirit of the chant. Each individual knocks a post and paces out his song. Then they publicly present *the heads of dogs*, which were cooked in the soup, to the greatest warriors to excite their courage. They shame the timid into enlisting by putting ashes on their heads. Only those who have proved their bravery may strike one of the assistants as if he were an enemy, and those who misrepresent pay forfeits of presents to the injured (Lafitau, 1724, vol. 1, pp. 521–523; vol. 2, pp. 189–191).

The Thanksgiving or Drum Dance takes its name from the skin-headed water drum on which the singer beats out the rythm for the dancers. As one of the Four Ceremonies attributed to the Creator, it is mentioned in the great Iroquois genesis myth (Hewitt, 1928, pp. 559, 563), which, however, may represent secondary rationalization. Before the time of Handsome Lake, at great celebrations Drum Dance afforded an opportunity for warriors and chiefs to cry out at the end of each song (wih ya'·') and recite their war records which they ended in a chant, crying (wa·hi'h); but now Twenty-kettles at Tonawanda believes that these old cries belonging to war speech should be abandoned. Handsome Lake interspersed the songs with prayers to the Creator returning thanks for the progressive stations of the pantheon (Fenton, 1936 b, pp. 14, 16; 1942, pp. 6–10).

War Dance came from some other tribe. Morgan (1901, vol. 1, p. 258) ascribes its origin to the Sioux; some informants said the Shawnee. The words and music do have a decided flavor of the Plains Indians, and possibly both derived it from an intermediary source (Fenton, 1942, pp. 27–28; Kurath, this paper, p. 288 ff.). The older Seneca call it ɛni''dje˙ and associate it with Sun, the great warrior, our elder brother, but hi''nǫ, the Thunderer, is particularly fond of it. Mary Jemison's narrative says that War Dance "originated about the time that the Six Nations commenced the old war with the Cherokees, about one hundred years ago" (Seaver, 1932, pp. 167–168). This would date its appearance among the Iroquois about 1724. Informants and historians agree that this dance preceded the departure and celebrated the return of a war party.

A war chief went into seclusion, and if a dream or a vision attended his fasting, he returned to the village and struck the war post. An old man went through the houses summoning the warriors to a feast of dog's flesh. They gathered at the war post or a post was driven into the ground, and they sat about it. The leader commenced reciting his exploits, punctuating his deeds by striking the post. As the drum quickened, others followed until all were dancing together without formation. Each warrior who struck the post pledged to follow the party. The following morning they departed, stopping at the edge of the village to leave their fine clothes with their women and pick up provisions for the journey (Parkman, 1851, vol. 1, pp. 175–176; Heckewelder, 1881, pp. 209–210; Zeisberger, 1910, p. 121). Zeisberger and Heckewelder concur that the Iroquois frequently met in peace to relate their war exploits, but that great store was put upon truth, and in reciting they rigidly followed one another in order of seniority.

In several instances bloodshed followed. Heckewelder, perhaps speaking of Delaware, relates an instance when an insulted chief stepped out of the circle and struck dead an impudent boaster (Heckewelder, 1881, p. 210). At the adoption of Thomas Morris in 1790, the Cayuga war chief Fish Carrier averted an impending brawl by pulling down the war post after an Oneida warrior had boasted of scalps taken from the other Iroquois during the Sullivan Expedition of 1779 (Stone, 1841 (edition 1866, pp. 43–45)). As late as 1812, Farmer's Brother bashed in the head of a Chippewa spy who had the temerity at a War Dance in the Seneca camp to boast of the Seneca and Yankees he had killed and scalped (Parker, 1919, pp. 35–36).

Moses Van Campen, Horatio Jones, and other victims of the border
wars of the Revolution leave vivid accounts of how returning war
parties stopped at Painted Post on the junction of the Tioga and
Cohocton Rivers to celebrate the Brag Dance. "Anyone could brag
and dance after making a small present to the 'master of ceremonies,'
usually the head warrior" (Harris, 1903, p. 404; Hubbard, 1893, pp.
238–239). Scalps were brought home as proof of their exploits.
Morgan has vividly described the modern War Dance which was performed in his honor at Tonawanda, December 3, 1849, and he published the greater part of his original notes including the speeches of
ridicule (Morgan, *in* Gilchrist, 1936, vol. 2, pp. 36, 123–143; 1901,
vol. 1, pp. 257 ff.; Parker, 1919, pp. 280 ff.). Any of these speeches
fit so well within the pattern of the modern Eagle Dance that I am
convinced that Morgan, had he known it, would have mentioned their
similarity. If War Dance has not changed since Morgan's writing,
it is still used in time of drought to bring rain, and it marks the rite
of male "friends."

Striking-the-stick Dance, which Morgan also marked as obsolete,
belongs to the class of fighting songs (hεnǫdi'o'hdahgwa'). He-
strikes-the-rushes has heard that it originated with the Shawnee when
they were allied to the Seneca, and that many of the present songs and
dances were derived from them. It was really a war dance performed
before the departure and on the return of a war party. Two lines of
dancers face each other, advance, and as they meet, they strike their
clubs; they pass, turn, and return. The dancers demonstrate how they
can fight and scalp. The war pole, which was diagonally striped with
red paint, was set up at one end of the place, for a speaker to strike at
the end of each song. Today, Striking-the-stick ordinarily follows the
War Dance. A Coldspring informant thinks that the speeches en-
couraging the dancers survive from encouragements which were
handed down to the warriors by old men, and that the ancient custom
of wishing good luck to a war party developed into wishing a host
well at a medicine dance. Gifts are distributed. The dance is now
believed to propitiate the Sun, the great warrior, whereas War Dance
is the property of the Thunderers. The association of war dances with
Thunder and the Sun is a widespread North American concept. Eagle
Dance is addressed to the Dew Eagle who, for the Seneca, shares the
function of watering the earth with anthropomorphic Thunderers who
perform the function of the Algonquian Thunder Birds.

The early historians did not always distinguish the various war
dances, and many were unaware that they described separate ceremonies under one rubric. Besides, the process of historic change has
altered the details of the old war feasts, and new dances have been
grafted to the old war-feast pattern. The most remarkable aspect of

this long historical perspective is the vitality of the war-feast pattern and its amazing stability in the face of changing conditions and functions. Having observed the modern medicine society rituals, particularly those which have developed around the war dances, one can pick out their essential elements in older literature of which the following account by Cadwallader Colden for the Mohawk is typical:

When any of the young Men of these Nations have a Mind to signalize themselves, and to gain a Reputation among their Countrymen, by some notable Enterprize against their Enemy, they at first communicate their Design to two or three of their most intimate Friends; and if they come into it, an Invitation is made, in their Names, to all the young Men of the Castle, to feast on Dog's Flesh; but whether this be, because Dog's Flesh is most agreeable to Indian Palates, or whether it be as an Emblem of Fidelity, for which the Dog is distinguished by all Nations, that it is always used on this Occasion, I have not sufficient Information to determine. When the Company is met, the Promoters of the Enterprize set forth the Undertaking on the best Colours they can; they boast of what they intend to do, and incite others to join, from the Glory there is to be obtained; and all who eat of the Dog's Flesh, thereby inlist themselves.

The Night before they set out, they make a grand Feast; to this all the noted Warriors of the Nation are invited; and here they have their War Dance, to the Beat of a Kind of a Kettle-drum. The Warriors are seated in two Rows in the House, and each rises up in his Turn, and sings the great Acts he has himself performed, and the Deeds of his Ancestors; and this is always accompanied with a Kind of Dance, or rather Action, representing the Manner in which they were performed; and from Time to Time, all present join in a Chorus, applauding every notable Act. They exaggerate the Injuries they have at any Time received from their Enemies, and extol the Glory which any of their Ancestors have gained by their Bravery and Courage; so that they work up their Spirits to a high degree of warlike Enthusiasm. I have sometimes persuaded some of their young Indians to act these Dances, for our Diversion, and to show us the Manner of them; and even, on these Occasions, they have work'd themselves up to such a pitch, that they have made all present uneasy. [Colden, 1902, vol. 1, p. xxii.]

Thus, war is an individual enterprise. The feast animal is a dog. The dance is accompanied by the drum which suggests (wasa''se' or wa·''ɛ'no'e·''), and individuals recite their previous exploits the night before their departure. Before leaving they record the expedition in red paint on bark, with clan symbols, and later return to the same place to make a record of casualties, scalps taken, and prisoners.[34]

Feasts on an animal head echo an earlier ceremonial cannibalism. The Huron, Mohawk, and Oneida tribes held feasts where the head, frequently the head of an enemy captive after torture, went into the kettle and then as a choice morsel went first to the chiefs. In the war feast the head, often a dog's head cooked in the soup, was presented to the captain who carried it in his hands inciting others to enlist. By

---

[34] Colden, 1902, vol. 1, pp. xxiv-xxv; O'Callaghan, 1849, vol. 1, pp. 5-8; Beauchamp, 1916, pp. 37, 41, 46, 100, 109. Mary Jemison's husband had a painted record of his achievements which he loved to relate (Seaver, 1932, pp. 104 ff.; Fenton, 1950, pp. 3-5).

the middle of the eighteenth century, the accounts refer to whole hogs being boiled in the corn soup and warriors successively danced with the hog's head in their hands. Thus, pork replaced the dog as the war feast food, and later it supplanted the bear and venison in all feasts, until today the pig's head is the ceremonial head, the pièce de résistance. Aside from the disappearance of the game animals, it is easy to understand the rapid introduction of pork as a ceremonial food, because the modern Iroquois have an almost insatiable appetite for fresh pork. The present use of the hog's head, nevertheless, evokes the same symbolisms involved in the ancient manipulation of a human or dog's head. On certain occasions, an individual may pick up the head and march toward the women's end of the longhouse, chanting a personal song, praising the exploits of his ancestors, or ridiculing his father's clansman's daughter. In all the medicine feasts, requiring the use of a head, except at Tonawanda and Onondaga where chicken is cooked for Eagle Dance, the head man or woman passes the head first to the ritual sponsor, who occupies the position of the ancient war leader, and after him among the singers, dancers, speakers, and other functionaries (Thwaites, 1896–1901, Jesuit Relations, vol. 10, pp. 181, 183, 229; vol. 50, p. 63; Megapolensis, 1792, p. 522; Lafitau, 1724, vol. 2, pp. 189–191; Colden, 1902, vol. 1, p. xxii; Beauchamp, 1916, p. 89; Zeisberger, 1910, pp. 102–103, 139–140; Loskiel, 1794, p. 146).

Contemporary traditions of earlier Eagle Dance meetings describe how the Iroquois abandoned recounting war records after the teaching of their prophet, Handsome Lake, about 1800. Other evidence for a shift of the Eagle Dance from a war society to a peacetime medicine society is of the same order as that cited for the four other war dances mentioned above. Seneca informants at Coldspring follow Djidǫ'gwas of the Wolf Clan:

Not very long ago the society met indoors early in the morning, and one hundred years ago they set up the striking pole outside and met there before dawn. Long ago they stuck up a pole and built a fire near it early in the morning.

The old people used to talk about war. They described the deeds they had achieved and the number of scalps they had taken. It made trouble, inciting further war, as they used to talk of war in gane''gwä'e·'. They would brag of how many people they had killed.

The old people decided, after the wars had begun to be fewer, that all this talk made for trouble. They agreed that it was bad to speak of fighting all the time as it might incite some young fellows to try it, that they, as old men, might also speak of prowess. They decided to give it up and speak only good words instead. Now gane''gwä'e·' is composed of only talking wi'·yo· or good. War dance— wasa'·se' [the Sioux War Dance]—was nearly the same kind of a dance as gane''gwä'e·'. They changed it also from a recitation of war records to wi'·yo· or talking good.

Striking-the-stick Dance has the same kind of history.

The same informant believes that the dances date from the Cherokee Wars, and he narrated a tradition of the peace negotiations which, unlike Curtin's record, describes the Cherokee coming to the Seneca. However, an earlier account, which Laura Wright took down from Esquire Johnson, who in turn had it from two Allegheny Seneca who accompanied the peace delegation, says the Iroquois went west and south to the Cherokee.[35]

Wood-eater, too, thinks that Eagle Dance was formerly used for a dance in war when the warriors threw a knife or a hatchet into a tree and proclaimed their bravery and willingness to follow a war party. However, Snorer insists that it was a peace dance.

Snorer enumerated the following ceremonies as formerly connected with war and the recitation of war records: Eagle Dance, War Dance, Personal Chant, and Striking-a-stick Dance.

Our leader, Handsome Lake, explained what he said he had heard from the "angels" [four messengers] that there was no longer any use in continuing this war business. We should cease telling war exploits and enlisting war parties. In olden times, when a man struck the stick, he would tell how smart he is, how clever a fighter, how many scalps he had taken on past raids! Now they have changed the speeches to begging and praying that the one who puts up the dance will have good luck and recover through this [ceremony of striking], which is powerful.

Snorer tells that War Dance was used in organizing a war party, that Striking-a-stick Dance followed their return, and Eagle Dance pertained to peace. His description, which I obtained on two occasions, fits the customary approach of the Calumet dancers. Taken together with Curtin's tradition of the Cherokee peace, these are quite interesting data.

That gane"gwä'e·' is a peace dance. When they have ceased fighting entirely, then they gather up a group of Seneca, as many as they can get, and approach the other party dancing the Eagle Dance. The dancers are out in front.

Many of the old folks, among them George Titus, used to tell this.

[Snorer has forgotten the names of the tribes involved, but] there had been fighting among the western nations, the Ojibwa and others. A great council convened "down west" near Detroit. The Senecas went down there because they wanted peace. They held a big dance and gathered up all the people there, and they made peace. They accepted the other nations. They shook hands and resolved never to fight again.

At this time the Seneca were living at "big hill" (djonǫdowa'·geh) when this trouble had occurred in the west. He thinks their village was then near the head of Seneca Lake.

There was to be a gathering of many nations near Detroit. When the Senecas arrived at the great council, the other nations were surprised because they ap-

[35] Caswell, 1892, pp. 259–262; Ms. notes of Mrs. Asher Wright's interview with Esquire Johnson (1876).

proached dancing the peace dance. They kept dancing. This was Eagle Dance which had been used in war.

[Snorer continued] Up to this time the other nations only had the scalp dances [Sioux War Dance and Striking-a-stick Dance], so the Senecas spread themselves among the other nations in order that the other nations might learn it. One of the Seneca chiefs made a speech to the effect that his people desired that there be peace between them and the western nations. The western Indians accepted.

Snorer thinks that this council occurred before Cornplanter's time, before the Seneca were living at Buffalo (diodo'šo·wɛ', "Moss on the creek bank"). This would date the council before the Revolution, and the place and dates suggest the time of Pontiac's conspiracy in 1763.

I realize the fallibility of relying on traditional history, but when tradition bears out recorded history, it should be heard. Albeit, I am inclined to think that Snorer's typical Seneca ethnocentrism has reversed the natural course of diffusion from the Central Algonquians, who were in possession of the Calumet Dance a century earlier, and who conceivably introduced the dance among the Seneca. Snorer's real contribution is the fact that he could describe his people as being in possession of a ceremony which they lacked before their western wars, and which also crops up in traditions of the same period, dated by the end of the Cherokee War, 1770.

A fragment of a tradition of the Great Fighter comes from Edward Cornplanter at Newtown, Cattaraugus Reservation, in 1905. The abbreviated notes of the recorder, Dr. A. C. Parker, are pertinent to our problem, and are quoted with his permission.

A Seneca war party saw the so-called bird dance among some tribe in the west [but this may also mean south, as the war path went west first to the Ohio settlements]. They saw some people dancing this in a house. They had sticks with feathers, long sticks with plumes. They were boasting what they did. The Senecas bragged back. They only struck the striped stick. They had pipes on sticks but they kept them in their pockets. The Senecas were afraid to use their pipes. It was Sioux (wasa'·se) smoke throwing. [??] They took captives, killing one, and taking the rest back to the Seneca country.

E. Cornplanter thinks that this started the Eagle Dance at Cattaraugus at the old longhouse before the others came from Geneseo.[36]

He-strikes-the-rushes is unfamiliar with this legend, although several old men at Newtown said that captives introduced foreign dances.

My father used to say, "We have many dances without origin legends, because captives brought them. Others came from animals."

The Eagle Dance is supposed to be purely Seneca. It may have been introduced by some other tribe, like some of our dances, but regardless of other tribes having Eagle dances, we claim it as our own. As a society, it is similar to the Medicine

[36] Parker, MS. The Seneca village at Geneseo was burned in Sullivan's raid, 1779. It was abandoned some years later.

Company, being limited only to members and often initiated into by sickness. The symptoms are such that the afflicted person gets visions or dreams of large white birds with blood all over their beaks. This is often followed by nose-bleeding to a large degree. I had my share when I first joined. Dad and I used to have it together. Like all medical society dances, the ceremony is performed with an Indian tobacco and the usual imitation of crows feeding over the pig's head. During the Midwinter Festival, those who follow the Eagle Dance from house to house have red paint on their right cheek. All of these dances—War Dance, Striking-a-stick, and Eagle Dance—are ended by someone striking a stick or stamping his foot and then making a speech. They tell tales of travel, jokes, but there is no blacking the faces of liars, as they stripe the faces of men who approach too near the women who are singing thanks for the crops. [Then a man's father's clansman's daughter may black his face.]

These rather lengthy statements of Seneca informants bear upon our thesis, and illustrate the way various Seneca individuals react to the queries of the ethnologist who often implies that some tribe "over there" has a similar ritual. Once the idea is conveyed to the inform- ant that another people may share a ceremony, he feels a sense of lost values and deflated pride in what he had considered to be the unique possession of his people. At such inferences, Snorer would close up, but He-strikes-the-rushes, as we have seen, usually ration- alized his people's customs, and added to my store of knowledge.

They say our Maker created the Dew Eagles for our benefit in order that they can assist him by rendering aid to chosen ones of us here. They seem to be pow- erful and rather sacred birds to us. But, as I say, if you travel among the tribes, even out west, you will likely find similarity in most of our customs and rituals. Then among us Iroquois, we differ to some extent. Take the ones in Canada and the Onondagas, they have a little different system than ours.

Uncovering the roots of the Eagle Dance has disclosed its relation- ship to a group of war dances featured by individual recitation. The content of speeches underwent a change about 1800. We have seen that the Eagle Dance was once used as an approach in peace treaties and that it was of foreign provenience. The idea that this sacred ritual may be of foreign derivation, and therefore spurious and not genuinely Iroquois, comes as a great shock to the present generation of Seneca Eagle dancers, who have passively accepted it as a vital part of their ceremonial life.

Two more problems remain as to its former uses: First, were the bundles taken on the war path? Second, how do we resolve the anomaly that western nations employing the Calumet Dance have attached the feather fans to so-called peace pipes which are foreign to Iroquois ceremonialism?

Hemlocks-lying-down said that Dew Eagle belongs to the Medi- cine Company, and that departing war parties used to sponsor the Eagle Dance to derive their luck from Dew Eagle.

They erected the forked striking pole and displayed scalps taken on previous expeditions. The speakers talked of killing and scalping, how many scalps they had brought home the previous trip, but our ruler sent word by his messengers through Handsome Lake for us to cease war speech. They changed over the society, changed the words to begging for good luck, health, and good behavior.

They did not take the pole and eagle bundle on the war path. They did not take the Little Water Medicine [meat powders], but the second kind, the medicine composed of more than twenty herbs [hadi'yawitha'].

When they returned, the leader put up Eagle Society again and described all that had happened on the war path. It is the leader's duty to sponsor the society to solicit aid from Dew Eagle when they go, and return thanks that they have got back.

Snorer and He-strikes-the-rushes both had heard that the war leader carried a bundle on the war trail. He carried his package of sacred medicine and a gourd rattle which he hung in a tree at night. If the gourd fell and broke, this was an evil omen, and the party returned home. "The oldest Little Water Medicine has the power to revive a person with seven mortal wounds, as long as the patient can swallow." My information does not state that the leader carried a forked pole which he inclined toward the enemy country. There is little likelihood that the Eagle Dance bundle was used outside the ceremony itself, and it is by no means a tribal palladium; the Eagle bundles are individually owned, whereas the Little Water Medicine is considered tribal property.

There are few instances of circuitous pipe passing in Iroquois rituals. The early sources speak of individual chiefs sitting in council, each smoking his own pipe incessantly. This pattern still prevails. Many foreign nations brought great pipes to Onondaga. Sir William Johnson gave them a handsome peace pipe, but the peace pipe has never become a vital part of council procedure. The dance fans are entirely divorced from any pipe notion. Unlike the Pawnee feathered Hako stems, they are not hollow shafts. The basic calumet idea, however, is the feathered stem, which, when it becomes also attached to the altar, symbolized by the pipe, combines the tobacco invocation concept with the fan that sweeps aside evil. The Iroquois have no ceremony which resembles the Pipe Bundle Dance of the northern Plains, but their Eagle Dance ritual more nearly resembles descriptions of the middle Mississippi Valley Calumet Dance with the feathered stems of the Pawnee Hako type.

The few instances of pipe passing in the Seneca medicine societies are confined to societies bearing no other relationship to the Pipe Bundle Dance. In the Dark Dance, the matron in charge, after the opening address and the tobacco-burning prayer to the "Little Folk" and the charm animals, lights a pipe of Indian tobacco. She uses any pipe. She passes it first to the beneficiary of the feast, then to the head singer, his helper, and to the rest of the members, going around the lodge counterclockwise. Everyone takes a few puffs. This is in Dark Dance only. In Bear Dance, however, the dancers file by and in turn puff from a pipe held out by the conductor. But in the ceremonies of the Medicine Company, members bring their own pipes, and a bowl of Indian tobacco is set before them as in Eagle Dance. An origin legend for the Medicine Company by Snorer describes the medicine animals at the cure of Bloody-hand smoking individual pipes between periods of singing. Thus, once more, the same ritual procedure connects the Eagle Society with the Medicine Company.

The Eagle Society, therefore, belongs to a group of linked societies in which the members impersonate the first animal members. To the Seneca of Newtown and Tonawanda especially, the Eagle Society is also the Medicine Society (honǫ'tcino''gę'). The Seneca distinguish three classes of members. The first includes the holders of the Little Water Medicine bundles, and all those who have been cured of wounds by taking the sacred medicine, and who renew their association with the mystic animals and prevent accidents recurring by celebrating a ritual called ye'i'do·s, or, collectively, hade'i'do·s. The second class of members includes those who have entered the society after a dream of impending misfortune, of bodily injury, or of hearing the songs (all dreams call for ye'i'do·s, the celebration ritual, to help or cure them). The third order of membership includes those who have dreamt of birds, have heard the songs of Eagle Dance in a dream, or have had its ritual performed at the suggestion of a clairvoyant. Falling-day at Tonawanda explained the three orders of membership.

They claim that they are all the same society, only they have different names. The Eagle Society belongs to Dew Eagle, but the three orders are all of the same medicine company. For instance, in ye'i'do·s, they bite off chunks of meat from the animal head as it goes around, crying like crows. They do this also in Eagle Dance. This is wa·diga'hga·, behaving in the manner of crows feasting on carrion. That's why they say ga'''ga''' [high tone] like crows. The celebration group [hade'i'do·s] and those who sing at the three all-night sessions to renew the strength of the medicine are members of the same medicine company; but Eagle Dance is a distinct order belonging to Dew Eagle, who is also a member of the great Medicine Company, like Wolf and Bear, and all animals who assisted at the cure of the good hunter.

Bear, Buffalo, and Otter Societies are distinctly of a different order. These are shamanistic societies and comprise a group with the Society of Faces, which set a high premium on possession as a sign of supernatural acceptance (Fenton, 1937, p. 228; 1941 b). Nor have the latter societies any specific connection with war or curing wounds. They are rather devoted to fulfilling traumatic derangements. Falling-day remarked that it was not required of him to participate in the rituals of the societies whose tutelaries have not accepted him for membership by making him sick. He is a chief and has lived around these rituals all his life, but he does not belong to several societies, although he has helped out at Midwinter Festival by singing for them. He mentioned how others who do not belong go and participate, implying that such behavior he considered both undignified and dangerous.

CLASSIFICATION OF DEW EAGLES

Informants differ as to the exact number of Dew Eagles. A Seneca's conception and classification of these mythical birds derives from how well he knows the rather extensive oral literature of his people. He rationalizes from a personal version of the origin myth, such as Boy Carried Away by Dew Eagle, and the oral traditions connected with sacrifices at the first kill, eagle baiting, and pit trapping, with which he couples his own observation of the habits of real birds, to the end that each Seneca has his own conception of the nature, habits, and powers of these supernatural birds; and these personal conceptions vary considerably with personal acuity and ornithological interest.

The Iroquois have observed real birds in their native habitat, and they have projected that behavior, magnifying size and character-istics, and granting corresponding powers, until they envisage mythological birds which "no one has ever seen." Such is the opera-tion of a principle: for everything in the known animal world, there is a great prototype in the supernatural world. The fact that super-natural birds are seldom, if ever, seen exalts their power, because, in Iroquois thinking, in order to be pure and free of contamination anything must be secluded from sight. Conversely, the only person who has rapport with "secluded" things is the one who has himself been kept apart from all contamination. Thus one who is born with a caul over his head will, if kept in seclusion, have powers of second sight. He becomes a pure person and has easy access to all those things which exist beyond the pale of vulgar persons who observe only the events and phenomena of the common world. Consequently men went into seclusion apart from women and purged themselves in order to lure down mere eagles, and a few were blessed by seeing the great Dew Eagles. Again, when a person takes the Little Water Medicine, he must go into seclusion during 4 days, and abstain from grease and salt, because the medicinal ingredients derive from birds and animals who are secluded (hodi′ya′dawa·dǫ′).

He-strikes-the-rushes, my extraordinary interpreter at Tonawanda, thinks that the concept of seclusion is what Hewitt, after intense study of the old cosmologies, termed "down-fended."

Down-fended . . . describes a feature characteristic of a primitive Iroquoian custom, which required that certain children should be strictly hidden from the sight of all persons save a trustee until they reached the age of puberty . . . the down of a cat-tail flag was carefully scattered about the place of concealment, so that no person could pass into the forbidden place without first disturbing the down . . . . Persons so hidden were regarded as uncanny and as endowed with an unusual measure of orenda, or magic potence. [Hewitt, 1903, p. 142.] The occasion of this seclusion was some omen or prodigy accompanying the birth of the child, which indicated that the child was uncanny. . . . It seems that children born with a caul were thus secluded, and the presence of the caul itself may have given rise to the custom. [Ibid. p. 255.]

The Dew Eagles wheel in flight among the clouds beyond the sight of mortals, and the Seneca call them "cloud dwellers" or "they of the vapors" ['o·'shada'ge' a·']. They are the greatest and highest of all the creatures of the air. Dew Eagle collects a pool of dew in the hollow in his back between his shoulders and when the Thunderers fail in their duty of watering the earth, Dew Eagle tilts his wings and the mists descend to refresh the crops. For the Seneca, Dew Eagle divides the task of refreshing the earth with "our grandfathers," the Thunderers, anthropomorphic beings, who for the Winnebago and Central Algonquians are the Thunder Birds (Radin, 1923, pp. 433, 447 (bundle feast), 439, 287 (disease); Converse and Parker, 1908, pp. 45-47; Curtin and Hewitt, 1918, p. 275; Parker, 1923, p. 16).

He watches over the Iroquois, and in time of great trouble descends to earth. His meat is in the Little Water Medicine, and his songs will revive a person who already has approached his grave. He is so tremendous that his wings obscure the sun and in landing his forward-thrust talons plow great furrows in the earth, leaving ravines. [He-strikes-the-rushes and Awl-breaker, Tonawanda.]

The Cayuga at Grand River and the New York Onondaga know Dew Eagle as ha''guks, and they ascribe to him similar attributes: the hollow-log kidnapping incident, agent of the eagle sickness, and it is necessary to sponsor his dance in order to cure a patient of convulsions which are thought symbolic of the eagle's manner of commencing flight (Waugh, Ms.: John Jamieson, Jr. (Cayuga), 1912, pt. B, p. 9; David Key (Onondaga), 1915, vol. 5, p. 18; John Echo (Onondaga), 1915, vol. 5, p. 35).

Several Seneca informants had specific information concerning the suborders of Dew Eagles. Wood-eater gave different names for them at separate sittings. On one occasion, he said:

The great crow [ga'hga'gowa''] is in continual flight across the earth. It is he who warns the Dew Eagle when the people are having a meeting. Dew Eagle is the highest above the earth. The head bird is red and called dja'hgwiyo' or dja'hgwiyo'go·wa·'. There are two others closer to the earth and to whom parts of the Little Water ritual are addressed.

Thus Wood-eater had two sets of names for the Dew Eagles: one descriptive of their markings, and a second set grading relative altitude and proportional greatness.

The Dew Eagles are of three kinds:
First, the one nearest the earth is large and white and black. He is called

the-lower-one [ne' i'da'genyane·'s]. He is also the-black-spotted-one [djɛsta'ɛ' o'dja'hgweonyǫ'], or the-striped-one [hodja'dagɛ''dja'kǫh]. He is nearly like a hen hawk and sometimes called swɛ'gäda'ge'·a·'.

The second is huge and white and a little higher up, and because of this is called ne' hetgɛ''osthǫ'—"the-higher-up-a-little," or "the ones that look white" [onowǫ'da'ɛ' nya'diya''dodɛ'].

The third, or red one, is biggest and flies highest; thus he is called "the highest" [ne'hetgɛ], or "the-red-appearing-one" [gwɛ'dä'ɛ·' nyaya'dodɛ·' or nya·niya'do·dɛ·'].

The red bird has a third name, dja'hgwiyo', and is sometimes called dja'hgwi-yo'go·wa·', the suffix meaning "great." He also belongs to the Little Water Company.

Hemlocks-lying-down knows of three Dew Eagles, but denies that they rate according to altitude: a red-appearing one (gwɛ'da'ɛ·'nya-ya'do·dɛ'), a blue-appearing one (djinyo'wai'nyaya'do·dɛ'), and a white one, as above; and he has heard of a brown-appearing one (o'gɛ'ɛ nyaya'do·dɛ').

SRE denies the reality of the blue one.

A third informant, Snorer (August 1934) names the Dew Eagles a bit differently and includes a blue one.

Having left the medicine animals of the ground, in going aloft above the earth Dew Eagle is the first of the birds. They are of several colors: a brown one; one like a hen hawk [swɛ'gäda'ge'·a·']; a black and white one (but one does not seek him for a charm animal); the great red one [dja'hgwiyo'go·wa·']; a blue one; and a white one [gano''gwiyo'ge·i'].

At Tonawanda, Hair-singed-off and Lightning, a sachem and a matron of Snipe Clan, spoke of another bird called gwiyo'ge'·i'. Chauncey Warrior at Allegany had given it as the name of a summer constellation and had mistakenly called it "loon." This constellation was observed on July 31, 1933, at 9:45 p. m. at altitude approximately 45° east, and declination approximately 65° north of the Equator. The Relation of 1660 mentions the constellation of the Eagle in connection with a comet visible at Montreal between January and March (Thwaites, 1896–1901, vol. 46, p. 205), but the two are probably not identical. Hair-singed-off claims that gwiyo'ge'·i' flies at night, and his meat is in the Little Water Medicine. He told a tale of how it destroyed a snake that was climbing to a flicker's nest.

All these birds are seldom seen because they are secluded from sight. Lightning thought that a pure man might see some of these birds: "One who never goes out, one about whom one hears nothing evil, probably a virgin, but anyway such is usually a single male who has gone into seclusion to become cleansed."

He-strikes-the-rushes had heard of gwiyo'ge'·i', the mythical night-flying bird of the Eagle family for whom the constellation is named gwiyo'ge·i' gadji'', "loon flying." He remembers that Converse was notably poor at writing down Seneca when she worked with his father years ago at Newtown. Her "ga-do-jih"[37] is "black feather" (ga"dadji'), any bird whose feathers are black. I have had this from other informants as the totemite for the Heron clan. Her sa-go-da-oh is not recognized by my informant.

Big Crow or Raven (gah'ga'go·wa·') is in continual flight across the earth as messenger (hadja'swas) for all the birds. He is not a vulture, but a great common crow, who like his miniature fellows hesitates in flight and cries out whenever he discovers any carrion lying there ('tgaya'swayε') or observes any strange event. The Great Crow notifies Dew Eagle whenever the people are meeting. "He gathers up all the birds and animals belonging to the Medicine Company. He is headman of the whole Medicine Company"(SRE). Wood-eater considers him "a tremendous crow," messenger for all the birds, "who flies continuously back and forth above the clouds," and he deems ridiculous He-strikes-the-rushes' notion that it flies above the trees. Hemlocks-lying-down agrees. Accordingly, in the earthly ritual when the host chooses a headman, he expects him to act first as messenger (hadja'swas) and then "take charge" (has-de·i'sdǫ')—conduct the meeting.

Big Crow comes in for special mention in prayers. Wood-eater says, "Big Crow should be mentioned in putting tobacco for the Society of charm animals, the Eagle Dance, and the Little Water Medicine of which he is the head one."

Wood-eater jokingly adds: "Snorer is Big Crow or head singer for the Little Water Company; may be he is the second one, whom He-strikes-the-rushes referred to as flying above the trees." This jibe at his rival is quite apt because Snorer lives at "high bank," above the Allegheny River, which the local Seneca amusedly call the sky place (ge'ǫya'geh) or "heaven."

The members of the Medicine Company, therefore, behave like crows. When the Seneca speak of the cooking preparatory to a feast or a dance of one of the Medicine Company's orders going on over yonder at the next house, they say 'tgaya'·sho', literally "they are preparing carrion," and the feast is set on the ground to symbolize a fallen animal ('tgaya'swayε'). Likewise, the members simulate the behavior of crows, and bite at the meat, and "they dip their bills in the soup." Finally, at the end of the meeting, "they scatter and fly wherever they are wont to frequent," as if the men transformed themselves into birds and flew off in the night, when actually they pick up their pails and depart. The sponsor puts up a feast for the scavengers who possess the power of carrying off his disease or ailments.

[37] Converse and Parker, 1908, p. 69. A manuscript, written by Mrs. Converse, now in the files of the New York State Museum at Albany, differs slightly from Parker's edition of her work. It mentions "gahdahjih" as chief of all the eagles, and that "shadahgeaah," the blue eagle, is his helper.

All these mythical birds rank above their smaller earthly counterparts. Bald Eagle (do'nyonda') is the totemite of all the Iroquois. The eagle perches atop the great tree of peace which is symbolic of the Confederacy. Warriors seek his feathers for their headdress. The revolving feather, like the totemite which it represents, looks in all directions, protecting the wearer. So Yankee Spring explained the relation of his people to Bald Eagle:

The Eagle is the symbol of the Confederacy.

The Iroquois, or the Five Nations, began as separate entities and became known as such when they formed the League. When they learned the great mutual law [gayaneshä"go·wa·'], the Creator told the people a way by which they might know each other. It should be by wearing of an eagle feather, because that bird was a far-seeing bird, and the Creator wanted his people to be far-seeing.

The great mutual law was designed for the future. It did not rest upon the past. The Creator chose the eagle feather by which they might recognize each other in the future. He chose the eagle as the totem of the Iroquois as a people, and he ordained that collectively the Five Nations should belong to one clan, that of the Eagle, which is called variously: oswf'gäda'ge''a'',[38] oshada'ge'·a·', "Dew Eagle," or do'nyonda', "Bald Eagle."

One feather he deemed enough for his people's headdress. In ceremonies they added to the single large whirling eagle feather by wearing a cap which had at the forehead a cluster of split feathers from which the quills had been removed. The one feather is worn as nearly straight up as possible. There was never any coup system. The feather was merely a means of recognition, a symbol of membership in the League. [Pl. 18.]

DREAM EXPERIENCES

Dreams have provided the rationale for Iroquois ceremonialism during 300 years. The Huron of Canada were pictured as preoccupied with traumatic experiences by Champlain and the Jesuit writers to whom we are indebted for the finest descriptions of the Iroquoian tribes. Dreams to the Huron had all the significance of the vision quest by fasting among the Central Algonquians. The Huron, moreover, consulted clairvoyants, persons reputed to be gifted at divining dreams and prescribing the proper ceremony to relieve certain kinds of sickness. Whole villages met at midwinter to guess dreams and pay the forfeits which custom prescribed for particular dreams. The whole Feast of Fools, so-called in the Jesuit Relations, has evolved from a random series of dream fulfillments to an organized Midwinter Festival by a gradual standardization of forms which differ according to locality (Fenton, 1937, p. 229; 1936 b, p. 5; 1951; Jesuit Relations, vol. 10, pp. 183, 185 ff., 209 ff.; vol. 22, p. 227; vol. 39, p. 21; vol. 54, p. 101; vol. 42, pp. 154–169; Lafitau, 1724, vol. 2, pp. 81–84).

---

[38] SRE says this is Hen Hawk or Sharp-shinned Hawk, totemite of the Hawk clan.

Bressani's Relation of 1653, concerning the Huron, says that clair-voyants, in order to reveal the motivations for dreams, consult their familiars (Oki).

They said they had this vision and virtue from an Oki—that is, from a powerful genie dwelling in them, which had appeared to them in a dream, or in watching, in the form of an eagle, or raven, or some other like animal.

The diviner determined what tutelary was involved by water scrying, or by the kind of hysteria possessing the patient, or he himself went into seclusion; and the patient paid in presents (Jesuit Relations, vol. 39, p. 21).

The Relation of 1642 tells how a Christianized Algonquin's strong faith prevented his return to paganism following a dream.

He saw, in a dream, a person who said to him, "Prepare an eat-all feast; if thou wilt be cured, put Eagle's feathers on thy body, in the manner that I shall tell thee; thou art a dead man if thou dost not obey. Above all, pray no more; it is prayer that has made thee ill."

The savages have no stronger belief than in dreams, . . . [but this fellow would not return to paganism]. [Jesuit Relations, vol. 22, p. 227.]

The extensive literature on the Iroquoian and neighboring tribes presents case after case of such behavior following dreams. Here a great chief, Cornplanter, relinquishes his title following a dream, and at another place his previously unimportant half-brother, Handsome Lake, during a long illness receives several epoch-making dreams which change the whole life of his people, and perpetuate elements of the old religion down to the present (Morgan, 1901, vol. 1, p. 205; Parker, 1913 a, pp. 14 ff.; Deardorff, 1951).

So today an Iroquois Indian joins a particular medicine society after a dream or following a sickness because a clairvoyant has pre-scribed the ritual of a particular society for his cure. He automat-ically joins just those societies, and is afterward duty bound to sponsor any combination of rituals that have assisted his recovery (Fenton, 1937, p. 226; 1936 b, p. 17; 1941 a).

Dreams, as we shall see from the following experiences of Seneca informants, are couched in cultural terms and reflect personal knowl-edge of and acquaintance with the oral literature of the ceremonies. In general, erudite informants like Wood-eater and He-strikes-the-rushes, the son of a Handsome Lake preacher, had rich dream expe-riences. I find a consistency between what they know and the content of their dreams. Their dreams, possibly, have been elaborated during subsequent rationalization, but the two informants have consistently adhered to the main facts when spontaneously repeating the dreams to me at intervals of 2 years. Another thing I notice is a change in dream content which parallels changes in the ritual. Among the Seneca of Allegany and Cattaraugus, dreams of a pig head are frequent, but at Tonawanda and Onondaga, where chickens are boiled for the feast, they dream of chickens. Almost no one dreams of eagles, which no modern Seneca has trapped. Classic Iroquois matrilineal reckoning, moreover, has affected dream life; and dreams may involve a whole maternal family, the descendants through females, of a certain woman; and dreams sometimes select a particular person in the opposite moiety who, during his lifetime, stands in a special relationship of "friend" to the dreamer. Thus even social organization creeps into dreams.

Dreams indicating membership in a particular medicine society do not have to be experiences of the beneficiary. Someone dreams something good about someone else, and they become lifelong friends, celebrating their friendship with annual rites of reunion. This was Wood-eater's explanation for the beginning of the Eagle Medicine Society.

THE FIRST DREAM

The first time a little boy got sick and no one could cure him. Meanwhile his mother had a dream that her son should prepare: First, tobacco; second, he should secure the head of some game animal; and third, he should have soup prepared for the Dew Eagles.[39]

In this dream, the Dew Eagle taught the woman the songs; that is why they have used the same songs ever since the beginning.

After the boy had this meeting and put up the feast, he was able to get out of bed and walk about without having to use any medicine. Later his mother had another meeting for him. That is why we put up anniversary feasts.

The bird did not say anything about having things on opposite sides [moiety functions], but the people put this in afterward.

The tobacco, the songs, the dances, and the feast are in honor of the bird.

The speeches are made to the man who is the host.

Poking fun has no relation to these, but was added by those people who divided things according to moieties.

WOOD-EATER JOINS EAGLE SOCIETY

Years ago, when Wood-eater was much younger, he was sick for nearly a year. It seemed as if something were continually clutching him by the shoulders. His arms were nearly paralyzed. They pained terribly.

And then pretty soon I go to sleep one night. While I am asleep I saw a huge red bird [dja'hgwiyo'go·wa·'] come alight on the ground nearby. It laid down and transformed itself into a man who approached me. The man had a red face and a hooked beak instead of a nose. He said, "You are pretty sick and I can help you. Your old people, who are all dead, used to put up the Eagle Dance, and you should do the same for yourself. Then later, if you have children, you must put it up for them."

---

[39] Note the "contract" theory whereby in return for certain things—tobacco, corn soup, or mush—which man has, spirits agree to bestow blessings and remove diseases (Radin, 1923, pp. 279, 289).

Then he transformed himself back into a bird and flew up into the heav and disappeared.

After that they put up Eagle Dance for me and the clutching sensation disappeared from my shoulders. I recovered. And this is why I still put it up; and this is why I have it yearly with my boy.

WHAT DJIDǪ'GWAS DREAMED

Djidǫ'gwas, a Seneca of the Wolf Clan, who was born in 1861 at Coldspring, customarily relates his experiences and folktales in the form of a dialogue. He lived with his mother who was quite advanced in years when she bore him. It seems that when he was young, he was very sick.

I had been down sick for three weeks. My throat was swollen so that it was nearly closed, and I could only drink the Indian medicines which my mother prepared for me from the herbs which she gathered. I did not get better. Sometimes at night I would hear my mother crying. She thought I was going to die.

I said, "Don't cry, mother, it's no use. If I am going to die, you can't stop it; I can't stop it; nothing can stop it." [40] Then she would cry more, and I would say, "Don't cry, mother."

At first they gave me the Small Dose Medicine, and after that I was confined 4 days, they let it go [with the ceremony of release]. Then a week passed. I still lay sick.

Now during the second week while I lay sick, one night I was asleep. Someone came to the door and entered. It was a man, but he was visible only from the waist down. I could not see his face. In one hand he carried a bundle. At one open end I could see fine feathers like the tufts on the feather fans where they stuck out of the bundle. He said twice, "This is here, if you want it. This is here, if you want it." Then he left.

The next day I told my mother. [Here he related the whole incident, repeating the conversation with his mother.]

Mother said, "He must mean that you want gane"gwä'e·' [Eagle Dance]."

My mother prepared hulled-corn soup and she bought the head of a pig which she boiled in the soup. That night a great crowd of people came to our house for the meeting. They made long speeches, hoping that I would get well.

Finally one day I got up. I staggered like a drunken man. My mother helped me by the shoulder. I was very hungry. I said, "Mother, I am hungry."

She said, "All right."

I said, "I am very hungry and I will try to eat something. Now you fix whatever there is." I sat down at the table and she set before me whatever there was in the house. And I commenced trying to eat.

Oh, the food stuck to the insides of my cheeks! They seemed stiff. I leaned over the table trying to eat. I swallowed hard. Presently, I heard a noise, žuk, žuk, žuk, žuk! [a sound which he made with distended lips, as if he were pointing at something]. It sounded like dripping. I looked down. It was dripping down my front, between my thighs, and onto the floor.

"Mother," I cried, "get the wash dish and put water in it. It has broken, the swelling beneath my chin has let go."

You see that scar? [He tilted his head back, raising his chin and protruding his lower lip so I could observe the scar which the eruption had left beneath his

---

[40] The old Senecas believe that death is predestined.

chin.] My mother placed the wash dish on the floor. The matter ran into the dish and filled it nearly full. Then I got better.

Yes, I have belonged to the Eagle Dance many years, and sometimes I burn tobacco before the meetings.

TEN-MORNINGS BECOMES A MEMBER, BY DJIDQ'GWAS

The question had arisen from my notes and the testimony of my interpreter, Clara Redeye, in 1934, whether several men who participated in the anniversary rite for Resting-sky are members of the Society. The problem also came up whether membership is a prerequisite for speaking at Eagle Dance meetings. After djidq'gwas had related so graphically his own experience, I asked him about his friend Ten-mornings.

Ten-mornings, whom we call da'hdot [Bear Clan], belongs to the Eagle Society. Once in a while he has a meeting over at his place. He once told me how he joined. Da'hdot was very sick. They thought he would die. He had no feeling in his body or his legs. He dreamed of a meeting of the Eagle Society. Someone was speaking. He said, "Da'hdot will get well if they hold gane''gwä'e·' for him."

Da'hdot related this dream to his mother, his wife, and his stepfather. The stepfather talked about it. He said that the dream must mean that they should put up an Eagle Dance for da'hdot. The stepfather and the mother prepared hulled-corn soup, and they got a head from a pig. Many people came to the meeting. They hoped that da'hdot would get better.

Two days later, da'hdot had recovered sufficiently to get drunk. He went about shouting, "I am well again; they had Eagle Dance for me. I feel fine."

The question of William Cooper's membership had also arisen and my interpreter was not sure whether he belonged. I have not had an opportunity to question him, and such personal information comes to the ethnologist only in bursts of confidence. Djidq'gwas is not sure whether William Cooper belongs to the Society, but he sometimes has meetings, so he must be a member. Hemlocks-lying-down an hour later confirmed djidq'gwas' feeling that membership is not an important prerequisite for speaking, stating emphatically that membership is not required in order to speak. "Anyone at Coldspring speaks at Eagle Dance meetings." Nevertheless, all the speakers whom I have heard have on investigation proved to be members.

THOSE WHO HAVE INHERITED

The Eagle sickness runs in certain families from generation to generation. This amounts practically to inheritance of the Society by the children of parents who have failed to sponsor the ritual. Among the Seneca, when the children of believing parents display the symptoms of ailments which the tutelaries of particular medicine societies are believed to cause, the old people say that the children are afflicted by the negligence of their parents. This faith plus the ever-present Iroquois preoccupation with traumatic experience insures the perpetuation of the medicine societies from generation to generation. A child may inherit his associations from either side of the house. However, some dreams require the participation of a whole maternal family.

Hemlocks-lying-down does not recall when he joined the Eagle Society. It is so long ago he cannot remember.

The trouble is that the old people do not put up their societies very often and therefore it goes right in his family; when I don't put up my societies, 'ie·i'do·s and Eagle Dance, as I didn't, so Great-night, my son, got sick. Great-night put up both of them, and now he is all right. Likewise, my father and mother did not have meetings for their societies and I got sick. The sickness follows in the family. They say my legs were cramped and bent. I could not straighten them.

Hemlocks-lying-down did not recall what clairvoyant his parents consulted.

According to Corn-husker's wife (Bear Clan), in whose house I boarded one summer, her husband Corn-husker (Hawk Clan) and three of his children, two older sons and a daughter, belonged to the Eagle Society. She and the two younger children, a girl and a boy of 14, were not members. Years ago Corn-husker's father (Wolf Clan) dreamed that he and his son should put up the dance together. Corn-husker has kept it up. Similarly, in the following generation, Corn-husker dreamed that Eagle Dance would help his second son who was always sickly, and so Corn-husker and his son have it together now like Corn-husker and his father before him. The oldest son was sick and dreamed that the Eagle Dance would help him, and the daughter had a similar dream. His wife has little faith in these things, and, interestingly enough, the two younger children have not revealed any dreams.

Wood-eater (Bear Clan) has Eagle Dance with his son, SRE (Snipe Clan).

The father and children in both instances are of different moieties, but Corn-husker's wife and Hemlocks-lying-down concur that a father may have a ritual with his sons regardless of moiety membership.

An example of a dream which involves participation of a whole maternal family in a medicine society is that of She-gave-her-the-name and all her daughters and their children of the Bear Clan at Coldspring, who sponsor the Bear Dance together; but their clanship may have no connection with the name of the society. Ha'nodje·nɛ's (Snipe Clan), who acted as conductor for Resting-sky's meeting, belongs to Eagle Society and sponsors a joint annual meeting with all surviving descendants of his mother's father, all Snipes. My informant, Hemlocks-lying-down, at first said that this meeting was for the whole clan, but then corrected himself by saying he meant that only the maternal family have been carrying it on ever since the old grandfather, and he stated that this meeting does not include SRE and his half brothers, children of another maternal family in the same clan.

CEREMONIAL FRIENDS

Ceremonial friends are principals in a supplementary or substitutive relationship that is cemented by common association in a ceremony which has been revealed in a dream or prescribed by a clairvoyant. One party is ill and requires the bond with a healthy person, or perhaps he needs the interpersonal relationships which have been denied him in a broken family; and the actual ties of blood relationship between him and his correspondent seem unimportant. Friendship operates on the principle, common among exotic peoples—particularly the Iroquois—of projecting everyone into some situation of real or fictitious relationship to one's self and others. Not only do the Iroquois rigorously apply their kinship system within the tribes of the Confederacy, but the principle of extending kin ties classes clansmen of member tribes as siblings; and in council the sachems of the confederated tribes call each other older-brother and younger-brother nations respectively, dividing themselves into two moieties, and they use remoter relationship terms, such as nephews, for the subjected Delaware, over whom they exercised an avuncular authority, and "children of our father's brothers" for the Chippewa (Jackson, 1830, p. 8). Use of the terms predicates behaving as if the implied relationships were real. The principle of fictitious kinship underlies adoption; it is at work in the concept of ceremonial friends; it is projected to the tribal level in the Confederacy; treaties confirmed by wampum belts make kindred of contracting parties; and father-son and uncle-nephew relationships unite tribes participating in the widespread Calumet Dance.

Among the Seneca, ceremonial friends may be of the same generation, sex, and moiety, but friendships are usually arranged between a child and an older person of the other moiety—preferably his father's clansman. The pattern seems to be this: A child is sick. Either the child dreams of another person, or someone else reveals a dream about the child and himself or involving the child with another person. The parents consult a clairvoyant, who divines that the child needs a friend, who is sometimes named. The parents seek the friend and pay him tobacco. The ceremony is confirmed with an exchange of presents. Often the older person presents the child with a talisman— a miniature object—symbolic of their association which must be renewed annually. The custom of presenting miniature talismen derives from the old Huron-Iroquois custom of dream guessing and celebrating the revealed rites at the Midwinter Festival.

Hemlocks-lying-down (Turtle Clan) frequently conducts Eagle Society meetings, but he has no "friends" through the Society. However, he has a friend in the Bear Dance Society. . . .

The little girl next door [in the Beaver Clan] was sick. She fell and nearly broke her arm. She could not move. Her mother dreamed that she had to have a friend, an old man. [The girl's father does not live with the family.] So they asked me, would I be her friend, and I thought I better do it. We put up the ceremony of the Bear Society and the next day her arm was all right.

Clara Redeye, my first Seneca interpreter at Coldspring, said that a boy would ask his grandmothers to interpret his dreams. Then the boy's mother or father would notify the father's clansman to make the boy a suitable miniature object: a lacrosse stick, a canoe, bow and arrow, a wooden mask, or a husk mask—something symbolic of the dream and the prescribed ceremony. He makes it and presents it to the boy at the ceremony. Thus a companionship grows up between the boy and his father's clansman.

A boy or a little girl may be sick at the time, or any sick person may have such a dream. The parents or old folks [grandparents] will ask that person to to be the friend. Older people sometimes dream of younger people. The clan does not matter. A ceremony is held to make them friends and presents are exchanged. They are true relations after this: the boy calls the man his friend (hononde"yo'); if a man dreams of a woman the same term is used, and it also holds for a girl and a woman. Most of the dreams are on the part of little children with older people as the dream subjects.

Neither Wood-eater nor his son's wife ever had this ceremony. The ceremony or dream rite for friends (ade'oshä') is held at the child's parent's house. It may resemble a social dance, but the older person is supposed to offer a present for the child.

My sister, Leaf-blowing-down [Hawk Clan] had one with gaweni"de' [Turtle Clan]. [They are both of the same generation, but of opposite moieties; they are close friends and constant visitors at each other's homes. The former's husband's younger brother, Days-old, married the latter's younger sister.] When the rite is held for two women, pieces of cloth are exchanged; a boy and a man give each other white shirts. The exchange of presents cures the sick child. They are supposed to renew this annually, but they usually do not.

If a child is sick and thinks of a certain man, or dreams of him, the mother may call in the man to give medicines. Corn-husker's wife (Bear Clan) called in O'pi (Heron Clan) when her son was down with pneumonia, because he asked to see him. O'pi prepared herbal medicines which cured the boy.

F. W. Waugh recorded a ceremony of friendship while at Tonawanda on an ethnobotanical field trip in 1912. According to his informant, Peter Sundown, the medicine dance was held at Louisa Ground's house for a little boy named Moses Bull, who was then 4 years old, and Twenty-kettles, who had been secured for the friend.

The ritual consisted of an invocation, the peach-stone game, in which the women defeated the men, the Eagle Dance, the rite of Personal Chant, Fish Dance, a social dance, and an exchange of presents. The feast was beef soup with hominy and was distributed at the end. Peter Sundown received a white-bosom shirt when he went through the friendship ceremony. In 1934, with Twenty-kettles as informant, I supplemented Waugh's notes on this ceremony, partly in text.

Moses Bull was pretty sick, but three or four days after the ceremony of friendship and singing of Personal Chant he felt pretty good. He is alive today (?).

The ceremony of friendship is called a'de'wishɛ', hnondɛ''ǫ', or ogya'tcih.

Moses was pretty sick and his mother used medicines and they did not seem to help him. She went to a woman fortune teller [yɛne'·ye'ǫ] to consult her. The clairvoyant said, "He wants his friend." So the old lady and the boy's father commenced hunting around for a friend for their sick child. I was here at home that night. The parents came to me saying, "I want a friend for my little boy." When the father told me that, he gave me Indian tobacco. It is just the same as when I go to gather herbal medicines. I take along Indian tobacco and make offerings to the plants I take. Likewise, they gave me tobacco because they wanted me.

When I went to his house, his mother asked me what kind of dances I wanted. The father suggested Personal Chant, and I agreed.

William Poudry the headman made an address, giving thanks to all the spirit-forces, and then he addressed the little boy's friend, Twenty-kettles. He told all those present that the purpose of this meeting was to cement a friendship between this little boy and his father's friend.

Then he put tobacco in the fire for Twenty-kettles and Moses Bull, the two friends. [Twenty-kettles did not hear the words of the invocation. However he should make the same kind of an invocation as one uses when going out after medicines. Then one tells the medicines what they are to be used to cure and the name of the person whom they must help.]

Before the Personal Chant singing, they sang the Eagle Dance. In Personal Chant every one sang to bind the friendship.

When we finished with the Personal Chant, he [Moses Bull] gave me 4 yards of cotton sheeting to bind my friendship. Long ago they used to give buckskin in these rituals.

This was thirty years ago. Sometimes I sing Personal Chant in the longhouse for Moses Bull. Sometimes at the New Year's dance I sing Personal Chant for my friend.

He-strikes-the-rushes, my interpreter, commented:

The boy has a friend who is an older person. He must help the child to grow up to be a man. He must advise the boy, acting as his counsellor. Twenty-kettles is of the Hawk Clan. Moses Bull's father was of the Wolf Clan. He had approached a friend of the other moiety to be a friend of his son, who was of the Turtle Clan. Twenty-kettles says that a man and his friend would be of opposite sides [moieties]: "My friend is on the other side. When one is ill, they choose a friend for him from the other side."

It is believed that the ceremony of making friends merges the relatives of the two principals into one kindred unit: The relatives of the man are linked with the relatives of the child.

The older man must act as an example to his junior friend. The older man's conduct shall be observed by the younger boy who considers the older friend a model of behavior. The Creator has ordained that these two be friends and it is hoped the younger one will grow up to be the fine man his older partner is supposed to be. Whatever he observes the older man doing, he shall do it. The old man bears the onus of the child's future. As a reward he will see the Creator when he dies.

When the two meet on the road, the older person speaks first. "Thanks you are well my friend? [ni'a·wɛ skɛ·noꞌ gyade'ǫh]." The younger one answers, "Truly thank you I am well my friend [dogɛꞌ·s nia·wɛh skɛ·noꞌ gyade'ǫh]." Every time he sees me, he calls me "friend (gyade'ǫh)."

HELPER AND HE-IS-COMING

Likewise, Helper, sachem chief of the Bear Clan, an old man of 70, has a young friend, He-is-coming, of the Snipe Clan, in the other moiety. Helper narrated his experience in joining the Eagle Society.

I pretty near die one time. I sleep. Then I wake, then it seems as if I sleep again. I see people sitting around. Among them was a large woman wearing a wide-brimmed straw hat and she was beating on a pan of ashes with a stick as if she were singing. She is the one who told me to put up the Eagle Dance.

He had been sick, the boy whom we call He-is-coming; he was little then, and he had a bad stepfather who licked him all the time. And the boy would cry all the time. And he thinks he is going to die. Now his mother, Lightning, felt sorry for him, and she consulted the old Pagan people around the Longhouse and they said she had better get someone to be his friend, maybe. Well, Lightning came to me saying, "I want someone to be a friend for my boy." [Helper is Bear Clan, and He-is-coming and his mother are Snipes in the opposite moiety.] Lightning said that she used to belong to the Pagans and I say, "all right." But I add that I do not want to go to the Eagle Dance for fear that I might become sick with the illness that the Eagle causes.

The old people had told me that one who does not belong to the Eagle Dance will become sick if he passes the dancers performing that dance on a floor. So I told Lightning that I don't want to celebrate our friendship with that ritual which would help her boy, but I will make a friend with gadžɛꞌꞌgeka·ꞌ [the Bowl Game].

In about two weeks I was sick. I cannot get up. I am stiff all the time. Sometimes I do not know who of my people comes to see me, I do not know them when they look me in the face. I am asleep some of the time. Then I see that old woman wearing the big straw hat and beating a pan of ashes with a stick. "You look outside," she says, and I look out and see my chickens lined up from the door to beyond the jog in the corner of the house.[41] The first chicken has no head. It is cut off and is hanging, but the blood is spitting from its mouth. I look way back beyond the chickens and there stands my friend, that boy named He-is-coming, and he is laughing and looking at me.

Right away I told them; and afterward I learned that they put up a dance for me at night. I don't know but they tell me. He-is-coming and I have it together now.[42]

He-is-coming has heard his mother, Lightning, say that she went to Buffalo to consult some woman whom the Tonawanda people recom-

---

[41] Chickens, instead of pork, are the principal feast at Tonawanda.
[42] See p. 54 for an account of their anniversary ceremony during February 1935.

mended. "This Indian woman told Lightning that I should have a friend."

From the same source it was learned that when Awl-breaker, Messenger Chief of the Wolf Clan at Tonawanda, was small, he was sick. His old people went to a fortuneteller and she prescribed the Eagle Dance. They put up the Eagle Dance ritual and he forgot about being sick. That old lady and her daughter were Oneidas from Green Bay, Wis.[43]

THE DREAM AND DELIRIUM OF HE-STRIKES-THE-RUSHES

I don't think the Eagle Dance and all its equipment were ever used outside of the Ceremony itself. In fact the common Eagle is not the one that has the dance—it is the Dew Eagle—a mythical eagle supposed to soar among the mists and clouds but never below. Hence his name, o'shada'ge'·a·', "mist dweller" or Dew Eagle. Dew Eagle is supposed only to be seen in dreams when the patient is being afflicted by their power for the purpose of putting on the Eagle Dance. I have seen it myself in a dream, or rather in delirium condition, when a small boy. To me they appear to be enormous birds—pure white, and they had fresh blood on their beaks. Oh yes, you have to be an Indian to be and see all we see.

When I was a little child, I was very sick. It was warm weather and I lay in bed. Everytime I dozed off to sleep I would see large white birds on the ground flapping their wings. They seemed to have blood on their faces.

In my waking moments, as I gazed up, the ceiling seemed to approach my face and stick to it. I was unable to shake it off. I felt as if a great weight were pressing down upon my head. Then again as I came out of it, I called my mother. She approached the bed where I lay, leaving her work about the stove. Her face appeared distorted and it seemed to come up close to mine and stay there as I stared at her spellbound.

A clairvoyant interpreted this short-focused vision and delirium, supplemented by my dreams, as symptoms of the sickness which the eagles cause.

Two years later, I recounted to this informant Helper's account of joining the Eagle Society, which prompted him to retell his experience.

Second version:

I remember a time back in the old homestead in Newtown. I must have been still in swaddlings for I remember being slung in a hammock across the corner of the room. (The people spread two wires with two sticks and they fasten the wires together at the ends and wrap the wires in blankets. This is an old Seneca contraption.) Now I was very sick. There was a knot in the ceiling above me and I kept staring at it. My head seemed to swell and the ceiling came down toward my face. I cried and my mother came to me and her face was distorted and seemed to tremble and her eyes bulged out. She leaned over me and her face came down close to mine until I cried. She, only knowing that I was fretful, went to a clairvoyant who recommended that they put up the Eagle Dance for me.

Meanwhile I slept intermittently and I kept dreaming of seeing great white

---

[43] All that apparently survives of Eagle Dance among the Oneida of Green Bay is the custom at certain curing feasts of pounding on the wall with a stick and then scattering candy and peanuts which precipitates a general scramble. But the word for it, guwanle' gwala'eks, "they throw club," is clearly cognate with gane'gwa''e·', the Onondaga name of Eagle Dance (Ritzenthaler, 1950, p. 38).

birds on the ground outside the house and their heads and necks were splattered with blood.

The clairvoyant told my mother that the cause of my sickness was my father's failure to put up the Eagle Dance. He had let it go by several years. I had got it from him.

Some years later and I had grown up and I was swinging my sister's hammock which was hung in the same corner. I looked up and saw the knot in the ceiling. Calling my mother, I recounted my experience as a sick infant, how I had seen the great white birds splattered with blood on the ground outside, and she told me then that I belonged to the Eagle Society, how she had gone to the clairvoyant who diagnosed the Eagle as wanting me because my father had neglected to put up a feast. I was perhaps fifteen when I learned this.

Dreaming that one hears the songs of the Eagle Dance, in the distance, indicates the sickness is caused by that bird.

Clairvoyants are consulted because they are people reputed to know the omens indicating membership in particular societies. They know what types of dreams reveal a need for membership in the Eagle Society.

They usually recommend the Eagle Dance, and if it succeeds, well and good, but if not, they may suggest 'ie'i·'do·s, which has nearly the same symptoms.

My father and I had an Eagle Dance bundle and a striped pole (ge'ǫdo·t). When we were ready to have a meeting, we called in sanǫ''gai·s (he-has-long-horns) of the Deer Clan to be the runner (hadja'swas) and conductor (hasde'i·sta'), because he was of the other phratry from my father. He took the pole and stood it up outside the house in the front yard. He tied the fans together end to end attaching them near the top of the pole, orienting the fans east and west when the pole was erected. He hung the rattles from the limbs of the crotch at the top of the pole. The striking stick is also hung up on the pole.

The pole is striped red from lower left to upper right. The red pigment was a clay [ogwę'·shä'], stained with the bark of a certain tree, the name of which is now lost. The pole itself is sycamore [gę'nsa], "scabs falling away."

When you are chosen by the Dew Eagle to be in league with him, you are given this pole. This is after a clairvoyant has named the Eagle Society by interpreting your particular dream or ailment. The pole becomes your charm and with it goes a striped striking stick [yene'gwa''e·sta' ga''nya'] which is similarly striped and which also is hung with the rattles when the contents of the bundle are displayed.

He does not say who makes the pole and beater for the novitiate. He does not know whether the crotch at the top of the pole is symbolic of the eagle's nest. Hemlocks-lying-down said, "No, the crotch is only a place to hang the fans."

Long-horns puts tobacco when he raises the pole. He was always master of ceremonies when my father had meetings, because he was of the opposite phratry, my father being [shoshǫdo'·wa·'] [Great Night] of the Wolf Clan. We [my father and I] held it together because my father did not live up to the requirements of the pact with the Dew Eagles when I was small, and I got sick. He and I had it together afterward.

The old folks claim that by erecting the pole and displaying the contents of the bundle that [ga'hga'go·wa·'] the giant crow who is flying *above the tree tops* will see it. He is messenger [hadja'was], for the birds. He goes all over, traveling everywhere over the face of the earth. Then he ascends above the clouds to the Dew Eagle [shada'ge'·a·'], because he never comes low down. He tells all the Dew

Eagles, for there are a lot of them, that they, the people, have remembered us again:

o·nɛh ai·'	djǫkiyasha''ǫ	ne·' yoɛdza'ge'
now once more	they us have prepared a feast (carrion)	they of the earth
o·nɛh ai·'	djǫki'yaswaye·ni	da'·ne'ho
now again	they for us have put up a feast (they have spread carrion)	so that's all

Now once more the people of the earth have remembered us with a feast. Now again they have put up a feast in our honor.

Having heard this, now the Dew Eagles will be expectant. All they will need is the fumes of the Indian tobacco to bear the message up to them, for them to hear their own songs and ritual. They have great esteem [hodiwanǫ''gǫ'—they have great respect] for their own songs and ceremony. This is why the performance of the ritual pleases them. Thus they are pleased and are then willing in return to help the person have good luck.

Carrion ['tgaya'swayɛ'] is the sustenance on which birds of prey—eagles, hawks, ravens, and buzzards—feed. The pig's head or a bear's head symbolizes the carrion. So when the members say Ga'·' ga'·' [high tone] they are imitating the birds, particularly the crows and buzzards, making all that fuss as they hover feasting on this carrion.

COMMENT

Membership.—A summary of biographical experiences gives two general methods of joining the Eagle Society: (1) By cure, or (2) through a dream. The child's parents decide that the ritual may help their sick child, or, the child is sick and they consult a clairvoyant. The patient may dream himself, or someone may dream that the ritual will help the person.

Clairvoyants.—A clairvoyant (hɛne'·yǫ') (male), (yɛne·'yǫ')(female) divines dreams for a fee. Some use tea or cards, and others employ certain herbs and put them under their pillows on going to sleep. Others perform divination by water scrying.

Sarah Snow (gadji''djɛ's) of the Bear Clan at Allegany, a much consulted clairvoyant (yɛne·yǫ') and herbalist (pl. 19), prescribes the Eagle Dance ritual for the following illnesses: "It is good for a cough and high fever, 104°, this is sometimes accompanied by nervousness; or the patient may be afflicted by a general weakness and lassitude which the Eagle causes; sometimes they fever, sometimes they cough, and sometimes they merely have violent headaches; sometimes it takes the form of lumbago. The patient gets well when he puts up the Eagle Dance."

Dreams.—To have the Eagle Dance ritual, the person usually has a dream of a bird flying around, or of one down on the ground, or sees chickens. The birds frequently have blood on their faces. Then the clairvoyant knows the sickness is caused by the Dew Eagles.

RITUAL EQUIPMENT

Members of the Eagle Society are supposed to own a bundle containing two feather fans, two small gourd rattles, a single feather, a whistle, and a package of sacred tobacco. They also should own a striped pole and a striking stick. Sometimes, as in the case of He-strikes-the-rushes and his father, a family may possess a bundle in common. When not in use, the bundle is hung up near the ceiling or in the rafters; and the pole, if not stood carelessly in the corner, is carefully laid overhead on the drying racks. However, bundles are frequently borrowed and loaned, and sometimes an old man of the opposite moiety promises to make a bundle for a young boy on the other side.

The bundle (dega'hudje·nyǫ, or preferably ga·'ho'·shɛ' or 'ohgwai'-shɛ') has a wrapper of newspaper or flour sacking, although anciently it was buckskin. I am uncertain as to whether a wildcat skin was ever used.

The Seneca feather fans are unlike the ordinary splayed calumet fans in that the feathers are invariably parallel to the handle. Each fan (gane'·'ɛ') has a wooden handle of no particular length, but is usually three spans of the hand and extended thumb (approximately 18 inches). The handle is sometimes striped with red dye. Snorer said, "The shaft (of ash or white hickory or soft maple) must be long enough for the handle to extend beyond the quills of the feathers. Put a string on it. There are three or four feathers, for the eagle's feathers are wide. The dancer holds the fan in his left hand and the rattle in his right." Hemlocks-lying-down has a bundle containing two fans of four eagle feathers suspended parallel with their quills pointed toward the handle (pl. 20,1).[44]

The feathers are attached with small silver rivets to two sets of red ribbons which pass over the shaft and down behind the feathers. The attachments have been mended with thread. Tufts of small

[44] Fans and rattles exhibited in the American Museum of Natural History were made at Coldspring by Hemlocks-lying-down (Cat. Nos. 50/62662, b, and c; also 50/5552, maker unknown).

Harriet Maxwell Converse donated to the American Museum of Natural History a fan which appears to be an Eagle Dance fan but with the following legend is strongly suggestive of the calumet fan. Four fans are frequently used in an Eagle Dance.

Iroquois Flag of Truce

"This is a flag of truce. The Indians say it is about two hundred years old. The feathers are those of the wild goose. The little bag attached to this flag is charm medicine. This was obtained on the Cattaraugus Reservation from an old Iroquois woman, or rather from her son. She had *four* of them. The story is that it was used by the captives of a nation who were exterminated by the Iroquois, evidently Western people. The women used these after the battle. It was the custom of the Indians to mutilate the dead captives; but when the women appeared on the field with these flags in their hands, waving them slowly, the Indians let them carry back as many of the dead as they wanted, perhaps a chief.

"The women would creep along with their little one, trembling, and the Indians never refused them their dead. That is, the women belonging to the captives would thus come. This was the flag of the enemy, but it was really a flag of truce. The bag of medicine is supposed to be a charm to prevent any disaster or to protect the bearer." (American Museum of Natural History, Accession Records: No. 50. 209; italics mine.—W. N. F.) [Caswell, 1892, p. 252.]

feathers are wound on the shaft at the tips and the middle of the shafts. The orientation of the feathers suggests the Hidatsa method of twining the feathers of an eagle's tail into fans to be carried home (Wilson, 1928, p. 170, fig. 11, b).

The ceremonial number four is common, but upward of five or six feathers, half of an eagle's tail, are also common. A bundle in the New York State Museum has fans of six feathers (pl. 20,2); and another set which I photographed while studying collections there in 1940 (New York State Museum Cat. No. 36876) measures 20 inches long and features a decorated thong which is wound with dyed and flattened porcupine quills and tufted with red horse-tail tips, as were originally the ends of the four eagle feathers which depend on buckskin thongs to which the quill is fastened by tapering it and tucking in the pointed end. The barb end is knotted. The wands are further decorated by feathers and ribbons. Judging by the materials and workmanship, this set of fans may be quite early and possibly came from the Plains. Converse and Parker illustrated fans, probably from Cattaraugus, having six feathers pointed proximally and bound with vertical ribbons; the distal ends of the wooden shafts are tufted, but the sticks do not appear to be striped (Converse and Parker, 1908, p. 73). However, a drawing, in the same publication, by Jesse Cornplanter, depicts four dancers facing each other in couples. Each dancer is holding a gourd rattle in his right hand and a fan of four feathers in the left hand, and the feathers are oriented proximally (Converse and Parker, 1908, p. 71). An example of five-feathered Eagle Dance fans from the Seneca comes from the collecting activity of S. A. Barrett at Cattaraugus for the Milwaukee Public Museum. I saw these specimens during a visit to the Museum in August 1947. They feature wooden shafts, and suspension by two ribbons, and a cord threaded through the quills. Rattles originally accompanied the fans (Milwaukee Public Museum, Cat. No. 24,064–5/6084; and personal correspondence, W. C. McKern, October 2, 1947). (Pl. 22.)

Sometimes turkey (o's'o·n) feathers are employed, mixed with those of the wild goose (ǫ'nga·k). A Tonawanda informant mentioned partridge feathers. White chicken feathers were used at Restingsky's anniversary. A Cayuga fan, which Dr. Frank G. Speck collected at Sour Springs, Ontario, has 60 osprey feathers suspended at intervals vertically by their quills (Speck, 1949, pl. X, A–B). The New York Onondaga also employ this type of fan. Some old fan handles are elaborately carved, and I suspect that their form was suggested by old shotgun cleaners.

A small rattle (gasta'wɛ'shɛ') is attached to the handle of each fan by a loop. It is usually a miniature gourd or pumpkin, or a tiny horn rattle. Tiny folded bark rattles (Parker, 1913 b, p. 124) are not now used at Coldspring. Hemlocks-lying-down, a careful craftsman, specializes in making gourd rattles. He selects a stick of dry white pine and whittles it down to the diameter of the cut-off gourd. He cuts a flange to receive the gourd, and trims the distal end of the stick and cuts it off where it protrudes from a hole in the end of the gourd. He bores a hole through the handle tip to receive a wooden cotter pin, which secures the gourd to the handle. Small seeds are inserted in the shell for percussion. Then the handle is waisted by cutting from the shoulder which supports the flange and from the proximal end of the handle both ways toward the middle. When the handle loosens, a few turns of string at either end of the gourd will tighten it.

The society used to employ a whistle (ga·'gɛnda'), which was identical to that now used by the Little Water Company, and it was kept in the bundle. Eagle wing-bone whistles were formerly used during the sessions to renew the strength of the Little Water Medicine, but both He-strikes-the-rushes and Long-horns deny that such a whistle was used in the Eagle Dance.[45] Hemlocks-lying-down does not know about eagle wing-bone whistles, but he has added a bamboo whistle to his bundle since I photographed its contents in 1933. He calls it (gano'·da'); it is 17.5 inches long, and has one hole and no stops. "Yendi has one and I have one. Someone is appointed to blow it at the beginning of every song." The note is shrill and the whistle is blown so that it oscillates between octaves. This represents the eagle's cry as it wheels in flight. "Whenever you hear it during the songs, that's what it means" (collection of M. H. Deardorff, Warren, Pa.; personal communication, May 9, 1951). The whistle is placed together with other bundle contents at the invocation.

Members provide a twined corn-husk tray filled with native tobacco (*Nicotiana rustica* L.) for the invocation and for members to smoke. The Seneca scatter the seed in their dooryard, and the tobacco plant comes up and then seeds itself from year to year. They seldom cultivate it. During the middle of the summer they pick the leaves and thread them on strings, which are suspended above the stove until the tobacco dries, and then it is crumbled and put away for smoking and for tobacco offerings. They call it genuine tobacco (oyɛ'gwa'ǫ·we).

The society used to employ a striking pole (gane''gwä'e·' ge'ǫda') or crotched pole (gaya''ihdo·t) at Coldspring. This was cut from the sycamore tree, and it was peeled and striped red, like the fan handle, but counterclockwise from lower left to upper right (pl. 21). They beat the pole with a striking stick (yɛne'gwä'e·sta' ga''nya'), or simply "stick" (ga''nya') which was similarly striped. The pole was above

<hr>

[45] Parker (1923, p. 255) illustrated the one having a single hole, no stops, and a cord and package of sacred tobacco attached.

the height of a man; and the beater, which was provided with a loop for hanging it on the forked pole, was of a convenient length. Just now poles have become obsolete, and canes have supplanted beaters at Coldspring; but at Tonawanda even the cane has gone out, and a speaker merely stamps his foot to stop the song.

Snorer commented, "There is no striking stick in War Dance; only in Eagle Dance. That is why in War Dance and Striking-a-stick Dance, frequently two or three speakers can strike at the same time. [This seemed amusing to him.] Each thinks he has the floor and he commences speaking."

The striking pole and beater, which is passed by the conductor, serves to regulate the sequence of speakers. The amusing dilemma of several speakers talking at once occurs now at Tonawanda in Eagle Dance where the striking stick passed by the conductor has gone out of use. Pounding on the wall with a stick survives among the Oneida of Wisconsin (Ritzenthaler, 1950, p. 38).

The singers of the Eagle Dance employ the water drum and horn rattle which provide the tempo for nearly all Iroquois dance music. Eagle Dance requires a small high-pitched drum, but the size of the rattles is unimportant. The water drum is definitely old with the Iroquois (Potherie, 1753, vol. 3, pp. 24–25; Lafitau, 1724, vol. 1, p. 193; Colden, 1902, vol. 1, p. xxii; Zeisberger, 1912, p. 18). But references to the horn rattle appear only in the recent source material; and He-talks-fast, of the Beaver Clan at Coldspring, has heard that a cylindrical bark rattle preceded the horn rattle, which seems to be of western provenience. I counted a dozen water drums at Coldspring, made by Corn-husker, Hemlocks-lying-down, Snorer, and Clarence White (pl. 23). Corn-husker and Hemlocks-lying-down also make horn rattles. The latter always has a dozen and he hates to part with them, but he brings them to the singers' meetings. Corn-husker seldom has any rattles. He always sells them. Hemlocks-lying-down introduced the waisted octagonal handle from Cattaraugus (pl. 24, a, b). Long-horns, at Newtown, however, prefers squat thick rattles with shorter octagonal handles which are waisted in the middle. Hemlocks-lying-down dyes the heads of his horn rattles red, and his rattles are as unmistakable to a Seneca singer from Coldspring, Tonawanda, Newtown, or even Grand River, as a genuine Stradivarius violin is to a violin expert. However, Corn-husker's rattles differ little from the run of the mill.

The Seneca stripe their sacred religious paraphernalia with a rare red pigment ('o·'gwɛ''shɛ·). He-strikes-the-rushes mentioned it, but only Snorer had any knowledge of its provenience. Snorer has heard that it was derived from a rock (possibly hematite) which was found in a certain face-paint (gagwɛ'šo') mine. It was a powdered rock which they used extensively, as late as a generation ago, at Cattaraugus for striping fan handles, the signal pole, and the striking stick.

Red paint, usually hematite, occurs in old Iroquois graves (Parker, 1922, vol. 1, pp. 424–427). Harrington and Parker found red pigment in graves on the Silverheels site (ibid., p. 227).

David Zeisberger speaks of wampum belts being smeared with red cinnabar as a sign of war, and states that the same pigment was used for dye and face paint. Men sometimes painted their whole head red, again half red and half black, and women painted a round red spot on each cheek (Zeisberger, 1910, p. 87).

Hulbert, the editor of Zeisberger's History of the North American Indians, writes: "A yellow ochre, found near Muskingum, when burnt, made a rich red paint, which Indians came from many miles to obtain. Vermilion River in Ohio derived its name from the clay there obtained for painting" (Zeisberger, 1910, p. 255). Vermilion was a favorite item in the lists of Indian presents from the mid-eighteenth century (Jacobs, 1950, pp. 47–48).

Pokeberries, bloodroot, and hemlock bark, when boiled, were also sources of red dye (Waugh, Ms., 1912).

RITUAL ORGANIZATION

SELECTING FUNCTIONARIES

Like every other organization in Iroquois society, the Eagle Dance Society has administrative functionaries who are appointed for the occasion. Among the Seneca, the recipient (ho'dɛ's) or the sponsor (hodɛ'ša·ni·; hodɛ'šo') selects a man from the other moiety to serve as messenger (hadja'swas) and later to conduct the ritual (hasde'i'stha'). The conductor is usually a near relative or perhaps a friend, and he should be a member. He is responsible for the ritual, appoints all the functionaries, and issues the invitations. The roles of sponsor and conductor fulfill an ancient Iroquoian custom (Thwaites, 1896–1901, vol. 6, p. 279; vol. 10, p. 181; vol. 23, p. 125). Erecting the pole and displaying bundle contents was the Seneca custom, with minor variations between Allegany and Cattaraugus communities.

At Coldspring, Jonas Crouse, an old man of the Hawk Clan, remembers that his grandfather put up Eagle Dance every fall before he went hunting. When Twenty-canoes (Bear Clan) was a boy, he remembers that his people set up the striped signal pole before the house and attached the wands and rattles to notify the Dew Eagle that the people were about to address him. Later on they abandoned setting up the pole and merely hung the fans and rattles on the front of a dwelling.

There was a special tobacco invocation for displaying the bundle, and according to Long-horns (Deer Clan) at Newton, the bundle contents were sometimes displayed to bring rain.

Chauncey Warrior, a Cayuga of the Turtle Clan at Coldspring, remembers how it was done at Plank road, Cattaraugus Reservation, before 1900.

"The morning before a meeting, the pole was erected outside the house and the fans and rattles attached to it, as a notice to passers-by that a meeting would convene there that evening. The priest burned tobacco."

He-strikes-the-rushes, in his account of joining the society (see p. 127), specified that the fans were oriented east and west, that the rattles and the beater were hung on the pole, and that a tobacco invocation accompanied the ritual of erecting the pole and displaying the bundle contents. However, Hemlocks-lying-down, also from Cattaraugus, asserts that the package of tobacco which was to be used for the invocation was hung on a prong of the forked pole (pl. 21), and that the notifier did not burn tobacco when he set up the pole.

"They erected the pole early in the morning, and everyone knows that they are going to have Eagle Dance today or at night. But the messenger goes from house to house just the same to tell them what time to meet. Otherwise, people would not know what they were supposed to do. The messenger says to this one, 'Go sing,' to another, 'Take your costume down there and dance,' (and pointing with his head and protruded lips) 'There is a feast over there, go there toward night.' " He denies displaying the bundle for rain.

Snorer, who was also raised at Plank road, Cattaraugus, speaks of having a messenger for the members of each moiety, which is consistent with the Cattaraugus pattern of moiety separation and with the ceremonial practice at Coldspring of appointing runners from each moiety to notify its members that a festival is going forward at the longhouse (Fenton, 1936 b, p. 14). Snorer also says that the sponsor erected his own pole and displayed the bundle.

I have to put up that society myself. I go tell *two* fellows of different clans, who are of each side [moiety] to notify the people. They gather the singers, the dancers, and speakers. They must secure *two* old fellows to speak first: the first speaker [hatha′ha′] to make the thanksgiving address to our Creator that we are living and the second to notify the Eagles by burning tobacco. Their clan does not matter, but they must be older men because young folks don't understand how to do this.

The messenger [hadja′swas] goes from house to house [hano′ndi·′ta′] notifying the members to gather.

Meanwhile, I must put up quite a mess of corn soup with a hog head boiled in it, to pass around when they get through so they can bite like crows [eǫdiga′hga·′] crying ga′·′ga′·′ like crows (which they are).

Early in the morning, when the sponsor [hodɛ′ša·ni·] first decides to put up a meeting, he erects a pole before his house and hangs the two fans and the rattles, the drum, a rattle, and the beater on the top of the pole where anyone passing may see it and know they are going to have a dance there that night. The sponsor erects the pole and displays the bundle, and the "notifier" [hadja'swas] takes down "the things" and carries them in and places them near the hearth where the priest will burn tobacco.

At Cattaraugus where I come from, they use the pole and striking stick, but here at Allegany they do not use it. The pole was erected early in the morning as a place to hang the fan. It is brought in at night for the meeting. [He illustrated how a speaker would support the pole with his left hand and strike it with the beater held in his right hand.] Frequently, they fastened the pole to the ceiling. In olden times, they planted a pole in the ground, like the war post. [However, Snorer had never heard an instance of its being struck down to end a meeting.] [Stone, 1841, pp. 43–45.]

I have no comparable data on organization of Eagle Society in Canada.

INVITATIONS

The conductor issues the invitations among the Seneca. He selects a drummer as first singer (hadɛ'no·tha'), usually from the moiety opposite the recipient, and a second singer who helps sing (hadɛnową''ase·'), from the other moiety to shake the horn rattle. He asks two or four boys to dance, selecting them equally from each moiety.

The headman [messenger] goes to the members' lodges and notifies them of their duties at the meeting accordingly.

If they are only to preach or talk, he will say: "You are chosen to go strike the stick [to talk, 'esǫga'·t 'ɛsne'gwä'eš'o''nǫ']."

"You are chosen to go hit the pole and talk—and give out presents when finished—" and he designates the time and place of meeting.

If the person is requested to sing, the headman will say: "You are chosen to sing for the Eagle [striking pole] Dance ['esǫgä'·t gane''gwä'e·' 'ɛshadɛno'danǫ']." This man will be the first singer.

When he reaches the dwelling of the second singer, he shall say: "You are chosen to assist in singing the Eagle Dance ['eso'gä·t gane''gwä'e·' 'ɛsadɛnową'-ase'·nǫ']."

ARRANGING THE MEETING

Most meetings are anniversaries of former cures; a member puts up a meeting every year lest his sickness return.

The person must put up a meeting every year, or get someone to put it up for him, otherwise his original affliction will return.

It is a matter of keeping in the good grace and in good standing with the other charm animals. This brings good luck. It is like paying one's dues in a society. [He-strikes-the-rushes.]

Frequently they sing the songs for a father and his son, as they did for Wood-eater and his son during the winter of 1934, or a mother and her daughter, who may be remnants of a family who once celebrated it together.

It is medicine for someone who is sick. Someone becomes ill and that bird is causing the sickness, and the nature of the disease is such that it will affect his legs. Once a (person) has been cured by this society, he should have a meeting at his house once a year, whether or not he is ill. [SRE.]

The host may ask the conductor to select a priest (hadɛ'nhi) or tobacco thrower (hayɛ''gontwas), or he may designate his choice. At Coldspring it is the priest's duty to give thanks (ganǫ'·nyǫk) to all the spirit-forces, an address which must precede all meetings, and "put tobacco on the fire" while making the invocation. The host furnishes the tobacco and provides the feast by having his woman or sister make corn soup and boil the pig's head which he has procured. Pork has now entirely replaced the flesh of game animals in those medicine feasts. The cook used to be of the opposite moiety.

Members should have bundles, but frequently a bundle is borrowed. The conductor often provides his own. Hemlocks-lying-down who acted as ritual manager for Francis Bowen's meeting frequently furnishes his own bundle when he conducts the ritual.

A new member usually borrows a bundle the first time. After that, they get somebody to give it to him. The other day Walter Jimmerson's wife came here about a meeting for her daughter. I had an extra set of [dancers'] rattles. I gave them to her, and Great-night, my son, made the fans. This is the second time [the first meeting following the cure]. Now they will put it up again soon so people will know they have the rattles to use forever.

This meeting is for her youngest daughter and herself. They are Heron Clan. [They came to members of the opposite moiety; a Turtle and a Wolf.] We just thought we would give it to them. You see the first time [they held a meeting] they used my fans. During the meeting, I told the old lady [she is about forty] that I would give her a pair of rattles. Then, after the next song, Great-night got up and said, "I will make the fans." Now after they get the fans and rattles, they will put it up again. That is the second time [their first celebration meeting].

At Coldspring, the feast is hulled white corn soup (ono'hgwa') with a hog head boiled in it. "They formerly used deer and bear heads, and pig was used when the game animals became scarce." The member also has to provide presents to be distributed after the speeches. "We used to give away fried cakes, cookies, and 'wheels' of boiled corn bread at Cattaraugus. They also used tobacco. It is not important so long as the dancers get something." Now they give soda crackers and apples.

The woman who is appointed to cook takes about six quarts of shelled white corn and leaches it with sifted wood ashes by boiling it twice in an iron kettle over a fire of hardwood and pitch pine. Then it is washed three times in a twilled splint washing basket, or an old pack basket that happens to be handy (pls. 25, 26). The hulled corn is now placed in the larger kettle and boiled with pieces of salt pork and the hog's head, and a few red pole beans are added

for flavor. They ordinarily cook outdoors in summer to avoid
excessive heat in the house. Corn-husker cut the necessary forked
poles of iron wood, and since his wife could never remember where
she left the pothooks, he ingeniously tied one end of a green hickory
withe to the kettle bail with an overhand knot, and a few deft turns
about the iron-wood travis suspended the kettle at the desired height.
The kettle simmers during the afternoon, and is then set aside until
the feast. Indoors, soup is ordinarily made in a wash boiler (Waugh,
1916, p. 90; Parker, 1910, p. 74).

MOIETY PATTERNING

The pattern of reciprocal services between moieties finds its
expression both in the selection of personnel and in their spatial
arrangement. A problem suggested by ridiculing members of the
opposite phratry is the relative priority of the sibs and the dual
division. Competition between moieties is also a socially sanctioned
way of draining off aggression directed at the in-group, as in the
Bowl Game, ceremonial Lacrosse, and in clan joking, which became
quite intense when the Iroquois could no longer take up the war
path and take it out on the Cherokee or some other tribe.

Seneca society is divided into eight exogamous sibs, which are in
turn grouped into two phratries, or moieties, of four matrilineal
clans each. The clans are not ordinally ranked, and enumeration
usually commences with the clan of the speaker and proceeds to the
rest in his moiety. Then the speaker refers to the clans "on the
other side," naming them in any order.

Moiety I:	Moiety II:
Deer	Bear
Snipe	Wolf
Heron	Beaver
Hawk	Turtle

Nomenclature and order of listing are somewhat arbitrary. The
order does not include my estimate of relative power but follows
Morgan's order of ranking. The Bear Clan has perhaps the greatest number of active functionaries in the Coldspring Longhouse, but
Beaver and Turtle are the largest clans; Heron and Hawk in the first
moiety. The moiety numbers are only convenient. He-strikes-the-
rushes believes the listing of the second moiety at Newtown Longhouse should read—

Wolf
Turtle
Bear
Beaver

They used to say that the Wolves are the dominating clan, and the Snipes in
the other moiety.

At Tonawanda Longhouse, they speak of the two moieties as the "four fireplaces" and the "five chimneys." Their order of importance, both in reference to numbers and political power, is: Turtle, Wolf, Bear, Beaver; and in the other phratry: Snipe, Hawk, Deer, Heron, and Eel; but the proper order of enumeration follows the enumeration of sachems on the Condolence Roll Call which recognizes reciprocal functions of the two halves: Turtle, Snipe; Turtle, Hawk; Bear, Snipe; and Snipe, Wolf (Morgan, 1901, vol. 2, pp. 214–215; Fenton, 1936 b, pp. 18–20; 1950, p. 57; 1951 a). "The people of one moiety call themselves by a term radically the same as 'siblings.' They call the members of the opposite moiety by a term whose stem is 'cross cousins.' Two similar officials, of opposite moieties, are spoken of as if they were a pair of cousins, or reciprocates" (Fenton, 1936 b, pp. 18–19).

In the evening of an Eagle Dance, the guests convene at their host's home and sit at random on benches and planks ranged round the wall. Women usually sit apart. Frequently a woman may be seen peering in from an adjoining room. The conductor who is invariably of the other moiety from the host, places the singers together at one side of the room, usually in the middle. The dancers face each other, or sit together. Sometimes when two persons combine to sponsor the meeting, and they are of opposite moieties, there are two dancers from each moiety who sit in pairs facing each other, but moiety alinement is diagonal.

$$X \qquad)$$
$$) \qquad X$$

If any two functionaries are of the same side (moiety), the conductor is *supposed* to borrow one from his moiety, and set him over on the other side, and later return him to his own clan with thanks when he has completed his service. It is not always done. At the meeting the conductor appoints a whooper, gift custodian, and men from each moiety who are to make presentation speeches before giving the wands and rattles to the dancers in their own moiety. These roles may be assigned when, as messenger, the conductor notifies the members when and where to meet and what is expected of them individually.

At Coldspring, it is the food distributor's duty to make the first speech after the presentation of the fans. He has no direct charge of the gifts, or basket of crackers, beyond his first speech. From this point each speaker chooses his own offering, depending on his whim.

Parker writes of the Newtown meetings:

The membership is divided into two classes by phratryship . . . . In the dance the members divide and stand opposite each other according to phratry, the animals opposite the birds. Two dancers from each phratry are chosen, and one singer from each. [Parker, 1913 b, p. 124.]

But at Coldspring, only a semblance of moiety seating occurs when Hemlocks-lying-down, who grew up in Newtown, conducts the ceremony. He and Snorer were constantly being accused of altering all Coldspring rituals to fit the Newtown pattern.

Djidǫ'gwas has heard old men discussing the problem of moiety patterning. They said that it was not fundamental, that it came later. When there are two dancers, preferably one should represent each phratry. Sometimes dancers are of the same phratry. My understanding of his explanation disagrees with Hemlocks-lying-down: A speaker of the first moiety should present the fan and rattle to the dancer from the opposite moiety, who sits across the room, and vice versa; a speaker of the second moiety reciprocates.

Sometimes we have four dancers at Coldspring meetings. Then the conductor gives the beater first to a speaker of my phratry who presents the fan to a dancer of the opposite moiety a (2).

Then a speaker of that phratry is appointed to present a fan and rattle to the dancer in my moiety, b (at 3). Now a second speaker of my phratry presents a fan and rattle to the other dancer of the opposite phratry, c (at 4). Then a last speaker of that phratry gives the last fan and rattle to the last dancer (at 1).

Or, he said, the presentation may follow from 1 to 2, 2 to 1; 3 to 4, and 4 to 3.

Hemlocks-lying-down is quite sure that Djidǫ'gwas and I have this mixed up. Explaining the moiety alinements with green and red apples, he said:—

Hawk is sick in your phratry. He gets a man of the other side, like me a Turtle, to take charge. Now when Hawk is sick, Turtle "strikes."

$$1(\qquad X4$$
$$2x \qquad)3$$

1. A speaker of the other side from the sponsor gives the fan to the dancer on his own side.
2. A speaker for the sick moiety presents a fan to the dancer on his own side.
3. Now a speaker of the opposite moiety presents a fan to the dancer in his own moiety.
4. Lastly, a speaker, for the sick phratry, presents the last fan to a dancer representing the sick one's side.

The singer must be of the same phratry as the conductor, the opposite side from the sick; his helper may be of the sick side, or he may be of the other side; it is preferable that the singers be of opposite sides. If you can't get anybody then they are both on the same side.

Spatial separation of the moieties into a dual division was not familiar to Coldspring informants. One had seen it years ago at Newtown Longhouse; another seemed unfamiliar with the arrangement entirely; and he remarked that if they divided into moieties, the custom must have changed recently at Newtown, after he left there. Coldspring sources deny that one moiety makes fun of the other. "Anyone may make fun of anyone else." Nor were they familiar with the custom of ridiculing one's father's clansman, which He-strikes-the-rushes described.

Snorer, however, who also came from Newtown, knew about the pattern of spatially divided moieties.

There was never room in a private dwelling. The conductor, singers, etc., must be of moiety opposite the one who puts up the dance, and the (2) dancers are of each moiety. In the olden days at Cattaraugus, when they met in the longhouse, they say they divided as in the Bowl Game, but not now-a-days.

Snorer never saw spatial separation. There has been no spatial arrangement according to moieties within his memory.

But years ago at Cattaraugus, the cousins sat facing each other: The men of five clans sat on one side; those of the four clans sat on the other, but lately this has been abandoned. The Seneca brought this [pattern] from Buffalo Creek Reservation [1840] to the old settlement at Newtown.

Similarly, raillery is said to follow the moiety pattern at Newtown.

The speeches are usually in praise of one's own clan and in derision of the opposite phratry. At the close the speakers all apologize for their clannish zeal, and say, as if everyone did not know it, that their jibes were intended only as jests. (Parker, 1913 b, p. 124.)

But anyone may be a target for ridicule in the Coldspring meetings, even one's clansman.

Snorer had heard of patterned moiety joking.

They had a quarrel between the clans. They talked rougher and rougher until they fight. That is why they stop. Now we only talk peace. We pray that it will be a help to the sick one. There is no more fun in gane''gwā'e·'.

One could joke, saying whatever he wanted to, about someone in the opposite phratry or his own, or else himself. Speakers can make fun of anyone whom they know to be good fellows. Some get mad awfully easy. If I [were about to] make fun on the other party, [and] if I know he is cross, I know I can't make fun of him, but [that] I have to speak straight words of peace.

Djidǫ'gwas gets mad easily. He is a good joker, though, but when they come to him, it is very different. He likes to make fun of others, but when it comes back to him, he gets mad. That won't do. It shows in his face and he quits striking.

It does not matter whom one makes fun of, particularly in the same clan, but often I make fun of someone in another clan. One tells jokes and funny stories to make people laugh; they are all the same people, only their clans are different. "I am Eagle [Hawk], my daughter-in-law is Turtle. It makes no difference."

Ceremonial ridicule along moiety lines suggests several possibilities concerning the development of Iroquois social structure. Moiety ridicule may be only native theory which was overridden, as prevailing patterns are now disregarded, in practice. Moiety ridicule possibly derives from the general pattern of reciprocal services between moieties which may have diffused to the Seneca independently of the clans which they embrace. We have the testimony of two informants, Wood-eater and Djidǫ'gwas, that arranging the personnel of medicine societies to permit the expression of the pattern of reciprocal services between moieties came after the introduction of the ceremony. Reciprocal moiety functions may have arisen in connection with moiety exogamy, or they may have colored the older clan exogamy. Morgan, Hewitt, and Goldenweiser have declared for the moiety as the original exogamic unit. Internal evidence leans both ways. There is a tendency to choose "a friend" for a child among his father's clansmen, and it is also preferable for "friends" to be of opposite moieties. Custom requires the donor of a miniature talisman, the dream guesser, to be of the opposite moiety from the dreamer to whom he presents the gift making him a "friend." One informant from Newtown, where ridicule between moieties has been reported, claims that it is customary to ridicule one's father's clansman, although no other informant has concurred; and several informants have described a joking relationship between a man and woman whose fathers were clansmen. If moiety exogamy once prevailed, such a joking relationship would exist between children of the same moiety whose fathers were clansmen in the other moiety. If the custom of ridiculing one's father's clansmen were extended to all members of the other moiety, which would include one's father's clansmen and one's cross-cousins, we have a possible explanation for the Newtown custom of intermoiety ridicule. One calls members of clans of the opposite moiety cousins. If one conducted a joking relationship with the children of one's father's sisters, who would then be of the opposite moiety, by extension all the members of the other phratry would be fit subjects for ridicule.[46] Also, if the custom of making dream objects was once performed by one's father's clansmen, it may later have been extended to the other moiety. As moiety exogamy disintergrated and the clans remained as the primary exogamic unit, outside of the maternal lineage, as they may have been originally and which is the case today, ridicule was extended to members of one's own phratry.

The internal evidence for the clans as the primary exogamic unit is just as convincing. The maternal family is the true kindred group, but lineage is not reflected in the kinship system by grouping the female members of one's father's maternal family with the father's sister, as among the Creek. The clans are composed of several maternal families. The irregular distribution of titles and clans among the

---

[46] I am indebted to the late J. N. B. Hewitt for this observation.

nations of the League and the irregular alinement of clans with moieties all point to the multiple origin of clans. Clans were formed by adopting women of other tribes; and clans have given rise to clans by fission. The moieties, moreover, are nameless among the Seneca. Maternal families compose clans which are grouped into moieties and these are primarily ceremonial divisions. Since much of my evidence denies the reality of moiety exogamy and patterned moiety joking, I am inclined to consider the possibility that the clan was the primary exogamic unit and the individual was the primary joking unit, and entertain the possibility that moiety influence may have marshaled clan exogamy just as it did interphratry joking for a time, and then disappeared.

The old Newtown Eagle Dance formation, with the moieties opposite each other, bears a striking similarity to the formation of an intertribal Calumet Dance of the Hako type. The Seneca Eagle Dance apparently had its beginnings among the Seneca band who settled on Cattaraugus Reservation, and there it reached its most elaborate development. If the Seneca Eagle Dance is derived from the Calumet Dance of the Hako type, it could have reached the Seneca at some intertribal meeting down the Great Lakes, or a western captive could have introduced it among the Seneca. The already existing pattern of reciprocal services between moieties and the two halves competing in athletic and gambling contests made a convenient substitute for the two tribes which negotiate the Calumet Dance. Whereas among the Prairie tribes one tribe honors its neighbor, among the Seneca one moiety performs for the other.

The priority of the sib or moiety was a burning issue in ethnological theory when I commenced this study, as it was in Parker's time, so I gathered all the information I could get on the subjects of clan and moiety function and carefully tagged each individual with clan label. The data on participation, consequently, enabled me to check native theory against practice. If the data for this monograph are loaded with such intellectual baggage the compelling reason may be ascribed to the climate of sociological theory during the 1930's. In reviewing these same data, some years since, current theory enables me to discern other things. Whatever the origin of Eagle Dance among the Seneca and the other Iroquoian tribes, the ceremony has undergone changes of function within the span of traditional history. At first a war and peace ceremony, by the close of the eighteenth century Indian wars were over, and any contest of bragging on war records was likely to generate internal hostilities which could no longer be projected on an enemy. A wise chief or two pulled down the war post, but the reformer, Handsome Lake, advocated changing the purpose of the rite. Eagle Dance became a Medicine Society, and the speeches aimed afterward to cheer the sponsor. But the Iroquois love contests, and they had a perfectly harmless way of conducting spirited contests within the community and between tribes of the League, without letting their spirits get out of control. Contrast, for example, factions, over which communities split and separate towns arose, with intermoiety rivalry at Lacrosse, in clan joking, and the Bowl Game, which are socially sanctioned and ritually sanctioned methods of releasing aggression without creating permanent rifts. It would seem that for a generation or so during the nineteenth century, the Seneca at Newtown developed intermoiety joking to an elaborate degree at large Eagle Dance meetings held in the longhouse. When it was no longer fashionable or possible to recount war records the men of Newtown raised the tall story to a fine art and started a tradition of joking which, when manifest in other communities by Newtown offspring, was not always appreciated. I believe that these data support a hypothesis recently advanced by Murdock to explain a problem previously noted by Linton (Murdock, 1949, p. 90; Linton, 1936, p. 229).

Still later at Newtown, it is said that intermoiety joking started a quarrel between the clans; and tension, which threatened the internal social structure, coupled with waning numbers of adherents to the longhouse ceremonies, by the end of the century, made it no longer feasible to hold big Eagle Dances at the longhouse. Within the memory of living Seneca, members have entertained the society in their homes, holding an occasional large celebration at the Newtown Longhouse at Midwinter. Today the Eagle Dance ceremonies at Newtown and Coldspring on Allegheny River are scarcely distinguishable.

THE RITUAL PATTERN

The Eagle Dance ritual shares the ceremonial pattern of other medicine societies. The order is: (1) Thanksgiving (ganǫ'·nyǫk) to the spirit-forces from the earth up to the Creator; (2) a specific tobacco-burning invocation directed to the disease-controlling agency who presides over the society; (3) the ritual proper, addressed to the presiding spirits, but with certain concessions to the patient; (4) a symbolic feast of an animal head and corn soup for the participating spirits, which is also recompense to human beings; and (5) a final blessing for all who have come to help out. One may discover this pattern of sequence telescoped many times within a morning of the Midwinter Festival. Even the great longhouse rituals themselves are preceded by a thanksgiving, and frequently terminate with daily feasts and a final blessing on all the celebrants (Fenton, 1936 b, p. 14).

OPENING

Snorer emphasized the importance of the conductor to the correct unfolding of the ritual procedure. His reason for having Eagle Dance in the morning was that a great many speakers employ Handsome Lake's good message which must be spoken before noon.

The first Speaker says, "Now listen," and then proceeds with the thanksgiving prayer [Fenton, 1936 b, p. 14; recorded in text from Wood-eater, 1934; on disk record at Iroquois Conference, 1945; on tape from SRE, 1948]. Then he tells why they have assembled and that they are about to have Eagle Dance. "Now it will go on." He tells who put it up, "he has prepared everything: Corn soup, genuine tobacco, and presents to distribute after speaking [yɛne'gwa''istha'] among the dancers, singers, and speakers. Then he prays to secure help for this person from Dew Eagle that the person may derive his power from him.

TOBACCO INVOCATIONS

The tobacco-burning invocation or prayer is addressed to the Dew Eagle. Etiquette demands that the conductor hand the fans to the priest and assist him by holding the tobacco dish (anciently a twined corn-husk tray), or place it within reach while he is addressing the bird. The prayer must cover a minimum of instances, but within this framework each man's version and manner of delivery varies.

Wood-eater, a proud, self-contained savant, sure of his forms, speaks evenly, but frequently inaudibly, and it is never said of him, as someone remarked of Snorer, "He talks so low, in throwing tobacco on the fire, that no one could hear him, not even the bird." To which the accused replied, "Dew Eagle might become angry if I talked too loudly."

Snorer continued his explanation:

One is not supposed to talk loudly when he puts tobacco. The reason is this: If I tell you something which I want you to do, and I talk loudly, you will be both surprised and mad and say, "He is scolding me." That is why I speak softly.

Further, when I pray or give thanks I speak in a low tone and easy. And preaching is a third [style of] thing and one should speak kindly. There is a reason and it happened long ago.

People are traveling from Cattaraugus to ohi'·o'. On their way they stop to camp over night. There is a young girl in the party and she is lying by the side of the fire, and she has no breath.

The old man went and procured his tobacco pouch, for men always carried tobacco, and he built a small fire, sprinkled tobacco, and whispered to our Creator, asking him to send this girl, his granddaughter, back to earth.

When the girl returned to this earth she told a story. A young woman came after me, saying, "I want you to come after me," and they went together. They went on a smooth path ascending the heavenly road. Finally on their way her leader stopped, saying, "Listen." They hear speaking—like the way I am talking—and it is plainly audible and loud. The words seemed to go by past the place where they are stopping. They understood these loud words. The young woman, her leader, said, "We must return because those words go on to the Creator who will send you back to earth when you reach him."

Thus, she told the old man, on returning, about hearing the loud words which, however, he had only whispered. So he decided it would be best to talk in a low tone, easy and slowly, because, when the smoke arises bearing the message, the tobacco magnifies the words and they appear loud to the Creator. This is why one only whispers when he is making a tobacco invocation at a medicine society meeting. A whisper is loud enough.

This young girl grew to be an old lady and died about sixty years ago [1870]. Like her grandfather, the Cattaraugus people had always talked easy. This vision brought a confirmation for an old habit. It helped the people. Their minds were easy.

Ordinary conversational speech or announcing is entirely too much noise. The spirits do not prefer a scolding fellow. The only time when one should really talk is when he is burning tobacco and making invocation to the Creator at the time the White Dog is sacrificed. They no longer burn the dog.

The tobacco prayer follows the general thanksgiving and it is usually given by the same man. He is *supposed* to be of the opposite moiety to the person who "puts up the meeting." Wood-eater's version was used at both meetings. In the first instance only he stood in the proper relationship to the host.[47]

(1) The priest grasps the fans by their handles in his left hand and sprinkles tobacco on the coals.

The smoke is now rising [from] the genuine tobacco. You [the Dew Eagle] who are soaring [or wheeling] high up above the clouds partake of this tobacco.

(2) Another pinch of tobacco falls on the fire. [Wood-eater omitted this section the first time he dictated the text.]

You also receive tobacco, you who are the leader, you [the giant raven] are gliding across the Earth at a great altitude.[48]

You are also volunteered to notify him [the Dew Eagle] when we are having a meeting.

(3) Again he sprinkles tobacco.

You [the Dew Eagle] who are in league with [the patient] [have accepted him] [listen]. So now he is ready this very night. He has fulfilled everything. He has prepared those things which you requested; they are now ready. They have remembered you. He has set tobacco down for you [on the floor]. He is ready. It is here.[49]

(4) He offers tobacco for the feast.

He has carrion, food for scavengers, lying here, that which was formerly running about the dooryard, especially that part which was preceding [the rest of it] [i. e., the head of a game animal].

---

[47] The following prayer was recorded in text. The English translation is as literal as clarity will permit.

[48] Wood-eater says he is addressing ga'hga'go·wa·' the giant crow (or Raven) who traverses the Earth above the clouds.

"Receive" is rendered in the sense of "accept," or "partake."

[49] Dew Eagle accepted the host to be associated with him in his society. Now the host has fulfilled all the requirements of the various origin myths and his personal dreams. In giving a feast, it is customary for the host to provide tobacco in a twined corn-husk tray, which the headman sets down on the floor after the invocation for the members to smoke.

(5) The pig's head receives tobacco.

That very thing, the part which was protruding [the head and snout]. It will go around [counterclockwise] when they finish singing.[50]

He has provided right here [gifts] to be distributed by the speakers.[51]

He has a kettle on the floor of corn soup. [He omitted to say that it was flavored with pork.] He will thank you with that, when it [the ritual] is finished.

(6) Tobacco is offered to the feast.

So now then, it rests with you. [For] he has fulfilled his part.[52] He has remembered you, you [who] elected him to be associated with. So now then, you are responsible.

(7) The Dew Eagle receives tobacco.
(8) And again:

Now you help him.

(9) Another offering.

Now he has done his duty [literally, he has fulfilled.] You are said to be able to thrust aside all manner of sickness.

(10) Tobacco is offered once more.

So now another thing. [You will arrange it.] He shall be able to walk around on this earth amidst all manner of hazards [misfortune]. [53]

(11) Another pinch of tobacco.

You said you collectively are able to resurrect someone when he is walking into an abyss [nearly in the grave].

(12) His song receives tobacco.

So now your song receives tobacco. He has supplied these things as emblems [the rattles and fans, the contents of the bundle], and they receive tobacco.[54]

(13) Tobacco is given for the drum.

That which regulates your songs [the drum and rattles] receives tobacco, for the ritual will require its use.

It is fulfilled.
So it is finished (da′ne′hoh).

---

[50] Naturally the pig's head precedes the body when it is running. The head is passed to the singers and members during the feast which follows the songs. All ritual circuits are strictly counterclockwise. "One goes around on the right—meaning his right flank is outside as he turns. The other direction is evil."

[51] Crackers will be distributed to the dancers, singers, and principal functionaries. Formerly they gave away boiled white-corn bread, or tobacco.

[52] The patient has fulfilled the requests made by the Dew Eagle in the origin legend. It is now up to the Eagle to fulfill his part of the agreement by curing the patient. The patient has fallen ill at some time, with symptoms which indicate that the Dew Eagle has chosen him his earthly correspondent. He will remain healthy so long as he fulfills his guardian's requests.

[53] Wood-eater says, "This world is full of all manner of misfortunes, bad luck, and accidents (which befall the poor human during his daily perigrinations); with the help of Dew Eagle Man Bowen be able to pass amongst these dangers without injury."

[54] This refers to the contents of the bundle, the rattles and fans as a unit, which the priest holds as he invokes the cloud dwellers, and which are emblematic of the Dew Eagles, and this manipulation in the ceremony is symbolic of their behavior. The red marks on the wand handles are symbolic of the songs. The noise of the rattles symbolizes the birds scratching in the gravel.

Here the priest sometimes sings over the first two songs of the ritual. Snorer says, "There is smoke for your song," then he sings. Djidǫ'gwas used a simpler invocation.

In the origin legend [55] the Dew Eagle told the little boy "When you dance that song gane''gwä'e'', put some tobacco and say:
Partake of the tobacco, cloud dwellers; it is ordained that at this time you receive tobacco, you very Dew Eagles.
So this is what I desire, that this [ritual] of striking do good when it is performed; everything now is ready, even the real tobacco, which is used to plead with; everything will happen for the best and this person will be of good health.
For there is corn soup which is meant for the ceremony; now it is fulfilled; I have everything ready! Let the ceremony of striking a pole commence.
In order that you will think this is true, you the inhabitants of the vapors, therefore we perform the ritual correctly, and we plead with this real tobacco, which we employ [to reach] wherever you are living among the clouds. So this is how far we carry this." [56]

After the prayer is finished, the headman takes the balance of the tobacco and sets it in the middle of the floor. The members pass at will, smoking it in their pipes.

FORM AND CONTENT OF SPEECHES

Descriptions of actual ceremonies show that speeches at the Eagle Dance adhere to a consistent pattern, with minor local variations. Custom prescribes the content of the first speeches; after that a man may ridicule himself or anyone else, preferably a man in the other moiety.

Then the conductor must make ready for the dancers. Everything rests with him. He presents the drum and rattles to the singer and his assistants, and he assigns the presentation of the fans to a speaker in each moiety. At Tonawanda and Newtown a presentation speech is made for the drum. At Newtown the drum is given alone; then the rattles and the fans and rattles are later presented by separate speakers. Fans are no longer used at Tonawanda.

In the drum presentation speech, he says that he was invited to come and present the drum to the singers. At Newtown he used to weave a story of a long journey to a foreign village which he had visited, using the story as an opportunity to expound on the proper conduct of the ritual, the songs, the agility of the dancers who picked up pennies or grains of corn with their teeth. He might say he witnessed the ritual there and that the singers he saw there looked like the very singers who are about to sing on this occasion. [He-strikes-the-rushes.]

Dancers still wear the full dancing costume, which is no longer truly Seneca, but is an adopted Plains "show" costume. They paint a red spot on each cheek, but all the members used to dress for meetings. Snorer says the old costume consisted of leggings, breechcloth, moc-

[55] See his version of the origin legend (p. 83).
[56] Usually only da''ne'hoh is said, which stands for the sentence, meaning "that's all."

casins, headdress with whirling feather, shirt, usually white but sometimes brown. He has never seen them dance stripped to the waist. "They paint a daub on each cheek of red paint." He designated each cheek by marking his in turn with his index finger.

Speakers do not paint their faces, and sometimes dancers do not. In War Dance, dancers paint their faces ad lib, and ribs on their bodies—always red, no other color. Other colors were introduced lately with show work. [Snorer.]

Married men may dance. Dancers need not be unmarried boys. Watching-water remarked that there would be an Eagle Dance that night. I asked whether Two-arrows-flying (Hawk Clan) would dance. Old Snorer laughed. "He can't dance Eagle Dance any more; he has a woman now! He is too young at 17." Snorer was 36 before he got married. "I never thought I would get a woman. My old woman finally came to visit me and she stayed there. We were married then. I was older than she." I inquired whether only virgins may dance. "Yes, married men can dance Eagle Dance, but Two-arrows-flying is too weak now!" Snorer rocked back in his chair to enjoy his joke.

According to Wood-eater, at Coldspring:

The first two men who speak have to be of opposite moities. They present the wands, with rattles attached, to the dancers [representing] . . . their own respective sides.

The whooper cries; the first song commences; and near the end, the first presentation speaker, a man from a moiety other than that of the host, strikes.

According to Snorer,

The speaker says whatever he wishes.

I used to see the best dancers during many years, and I think of one fine dancer, and now I think I see here a man just like him. I have been keeping these fans for many years, and now I give them to that fellow to play with, because he looks about like the one I recall. I have been saving them all these years to present.

This recollection is calculated to stir memories of the past in the minds of his listeners. The speaker may also refer to himself, they will remember him as a great dancer, and there is the additional note of humor. "I give them to that fellow to play with." Fine speakers are chosen to give the ceremony a good start.

"The speaker must be of the same side as the dancer."

Whoop. Song II. and strike: Second fan presentation!

The next speaker repeats about the same thing to his dancer, in the opposite phratry, but he urges him to beat the other dancer. Try the best you can.

After the presentation and introductory remarks, says Wood-eater:

Speeches in the Eagle Dance should follow a set form. One should preach first to the man or woman who is having the meeting, wishing him luck and good health; then one may say anything he wants to about a man in the opposite moiety or about himself.

Djidǫ'gwas says one should say after striking the signal pole:

So now I plead that this ritual of striking the stick, which is taking place, be performed for you; that you may depend on it when you shall travel about the earth; that you shall have good luck as you go to and fro on the earth's surface; that everyone will love this man and that he in turn will love everyone. Thus it is well that you shall have good luck; you will be good to everyone when you are traveling about the earth. Thus it is nice that everyone collectively will be on good terms with this man.

Several informants specified that anyone may talk at these meetings, but one cautioned, "If you talk and are not a member, you might get a dream." In practice all the speakers whom I have observed are members.

After the first speech, one may make a joke (gowɛnowe'hdashɛ'). Sometimes jokes are unintentional, or quite impromptu.

Two-arrows-flying [Hawk Clan] spoke at Fast-talker's [Beaver Clan] once, hoping his host would continue to be well and have many children. He already has five or six kids, so everyone laughed. [SRE.]

Here follow some interesting theoretical observations which, however, are overridden in the meetings for which I have information: "The opposite moiety tells jokes and stories on the other moiety. One does not make fun of a man on his own side."

For a contradiction of the above statement, the reader has but to look at the controversey between Stick-lodged-in-a-crotch (W. C., Snipe Clan) and Corn-husker, who are all of the same phratry, and who ridicule each other at Resting-sky's anniversary.

At Newtown, bragging of traveling is common, or one makes jokes on a friend in the opposite phratry. It is all in good fun.

At Allegany, men used to become very angry with one another. Once Great-elm [Bear Clan] had a meeting. ARE [Heron Clan] [the other moiety] said Great-elm should not go up to Esther Fatty's [Hawk Clan]; then everyone repeated it and enlarged upon it until the host became angry.

In a way this last example both corroborates and denies native theory. The speaker was tormenting a man in the other phratry, but also a woman in his own. Great-elm, although a Faith-keeper in the longhouse, is the object of many practical jokes, originating with children as well as grown-ups. Deficient in speech and intellectual power, he is, nevertheless, a hard and faithful worker about the longhouse. He casts his vote in councils, although he does not talk from the floor. He belongs to a great family, and his good disposition gets him by.

Toward the end of the ritual, when the presents are distributed, the Speaker, who has on his hands what is going on, must say this: he makes an announcement that whoever will strike again must "put up" himself whatever presents he gives away. A speaker must have something to pay when he talks. He can give to the patient or anyone there he chooses.

Again, at the end of the ritual, the Speaker rises. "We are finished with what we had to do." Again he must thank everything which he returned thanks for at the beginning. He thanks those who took part. He bids all goodbye and begs the Great Spirit to tell the Four Persons to protect everyone on the way home. [Snorer.]

THE DANCE AND SONGS

The movements of the dancers symbolize the behavior of the birds as described in the origin legends. The dance and the songs are essentially the same among the three Seneca groups. Minor variations in Canada are described by Kurath. Each song is preceded by a whoop, which the members answer. At Coldspring they appoint a special whooper, but at Tonawanda he is one of the dancers. There are three or four introductory songs before the dance commences on the fourth song at Coldspring, but at Tonawanda there are two introductory songs, and the dance commences in the middle of the third song, when the tempo changes.[57]

The whooper cries. The drummer, or first singer, strikes the drum and, beating vibrato, sings the signature (waheya waheya heyonǫ'). The dancer sways on his chair, looking from side to side, and flutters the fan held in his left hand and shakes the rattle with his right hand; this is the bird on the perch. The singer repeats the signature, and then his helper accompanies him with the horn rattle.

Now the tempo changes to an accented beat (goya heya heyonǫ'). The dancer crouches on the floor and advances in birdlike hops turning from side to side, shaking the fan and rattle with the music. This is the bird advancing toward the meat.

Halfway in the song, once more the drum beats vibrato. Here the dancer charges, weaving his shoulders and vibrating the fan and rattle far out on either side. This movement symbolizes the bird stooping to feed (pl. 28).

Then he raises up and retreats toward his seat; this posture is the eating bird looking around. They used to stoop twice during each song, but now only once. The second time the bird is eating very rapidly. The dance ends with three quick beats which the dancers duplicate with their heels and rattles and return to their chairs. Here the bird returns to its perch. The Seneca dancers must continue until someone strikes. They are frequently interrupted midway in a song. At Grand River, strikers wait until the song stops.

All of the songs are quite similar. They are composed of meaningless words of burden syllables which follow definite patterns in Iro-

---

[57] The reader is referred to Kurath's paper for the analysis of the choreography and the transcription of the music of Eagle Dance, both in its Seneca variants from Coldspring and Tonawanda, and from the Onondaga and Cayuga of Grand River, where she herself observed the ceremony and describes the dance.

quois music. The first song shows a similarity to some of the songs of the Medicine Company. There are some 18 songs in all. At a long meeting, they use each song twice, and then thus frequently omit several. There is a final song, always the same, when the dancers lay down the feather fans (yowadjine'he· gonǫdiya'awe·). "The dancers know that this is the end of the dance."

In the accompanying painting of the Eagle Dance by Ernest Smith of Tonawanda (pl. 27), the four dancers are midway in the song. Frequently an object, such as meat, or corn, or a penny, is placed on the floor, and an agile dancer will pick it up in his mouth without touching either hand to the ground. The women and men are dressed in costumes of the Federal Period, except that the stripe of beads should fall on the instep of the men's leggings. We see the first and second singer, and a speaker who has arisen to strike the forked pole interrupting the dance. At his left are the basket of gifts and a tray of corn bread which speakers present to the dancers and the singers when they have concluded speaking. The matron watches the kettle of soup at the far end of the longhouse, and a few speakers are indicated on the lower berth beneath the observer. The recipient is one of the three men seated on the far bench.

THE FEAST

The conductor has charge of distributing the feast. The following account, obtained from Snorer, supplements my own observations and the testimony of the two Tonawanda informants.

Now the conductor picks up the hog head, saying, "Let us pick like crows, now, you of the medicine company!" [ɛdwa'gahga·' o'·nɛh swatcinǫ'gɛ"shǫ']. Then he passes it to the host first, then the dancers and singers and lastly the crowd. They bite. Some try and get the whole hog. The members are supposed to bite, because the Eagles bite. Years ago, I used to bite it, but now my teeth are no longer strong enough. I support the head with my left hand and pull at it with my right. They cry like crows and clamor for the head if one hovers too long over it.

At the same time the head goes around, the [matron] gives chunks of meat to the officers: To the singer, his helper, the dancers, the headman, the Speaker, and the tobacco burner.

They bring in the kettle of corn soup, our feast (wa·diya'kǫ'), and set it in the middle.

Now the conductor cries, "Ho now, set down your pails" (ha' o'·nɛh dzinǫ'dza'ge'ǫ').

They slide their pails toward the kettle. The recipient, or some relative of the person who is sponsoring the feast, fills the conductor's pail before he fills the other pails. This is etiquette.

Having filled the pails equally, going in a counterclockwise direction, he cries, "Ho now, pick them up, take them away" (ha' o'·nɛh nɛ dǫsadje·k dǫsadinǫ'dzak).

It is all over now. Then he says, "Scatter, go wherever you can find something to pick at!"

This custom of the guests bringing pails to the feast is ancient. It has its antecedents in the old custom of guests bringing their own dishes to a feast and then carrying food home to their women and children (Thwaites, 1896–1901, vol. 6, pp. 279, 281, 285; vol. 24, p. 201; vol. 67, pp. 91–93), a custom throughout the continent east of the Mississippi. However, Iroquois children may not eat feast food until it has first been tasted by their parents.

DOCUMENTARY HISTORY

Having first described the Seneca Eagle Dance at Coldspring on the Allegheny River and having shown how the contents of Eagle Society meetings are affected by participating personalities, I next observed the ceremony at Tonawanda, and then sought comparative data at Onondaga Valley, and on the Grand River in Canada. With these observations on the living culture, social interaction, and personality fulfillment in several localities, I was prepared to discuss the Eagle Dance as a cultural phenomenon, here presenting folklore and traditional history of the Eagle Society, rationalizations of local lore, how informants classify Dew Eagles, and their dream experiences which foretold membership in the Society. I next described the ceremony systematically, employing as the table of contents for that section the ritual program of the ceremony itself; and in this manner a cultural phenomenon is described in terms of its own internal organization. It now remains to place the ceremony and its cultural baggage in its proper historical and ethnographic perspective.

Ethnology among the Iroquois carries Eagle Dance back a century, but traditional history records that about 1800 Handsome Lake, the prophet, altered its purpose from a war and peace ceremony to a medicine society. Thus the process of "upstreaming" takes us back 150 years. Beyond the turn of the nineteenth century there are vague ethnological memories of contacts with tribes "down the Lakes," of war parties that went off to the south and west, and stories that adhere to certain dances, which were brought from other tribes. But the tradition of the Peace with the Cherokee which ended the century-long war with the Southeastern tribes finds confirmation in documentary history. It is one of the most satisfactory aspects of Iroquois ethnohistory that by proceeding upstream against the current of time one can often reach the flood of recorded history and follow it chronologically. Tradition ascribes the Iroquois Eagle Dance to a peace-making ceremony and links it to the names of Southeastern tribes—the Cherokee in particular. The next section endeavors to connect what tradition describes with what history records.

The stream of history has many sources. Besides the stream which reached the Iroquois from the Southeast, another tributary came in from the West. At the mideighteenth century, colonial governors made a valiant attempt to stabilize relations between Indian tribes living on the frontiers of their colonies. For a half century Iroquois war parties had received French encouragement to go out against the "Flatheads," or Catawba. The Catawba took a toll of Iroquois prisoners and Catawba who were not burned lived in several Iroquois settlements. In an effort to straighten out such exchanges of persons the Catawba delegation brought the Calumet Dance to Albany. The other stream of diffusion flowed down the Great Lakes from the Far Indians—Chippewa, Ottawa, Pottawatomi, Fox, Miami, and others of the mobile Central Algonquians. From these nations who came to Oswego and Albany to trade, in years that they denied the French, ceremonies associated with the Calumet reached Onondaga during the first quarter of the century. With this preview of events in mind, let us follow the stream of Iroquois history before exploring the tributaries.

A SURVEY OF THE LITERATURE

Clear-cut descriptions of an Eagle Dance do not appear in the historical literature on the Iroquois before 1850, although several elements in the complex ceremonial pattern which we have described appear in the very earliest sources. I shall take counsel from Cadwallader Colden, who was one of the most considerable minds in the Colonies and was himself concerned with the History of the Five Indian Nations, and relate the "several Transactions in the Words of the Registers" . . . so that "When this is once done, he that shall write afterwards need not act with so much Caution" (Colden (1727), 1937, vol. 9; 1902, vol. 1, p. 1v.).

From 1634 on, one finds descriptions of feasts and the antics of the so-called "confraternities" among the Huron which suggest activities of the modern Iroquois medicine societies, and the two sets of phenomena, although separated by a span of 300 years, share a number of traits and seemingly follow the same ritual pattern (Thwaites, 1896–1901, vol. 10, pp. 175 ff.). But nowhere until 1673, when Marquette encountered the Dance of the Calumet among the Illinois (Thwaites, 1896–1901, vol. 59, pp. 115–119), have I found a record of a ceremony which suggests the crouching eagle dancer shaking a feather fan. The ceremony which came to be called the Calumet Dance, and from which I believe it can be demonstrated that the Iroquois Eagle Dance is an offshoot, was not unknown to the Iroquois of the French period, although they themselves at the time did not celebrate or quite respect the Calumet. The Iroquois had other protocol for greeting strangers, and the Dance of the Calumet rather pertained to the mobile Central Algonquians.

In 1667 an Iroquois chief passed through the Miami, Mascoutens, and Kickapoo villages, "where he was received with the honors of the calumet, and loaded with presents of beaver skins" (Blair, 1911, p. 350). La Potherie, contemporary historian of the savages attached to New France, comments in concluding his chapter that it is notably "useless to make peace with the Iroquois" (ibid., p. 351).

From earliest times Iroquois chiefs have affected the pipe, and "to smoke together" is almost synonymous with "holding council," but there is a vast difference between individual chiefs appearing in council and at once taking fire to light their pipes, which they scarcely remove from their mouths during the entire council, on the supposition that good thoughts come while smoking (Gallinée, Relation of 1669, [Seneca], *in* Margry, 1875, vol. 1, p. 129), and passing a large council pipe in rotation, from which all present take a puff and exhale to the sun, and the Dance of the Calumet in which the decorated pipe stem was the central object to which the pipe, usually of catlinite, was frequently attached. I can say for certain that a calumet is not intended when the Iroquois, in the parlance of the League, refer to the Cayuga as "The Great Pipe," for the allusion is to an incident at the founding of the League when Deganawidah met the leading Cayuga chief who was smoking an enormous pipe. Of such a nature, I believe, are most of the references to council pipes and pipe smoking in the literature of the Atlantic coast tribes, although large and multiple-stemmed council pipes were a feature among Virginia and Carolina Algonquians, among the Catawba, and the Cherokee (McGuire, 1899, pp. 547–548; Milling, 1940, p. 264; Swanton, 1946, p. 547).

It is just as difficult to determine, moreover, whether the early descriptions of so-called calumets and calumet dances refer to the northern Algonquian type of medicine-pipe bundle dance or to the Central Plains ritual with the feathered stems, of which the Pawnee Hako is the archtype. Certainly, as Wissler wrote, "Every pipe was not a calumet and every smoking ceremony not a calumet ceremony" (Wissler, 1912, p. 168). Calumet is a Norman French word meaning *cane* or *reed*, "and the calumet of the Indians is properly the stalk of the pipe but under the name is understood the whole pipe as well as the stalk." The stalks were "of a light wood, painted with different colors, and adorned with the heads, tails, and feathers of the most beautiful birds . . ." (Charlevoix (1761), 1923, vol. 1, p. 304).

With these considerations in mind, I now propose to examine critically the history of contacts between the Iroquois and tribes who were in possession of the true calumet ceremony to place and date the introduction of the Calumet Dance among the Five Nations and connect history with tradition.

Beauchamp (1907, p. 431) credits Lahontan with being the first observer to mention the calumet among the Iroquois in the council at La Famine in 1684, and then as distinct from the ordinary pipe. Garangula, the Onondaga orator, met the Governor of New France, De la Barre, and sat in council "with his pipe in his mouth, and the great calumet of peace before him" (Lahontan, 1735, vol. 1, p. 35; Colden, 1902, vol. 1, pp. 63 ff.). The Onondaga orator thanked the French Governor for bringing into their country the calumet which his predecessor had received from their hands, and then proceeded, in a famous address, to call the Frenchman's bluff and assert the sovereignty of the Five Nations. Had they not knocked the Twihtwies (Miami) and Chitaghicks (Illinois) on the head for cutting down the Tree of Peace and hunting beaver on Iroquois lands, contrary to the custom of all Indians? With a final belt of wampum he warned the French Governor that so many soldiers in so small a space threatened to choke the Tree of Peace, but assured him in the name of the Five Nations, "that our Warriors shall dance to the *Calumet of Peace* under its leaves and shall remain quiet on their Mats . . ." until attacked by the French or English (Colden (1727) 1937, pp. 86-88; 1902, vol. 1, p. 67).

What the old Onondaga speaker was saying was that beaver had already become extremely scarce in the home country of the Five Nations and their warriors were then ranging far afield in search of furs. The Iroquois role became that of middlemen between the traders of Albany, mainly Dutch, and the "Far Indians" (Ottawa, Miami, Illinois, etc.), and largely determined whether the trade came into Albany via Oswego or went to the French at Montreal. At least two historians have made a case for the thesis that the Iroquois fought punitive wars with the Huron, Illinois, and Fox Indians largely to control the trade in rum and beaver skins (McIlwain, 1915, pp. xlii et passim; Hunt, 1940). One has but to read the Colonial Documents to see that trade and Indian policy were inseparable, and the circumstances which affected the movement of furs also influenced the spread of the Calumet from the Great Lakes into the Iroquois country.

Toward the close of the seventeenth century the Calumet Dance was in vogue among the Central Algonquians for cementing intertribal treaties in every case where the Iroquois used wampum belts. We find that about 1690 the Ottawa sent the Iroquois red stone calumets and bales of beaver skins in exchange for eight wampums which had been sent to secure an alliance (La Potherie *in* Blair, 1912, vol. 2, p. 96; Wraxall, *in* McIlwain, 1915, p. 15). That year certain of the Huron, who for more than a generation had been refugees among the Ottawa and even among the Sioux (Robinson, 1904, pp. 31–32), made a pretext of going to Saginaw to gather herbs but went from Michilimackinac to the Iroquois bearing a calumet ornamented with plumes, and several collars (of wampum) to confirm the message of the Ottawa asking for a full union with the Iroquois, which action indicated a desire to abandon the side of the French in order to put themselves under the protection of the English (La Potherie *in* Blair, 1912, vol. 2, p. 106).

Dates for this period are deceptive and confusing, but Beauchamp credits Colden and Smith for having noticed a council of the League held January 22, 1690, although Wraxall's Abridgement dates it February 3, 1689, at which Cannehoot, the Seneca speaker, reported negotiations conducted the previous summer between the Seneca, on behalf of the League, and a band of Ottawa who had concluded a peace for themselves and several western nations, who gave "a red Marble Sun as large as a Plate" and "a large Pipe of red Marble" which "Presents were hung up in the House, in the Sight of the whole assembly, and afterwards distributed among the several Nations, and their acceptance was a Ratification of the Treaty" (Beauchamp, 1905, p. 237). Three Ottawa, who were present, according to Wraxall's Abridgement, "promised to use their best endeavors to bring the 'Tobacco Nation and the other Ottawa bands' into the Alliance." (Wraxall, *in* McIlwain, 1915, p. 15.)

Although we have gone to some pains to establish the introduction of the calumet—both the pipe and the fan—among the Five Nations prior to 1700, nevertheless, Iroquois sachems continued to sit in council smoking pipes individually, and the council went on using wampum belts for all purposes for which their western neighbors employed the calumet (Beauchamp, 1907, p. 433).

The French for reasons of personal inviolability influenced the rapid spread of the calumet about 1679. Intimate trade contacts with the Ottawa and their allies about the Straits of Mackinac, and among the Illinois, to the south, brought the calumet sooner into prominence in Canada than in New York (McGuire, 1899, p. 554; Beauchamp, 1907, p. 432). Contemporary writers support McGuire's thesis. Charlevois wrote in 1721, "It is more in use among the southern and western nations, than among the eastern and northern, and is more frequently employed for peace than for war" (Charlevoix, 1923, vol. 1, p. 304).

Lafitau, the Jesuit ethnologist and missionary among the Christian Abenaki and Mohawk in the St. Lawrence Valley during the second decade of the eighteenth century, declares that the Iroquois and the Indians near Quebec did not use the Calumet of Peace.

The law of nations is much more respected among the nations of the interior who dwell towards Louisiana along the shores of the Mississippi, who observe the custom of the calumet, which the Iroquois lack, as much as the natives near Quebec and in the Lower St. Lawrence River. [Lafitau, 1724, vol. 2, p. 314.]

A captive from the Fox, brought to the mission where Lafitau was staying (ca. 1720), introduced the Calumet Dance among the Christianized Abenaki. "The nation assembled often in the cabin where he [the Fox] had been adopted—to see him dance and hear him sing." Lafitau personally derived nothing but pleasure from witnessing it (ibid., vol. 2, pp. 324–325). Jacques Eustache Le Sueur, himself a Jesuit missionary at Three Rivers, Quebec, from 1716–1760, in 1734 wrote a brief history of the Calumet Dance, describing its introduction among the Abenaki by the Fox in 1719 and the appearance of the dance the next year (Le Sueur, 1906, p. 191). The missionaries of the Jesuit Order, who themselves had carried the Calumet down the Mississippi, opposed its spread to the suburban Indians of Quebec because the Fox endeavored to seduce the St. Lawrence tribes from a French alliance and the Fathers thought the ritual endangered the progress of Christianity. Chroniclers of New England mention no ceremonial use of the calumet along the Atlantic Coast, other than convivial smoking. "They are joyful in meeting any in travel and will strike fire either with stones or sticks to take tobacco, and discourse a little together" (Williams, Rodger, 1827, p. 75; Rainey, 1936, p. 55; Flannery, 1939, p. 68).

After the turn of the eighteenth century, the ceremonial pipe and feathered stem is mentioned occasionally in reports of New York councils, but as something remarkable and connected with distant nations (Beauchamp, 1907, pp. 432–433). The Indian Records for the first decade of the century roundly score the French for inciting Iroquois war parties to go out against the Catawba and Cherokee at the back of the English colony of Carolina and for continually fomenting trouble between the Five Nations and the so-called "Far Indians" who wished to come to Albany to trade (Wraxall, *in* McIlwain, 1915; Colden, 1937). Deputations of Far Indians came annually to the western door of the Longhouse, seeking admission, and giving ". . . a large redstone Pipe, the greatest present or Token used by those nations in their Treaties" (Colden, 1937, p. 364), until finally in 1710 the League council convened at Onondaga to receive, in the presence of Albany commissioners, Ottawa delegates who sought a passage through the "Longhouse" to Albany. Captain Evert Banker and David Schuyler went.

4 June . . . . When we came into the Castle we were sent for into the Gen[r] Assembly, Where we found 3 Wagenhaes or Uttawawas singing the Song of Joy. They had long Stone Pipes in their hands & under the Pipes hung Feathers as big as Eagles Wings. When they left off singing well we filled their Pipes & let them smoake, when They had done, They filled the Pipes for us to Smoak—this is the token of Friendship. [Wraxall, *in* McIlwain, 1915, p. 70.] 8 June . . .

they gave Two Stone Pipes to remain at Onondaga as a memorial of this Treaty for each Party to smoke out of whenever they hereafter met . . . . . [Ibid., p. 73.]

In 1712, when the Delaware got ready to carry their annual tribute to Onondaga, they sent for the Governor of Pennsylvania and laid out on the floor 32 belts of wampum in which various figures had been wrought by their women, and a large calumet which they said had been given to them a generation previously when they submitted to the Five Nations, who had told them to show it whenever they came to a new place and on returning to Onondaga as symbolic of their friendship and subjection to the Five Nations. The calumet, which attracted some attention and is variously described in the records, had "a stone head, a wooden or cane shaft, and feathers fixt to it like wings, with other ornaments" (Provincial Council of Pa., Minutes, 1852, vol. 2, p. 546; Hanna, 1911, vol. 1, pp. 101–102 [slightly different]; Weslager, 1944, p. 383).

It is interesting that the Delaware, who were then the southern neighbors of the Iroquois, employed wampum in far greater proportion to the lone calumet. Wampum, of course, originated with the coastal Algonquian tribes from whom it spread inland under Dutch and English stimulus with the trade. Tribes beyond the mountains had little wampum and prized it greatly and they could only obtain it through Iroquois or Delaware middlemen. No one understood this situation better than the Moravian missionary Zeisberger, who wrote in 1780, from a lifetime of observing Iroquois, Delaware, and Shawnee then living in settlements along the Ohio River, that the wing of a large bird was formerly used by people coming to the Delaware, who possessed no wampum, nor had they seen it (Zeisberger, 1910, p. 32). The Shawnee and Miami were then the next tribes west, and the former having once lived near the coast were familiar with wampum.

I infer from the records that the Tuscarora, who left the Neuse River in Carolina about 1711 and returned to the fold of the Five Nations in 1714, came north too early to have brought the Calumet Dance. They were living along the branches of the Susquehanna in 1716 when they became the sixth nation of the Iroquois Confederacy; but the Tuscarora first appear in the Albany records as participants at a Governor's council held during August 1722, representing a village situated between Oneida and Onondaga, after which the Iroquois were known to the English as the Six Nations (Wraxall, in McIlwain, 1915, pp. 101, 115, 143, 144; O'Callaghan, 1857, vol. 5, p. 671).

Meanwhile an illicit trade had grown up between the Albany Dutch and Montreal fur buyers in which Caughnawaga Mohawks were the bearers. Prices on the black market were cheaper than prices of the French monopoly. But the English wanted to confine the trade to Albany, and Governor Burnet prohibited the trade in 1720, after which the Indians from around Detroit commenced once more to come to Albany on the invitation of the Seneca and English, and in 1722, even some Ottawa braved French displeasure (McIlwain, 1915, p. lxviii).

In the beginning of May, 1723, a Nation of Indians came to Albany *singing* and *dancing*, with their Calumets before them, as they always do when they come to any Place where they have not been before. We do not find that the Commissioners of Indian Affairs, were able to inform themselves what Nation this was. [Colden, Report of 1724, 1902, vol. 2, p. 26; Wraxall, *in* McIlwain 1915, p. 140.]

At the end of May, 80 more of the same people from Michilimackinac arrived with a Six Nations interpreter, seeking admission as a seventh nation of the League, and they left a calumet at Albany besides sending others among the Six Nations. The delegation probably comprised mixed Huron and Ottawa, but the alliance was of no duration. Their chief Sakena, in explaining the custom of smoking the peace pipe, told how the previous spring he had sent two calumets by canoe to Onondaga, but that his emissaries had been intercepted by the French near Oswego. In the faith that the gift of a calumet and smoking together were tantamount to an alliance as the seventh nation, he gave a beaver coat to wrap and preserve the pipe (Wraxall, *in* McIlwain, 1915, pp. 144–145; O'Callaghan, 1853–57, vol. 5, pp. 693–695 [where the date appears as August 29]; Beauchamp, 1905, p. 269; 1907, p. 433; Schoolcraft, 1847, p. 113).

For all the Far Indians that filtered through the Longhouse to Albany, many more contacted the Seneca who were Keepers of the Western Door. And hunting parties of the Seneca and Cayuga ranged into Ohio and Indiana. In the eyes of the old men who sat at Onondaga, the Iroquois who had settled on the Ohio were for the most part young people who had gone there to hunt for meat and peltry and settled down a season later. The Longhouse was decaying at its corners, and to offset the growth of satellite authorities, which they foresaw were bound to spring up and threaten the integrity of the League, the sachems of the Six Nations about 1747 appointed a "half king," or civil governor, named Scaroyady, who was to stand for the League in all the Ohio country (Wallace, Paul A. W., 1945, pp. 258 ff.). The Half King made his headquarters at Logstown, where he received messengers of colonial governments including Weiser, Gist, and Washington, and from which he led deputations of Shawnee, Mingo, and Miami chiefs to Lancaster, Pa. Here was an official liaison between the great fire at Onondaga and the Miami bands centered on the Great Miami River who publicly celebrated such alliances with the Calumet Dance. Compared to the few public records of its celebration, one wonders how frequent were the informal contacts in which individual Seneca learned the ceremony.

Between 1667 when an Iroquois chief received the honors of the Calumet Dance in the Miami, Mascoutin, and Kickapoo villages (La Potherie *in* Blair, 1911, vol. 1, p. 350), and the series of treaties and conferences with the hostile Indians of the Northwest Territory which terminated in Greenville in 1796, many such occasions brought delegations of the Six Nations into the presence of the Miami. But we need not infer diffusion when it can be documented.

Of the many descriptions of the Calumet Dance, that of Father Marquette is the most detailed and has been most frequently quoted (Thwaites, 1896–1901, vol. 59, pp. 115–119, 131–137), but it is not the earliest. Marquette says he was received by the "Illinois," to whom the dance is most often attributed by later authorities, but some of these references to the Illinois possibly mean the Miami, since the term "Illinois" was in frequent use for all the tribes immediately south of the Great Lakes (Kinietz, 1940, p. 190). Allouez, who preceded Marquette up the Lakes first saw the Calumet danced in 1667 by a branch of the Illinois, or Miami (Kinietz, 1940, p. 192), and his account stresses veneration of the pipe, which is placed in the center of the room, individuals dancing in turn, pantomine of war danced to the drum about the pipe, circuitous passing of the pipe to all principals by rank, which reminded Allouez of the French custom of drinking from one glass, and entrusting the pipe to a keeper who is the honored man and who holds the bundle as a pact of peace or friendship (Thwaites, 1896–1901, vol. 51, pp. 47–49).

French observers stress ornamentation of ceremonial equipment and the emotional and physical effects on themselves of the ceremony. Perrot was impressed by the calumet and its brilliant feathers. He notes the old man pointing to the sun and invoking spirits, and also pointing to the cardinal directions, after first presenting the calumet to the honored guest, the Frenchman, who was then massaged; and the French were embarrassed at the thought of being carried. The great chief of the Miami came to meet them at the head of 3,000 men, and each of the village chiefs carried a calumet but was naked save for embroidered moccasins; but they approached singing and dancing, bending their knees in turn almost to the ground. A feast followed, after the manner of Iroquois Eagle Dance (LaPotherie *in* Blair, 1911, vol. 1, pp. 325–330).

The so-called Calumet Dance is not properly a dance at all, but a ceremony for greeting strangers and forming pacts between individuals and nations. Hewitt pointed out years ago that the motive of the ceremony is to create a sacred kinship, and that the purpose of the dance is to honor the calumet, which is the essence of good (Hewitt,

1912).   It is a complex ceremony, moreover, composed of many parts, and it varied with the occasion, and whether it was performed out-doors in summer, at the margins of the village in greeting strangers, in an especially prepared arbor, or in a house in winter.   French writers after Marquette and including Charlevoix and Lafitau, many of them priests, mention offering the calumet to the sun, a feature which they thought was intended by the Indians to call the sun to witness engage-ments then enacted.   Charlevoix stated that the calumet was as sa-cred among the western tribes bordering on the Missouri as wampum was to the Iroquois, and he could think of no example of a compact broken which had been entered into by smoking the calumet (Charle-voix, 1923, vol. 1, pp. 304–305).   Perrot, the trader, however, knew of such treachery by an Ottowa chief to the Sioux, and by the Iroquois, both eastern tribes; and both writers agree that the prairie tribes held the calumet in greatest veneration and respected its contracts.

The Calumet Dance has a pattern of sequence much like that of the Iroquois Eagle Dance.   Following the reception for greeting stran-gers at the margins of the village and bearing the guests to the theater prepared for the drama, the play has several acts.   The necessary ritual properties are prepared and laid out with war bundles, "and at the right is placed the calumet in honor of which the feast is given," and all about are piled the weapons of war.   Appointed singers are possibly berdaches, and women assist.   The first act is the Calumet Dance proper, second comes the Dance of Discovery, and third, the Striking Dance and recitation of war records, with gifts.   The pipe is then passed and there is a feast (Marquette *in* Thwaites, 1896–1901, vol. 59, pp. 135–137).

Raudot and Charlevoix have described Discovery Dance and Strik-ing-the-post, which, Kinietz has noted (Kinietz, 1940, pp. 194, 195), form the second and third acts of the Calumet Dance in its complete description by Marquette.   The Miami excelled at the Discovery Dance, according to Raudot, which I judge from Charlevoix's de-scription may be equated with Seneca Striking-a-stick Dance.   The other as the name implies was the means of reciting war records or counting coups, a feature found almost universally in the Mississippi watershed.   The Iroquois Eagle Dance and its relatives, War Dance and Striking-a-stick Dance, embodied the salient features of the three main acts of the Calumet Dance, Discovery Dance, and Striking-the-post, as they were severally known to French writers.

But the Miami were to come over to the English interest at the mideighteenth century through the agency of Scaroyady, the Iroquois vice-regent, and the young warriors proposed to kindle a council fire on the Ohio and invite the surrounding tribes in defiance of the old men of Onondaga, who as usual decided to remain neutral in the war with France. The conflict between the generations beset the League throughout its history as the councilors endeavored to maintain polity and negotiate disputes, and the warriors escaped from their arms to fight. This time the warriors came to Pennsylvania for provisions and arms, and they were followed the next July by a deputation of Twightwies, a great nation of 20 towns on the River Wabash, who brought to Lancaster, Pa., 30 beaver skins and a calumet pipe "with a long stem, curriously wrought, & wrapp'd round with Wampum of several colours . . ." (Wallace, Paul A. W., 1945, p. 261). If we assume that young men were the agency through whom the Calumet Dance reached the Iroquois in the Ohio settlements, we have a hypothesis which would explain why the Seneca have the Eagle Dance in its most elaborate form.

To support such a hypothesis the Miami afford two other bits of evidence, one historical and the other traditional. A description of "Warriors Feather Dance" by Gist, who saw it performed February 28, 1751, at Pickawillany, the chief town on the Big Miami River, resembles what the French call "Striking-the-post" and comes the closest of the early descriptions to the Iroquois Eagle Dance. The affair was sponsored by the chief of the Piankashaw Band of Miami at the council house.

Thursday 28.—The crier of the town came by the King's Order and invited Us to the long House to see the Warriors Feather Dance; it was performed by three Dancing-masters, who were painted all over with various Colours, with long Sticks in their Hands, upon the Ends of which were fastened long Feathers of Swans, and other Birds, neatly woven in the Shape of a Fowls Wing: in this Disguise they performed many antick Tricks, waving their Sticks and Feathers about with great Skill to imitate the flying and fluttering of Birds, keeping exact Time with their Musick; while they are dancing some of the Warriors strikes a Post, upon which the Musick and Dancers cease, and the Warrior gives an Account of his Achievements in War, and when he has done, throws down some Goods as a Recompense to the Performers and Musicians; after which they proceed in their Dance as before till another Warrior strikes ye Post, and as long as the Company think fit. [Darlington, 1893, pp. 53–54.]

The feathered sticks recall the feathered pipe stems of the calumet, but suggest modified fans of the Iroquois Eagle Dance. Gist does not say whether the three dancers performed singly as in the three constituent parts of Calumet Dance or together as now among the Iroquois. The feature of striking a post, to stop the song, gave its name to one dance, but recital of war deeds belonged also to the Discovery Dance, and survives in three separate Iroquois rites. The added element of speakers making gifts to the dancers and singers, which Kinietz says is not reported by French authors, is an Iroquois trait.

Tradition in the hands of a clever ethnologist will often pay off where historical sources fail. The Miami retained cultural memory of the calumet ceremony into the first quarter of the nineteenth century when Trowbridge wrote down their traditions for Gov. Lewis Cass (Kinietz, 1938, pp. 27–29). Trowbridge clears up a number of items mentioned in earlier sources. In making peace, Miami ambassadors carried a pole, on the end of which was hung the white hinder part of an eagle skin, and a "grand calumet ornamented with bones and feathers." He painted a blue streak across his forehead and a heart on his chest. When, as Zeisberger said, the Whites introduced wampum and flags, he carried a white flag in one hand and calumet in the other, but added a belt of white wampum. He inquired for the chief town and the residence of the Chief and went there. Passing over preliminaries of smoking, and the method of mutually publishing to their warriors that the road is open between their towns, we came to a description which is quite familiar. Note that there are four dancers, that a pole is erected and that the feathered stems are presented to the dancers by four speakers who in turn strike the pole with the feathered stem and recite individual achievements. Drum and gourd rattle accompany singers. The dancers evidently go in turn, which seems to have been the original way. Distribution of presents is implied.

After a little time they invited the villagers, their late enemies to come and partake of a grand feast, in commemoration of the cessation of hostilities. At this feast the common dance is the dance of the calumet (Pwaukāūna mēēhendgee). It is danced by four persons only. Four grand calumets are laid upon a mat on the ground, ornamented in full with the feathers of the eagle. A pole is placed in the ground near this, and when the dancers are ready to commence, one of the war chiefs marches to the place of deposit, picks up a pipe and striking the pole with the stem, recounts in a loud voice the many feats of bravery which he has performed, and in conclusion says that all those things are smoothed down by the late happy agreement between the contending parties. He then turns about and selecting some active young man he gives him the pipe and desires him to dance. The young man leads off, keeping time to the musick of a drum & gourd which are in the hand of some of the bystanders. He does not dance long before another chief or great warrior goes to the mat and taking another pipe, pursues the same course just described. In this way the pipes are all distributed, and the dancers are occasionally relieved by the speech of a warrior who rises, picks up a piece of tobacco or a knife and striking the post therewith recounts his deeds in war.

The guests after returning home reciprocate the compliment and the like cermonies of feasting, dancing & boasting take place. When this is done the way between two villages is considered plain & cleared of thorns. [Kinietz, 1938, pp. 28–29.]

Use of the calumet ceremony for welcoming strangers was in process of diffusion throughout the Mississippi watershed late in the seventeenth century. It had reached the Great Lakes in Marquette's time, and in 1687 the Cahinnio, a Caddo tribe, so welcomed Joutel, but it did not reach their neighbors farther west until 3 years afterward (Joutel, *in* Margry, 1875–86, vol. 3, pp. 418–419). The French were partly responsible for its rapid diffusion down the Mississippi and into the Southeast, although its spread accompanied the dispersion of tribes in that direction from the confluence of the Ohio and Mississippi which was its center. To the east it reached the Creeks in an attenuated form (Swanton, 1928 a, p. 703; 1946, p. 547), and presumably thence to Cherokee and Catawba, soon after the French settled Louisiana. Its next recorded appearance in New York is from that quarter.

Throughout the first half of the eighteenth century the Iroquois were at war with the "Flathead" or Catawba in Carolina, a cause in which their young men gained prestige by taking scalps and bringing home prisoners to replenish losses of manpower, although many Catawba were tortured. French agents among the Five Nations greatly aided and abetted these campaigns to the great distress of the English colonists who suffered depredations along the Warriors' Path, which roughly followed the fall line east of the mountains from Pennsylvania to Carolina. British policy was to secure these Indians against the French, and the colonial governors were instructed to make peace between the warring tribes. As early as 1741, the Cherokee and Catawba agreed to consider a peace settlement which the Six Nations offered through the good offices of the Governors of New York and Carolina. The Cherokee sent some beads, a pipe, an eagle's tail, and a white flag which they had taken from the French. The Catawba sent a wampum belt, a pipe of peace, and tobacco. The belt which the Iroquois had sent was to be kept in one of the principal Cherokee towns (O'Callaghan, 1855, vol. 6, pp. 208, 210–211). The Creek also told the Carolina authorities that they desired peace, but the Catawba ended by refusing all such propositions and calling the Cherokee "Old Women" (Milling, 1940, p. 243). Raids continued.

It took another 10 years to bring the Catawba chiefs to Albany. With them came several Iroquois warriors, prisoners of the Catawba, whose return the sachems of the League had insisted on as a precondition to peace. Having embarked at Charleston, Lt. Gov. William Bull, King Haigler, and the Catawba delegation reached Albany in July of 1751, where on arrival the Catawba performed the Calumet Dance, of which we have three accounts. Conrad Weiser was a central figure in the negotiations leading to the Albany conference, of which there are New York and Carolina versions (Wallace, 1945, p. 300 et passim; O'Callaghan, 1855, vol. 6, pp. 717–726; Milling, 1940, p. 244; Speck and Schaeffer, 1942, pp. 568–569). Weiser had been to Onondaga the previous year to invite the Six Nations to come halfway, but when the Six Nations declined to attend a conference at Fredericksburg, Va., William Johnson took the negotiations out of Weiser's hands (Wallace, 1945, p. 304; Johnson Papers, 1921-1939, vol. 1, p. 359; vol. 9, pp. 75, 83). Weiser's journals contain the whole story, since he also accompanied the Catawba and William Bull from New York City.

Of significance for this study of diffusion, one of the Catawba spoke Onondaga very well, having been a prisoner there previously, and Weiser appreciated that he knew what they were up against, should the Six united Nations not come to terms (Wallace, 1945, p. 324). Clearly the Carolina Government was more interested in the peace than the Indians. The party arrived in Albany June 27, and Weiser talked "in the bushes," with Iroquois friends who counseled that he keep the Catawba party out of sight until a speech was made, lest someone cut their throats on sight (ibid, p. 326). The preliminaries took a week, and on the 8th Weiser presented Mr. Bull. Then the Mohawks and Governor Clinton sent Weiser to meet and conduct the Catawba to their proper place; "they Came along singing with their Collabashes dressed with feders in their hands, they Continued Singing for a while after the Sat down. in the mean time. the Calumet pipe was offered by the Catabaw King to all the Chiefes and old people of the Six Nations, and after this another Calmet was offered by one of the Warriours of the Catabaws, and the Six Nations Indians Smooked out of Both" (Wallace, 1945, p. 327).

By Iroquois standards, the speech of the Catawba king was a flop, he being too much in awe of his hosts. But at the end, to make up for his loss of words, he "gave a large Belt of Wampum and Some Indian pipes & the feders! that was died to a post after done Singing . . ."

The Six Nations replied in 2 days, giving a belt. When the Catawba requested that several Iroquois hostages accompany them to their own country, the Six Nations said that they never customarily sent any "of our people with messengers of peace" the first time. But the Six Nations relented, and after receiving the Catawba in open arms in all their country, many of the Northern Indians accompanied the Catawba home (Milling, 1940, p. 244). I can imagine no better opportunity for the singers of the Six Nations, particularly in Mohawk, Oneida, and Tuscarora towns, to acquire the new songs and the ceremony.

If the Albany conference of 1751 was another Clinton fizzle, out of which nobody got anything but William Johnson (Wallace, 1945, pp. 331-332), at least the eastern Iroquois saw the Calumet Dance.

The official New York version contains only one detail about the Catawba performance not in Weiser. It says they ". . . Came down from their Quarters, Singing, with their Colours pointed to the Ground . . ." (O'Callaghan, 1855, vol. 6, p. 723). What this minute evidently means by "Colours" is either the feathers mentioned by Weiser, or flags which the Indians of the Southeast soon adopted.

Feathers had a special sacred character among the Catawba, who employed entire wings of turkeys, geese, herons, and hawks for sweeping premises and for purification, and a Catawba chief carried a staff of feathers of some worthy bird (Speck, 1939, p. 39). Pipe smoking was also a regular feature of Catawba council procedure, and as among the Cherokee, the size of the cloud foretold unanimity. Speck and Schaeffer investigated my problem among the Catawba remnant and found both feathers and wampum belts used in peace agreements, attributing the former to the old Southeast with its feather symbolism and the latter to the influence of Iroquois delegates on the Catawba and their neighbors (Speck and Schaeffer, 1942, pp. 568–569). The Carolina version of the Catawba performance (after Mills, 1826, p. 124) is quoted from their paper:

. . . At this time the Catawba king, and his chiefs, approached the grand council, singing a song of peace, their ensigns, on [or?] colored feathers, borne horizontally, not erected; every one present admiring their descent, dignity, and behavior, as well as the solemn air of their song; a seat was prepared for them, at the right hand of the governor's company. Their two singers, with the two feathers, continued their song, half fronting to the center of the old sachems, to whom they addressed their song, and pointed their feathers, shaking their musical calabashes; while the king of the Catawbas was busy preparing and lighting the calumet of peace.

Then the Catawba singers ceased, and fastened their feathers, calumets, and calabashes to the tent pole; after which the king stood up and advancing forwards, he began his speech to the Six Nations, speaking of making peace. . . . And I give a belt, with all my towns upon it, signifying that they all join in my desire. . .

The next morning the Mohawks withdrew from the Council, saying they were for peace with Catawba, and that those who were not, might deliberate further. Others soon agreed to peace. The Six Nations demanded prisoners from the Catawba, and said that when the latter returned with the prisoners, the peace would be concluded. . . .

The war between the Six Nations and the Southeastern Indians was to go on for another generation after the Albany Conference of 1751 with delegations of Catawba and Cherokee coming to the frontier towns of the Six Nations suing for peace. The calumet-waving peace ambassadors were being pushed by the southern governors whose colonists had tired of Iroquois raiders skulking at the back country. As the French and Indian War heightened the struggle between France and England for control of North America, British agents endeavored to consolidate Indian tribes who were at peace with the English. The French had succeeded in alienating the affections of the Delaware, Shawnee, and the Miami of Ohio. To secure the Six Nations as allies and prevent their defection to the French became the guiding British policy in all their subsequent dealings with the Indians, particularly after Braddock's defeat near the forks of the Ohio. The consistent policy of the old men of Onondaga was to remain neutral as long as possible, extracting concessions from both sides.

George II himself took a hand in these affairs and sent his cousin, the Earl of Loudoun, to America with instructions to secure the Six Nations. Sir William Johnson was continued as Superintendent of the Northern Department and Edmond Atkin and William Byrd actively engaged in enlisting the Catawba and Cherokee to mobilize at Winchester against the hated Shawnee and Delaware. But such a maneuver was impossible without first composing the feud with the other Northern Indians, the Six Nations (Fenton, 1951 a). Johnson was at this task the rest of his life and spent a king's ransom in presents to Indians.

Johnson's addresses to the Six Nations following 1753 fairly bristle with Indian metaphors, including analogies to the calumet, which he learned from Iroquois tutors. In councils of the League, speakers allude to a symbolic white wing, which the founders of the Confederacy gave to the Onondaga fire keepers, for brushing aside evil influences brought into the council by unfriendly strangers (Parker, 1916, p. 31; O'Callaghan, 1849–51, vol. 2, pp. 634, 638; Johnson Papers). On one of these occasions he presented the Six Nations with the largest pipe in America with instructions to keep it at Onondaga and use it in councils, thus establishing a custom that had not always been fixed among them (O'Callaghan, 1853–57, vol. 7, p. 64).

The Cherokee and Catawba responded to Atkin and Byrd with an alacrity that no one had anticipated and began to arrive at Fort Cumberland, barefoot and hungry, and in such numbers as to embarrass young Washington, who had warned the colonial governors to send up supplies. Virginia and Carolina traders had long vied for the Cherokee trade, but the presence of Cherokee and Catawba warriors in large numbers near the border settlements of Virginia, Maryland, and Pennsylvania alarmed the settlers who had seen northern war parties every year passing south for scalps and prisoners. No one was ready for the southern Indians, not even the Six Nations. The Iroquois declared they would never fight as allies of the despised Cherokee (Volwiler, 1926, pp. 116, 129–131; Thwaites, 1904–1907, vol. 1, pp. 34, 238–241; Loudoun and Abercromby Papers in Henry E. Huntington Library).

Among the Cherokee deputation that came north in the summers of 1757 and 1758 were counted 11 Cherokee, their women and children, and 3 Mohawk carrying messages from the chiefs of their nation to the chiefs of Six Nations. Detained at Philadelphia by illness of their leader, the party had Governor Denny write to Governor DeLancey to clear the path for them to Sir William Johnson's and their destination at the upper Mohawk Castle (William Denny to Governor

DeLancey, Abercromby Papers, AB 374, Huntington Library). The previous July a few Cherokee had come to the Mohawk to confer with Johnson and chiefs of several of the Six Nations; they had condoled one another, and gotten drunk as only Indians can, and meanwhile the Iroquois sachems had advised their warriors not to follow the war-path to the Cherokee country until the Six Nations could reply. Finally on September 19 came the answer of the Six Nations. Four Cherokee delegates were introduced to the council by Montour and were seated in as many chairs.

Sir William then lighted the Calumet or Pipe of Peace & friendship & after smoaking a Whif or two presented it to the four Cherokee Deputies holding to them while each drew a Whif . . . and [so] to every Indian present. The To-bacco from whence it was filled was then put into a Bag to be carried home together with the Calumet by the Cherokees. [Johnson Papers, vol. 9, p. 848.]

They were also given a white peace belt and a Seneca chief was to accompany them as far as Philadelphia, and farther if his shoes held out. The meeting broke up over a pail of punch (O'Callaghan,1853–1857, vol. 7, p. 327).

When the Cherokee delegation first mentioned returned the follow-ing year, they recommended that Iroquois warriors coming their way should attach a bunch of feathers to their gun muzzles to distinguish them from enemies passing from tree to tree along the war trail. The Cherokee women advised their Iroquois sisters to provision their warriors; then the speaker concluded,

BROR:

We hereby present you with a Calumet and Wing as the manager of the affairs of our Confederacy, and beg you will keep it in Remembrance of our nation, at this place of public Consultations of the Confederacy, Light the Pipe whenever you meet upon public affairs, and dont let any people yt carry false & trifling Reports Smoke out of it. Any time hereafter if we should come to your Fire Place upon Business we hope to find this Calumet and Wing, in order that we may light it and remember the agreement now made between each other. [Speech of a Cherokee Ambassador to Sir William Johnson, in O'Callaghan, 1849, vol. 2, pp. 765–768.]

The Iroquois speaker acknowledged the calumet and wing with directions, together with the Road and Peace belt; "And if we desire you will with equal Care preserve the Calumet you received here last year, and observe the rules we then recommended to you" (Johnson Papers, vol. 9, p. 959).

But the Cherokee-Iroquois war dragged on another decade until Sir William Johnson's treaty at Fort Stanwix in 1768 (Mooney, 1900, pp. 202–203, 351–352; Ramsey, 1860, p. 74; Seaver, 1932, pp. 53, 105–106, 117, 376). The Cherokee gave "11 belts and three strings. One for Sir William had a calumet and eagle's tail attached" (O'Callaghan, 1853–57, vol. 8, pp. 38–53; Beauchamp, 1905, p. 332). But even this effort had not ended the old feud by 1770 (Manuscripts of Sir Wm. Johnson, O'Callaghan, 1849, vol. 2, p. 949; Beauchamp, 1905, p. 336). Sequoya, the native Cherokee grammarian and inventor of the syllabary, is said to have been 10 years old that year when an Iroquois peace delegation visited the Cherokee town of Echota (Mooney, 1900, p. 109).

War was no hindrance to aboriginal trade. The Cherokee carried on a lucrative trade with tribes to the north, trading white stone pipes and other articles with the Delaware in the Ohio settlements (Zeisberger, 1910, p. 54). Catlinite passed south from the quarries in Minnesota. Firearms, rum, silver, jewelry, and wampum filtered west from the Atlantic settlements, and eagle wings and tail feathers, new ceremonies and their dances came east and north from the south and west. The Iroquois knew the country west to the Black Hills of South Dakota, whence they returned with prisoners; and they went from New York to South Carolina to attack the Catawba and into Florida against the Creeks (McGuire, 1910, p. 800; Myer, 1928, pp. 735 ff.). In 1750, Cammerhoff and Zeisberger were entertained by an elderly Seneca chief who had been down the Ohio and Mississippi to the Spanish settlements, and he described the country, its people, and its resources (Journal of Cammerhoff and Zeisberger, 1750, *in* Beauchamp, 1916, pp. 80–81; Charlevoix, 1866–72, vol. 3, p. 45). It was during these raids and trading excursions, frequently of 2 years' duration, that individuals learned new songs and dances. "A friendly visitor with a new sacred or social dance was always welcome in any Indian village, and great pains were taken to learn it" (Myer, 1928, p. 735). Iroquois war leaders brought home captives, either to replace fallen members of their expeditions or at the request of some house mother who had lost a relative on a previous expedition. When adopted, captives continually replenished the population, and they introduced new elements of culture.

A century after the Potawatomi and Illinois received Allouez and Marquette with honors of the calumet, the ceremony was still in vogue among the Ottawa. In 1763, the Seneca alone of the nations of the Iroquois Confederacy joined in the plot with Pontiac to destroy the English. They were incensed at English intrusion on their lands, and they were farther removed from Johnson's influence than the other Iroquois whom he barely kept quiet. On the first of May 1763, Pontiac, leader of the confederated Ottawa, Ojibwa, and Potawatomi, appeared at the gate of Detroit with 40 Ottawa and under pretext of dancing the Calumet Dance, 10 men inspected the fort while 30 proceded to recount their warlike exploits (Parkman, 1851, pp. 185 ff., 203, 217; Burton, 1912, p. 34).

Contacts between the Iroquois and tribes of the Great Lakes region who had the Calumet Dance thus extended over a century and bear importantly on contemporary traditions of early intertribal Eagle Dances. Beyond the first contact of the Iroquois with the ceremony among the Miami, where had it started? Evidently the French wondered, for Nicholas Perrot, in discussing the Ottawa variant, wrote:

"The savages believe the sun gave it to the Panys, and since then it has been communicated from village to village as far as the Ottaouas" (Blair, 1911, vol. 1, p. 186). The Illinois got it from the Panys and the Sioux from the Illinois during their wars (ibid., vol. 1, p. 182). Charlevoix also ascribes its origin to the Pawnee (Charlevoix, 1923, vol. 1, p. 306).

Hopes of finding definite Seneca and Pawnee contacts are admittedly slim. Then, contact does not necessarily mean that the ritual passed to the second tribe. However, we do know that Pawnee captives became widely distributed during the eighteenth century. About 1700 when the Pawnee were settled west of the Missouri in the present State of Nebraska, the Illinois obtained so many captives from them that Indian slaves became generally know as *Panis*. An ordinance on April 13, 1709, recognized their slavery in Canada along with Negroes. During the first quarter of the century, the French likewise encouraged the Fox to make war on distant tribes such as the Pawnee. By 1763, Pawnee slaves, whom the Sauk and Fox had brought as captives for sale to the French settlements, were to be found in the principal families of Detroit and Michilimakinac (Thwaites, 1896–1901, vol. 69, p. 301; Charlevoix, 1866–72, vol. 5, p. 224; Strong, 1935, pp. 12 ff., 16; Wedel, 1936, pp. 3, 99–102). There was a "miserable Panis," apparently living among the Shawnee, in 1749 when there were Delaware-Seneca and Shawnee villages neighboring Logstown and Scioto in the Ohio country. He nearly precipitated the torture of Bonnecamp, De Celeron, and Joncaire, when he cried out during a council at the Shawnee village that the French only came to destroy them, and the Shawnee might have executed his threat had an Iroquois, who happened to be present, not persuaded them that the French had no evil designs (Bonnecamp's Relation, 1749 *in* Thwaites, 1896–1901, vol. 69, p. 179). The sources do not say that this Pawnee introduced a ceremony of the Hako type among the Shawnee and Seneca in the Ohio villages, but if he brought it to the Miami, who had it, it spread from there east to the Seneca towns.

In 1771, Sir William Johnson commented on the possible origin of an alleged Shawnee Indian whom he interviewed at Johnson Hall and who later applied to the Governor for protection from slavery. "It is certainly a common practice amongst the Western nations to sell their captives of the *Panie* Nation, as well as some others their next neighbors under that Denomination, and Canada . . . depends a good deal on their labour . . ." (Manuscripts of Sir William Johnson, O'Callaghan, 1849–51, vol. 2, p. 984). Slavery was abolished in Canada in 1793, but the last public sale occurred at Montreal, 1797 (Thwaites, 1896–1901, vol. 69, p. 301). If, in the absence of other data, we resort to the often criticized procedure of arguing cultural diffusion by inferred individuals, we must not overlook the possibility that, through some one of these contacts, the Pawnee Hako ceremony spread to the Seneca. Modern informants and the historical sources agree that the Iroquois raided and controlled the country west nearly to the Mississippi; they knew the Pawnee, but, since we have discovered no definite instances of intertribal meetings at which the Hako was celebrated, it is more likely that the ritual reached the Seneca in an attenuated form after passing through the Illinois and Miami.

DISTRIBUTION AND COMPARISON

Having surveyed the history of Iroquois contacts with tribes having the Calumet Dance, in which the documents gave the time and places when the Iroquois could have acquired the complex of traits which it comprises, the task now remains of comparing the Iroquois Eagle Dance with neighboring variants of similar ceremonies to place it in its proper ethnographic perspective. The comparative method, which Boas, Wissler, and Spier have so ably used to infer history in the absence of records, has encountered criticism. The direct historical evidence for the present study is considerable, but to evaluate the historical record properly it is still necessary to engage in the same type of analysis and comparison. Until we know that the Eagle Dance is a variant of the Calumet Dance the historical record is of no use.

If the hypothesis is correct that the Iroquois Eagle Dance derives from a variant of the Calumet Dance, the direct historical evidence indicates how the Iroquois possibly acquired it several times and from several quarters. The Calumet Dance possibly came to the Iroquois from the Miami during a century of intertribal relations in the Ohio country after 1670. Meanwhile, the Seneca and Onondaga were also hosts to the Far Indians—Chippewa, Ottawa, and Huron—who came down the Lakes to Onondaga and Albany, where they brought calumets in the interest of trade. The other main line of diffusion was from the Southeast, also at the midcentury. Since, however, the Calumet Dance spread into that quarter from a mid-Mississippi source among the village tribes of the central prairie around the turn of the eighteenth century, I am inclined to consider the Southeast a secondary source and favor the Ohio Valley route to the Miami, Illinois, Fox, and Pawnee as direct and historically valid.

The Iroquois Eagle Dance is a congeries of elements which are found in varying degrees among neighboring peoples. The ritual complex, then, apart from individual, local, and tribal historical aspects, already treated, may be considered from its distributional aspect which reflects either archaic residue or diffusional content arising from intertribal contacts and the adoption of individuals from one tribe into another. At the outset I suspect that archaic residue accounts for the Iroquois ceremonial pattern to which the Eagle Dance conforms, but the unique features of the ceremony may be sought outside of Iroquoia. From the point of view of their geographical position, being situated but one remove from the marginal tribes of the Northeast, at the sources of the major eastern waterways, the peripheral Iroquois afford a poor springboard for a distributional study. Nevertheless, I shall indicate broad movements of rituals which resemble the Iroquois Eagle Dance.

For comparative purposes, the Iroquois Eagle Society may be characterized as one of a series of linked medicine societies, membership in which includes both men and women who have suffered similar dreams or ailments which a clairvoyant has diagnosed as Eagle sickness. These societies have two types of origin legends: the good hunter restored by a council of animals and the lost boy abducted in a hollow log by a giant bird. Sacrificing the first kill facilitated eagle shooting and autumn pit trapping. Eagles higher up have power to cause and remove sickness, and danger of illness attends being bitten by bird lice. Giant Crow is man's intermediary with Dew Eagle, and messenger for the birds. A feature of the ceremony is striking the post, which stops the song and dance, to recite war records, travel anecdotes, humorous stories, or to ridicule another member, a pattern which has its roots in the old war feasts, but in modern performance links Eagle Dance with War Dance and Striking-a-stick Dance, with which it appears in combined performance, and with Drum Dance, now a religious rite. A second salient feature, common to all the cycle of war dances, is using the ritual to cement friendships or create a fictitious kinship between two persons of opposite moieties of Iroquois society, which when projected to the intertribal level is the avowed purpose of the Calumet Dance.

In a third feature, members own buckskin bundles containing two fans of feathers parallel to the wooden shaft, two gourd rattles, a whistle, a feather, and a package of sacred tobacco, and each member may possess a forked striped pole and a beater. Water drum, horn rattle, and painting a round red spot on each cheek are generalized Iroquois traits. Preliminary ritual organization is shared by other ceremonies. Annual renewals of medicine society rites occur mostly in winter. A male conductor, called Big Crow or Big Raven, issues invitations, selects speaker, priest, whooper, singer and assistant, and two, three, or four dancers. Moiety patterning prevails, and when the society divides spatially the dual divisions resemble two tribes.

The usual Iroquois ceremonial pattern regiments the ritual: thanksgiving and announcements, tobacco-burning invocation, ritual proper, blessing, and a terminal feast of animal-head and corn soup which is divided and taken home.

The Eagle Dance has a sequential pattern of its own and unique concepts. Bundle contents are displayed on the forked striped pole, orienting the fans east and west. Ritual manufacture of fans survives, but the fans lack sex or color symbolisms. Honored old men present drum and rattles to singers and fans and rattles to dancers. There is a whooper, whistle blower, and the singer strikes notes of approval during the speeches. The headman passes tiny pieces of meat to host and members. Speakers interrupt dancers by striking or stamping and distribute gifts following each speech. Women may speak. Dancers hold the fan in the left hand and the rattle in the right, crouch like birds, and pick up objects in their mouths. Rattles represent the noise of birds scratching and the fans symbolize wings which sweep aside evil, and the rattles belong to the fans. A special song precedes laying down the feather fans, which are rewrapped together with the rattles.

Four and ten are sacred numbers, and all circuits are counterclockwise. The head goes first to the host and then to the members who cry like crows; workers receive chunks of meat; and the host fills the headman's pail before he distributes all to the guests, who take home shares to children who may not eat until their parents have first tested feast food.

The bundle and its manipulation before and during a peculiar crouching dance are what externally distinguish the Eagle Dance from other Iroquois curing ceremonies. We shall accept as a typically Iroquoian the basic ritual pattern which regiments all Iroquois ceremonies so that performances today conform substantially to descriptions of Huron ceremonies written 300 years ago. Traits peculiar to the Eagle Dance should occur among neighboring tribes, and in looking for them I recall Wissler's caution: ritualistic ceremonies are "constructs," and one "must expect to find common elements in quite otherwise different wholes" (Wissler, 1912, p. 168).

The mythological motif of the lost boy abducted by a giant bird, Roc, to its nest on a mountain top, from whence with the aid of the young birds he gets home, is widespread in North America. Thompson (1929, pp. 151, 318) assigns the Roc motif number 31.1 in his index. It occurs everywhere eagles are trapped: among the Iroquois, Ojibwa

(Radin and Reagan, 1928, p. 87), Shawnee (Voegelin, MS.), Cherokee, Creek (Swanton, 1928 b, p. 36), Natchez, but of Southeastern tribes especially among the Alabama, Koasati, and Hitchiti (Swanton, 1929, pp. 90, 154, 193, 272); the tale occurs in the Southwest among Pueblos and Hopi (Hodge, 1912, pt. 1, p. 410; Fewkes, 1900); on the Plains among the Arapaho, Gros Ventre (Kroeber, 1907, p. 61), Assiniboin (Lowie, 1919, pp. 170, 240), Crow and Hidatsa (Lowie, 1918, pp. 144, 147), besides the Ponca, Shoshone, Uintah Ute (Thompson, 1929, p. 318); but the Plateau and MacKenzie areas afford even more examples: among the Chilcotin, Shuswap, Thompson, Okanagan, Sanpoil, Kutenai (Boas, 1918, p. 286 and footnote 1); and Beaver, Hare, Chippewyan, Kaska, Dog Rib (Thompson, 1929, p. 318). A tale so widespread can scarcely be considered diagnostic, but it is interesting, nevertheless, that some Iroquois informants at Allegany told the tale as the origin legend of Eagle Dance. I have no references to the Roc episode among Pawnee, Omaha, and Osage—classical Hako tribes—but the Pawnee hero dreamed of the Water Monster who instructed him to trap eagles and to seek the eagle's nest, where he conversed with the birds and received instruction on the ceremony (Dorsey, George A., 1906, pp. 52–56). Possibly related are animal abductors. Among Northeastern Algonkians, Fisher (1946, p. 253) notes: Eagle or mythical bird—Micmac, Passamaquoddy, Malecite, Montagnais-Naskapim, Cree, Ojibwa, Potawatomi, besides Menomini, Gros Ventre, and Cheyenne; absent or unnoted for—Penobscot, Algonquin, Fox, Sauk, Kicpkapoo, and Arapaho.

Iroquois eagle shooting and pit trapping is peripheral to a widespread distribution in the Southwest among the Hopi, Taos, Jemez (Parsons, 1939, p. 29); generally on the Plains north to the village tribes on the Missouri; and in the Southeast professional eagle hunters are reported from the Cherokee, Creek, and Shawnee, and their methods closely resemble the Seneca (Beaglehole, 1936, pp. 25–26; Wilson, 1928; Mooney, 1900, pp. 281–283; Swanton, 1928 b, p. 495). There was a lodge of eagle trappers among the Dakota (Beckwith, 1931, pp. 30–31). A young Dakota must learn to distinguish real from false claims to the red eagle vision (Beckwith, 1930, pp. 343, 385), which suggests Seneca distinctions between various colored eagles.

A central purpose in celebrating the Calumet Dance and also in Iroquois Eagle Dance is creating ceremonial friendships of the cross-cousin type or father-son relationships between individuals who, when members of separate tribes, become the agency of peace between warring parties. Besides the Iroquois, such associations were recognized among Shawnee, Miami, Illinois, Potawatomi, Chippewa, Pawnee, Omaha, one division of Caddo, Cherokee, Sauk and Fox, Menomini, Eastern Dakota, Oglala Dakota, Winnebago, Hidatsa, Mandan, Crow and Cheyenne, Plains Cree, and Zuni (Hocart, 1935 a, b; Mandelbaum, 1936, p. 206; Michelson, 1937). In the Hako type of Calumet ritual, the visitors set themselves up as parents, and the hosts find one of their number to be the honored son. This parent-child relationship is of interest in connection with Iroquois moieties, which sometimes function as parent and offspring—a relationship which finds its most elaborate expression, at the intertribal level, in the Condolence Council (Fenton, 1950). The distribution of ceremonial friendship coincides with the Calumet Dance.

Besides the Roc legend, pit trapping of Eagles, and ceremonial friendship, some 50 elements comprise the Iroquois Eagle Dance complex, but, unfortunately, data are not forthcoming for plotting the distributions of all of them. Two elements, for example, the water drum and the horn rattle, for which data are available, probably originated in the Southeast; they are recorded late for the Iroquois, and do not extend much beyond them, gaining no mention from early writers on New England. The Turtle rattle is more generically Iroquois than either the water drum or horn rattle, and the latter is ascribed to "western" sources by informants, who say that it was preceded by a cylindrical bark rattle (Flannery, 1939, p. 83 and footnote, and pp. 85–86). I consider these elements nondiagnostic for this problem.

Belonging to the archaic residue of Huron-Iroquois culture are the traits relating to the organization and rationale of medicine societies based on dreams and cures. We read in the Jesuit Relations that the Huron have fraternities organized to honor certain spiritual masters or tutelaries to whom the sponsor appeals in making a feast, and that all those persons once the object of such a feast become members, a child succeeding his father (Thwaites, 1896–1901, vol. 17, p. 197). The Eagle is one such tutelary. The same people anciently sought the clairvoyant to interpret dreams. Algonquians west and east of the Iroquoians shared these customs, more so in the Great Lakes area.

Casting tobacco in the fire with prayer, the most common form of offering among the Huron-Iroquois, was widespread in the northern woodlands from the Abenaki westward to the Winnebago, among the mobile Algonquians including Delaware, and possibly in Virginia and Carolina (Flannery, 1939, p. 140; Radin, 1923, pp. 330, 447, 451). The basic idea of communion with spirits is elsewhere transferred to the pipe, which becomes the altar.

While individual pipe smoking at councils was a well-developed Iroquoian trait, ceremonial smoking, as we have seen, had its development elsewhere. The idea that those who smoke together become friends was found among Coastal Algonquians from Virginia northward, but the pipe of peace idea grew in importance going west up the Lakes, where the true calumet or feathered stem was found, and down the Mississippi to its confluence with the Ohio and Missouri and faded toward the Delta (Flannery, 1939, p. 68).

Possibly unrelated to the Iroquois custom of making a present to a dancer or other person after a speech, a feature of feasts at which dances of the war cycle are performed, is the custom of holding feasts at which presents are given away (Flannery, 1939, No. 291, p. 143). Dancing away one's property was a custom among the Massachusetts Indians, in which individuals one after another competed, dancing singly after the manner of Iroquois Personal Chant. The Narragansett celebrated this custom after the harvest, potlatching the whole community, and the sources imply that a similar custom was known at Martha's Vineyard, around Manhattan, and among the Delaware, where payments were in wampum, particularly to participants in the Green Corn Feast. The chiefly families of Mohawk Iroquois gave presents of wampum to each other, and there was a dance called *Gannisterohon* [58] which only members of that rank might sponsor, and in which they distributed wampum to those invited (Beauchamp, 1895 b, p. 218, citing Bruyas, 1862, p. 79). Likewise among the Cherokee, Timberlake reported that warriors danced individually, recited exploits, and threw wampum onto a large skin spread for the purpose. All these instances are obviously not related to the same culture trait, although Flannery noted an underlying similarity (Flannery, 1939, p. 145); and I can add that the privilege of reciting war records carries the responsibility of paying presents in all the Iroquois striking dances, but distributing goods is also a feature of two feasts sponsored by women: Death Feast (Fenton and Kurath, *in* Fenton, 1951 a), and Quavering (Fenton, 1947, p. 10). The presence in Iroquoia alone of two kinds of feasts at which presents are distributed, besides the Condolence Council in which the mourners are requickened with wampum strings, suggests that the sources cited by Flannery relate to several things.

The concept of the "head" permeates Iroquois feast symbolism. A human head, a dog's head, a bear's, a deer's, and a boar's head have all figured in successive periods as the central object of attention, symbolizing the feast of war and as the pièce de résistance at certain of the modern medicine societies. In fact, the fund levied for the Midwinter Festival at Tonawanda Longhouse is still referred to as the "head" (Fenton, 1941 a, p. 161). We have seen that dancing with the head preceded going to war. Presenting the head to the chiefs first, or by preference over other parts, goes back to wartime

[58] The modern Delaware "skin-beating" dance is still known among the Onondaga of Six Nations as gani'stǫgeka·' and by the Seneca ganisdǫgä'e·'.

cannibalism (Flannery, 1939, No. 257, pp. 126–127). The concept may be attributed to the Iroquoians, although we shall find precedents in the prehistory of Ohio and in the ancient Southeast.

All of the head is eaten at the feast, but the soup is taken home. This type of feast is not the true eat-all feast of the Huron and their neighbors, so frequently described in the Jesuit Relations, in which everything must be consumed on the spot. And the custom of bringing bark dishes, spoons, and lately pails to carry home the feast prevailed throughout the woodlands from the Caddo to the Malecite, so that trait is nondiagnostic for the present problem, although "they who carry pails at night" is a constantly recurring theme of modern reservation life among the Longhouse Iroquois.

If we proceed on the assumption that the Iroquois Eagle Dance is related to the ceremonial complex known as the Calumet Dance, it seems logical to isolate those elements of Iroquois Eagle Dance which are unique to that ceremony in Iroquoia and to then compare the reduced complex with neighboring complexes most like it. In ordering the comparison the logic of history and geography is compelling. Culture diffused in eastern America along paths and watercourses connecting ancient habitations, villages, and tribal hunting territories. The warpath was the line of travel outward in aggression; the same route was followed by peace embassies carrying the calumet. The calumet and its ceremony has a riverine distribution, and for purpose of discussion the distribution segregates along four great watercourse systems: the Ohio-Wabash, of which there is direct historical evidence; the Upper Mississippi and Great Lakes, only partly documented; the Upper Missouri, by inference and later documents; and the Lower Mississippi and its tributaries. Beyond the direct evidence of history and the inferential evidence of ethnological spread, there is some evidence for reconstructing a putative Eagle Dance substratum to account for certain common elements of well-nigh continental distribution, extending from the Southwest to Iroquoia. Finally, such speculation receives support and encouragement from a well-developed archeological literature on the so-called "Buzzard" or "Southern Cult," in which various interpretations for bird symbolisms range from Middle American influence to the more prosaic, and I think correct, theory of relationship to the Thunderbird concept of the Central Algonquian and Siouan Indians, or to some giant mythical bird, most frequently the Eagle—a character whom I hope the ritual of ethnology has requickened by the publishing of this monograph.

Returning to the perspective of living ethnology, the climax form of the Calumet ceremony was the Pawnee Hako, an elaborate ritual of 20 parts and four days' duration, which lived in the memory of Fletcher's informants late in the nineteenth century. The Hako embraces most of the features involved in the widespread ceremony of earlier times when living sources ascribed its origin to the Pawnee. Four conspicuous features of the Hako suggest a relationship to Iroquois Eagle Dance:

(1) The use of feathered stems.
(2) A dance in honor of Eagles.
(3) Presentation of feathered stems by honored old men to the dancers.
(4) Friendship (or peace) as the leitmotiv.

In demonstrating the relationship of Iroquois Eagle Dance to the Calumet, there are some 25 traits to be accounted for.

Peculiar features of Iroquois Eagle Dance

(1) Ritual addressed to Eagle
(2) Luring down birds (pit trapping) *
(3) Eagle sickness: contamination by bird lice or dream
(4) Raven messenger
(5) Eagle Dance songs
(6) Crouching bird dance mime eagles
      (a) rattle right hand; fan left
      (b) pick up object in mouth
(7) Medicine bundle: tobacco, gourd rattle, fan (whistle)
(8) Display bundle on pole
(9) Striped pole and signal beater
(10) Roc *
(11) Friends (adoption) *
(12) Messenger and conductor
(13) Appointed whooper
(14) Appointed singer
(15) Appointed dancers
(16) Pipe-passing *
(17) Honored men present fans and rattles to dancers
(18) Striking and counting coup
(19) Gift distribution after speech
(20) Song for laying down fans
(21) Pass head and mime bird cries
(22) Wings brush aside evil
(23) Meetings mostly in winter
(24) Lack sex and color symbolism
(25) Moiety spatial seating

The Pawnee are credited with originating the Hako type of Calumet Dance and from the eighteenth century forward observers recorded the tradition that the Pawnee were the agents of spreading it east, south, and westward on the Plains. For the moment we shall not be concerned with the recent diffusion of the Hako to the Teton Sioux (Walker, 1917, p. 122), or how the Arikara, after splitting away from the Pawnee, gave the pipes first to the Omaha (Fletcher and LaFlesche, 1911, pp. 74, 376), and later were the agents of its introduction to the

---

* Already discussed.

Hidatsa and Crow during the second half of the nineteenth century
(Lowie, 1915, p. 239; Curtis, 1909, vol. 5, p. 150); but we shall first
compare the composite Pawnee ceremony with Iroquois Eagle Dance
to see what they have in common before chasing the distribution of
the Calumet Dance. In making the comparison, two ritual constructs
of approximately the same time level are being contrasted. Earlier
and later forms of the Calumet Dance can then be treated in proper
perspective.

With all the elaborate bundle complexes of the Pawnee, it is not
surprising that one division of the Pawnee had an Eagle Dance
(Murie, 1914, p. 640), and the Young Eagle Society Bundle, which now
reposes at the Chicago Natural History Museum, exclusively required
songs which "resemble those doctors use, which as a class differ from
songs for bundles" (Murie-Wissler, MS., p. 157). The relationship
of these two briefly mentioned rites to Hako is not clear, unfortunately.
The Hako is one of four ritualistic procedures which were not compo-
nents of the yearly cycle—Morning-star sacrifice; Calumet ritual;
North Star Bundle ceremonies; and the New Fire Ceremony, or the
Scalp Dance (Murie-Wissler, MS. p. 8).

In the latter respect Hako resembles Eagle Dance.

At the expense of distorting the pattern of sequence which Hako
presumably shares with other Pawnee rites, the Pawnee data are now
brought into parallel sequence with Iroquois Eagle Dance. First,
the Hako is addressed to eagles, and its very name may be remotely
cognate with the Iroquoian name of the rite: Pawnee ruktaraiwarius,
"shaking a stick, or feathered stem," suggests its Iroquoian synonym,
gane'onda·don'.

Lacking data on luring down birds and contamination, I note that
Eagle Dance is held for a sick youth and the power of running water
figures prominently in the cure as it does in the Iroquois Little Water
Medicine Company; and dreams and visions are stressed, having their
locus among eagles, as the origin of the ceremony.

Eagle instead of Raven is man's mediator with the supernaturals.
A brown female eagle is associated with north, peace, and heaven.
A white male eagle signifies war, the earth, and is south. All the
birds on the stem are leaders: the eagle presides over day; the owl
presides at night; the woodpecker presides over trees; and the duck
over water.

Elaborate bundle equipment includes two hollow feathered stems,
(feathered with eagle feathers and decorated near the mouth with duck
and woodpecker heads); decorated gourd rattles (one for each stem);
wing-bone whistles to mimic eagle cries; an ear of corn; a crotched
stick symbolizing the eagle's nest to rest the stems; and a wildcat-skin
altar, but no beater. When displayed, fans are oriented north and

south on a tent pole, and an elaborate ceremony attends the making of new fans. Fat offerings symbolizing plenty exceed tobacco offerings, but the emphasis on ritual smoking contrasts with Iroquois.

The Hako is a summer ritual of five days, of which the nineteenth part is most like the Iroquois Eagle Dance (Fletcher, 1904, p. 253 ff.). Dancers hold a rattle in the right hand and fan in left, they sway in mime of eagles but do not squat, there is preliminary ceremonial feeding of children (eaglets); and there are special songs for laying down the feathered stems, which represent the eagle descending to its nest.

Officialdom is more elaborate than Iroquois, and the conductor appoints main participants, including singers and dancers. The conductor appoints an honored warrier to present both fans to the two dancers, who are north and south. Holding the rattle in his right hand and the fan in his left hand, the privileged one recounts his war record and then presents the fans. There is no striking post, but other warriors may interrupt the singers by stepping forward with upraised hand. Gifts are distributed in the twentieth ritual ceremony.

Cosmogonic symbolism pervades the Hako. The wing of the eagle (not raven) is the doctor's sign; ceremonial swaying of feathered stems stands for power of birds to disperse evil by flapping wings, blowing out impurities like Iroquois False-faces; the lodge is the nest of the eagle, symbolized by crotched stick; color figures prominently; directions and motion also figure prominently; four is the sacred number; and the honored child is the symbol of life and generations to follow. In winding up the equipment he is told of the good which will come to him.

The purpose of the ritual is twofold: it forms a sacred kinship, as of fathers and sons, the latter becoming fathers to others, and the rite renews such associations. Moiety reciprocity between clans, which are most frequently of different tribes, is a focal factor in an area rent by factions.

If the Pawnee and the Iroquois were never in direct contact, at least several elements in the Hako suggest to me a more easterly and woodland habitat for the Pawnee in former times: substitution of the buffalo for the deer in feasts; maize symbolism reminiscent of former more intense agriculture; and the peculiar treatment of water, on which ground Miss Fletcher argued that the ceremony originated in a semiarid region; however, both the Iroquois and Cherokee employ the power of running water in cures (Fletcher, 1904, pp. 253–282).

While it is certain that the path of diffusion of the Calumet Dance from the Pawnee to the Iroquois lay through other tribes, such as the Iowa, Fox, Illinois, and Miami, the route of transmission cannot be documented for each tribe. Nor are the accounts of the dance among various tribes of comparable age.   The dance in honor of the calumet among the Illinois, which term may infer the Miami and related tribes south of the Lakes (Kinietz, 1940, p. 190), was first described by the Jesuit Fathers Allouez (1667), who first saw the ceremony performed in the Green Bay region, and Marquette (1673). They discovered in this remarkable ceremony of friendship a passport which was to carry them safely among hostile tribes living along the banks of the great river which the French were about to explore. The Miami band, which was visited by Allouez, was then much reduced by wars with the Sioux and Iroquois; they made a dance in honor of a single pipe which was ceremoniously placed in the middle of the room; individuals danced successively to the drum, pantomiming stages of warfare from preparing arms, dressing, running, discovery, the cry, the kill, scalping, and returning in victory; and finally the pipe was presented to the honored guest as a certain pledge of peace so long as he shall keep it (Thwaites, 1896–1901, vol. 51, p. 47).   Its use in making peace, according to Allouez, was even greater among the Sioux beyond La Pointe.

Seven years later the Illinois greeted Marquette with the full course of the Calumet Dance and his famous Relation is too well known to repeat except to underscore those features which the Iroquois keep alive as weak images.   He describes a summer ceremony in an arbor, although in winter it was performed indoors.   The ritual addressed the sun, if not the eagle, like the Pawnee: naked priests stared at the sun through spread fingers held at arm's length, and dancers pointed the pipe at the sun.   Weather control is implied. Pipe bearers greet strangers and conduct them to the village, and at each village entered the honored guest is offered the pipe and is hand-fed four times.   A special set of songs accompany the Calumet Dance, with drum and rattles.   Single dancers take up the pipe in succession and "   . . .   make it spread its wings, as if about to fly . . .".   Part two is the Discovery Dánce, described by Allouez, and which resembles Iroquois Striking-a-stick Dance.   In part three, individual warriors one after another take up the calumet and recount war exploits, for which the conductor rewards the coup counters with presents of beaver skins.   The calumet goes to a neighbor and finally to the honored guest.   The Illinois calumet, the large feather fan, is attached to a red-stone pipe which is smoked, and the hollow stem is ornamented with the heads and necks of various birds—red, green, and other colors—the war calumet being predominantly red. As at Fox war-bundle feasts, the calumet, various dream objects which comprise the bundle contents, and weapons of war are displayed on a mat where the honored guest is seated.   The ceremony has its own officials, including a conductor and pipe messengers, and the role of singers falls to berdaches who occupy special seats but are not permitted to dance, a role reserved for warriors. Emphasis on pipe passing and smoking is absent from Iroquois, but in the end as in Iroquois Eagle Dance, Marquette, the guest, received the calumet, which had gone through the hands of boasting warriors, as a token of friendship. Thus the calumet became a symbol of peace and a passport. The ceremony was usually given to honor another tribe, and its principal symbol functioned to end disputes, strengthen alliances, and to speak to strangers (Thwaites, 1896–1901, vol. 54, p. 191; vol. 59, pp. 115–137).

Having accepted the calumet, the French soon found out how far the newfound passport would take them. La Salle met a similar ceremony among the Akansa and noted that calumets differ from tribe to tribe. The Akansa put up poles on which to display gifts, they seated the guests and chiefs near the middle, and the singers accompanied themselves with pot (water) drums and gourd rattles. Here is the first mention of a war post, planted in the center of the group, which the warriors struck with war clubs and counted their coups, but a liar risked having the pole wiped clean of his lies with a skin. Speakers made gifts to the recipient of the feast. Again I note considerable passing of the pipe. Elsewhere La Salle says that the Iroquois have no respect for the calumet and keep at an enemy until they destroy him, and he implies that the Iroquois had rejected such peace overtures from the Illinois. A still later account mentions corn soup at Akansa feasts (Margry, 1875–1886, vol. 1, pp. 553–554; vol. 2, p. 33; and Thwaites, 1896–1901, vol. 67, pp. 249, 251).

In 1680, Sauk and Fox and various divisions of the Eastern Dakota, the Ottawa, Potawatomi, and probably those Chippewa living south of the Lakes, employed the calumet ritual for creating father-and-son relationships (Hennepin, 1880, pp. 105, 112–113, 190, 205, 208, 213, 226–227; 1903, vol. 1, pp. 125–127; Perrot, in Blair, 1911, vol. 1, p. 185). The Winnebago and Sauk honored the French commandant of Michilimackinac in 1721, and Charlevoix, an eyewitness, credits the Winnebago with a better performance. All of the participants were very young persons, including drummers, assistants with rattles, and dancers who were painted for war and were holding feather fans. The calumet had the honored place. "Orchestra and dancers were seated quite around, the spectators being placed up and down in small bodies, the women apart from the men . . . ," as in Iroquois feasts. Between the honored guest and the singers, a post was erected for the warriors to strike. Near the end of each song a warrior would stop the dance by striking the post with his battle-ax; profound silence followed, and he proclaimed his achievements. The company applauded, but instead of wiping the post clean, he smeared ashes on the heads of liars.

Charlevoix, who had read Marquette's Relation, but who became quite bored before both tribes had gone through the ceremony, says specifically that the commandant was not placed on a new mattress, feathers were not placed on his head, and he saw no calumet presented to the commandant. Nor did he see any naked and entirely painted pipe-bearers. A description of the Dance of Discovery follows, ending with recitation of war records. Evidently the ceremony here was not as elaborate as among the Illinois (Charlevoix, 1923, vol. 2, pp. 63–66).

Meanwhile the Fox Indians had introduced the Calumet Dance among the Abenaki near Montreal, and since the Fox were the close kindred of the Sauk, whom Charlevoix observed, and later merged with them, the Fox Pipe Dance merits consideration. My analysis is based on the rich published and manuscript materials of the late Dr. Truman Michelson and the observations of Mrs. Kurath (p. 268), who saw the Fox perform the Pipe Dance at Rock Island, Ill. Historic contacts between the Fox and Seneca were frequent, and the number of correspondences between the Fox Pipe Dance and the Iroquois Eagle Dance is not surprising. Fox bundle feasts follow a consistent pattern of sequence, which also seems to be characteristic of Sauk, Kickapoo, Prairie Potawatomi, Ottawa, Iowa, and Winnebago feasts, a discovery which we owe to Dr. Michelson (Michelson, 1928, pp. 545–546; Jones (Fisher, ed.), 1939, pp. 144–145, and references cited therein). The Fox pattern, moreover, is quite different from the Iroquois feast pattern, and comparison requires wrenching the data out of context and rearranging them. This is one of the unsatisfactory aspects of comparative studies, since no two sets of ethnic phenomena are ever quite the same.

Society emphasis is marked among Fox, and Eagle gens dominates membership in the Eagle Dance Feast, at which others "sit as children" to regard two feathered pipes, the emblems of the Eagles (Jones (Fisher, ed.), 1939, pp. 88–89, 97–98; Michelson, B.A.E. Ms. No. 2756).

Besides the Pipe Dance of the Eagle Society, the Fox have another rite called Wapanowiweni, which is exclusively for birds, who are presided over by four "great-grandfathers," the sacred number, who reside at the four quarters, and correspond to the dual divisions of White and Red, generically similar to Iroquois (Michelson, 1932, pp. 12–13).

Besides a variant of the Roc myth, a hero dreams of a bird and is instructed to tell the people, and public health depends on performing the rite of the pack (Michelson, 1932, p. 29). The Crow is a wise bird who knows medicines, and is grandfather and scout for the council of animals.

Sixteen dancing songs, divided into four periods marked by drum beats, involve vicarious participation by eagles. The Eagle Dance is not described, but the songs show close correspondence with Iroquois (see Kurath, this paper, p. 297). The dance in honor of the Eagle bundle resembles other Fox pack dances: shamans dance individually carrying Eagle fans in White Buffalo (Michelson, 1925, p. 11), and in clusters, women facing in one direction, and the men in one spot (Michelson, 1932, p. 121); and at their feast Eagles leave the dancing to guests.

Fox bundles call for special handling (Michelson, 1928, p. 5); tobacco is used for supernatural mediation (Michelson, 1932, p. 9); two redstone pipes, with eagle-wing fans, stand in a vessel (Michelson, 1929, pp. 97–98); and a ceremonial flute is blown to quarters. When displayed, the bundle is not on a pole, but a feathered pole, which brought people through an ordeal, is erected at the door of a lodge and painted red (Michelson, B.A.E. Ms., No. 1850).

Roc lives in a land of rocks, the winter home of birds, and Eagles are lured down with tobacco (Jones (Fisher, ed.), 1939, p. 22).

The ceremony has two sides, givers and guests, and the Fox employ a headman or conductor, ceremonial runners and waiters, as do other central Algonquian and Siouan tribes (Michelson, 1927, pp. 2–3 for distribution; 1928, p. 4). Singers are appointed, and there are four dancers (like Iroquois) who symbolize world quarters, and the four similarly colored birds. Eagle Pack features pipe passing, but the tobacco offerings suggest Iroquois, and as in Iroquois False-faces and Pawnee Hako, pipes and fans are fed with grease.

It is not clear that anyone presents fans, but speakers pray for long life, as do the Iroquois; nothing occurs on gift distribution, nor is there a song for laying down fans. Dog meat is the Fox feast food, but note that a hog head is now substituted and is used widely in the area (Michelson, 1928, p. 6; 1929, pp. 8–9). Summer meetings predominate. Color symbolism is marked as noted, four feathers being placed at cardinal points (Michelson 1928, p. 13; 1932, pp. 12–13).

While it is not safe to compare ceremonies of different historic periods, the analysis of Iroquois Eagle Dance correspondences with Fox, apart from the historic record of contact, would argue for an original connection between the two ceremonial complexes; but I judge that the Calumet Dance, in the course of being transformed to the Red Stone Pipe ceremony of the Fox Eagle Gens, has been fitted into the consistent pattern which guides all Fox bundle feasts, just as it has been adapted to the pattern which governs the medicine society complex of the Iroquois.

If the first path of diffusion of the Calumet Dance led up the Ohio to the Iroquois through such tribal links as Pawnee-Iowa-

Fox-Illinois-Miami, diffusion can also be inferred from a northern Mississippi River center, hypothetically located at the Pipestone Quarry near the Falls of St. Anthony, where surrounding hostile tribes met on neutral ground to mine catlinite. The quarry may be called the focus of the "peace pipe" concept, and just east of it lay Green Bay, the rendezvous of the "Far" Indians, certain bands of Chippewa and Ottawa, who were agents in spreading the use of the peace pipe eastward to the Iroquois between 1680 and 1725. From the same center, the westward drift of the Chippewa and Dakota during their wars produced a westward spread of the catlinite pipe and feathered stem presumably to the Plains Ojibwa, Assiniboin, Plains Cree, Blackfoot, and possibly the Cheyenne. It is in this northern Plains area where the Pipe Bundle Dance occurs, involving a bundle, a sacred pipe, and a rite. That the Medicine Pipe Bundle and the Hako are distinct types of ceremonies was first seen by Wissler, to whom it appeared that the former prevails on the northern plains and the latter on the southern, and from the fact that the Teton Dakota have both (Wissler, 1912, p. 167). Diffusional influences from the Hako area also passed overland from tribe to tribe as far as the Ottawa above the Straits of Mackinac and to the Sioux.

A certain Ottawa chief received the honors of the calumet from the Sioux for saving prisoners from death at the hands of the Saulteaux (Ojibwa), circa 1665. Perrot comments:

The savages believe the sun gave it to the Panys, and since then it has been communicated from village to village as far as the Outaoüas. [Blair, 1911, vol. 1, p. 186.]

It is said that the Illinois got it from the Pawnee, and the Sioux from the Illinois during their wars (Blair, 1911, vol. 1, p. 182).

The Potawatomi and Menomini of Green Bay, Wis., followed the custom further south of carrying the honored guest on their shoulders (Blair, 1911, vol. 1, pp. 309, 311). Perrot who had wide experience with the Calumet Dance received similar honors from the Iowa. Outside a village which was inhabited jointly by Miami and Mascoutin, he was greeted by pipe messengers, and while musicians kept singing, the dancers alternately bent their knees almost to the ground; they presented the calumet to the sun with the same genuflections, a feature which recalls Eagle Dance crouch. Whereupon the war chief raised Perrot on his shoulders and the whole troop of musicians conducted him to the village, where he was taken to the cabin of the Mascoutin chief (ibid., pp. 327–330).

A degenerated form of the Calumet Dance persisted into the present century among the Menomini. Skinner notes several survivals of comparative interest. When prolonged drought threatens, they sometimes give the contents of a bundle a somewhat sacrosanct airing on a pole, displaying a drum, gourd rattle, and eagle-feather fan (Skinner, 1915 b, pp. 206–207; 1921, pp. 60, 99, and pl. 11). The Tobacco Dance, so-called, is held to honor an ancient pipe; it has its own opening speech and songs, it features an individual dance contest, alternating with "brave" dances, and is restricted to veterans of the Civil War. Each dancer carries a gourd rattle, but no pipe is mentioned. It is held usually in the open, sometimes indoors. Losers make gifts of clothing, or more appropriately red-stone pipes, to the winners, especially when an intertribal contest is held with a friendly tribe such as the Potawatami or Winnebago, and then a feast is held (Skinner, 1915 b, pp. 211–212). One of the important duties of Menomini chiefs, of whom one was pipe holder, was to prevent brawls attending a murder (Skinner, 1913, p. 24). Skinner and Wissler were among the first to note the widespread juridical function of the pipe holder among the Plains tribes (Skinner, 1913, p. 28).

For the Chippewa, there are two descriptions of the Calumet Dance from the first quarter of the nineteenth century by George Boyd and Peter Grant (Kinietz, 1947, pp. 92–94). These descriptions may be considered typical of the dance among the Chippewa, Ottawa, and Potawatomi (Kinietz, 1940, pp. 270, 325). The Chippewa baited a giant bird (Eagle) with deer, prizing its feathers (Kinietz, 1947, p. 106). Grant distinguished the Discovery Dance from the Grand Calumet Dance, of which the southerly bands of Ojibwa claimed superior knowledge. The single dancer held the rattle in the right hand and in the left the war-pipe stem, from which depended a quarter circle of eagle-tail feathers. Kurath has analyzed his maneuvers. Passing the implements to the next person was esteemed a compliment and the succession of single dancers continued.

The Sioux in the late seventeenth century still occupied much of Minnesota and Wisconsin, and the Jesuit Father Allouez called them "the Iroquois of the country beyond La Pointe," and it is "they who chiefly adore the calumet," they feast in silence and greet a stranger by feeding him with a wooden fork as one would a child (Thwaites, 1896–1901, vol. 54, pp. 191–193). But probably no one had more varied experience among the Eastern Dakota, the Iowa, and the Illinois or suffered more abuse in the name of the calumet than Father Hennepin, the Recollect. Emphasis on tears or ceremonial weeping on greeting strangers recalls the reception of visiting tribes in Iroquois Condolence Council and may tie in with the weeping-eye motif of the Southern or Buzzard Cult. They lay hands on the head and massage the legs of a visiting traveler.

Hennepin saw successive dancers contest for honors. He mentions the gourd rattle and much pipe passing. The ceremony created father-and-son relationships with distant tribes (Hennepin, 1880, pp. 205–230). In the same year the Sioux who were at war with all others but the Saulteaux (Ojibwa) and the Iowa came to Michilimackinac bearing calumets, they carried the honored guest about the village on their shoulders, and they wept over his head like the Iowa (LaPotherie *in* Blair, 1911–12, vol. 2, p. 31).

How these performances of the Calumet Dance, so-called by French writers, tie in with the Medicine Pipe Bundle ritual of the northern Plains tribes, as described by modern ethnologists, and how the former seventeenth-century descriptions relate to the Hako type of Calumet Dance remains one of the unsolved problems of this study. It is a marginal problem, moreover, and leaving it as a legacy to later scholarship does not affect the attempt to trace the historical roots of the Iroquois Eagle Dance. Whatever common traits were shared at first by the tribes west of Green Bay who first felt the influence of the Pawnee Calumet Dance on their own sacred Pipe Dance, several centuries and the westward dispersion of tribes gave time and space for developing distinct ritual patterns and complexes of traits which by the twentieth century appeared quite unrelated. Wissler and Lowie, whose knowledge of the northern Plains tribes will never be equaled, attribute the Medicine Pipe Bundle ritual and the Pawnee Hako ceremony, despite superficial similarities which no doubt reflect borrowings, to separate sources. Wissler's work with Murie on Pawnee ceremonies, after prolonged field work with Blackfoot and Dakota, commands respect for his comparative notes on the distribution of the Medicine Pipe Bundle; its distinction from the Hako; his general reservations about all smoking ceremonies not being calumet ceremonies; and the probably distinct origin of the Hako and the Medicine Pipe (Wissler, 1912, pp. 165–168). The Blackfoot type of Medicine Pipe Bundle Wissler found distributed among Sarsi, Gros Ventre of Fort Belknap, Western Cree, on the authority of Mackenzie and Kane, and Teton Dakota; the Arapaho, Gros Ventre, and Cheyenne possibly shared the flat pipe of an analagous type (Kroeber, 1904, p. 308; 1908, p. 272; Dorsey, James Owen, 1884, p. 278); Wissler doubted that the Assiniboin had something similar, but Denig rather confirms it (Denig, 1930, pp. 446–448), and the Assiniboin borrowed from the Cree a crouching dance with rattles in mime of prairie chickens, which is probably unrelated to Iroquois Eagle Dance (Lowie, 1909, p. 57; Skinner, 1914, p. 531), and the Horse Dance utilized wing-bone whistle and pipe. Leaving the Pipe Dance to students of the northern Plains, let us take up the path of the Hako.

From its center among the Pawnee the ceremony was carried up the Missouri to the village tribes presumably by the Arikara. The Omaha and the Osage had the ceremony after the Arikara (Fletcher and LaFlesche, 1911, p. 74), and the Iowa who claim to have originated it probably had it from the same source, if not from Omaha or Pawnee, while the Ponca, Oto, Kansa, and Caddo were in direct contact with Pawnee (Skinner, 1915 a, p. 706). Cheyenne, Arapaho, and Kiowa were all contiguous to the Pawnee on the west, but I find no clear-cut statements that they had the Hako, other than the Omaha tradition of the coming of the peace pipe (wa^{n}wa^n) from the Arikara. Omaha tradition maintains that the Arikara were the agents of spreading the ceremony to the Omaha, Ponca, Iowa, Oto and Cheyenne at a village then situated on the Big Sioux River, where the Arikara were found living a sedentary life later taken up by the Omaha. The Cheyenne later lost the rite (Fletcher and LaFlesche, 1911, pp. 47, 74, 376).

The date for the appearance of the Hunka (or Hako) among the Teton Dakota is given in a calendar as about the year A. D. 1805, "when They Waved Horse-tails over Each other," which is what the Oglala call the ceremony (Walker, 1917, pp. 122–123). Sometime in the second half of the century, the Crow adopted "a Medicine Pipe Dance of the *Hako* type . . . from the Hidatsa . . . and the Hidatsa remember that their Medicine Pipe ceremony was in turn derived from the Arikara" (Lowie, 1913, p. 150; 1915, p. 239). Just how the ceremony reached the Plains-Cree is uncertain, and Skinner's description fits the Blackfoot type of Medicine-pipe more nearly than the Hako (Skinner, 1914, p. 536; 1915 a, p. 706; Mandelbaum, 1940, p. 278). Surely it was the central Siouans and the Caddoans, the southern and western nations of Charlevoix, among whom the calumet was more in use "than among eastern and northern tribes, and more frequently for peace than for war," and, specifically, it was the Pawnee to whom "the sun gave the calumet" (Charlevoix, 1923, vol. 1, pp. 304, 305).

Of the central Siouans, the Omaha Calumet Dance is the best described, after that the Iowa, and the Teton Dakota version exhibits interesting differentiation. In the Omaha form of the ceremony War Eagle figures prominently, supplanting Corn in the Pawnee Hako, as the "Mother" tutelary of the rite. Otherwise the articles used and their symbolism is identical (Fletcher and LaFlesche, 1911, pp. 379, 381).

In this area Woodpecker replaces Raven as messenger for the birds and mythology connects him with the sun.

A specific song accompanied by rhythmic movement of pipes is called "shaking or waving the pipes or feathered stems." The whole ceremony is called wa^{n}wa^n, "to sing for someone" (Fletcher and La Flesche, 1911, p. 376.)

Two dancers simulate the movements of eagles, but do not crouch.

The stems taken up from the wildcat skin are waved to the rhythm of rattles shaken with an accented beat, and in this part no drum is used (Fletcher and LaFlesche, 1911, p. 383). Elsewhere, the Omaha use a water drum of partly hollowed tree; they know the Iroquis technique of tipping the drum to keep the skin head wet, and they beat with a rebounding rhythm (ibid., p. 371). In the part which resembles Iroquois Striking-a-stick Dance, the calumet is grasped in the left hand by the duck's neck, the gourd rattle in the right, and the dancers follow the drum and pass backward and forward, imitating the actions of War Eagle, constantly waving the calumet and shaking the rattle in time with the drum (Long, 1823, vol. 1, p. 332).

The paraphernalia comprises 2 feathered stems of ash which are 7 stretches of thumb to tip of forefinger in length; the blue or female one has 10 mottled feathers; and the green or male has 7 white feathers which are war honors. At rest against red crotched sticks, head down on a wildcat skin, each stem has a decorated gourd rattle; there is a bladder pouch of tobacco; an eagle wing-bone whistle; three downy eagle feathers; and sweetgrass which completes the ritual equipment (Fletcher and La Flesche, 1911, p. 377). I do not find that the bundle is displayed on a pole for weather control. Long saw a striking post (Long, 1823, vol. 1, p. 332).

Ceremonial friendship as in Pawnee and Iroquois was its purpose, and the two parties, the one who presented the pipes and the recipient, assumed a father-and-son relationship. Analogous to the friendship pact created by the Iroquois Eagle Dance between a sick boy and his father's clansman who had dreamed of him, the child in Omaha represents the coming generations and often a generation separated him from his "father." On one such occasion the Oto gave a child to the Pawnee, who mounted him on a fine horse and sent him back (Long, 1823, vol. 1, p. 332).

The sponsor sends a messenger bearing tobacco to fill a pipe which, when accepted and smoked, seals the contract, but may be courteously refused on grounds of poverty. Presumably there is a conductor because the guest has two servants, his dancers. There is a crier. Singers and the two head dancers are obviously appointed (Dorsey, J. O., 1884, p. 277). Two young men of the party are chosen to perform the final dance (Fletcher and La Flesche, 1911, p. 399); they wear only breechclout. Drummer and singers sit in the middle, and the child, or honored guest, is with them, his head sprinkled with eagle down. Nearby are the two dancers wearing only breechclouts and both have the sign of the ceremony painted in red on their faces (Dorsey, 1884, p. 281). Each holds a wand in the left hand and a gourd rattle in the right. Otherwise no regular pattern of seating obtains.

I am uncertain whether honored men present fans and rattles to the dancers, but Long said striking the post, or touching one of the dancers was the accepted means of counting coup. A man would advance and stop before one of the dancers who handed him the pipe, the music ceased, the man recounted his deeds and laid the pipe on the ground, which challenged other warriors to take it up and recount deeds of equal valor (Fletcher and La Flesche, 1911, p. 399). I gather from Long's account that warriors had to validate their intention of striking by assembling horses and guns as gifts at the post, which was announced by the crier. The donor then struck the post, counted coups, and occasionally one would take the drum and beat out the number of his accomplishments, which stopped the ceremony and no one might touch the drum until another could top his record, whereupon the drum was returned to the performer (Long, 1823, vol. 1, p. 332). Presents at Omaha and Pawnee dances sometimes ran to excesses, but the "son" received the ritual equipment which he customarily gave away to those who had assisted him (Fletcher and La Flesche, 1911, p. 400). Visitors also made presents to the hosts. Dorsey says that the child's parents usually kept the sacred stems, and with them went the privilege of adopting others in the same manner (Dorsey, J. O., 1884, p. 281).

The Omaha, too, had a special song for laying down the feathered stems; the rattles were attached to the wands, and the dancers simulated eagles settling on the nest (Fletcher and La Flesche, 1911, p. 384).

The concept of the animal head does not appear, but I note the idea that wings brush aside evil.

It was a summer ceremony of several days duration, with a special rite of putting the calumet to rest each night. Symbolism reached elaborate proportions, special colors standing for sex, sky, and earth, the moieties or tribes; and the innocent child represented the oncoming generations, peace and the contrast of the warlike spirit of the Plains. The design painted on the child's face and on the gourds, which symbolize birds' eggs, shows horizon, the path of the four winds; red face paint symbolized the light of the sun. Red woodpecker feathers are a sun symbol. Green stood for earth, blue for sky, and red for the sun and life. It all added up to peace and friendship (Fletcher and La Flesche, 1911, p. 380). The very spatial seating of the tribes met for this purpose constituted a focal force in Plains life counteracting the centrifugal tendency of factions and war.

The Ponca had the same ceremony in a somewhat attenuated form, supposedly having received it from the Arikara with the Omaha. Dorsey said they were not fully acquainted with the dance and had only one pipe (Dorsey, 1884, p. 282), but in Skinner's time they had a full bundle of two feathered wands, male and female, wrapped in a wildcat skin (Skinner, 1915 a, p. 789). The closing act, called "blessing the child," which was secret among the Omaha, was open with the Ponca, and differed in some minor details (Fletcher and La Flesche, 1911, p. 401).

If tradition can be trusted, and the Iowa acquired the Calumet Dance from the Arikara with the Omaha, the Arikara must have separated from the Pawnee, in the middle of the seventeenth century, and conveyed the ceremony a decade or two later, because the Iowa were reported already in possession of the ceremony by 1680 (Thwaites, 1896–1901, vol. 60, p. 203; Blair, 1911, vol. 1, pp. 368–369). Father Louis André, who was among the Winnebago at Green Bay in 1676, writes that they were visited by seven or eight families from a tribe called Aiaoua, who are neutral between our savages and the Nadoessi (Sioux); they inhabit a large village some 200 leagues west from Green Bay, and they are quite poor, "for their greatest wealth consists of ox hides and of Red Calumets" (Thwaites, 1896–1901, vol. 60, p. 203). Possibly these same Iowa annointed Perrot with "saliva, snot, and tears" (for they were great weepers) when he visited their village situated some distance beyond the Mississippi at 43°North latitude. "Twenty prominent men presented the calumet to Perrot, and carried him on a buffalo skin into the cabin of the chief, who walked at the head of this procession . . ." More weeping followed, after which he was presented the calumet again, and he was ceremonially fed with pieces of Buffalo tongue, which he proceeded to spit out with the smoke from the calumet. The chief asked Perrot whether he would accept the calumet, "which they wished to sing for him . . . an honor . . . granted only to those they regard as great captains" (Blair, 1911, vol. 1, p. 369).

The later-day Iowa had both the Calumet Dance and an Eagle Dance, which Skinner placed with his Forked-tailed Kite Dance (Skinner, 1915 a, pp. 706–709, 715–716; Catlin, 1844, p. 21). All three have traits in common with Iroquois Eagle Dance. Catlin's Eagle Dance was a war dance in honor of eagle to whom the song appealed. Each dancer imagines himself an eagle soaring. The dancers advance from behind musicians, hover, appear to stoop, and are blown back. They carry whistles in hand and mime eagle cries (Catlin, 1844, p. 20). Each dancer has a fan in his left hand made of an eagle's tail (Catlin, 1852, pp. 17–18 in Skinner 1915 a, p. 716). Catlin's term "ha-kon-e-crasse" strikes no response, but waioⁿewaci, the Iowa term for Calumet Dance bears a tantalizing resemblance to Iroquois wa'e'no'e·', Striking-a-stick Dance. Moreover, in Iroquois fashion, the mythical founder of Iowa calumet dance dreamt of two eagles, one white and one dark. Skinner further regards Catlin's description as of an eagle cult, or one connected with a war bundle (Skinner, 1915 a, p. 717), and the Forked-tailed Kite Dance has therapeutic power. Two wand bearers dismount and dance in the Iowa Calumet Dance, halting four times on their way to the village, calumet in left hand, rattle in right. Both of the Iowa wands are male, they are perforated, a deer bladder painted blue holds tobacco, a forked stick supports the reclining calumet, and a wildcat skin spreads on the ground behind the crotched stick where two gourd rattles rest (Skinner, 1915 a, p. 707). In another paper, however, Skinner illustrates both male (white tipped with black) and female (dark feathers) wands, a tobacco bag of a buffalo's heart, with buffalo wool and sweetgrass attached (Skinner, 1926, pl. 37). Displaying the bundle on a pole and heaping tobacco beneath precedes Forked-tailed Kite Dance and suggests Iroquois, and in the Calumet Dance a special song accompanies the setting up of the forked stick in the lodge. A runner bears the tobacco bladder and the recipient becomes the adopted son of the donor. Catlin said the Eagle Dance was given to compliment a warrior, and to initiate friends to brother-and-sister relationships. The owners of the seven gens pipes delegate one of their number to conduct the one who wishes to make a friend. Early Iowa accounts mention pipe passing. Catlin says that to commence the Calumet Dance, the two sets of pipes and rattles are handed to the dancers by the greatest warrior present who boasts as he makes the presentation a fact of which the honored one may brag all his life (Catlin, 1844, p. 21 *in* Skinner, 1915 a, p. 709). And in Catlin's accounts of the Eagle Dance, at the end of the song, without striking, warriors step forward, stop the dance, and count coups, which gives the dance momentum (Catlin, 1852, pp. 17–18 *in* Skinner, 1915 a, p. 717). All invited bring presents, some even sending gifts as an investment, in expectation of returns (Skinner, 1915 a, p. 708), for the honored one is expected to make handsome presents (Catlin, 1844, p. 21). The ceremony lasts several days, ending with painting the sacred child who is ceremonially captured by warriors who rush the tent and count coups, after which he is returned to his kin bearing the wands (Skinner, 1915 a, p. 709). Renewals are held over a period of four years, the magic number. Other details are lacking.

The Oglala Division of the Teton Dakota were the highwater mark of true Hako diffusion on the northern Plains. The Sioux Hunka, first described by Curtis (1908, vol. 3, pp. 71–87) and with greater detail and authority by Walker (1917, pp. 122–140), is synonymous with Pawnee Hako; but "waving horse tails" has replaced "waving the feathered stems" in the minds of Dakota horsemen. We noted that dreams of eagles occur in Dakota folklore. The rite has its own songs, and two dancers are appointed to bear the two wands, stem in left hand and rattle in right. I take it that the two Hunka wands are decorated and so named Horse-tails in lieu of feather tufts, and a rattle goes with each. Besides, Walker lists (p. 124), as provided by participants: an ear of corn, fire carrier, counting rod, scaffold, and drum; equipment provided by the conductor, a shaman, included the ceremonial pipe, buffalo skull, and fetish. He lists other materials, including sweetgrass, and paints (red, blue, yellow, and green), and other typical Dakota props.

The Hunka relationship is one of ceremonial friendship and all the initiates share a name but they do not constitute a distinct society in the Plains sense. Like Iroquois, the relationship often overrides generations, and with a young boy requires parental consent. The conductor is a shaman, one entitled to paint his hands red, and the decision rests with him whether and how to compound the rite; pyramiding rituals is characteristic of Dakota. The conductor may also appoint a policeman; he appoints an assistant, and a register; and the two principals and their two friends who carry the messages agree on two men to have charge of the wands, a custodian of the ear of corn, and a drummer. Invitation wands are sent out. Much pipe passing precedes the ceremony, followed by symbolic capture; there is a meat offering, and the conductor waves the horse tails over the principals, an act which is supposed to have therapeutic power and to guarantee long life. Pronouncing them Hunka calls the sun to witness. It is an outdoor ceremony of several days duration. It is marked by exchange of gifts. And the use and connection of ceremonial red paint with sun, long life, and "good" reaches eastward to the Iroquois.

From a Hako center among the Pawnee the fourth path of diffusion carried the ceremony down the Mississippi from the Pawnee and Osage to the Caddo and the Natchez, until it reached the Chitimacha on the Gulf of Mexico. From the Natchez or one of their neighbors the ceremony passed to the Creek, the Cherokee, and finally to the Catawba in a diluted form. From the southeast the calumet ceremony returned to the Iroquois in the hands of Catawba and Cherokee, as we have seen from direct historical sources. The Shawnee occupied an enigmatic position between the Southeast and the Northeast, and their Eagle Dance had elements that reach to the Southwest, other elements reaching to the Iroquois, and still others to an ancient Southern Cult.

The Calumet Dance spread rapidly down the Mississippi within a few years following 1687. Two related causes contributed to the rapid diffusion of the rite and both were set in motion by the coming of the white man. The beaver had disappeared from the Iroquois country and the Indian traders soon backed up demands for peltry with raiding war parties which drove down the Ohio River to the Miami and Illinois and are credited with dispersing the Mosopelea or Ofo and other Siouan-speaking villagers who sought refuge further downstream (Swanton, 1946, p. 166). In fact, the Dhegiha group of

Siouans, comprising Omaha, Ponca, Kansa, Quapaw, and Osage, are supposed to have once been a single body living along the lower course of the Ohio (Swanton *in* Hodge, 1912, pt. 2, p. 156). More or less elaborate forms of the Calumet Dance are reported for the Ponca (Skinner, 1915 a, p. 789), and the Kansa (Skinner, 1915 a, pp. 759–760); the Osage knew the ceremony in elaborate detail late in the nineteenth century (La Flesche, 1939). By 1673, however, the Osage were located on the Osage River, so the removal from the Ohio got started ahead of the Illinois war of the Iroquois. If southern Siouans did not already possess the ceremony before the break-up, they acquired it soon after from Caddoan-speaking people. The second cause was the French themselves who carried the calumet for reasons of inviolability clear to Louisiana. It is not reported by members of the De Soto expedition, but LaSalle found it good among the Akansa, and Joutel; his companion, found the rite practiced by the Cahinnio, the Caddo tribe nearest to the Mississippi, but not by the Caddo tribes on the Red River beyond. When the French settled Louisiana, the calumet occurred among the Natchez, Chitimacha, Choctaw, and Chickasaw, and its use extended as far east as the Creeks, but with somewhat different significance, and the Cherokee had it soon after (Swanton, 1928 a, pp. 702–703; 1946, pp. 546–547; Bourne, 1904, vol. 1, p. 41; Thwaites, 1896–1901, vol. 68, pp. 123 ff., 159, 161, 201, 203; Mooney, 1900, p. 493).

La Flesche described the Osage ceremony at the peak of his career, after gaining comparative knowledge from field work among related Siouan groups. The Wazha'zhe or Osage, whose tribal name suggests Iroquois wasa·'se, War Dance, address their Wa'wa-tho⁷, or Peace ceremony to the spirits of birds—Golden Eagle, Pileated Woodpecker, Mallard Duck, Owl, Cardinal, and Bluejay—who inhabit the clear sky, when the storm clouds of war and lightning abate, in times of peace. Raven does not figure prominently. The rite has a special set of songs, one movement being addressed to birds, and the order is preserved for singers by reference to two sets of mnemonics, rods and carved flat sticks, a typically eastern trait (La Flesche, 1939, pp. 213–214; Fenton, 1950). Two dancers simulate movement of birds, rattle in right hand and feathered stem in left, keeping strict time with the drum. The dance ceremony corresponds to the final dance of Omaha, Ponca, Oto, and Pawnee (La Flesche, 1939, p. 246). Elaborate ceremony attends procuring the materials and making the ritual equipment (ibid., p. 206 ff.), which requires tail feathers of young and mature eagles, down, a forked stick, fat, leaves of cattail, arrowshafts for pipestems, owl feathers, skins and heads of two pileated woodpeckers, and duck heads. The stem is of ash, painted green, and like Seneca wands is not perforated (ibid., p. 253); streamers of horsehair recall

Dakota, and, as with the Omaha, the pipe is feathered with three wing feathers of eagle, which are split and tied, as in fletching Iroquois arrows; the Osage calumet fan has seven tail feathers of the golden eagle, and contrasted with Omaha and Pawnee pipes, Osage pipes appear crude (ibid., p. 255). Rattles resemble those of Omaha, one belonging to each eagle or stem, like the Pawnee. The wing-bone whistle is also part of the equipment. The ceremony of erecting the rack (ibid., p. 242) and setting up the pole for coup counting and tethering the gift horses compares with traits No. 8 and No. 9 of the Iroquois (see p. 134). Making ceremonial friends in the father-and-son relationship is the avowed purpose of the ceremony of the Osage who preserved the intertribal character of the rite in an elaborate intra-tribal dual division symbolizing sky and earth. In all probability the former was a projection of the latter. Its vital principle extended to peaceful relations between the Osage and other tribes, and the Osage, Omaha, Ponca, Kaw, Oto, and Pawnee all practiced this rite (ibid., pp. 204, 251). The right to perform the ceremony carries the privilege of employing a "prompter" (conductor), and the preparation of the props, and the conduct of a composite rite entails considerable organization. The servant or messenger obliges lovers by carrying and keeping secrets. Messengers also acted as clowns, mimicking domestic quarrels of the moment. All functionaries were appointed. Despite what earlier writers observed, La Flesche insists that striking the post and recounting war honors on these occasions were not practiced by the Ponca, Oto, Omaha, and Pawnee, although provision for counting coups was usually made (ibid., p. 243). Striking the post or shield hanging there was the Osage practice, and a warrior's wife stood there to validate his honor with gifts. Presents were reciprocated by the sponsors. I note something resembling a song for laying down the feather fans (ibid., p. 216). Lacking, is the concept of the head, but ceremonial feeding of props with ceremonial fat occurs. Wings brush aside evil. They perform in summer for several days. Color and spatial symbols abound—north and south, sky and earth, blue and green—the dual divisions all mean enduring life; the number four; red paint and the woodpecker head mean the sun and perseverance; and the little red groove running the full length of each pipe is the path of the sun and of life; the crotched stick, where the pipes rest, represents elk horns, not the bird's nest; and the whole ritual aims to control the weather, to create a clear sky, the habitat of happy birds, whose enjoyment symbolizes peace on earth. So strong is this cosmic picture to the Osage that even poor replicas of the proper ceremonial equipment can recreate the proper significance of the ceremony, and Osages have been known to accept "pipes" or corn husk when offered with proper dignity and sanctioned with ritual. This is a profound lesson for ethnologists since it goes far to explain the stability of Indian culture in the face of material change.

The custom of greeting strangers with loud wails and weeping, which we noted for the early Iowa and Illinois, and in the Iroquois Requickening ritual, does not carry over to the nineteenth century performances of the Hako type of Calumet Dance, but it was certainly a habit of the Caddo and their neighbors in the late seventeenth century. De Soto was met by a weeping messenger of the Tula chief, Joutel was greeted by wailing women of the Hasinai, and even Mooney experienced being greeted with tears on his returns to the Caddo because ". . . he reminded them of those who had died since they last met" (Swanton, 1942, p. 176). This preoccupation with death and the tendency to manifest grief may be a trait having stability since archeological times, as witness the weeping-eye motif of the Southern Cult. Carrying a guest into the village pick-a-back was accorded visitors to the tribes south of the Lakes. It crops up again among Caddo (Kadohadacho of Joutel) (Margry, 1875–86, vol. 3, pp. 404–406; Swanton, 1942, p. 178), and it leads logically to the use of litters among the southeastern Indians (Swanton, 1946, p. 598).

Of the Caddo tribes only the Cahinnio had any knowledge of the true calumet of peace, according to Joutel, who in July of 1687 was met at the frontier by an Indian carrying a "sword ornamented with feathers and two hawk bells . . ." the noise of which he heard. Nearer the settlement a throng greeted him and conducted him to the chief's cabin in the town, where a bearskin was laid down for him to sit on. Presents were brought and exchanged with old men next day when he experienced the calumet ceremony for the first time among Caddo. La Salle had been mistaken about the ceremony of the previous year among the Hasinai. Joutel gives the following order of events: a messenger bearing calumet led a procession of old men followed by young men and a few women singing to his door; they paused to sing and entered; they supported the guest and led him outside; at a prepared place, one put sweetgrass under his feet, two others washed his face; he was seated on the skin; old men sat near the guest, and the conductor laid the calumet over a scaffold supported by a reddened crosspiece laid on two crotched sticks and covered with skins; men were singers joined by women and accompanied by gourd rattles; one was appointed to support and sway the guest with the music; for the first time we encounter two girls bearing gifts who are then seated so as to support the honored person's limbs; a feather was placed in his hair; the ceremony terminates daily on whim of the guest who is supported back to his cabin to rest; the same processional starts the second day; ceremonial pipe passing first to the honored guest, then to others; and putting the calumet to rest each evening; and finally the pipe goes to the honored guest as a passport among allied tribes (Margry, 1875–86, vol. 3, pp. 416–419; Swanton, 1942, pp. 179–180).

The Natchez form of the Calumet Dance, from Charlevoix, Du-Pratz and Le Petit—French observers of the early eighteenth century—has been described by Swanton (1911, pp. 123 ff., pp. 134–138). It bears certain resemblances to those described farther up the Mississippi, although Kurath classes it with a southeastern type, employing several dancers. Its war aspects are stressed as among the Iroquois. Natchez temples were decorated with wooden eagles, and were the point of departure and return of war parties. The leader erected two red posts, decorated the posts with feathers and war clubs, and indicated the mission with pictographs. Volunteers took emetics in the leader's cabin, and the calumet of war hung on the door of the war chief during councils. Dreams were important augurs, and the leader carried a bundle which he hung at night on a pole inclined toward the enemy. DuPratz says the calumet of war was displayed on a pole outside the war council, that in declaring war, the Great Chief was consulted and matters of policy were cleared, for the opinion of old men always prevails, and some ancient and wise warrior might be detailed to lead a party bearing a calumet and without presents to state a wrong, to parley, and to initiate the drama of war. Invitations to friendly allies were issued by a messenger bearing a calumet of peace, which he describes (Swanton, 1911, p. 128).

At treaties of peace, guests occupied honored places, a procession approached with singers shaking rattles, and six women came last. They stop, and, when invited, dancers approach the chief to wave fans over him, and rub him down head to foot. The calumet rests on forked sticks, while pipe passing goes the circuit. An appointed master of ceremonies conducts the rite, which takes several days. Hometown warriors strike a post and recount exploits, making presents to the ambassadors, who are then given the freedom of the town, and provisioned for their return (Charlevoix *in* Swanton, 1911, p. 134). Le Petit says that the great chief orders the master of ceremonies and all duties and expense fall on his subjects. Sweeping the plaza, as among the Pueblos, precedes the ceremony.

The Chitimacha had the same type calumet ceremony as the Natchez, although Du Pratz mentions the use of flamingo feathers (Le Page du Pratz, 1758, vol. 1, p. 118). There is little to distinguish Adair's description of the Chickasaw ceremony, which Swanton also cites in his Creek report, except the swan's wing; the person visited appoints a half dozen youths as dancers to wave the fans of eagle tails. They dance in bowing posture, then raise erect, eagle tail in right hand, small gourd rattle in left, with which the dancer touches his breast, pointing the fan to heaven (Swanton, 1928 d, pp. 238–239; 1928 b, pp. 442–443). Multiple dancers characterized this area. Feather fans were a common dance implement in the southeast. Besides those already mentioned, Yuchi, Creek, Chickasaw, Coasati, Catawba, and Cherokee used them (Speck, 1909, p. 52; Swanton, 1928 b, pp. 299,442).

The Choctaw had the same ceremony to all appearances. They acknowledged the Illinois country as the source of pipe stone (Swanton, 1918, pp. 56–57, 66–68), but they also had an Eagle Dance, which impressed Catlin so much that he made a sketch and also left a description (Swanton, 1931, p. 222). The dance was organized by young men to honor the eagle. A dozen or more young men, who painted themselves white like neighboring calumet dancers, arose in groups of four to the beat of a tambourine drum and a wood rasp, brandishing weapons in right hand and the eagle-feather brush in the left. The jumps impressed Catlin as different from anything else he had seen, and he commented on the strain of the squatting posture, which he illustrates.

Dancers of social dances in the Southeast generally painted a round red spot on each cheek like the Iroquois. Bird or Eagle sickness occurs among Creek, Chickasaw, Yuchi, and Cherokee and is usually associated with poisoning from bird lice contracted while procuring eagle feathers. A buzzard feather is the doctor's sign, moreover, among Creek, Cherokee, and Shawnee, and the Iroquois probably derived their concept of giant crow from the carrion crow or black vulture of the Southeast. The Creek had a Buzzard Dance, and southeastern doctors cry like ravens, but medicine societies as such, a generic trait of the Central Algonquians, apparently did not develop here (Swanton, 1928 a, p. 644; 1928 d, p. 267; Speck, 1911, p. 219; Mooney, 1900, p. 281; Speck and Broom, 1951 and correspondence; Voegelin, Shawnee Field Notes, and correspondence). To balance the other comparisons, to bring this monograph down to date, to link the Southeast with the Iroquois, and to regain the perspective of modern ethnology, I end this comparison with an analysis of the Cherokee data of Speck, and field materials on the Shawnee Eagle Dance collected for me by Dr. Erminie W. Voegelin.

Eagle Dance presents one of the more interesting parallels between the northern and southern Iroquoians. The studies of Mooney who first called attention to folk resemblances between these ancient linguistic relatives have since been supplemented by modern field studies of Cherokee ceremonialism by Gilbert (1943), Speck, and two of his students, Witthoft (1946) and Broom (Speck and Broom, 1951). The writer made a brief field trip to the Cherokee in the winter of 1946, gaining the quick impression that Cherokee ceremonialism is a thing of the past, which makes the living ceremonialism of the northern Iroquois all the more remarkable.

The Cherokee Eagle Dance honored the Eagle for victory in war (Mooney, 1900, p. 496) and was held in recent years to celebrate winning the Ball Game (Gilbert, 1943, p. 263), and, as such, represents a survival from an older variant of the Calumet Dance. The eagle was the most honored bird among the Cherokee and a special class of eagle hunters braved the contamination of bites by bird lice which caused Eagle sickness (Mooney, 1900, p. 283; Witthoft, 1946 b, p. 376). The dance was performed to welcome visitors and to welcome the dead eagle to town. Eagles were lured down to high places and were both trapped and shot, according to Will West Long. I am uncertain that Raven is messenger for the birds, but the "High Priest of War," leader of the red organization, is sometimes called the Raven. He wore a raven skin and went forward to scout the enemy and gave a raven call of alarm (Gilbert, 1943, pp. 348, 353). Fourteen Eagle Dance songs are arranged in three periods or movements, involving a processional formation, counterclockwise wheeling, trot, and a crouch. Speck has described these maneuvers and Kurath comments on them. The first period is Victory Dance, clearly related to the Scalp Dance of wider distribution; and the Eagle Dance is related to Iroquois and to the Calumet Dance. Speck disagrees with Mooney and says that Eagle Dance is never a means of curing sickness as among Iroquois (Speck and Broom, 1951, pp. 40–51). Fans and rattles are carried in right and left hands, evidently interchangeably (my own photographs (pl. 28), and Speck's and Gilbert's). The bundle concept is not developed; the fan in the U. S. National Museum collected by Mooney has 12 feathers depending from a solid sour-wood stick (Mooney, 1900, p. 282, fig. 1), and my own photographs show five feathers with a bentwood spreader; Mooney gives seven, for the number of Gentes (Witthoft, 1949, p. 58; Speck and Broom, 1951, p. 39). And the modern Cherokee dance wands have no pipe attachment, contrary to early descriptions and one illustrated in Catlin's portrait of Black Coat (1836) (Witthoft, 1949). Skinner, in describing a Cherokee Eagle Dance fan in the American Museum of Natural History, notes the resemblance to Iroquois Eagle Dance wands along with other Cherokee-Iroquois parallels (Lowie, 1910, p. 286). The bundle was not displayed on a pole, and I find no mention of striped pole and beater, but the Uku's standard was a long white pole with bird carved or painted on the top (Gilbert, 1943, p. 332). Tlanawa is Roc, but the bird abduction myth is not the origin myth of Eagle Dance (Witthoft, 1946 b, p. 376; Mooney, 1900, pp. 315–316). Gilbert found the dance functioning to provide a setting for releasing permissive joking relationships, and is no longer connected with removing contamination from killing eagles (Gilbert, 1943, pp. 263, 284). Friendships sometimes ripen from these occasions, and the dance seems to be related to so-called Friendship dances (ibid, p. 257). A conductor picks the other functionaries and acts as caller. As with the Shawnee, dancers are the whoopers. Pipe passing punctuated eithteenth-century accounts by Timberlake (1765, p. 107), and Cuming (Williams, S. C., 1928, pp. 125–126, 135). Honor attached to presenting eagle tails to visitors and frequently they were sent abroad to kings; the guest was massaged from head to foot with the fan, as among Muskogeans generally. An even number of male and female dancers—4, 6, 12, 16 (Mooney says 6)—parallels earlier descriptions for the Natchez which mention 6 females at the end of the line, but only men dance in the Victory Dance. A dancer may stop the song with a cry, leaping out in front and raising an elbow for attention, to boast. Boasting of war records has of late degenerated to teasing (Gilbert, 1943, p. 263; Mooney, 1900, p. 293). Gilbert comments:

Not only do the familiarities of the sexual type find their best expression in the dances but also the familiarities of the ridicule-sanction type also seem to be brought out in fullest form . . . in Eagle and Friendship Dances. [Gilbert, 1943, p. 284.]

Will West Long said Cherokee dancers want a present beforehand; Iroquois dancers receive them after each song. I find no special song for laying down the feather stems, and a head is not passed. As in the north, however, killing frosts precede and terminate the proper ceremonial season and the rite is thought too strong for summer (Speck and Broom, 1951, p. 42); but Gilbert observed the dance in summer, although he noted the danger felt of snake bite or cold weather ensuing (Gilbert, 1943, p. 257). An evil omen attaches to dropping a fan.

The Cherokee Eagle Dance would have long since disappeared but for the activity of Speck and certain ethnologists who kept the people of Big Cove supplied with imported feathers (Gilbert, 1943, p. 367). How considerable has been the change in Cherokee ceremonials is apparent from a comparison of the preceding modern accounts with traditional accounts of the Seneca-Cherokee Peace by Seneca and Cherokee informants and with the descriptions of eighteenth-century travelers.

Between the Cherokee and the Iroquois during much of the eighteenth century lay two Algonquian-speaking tribes who were horticulturists and hunters, the Delaware of eastern Pennsylvania and the Shawnee, probably the most mobile tribe in America. The Delaware, who were first met at Philadelphia and ranged between Jersey and the State of their name, drifted westward in a series of land sales and removes which marked the advancing frontier, trekking from their own river to the Susquehanna, to the Allegheny, and to the Muskingum, north of the Ohio. The Munsee of New Jersey ended their migration among the Six Nations in Canada, the Ohio groups going to Indian Territory. Whether the Delaware had originally an Eagle Dance or a full Calumet Dance is uncertain, but certain elements of both survive in the ethnological literature.

Most like the Iroquois Eagle Dance is the Nighthawk Dance, noted by Speck among the Munsee-Mahican of Six Nations Reserve, Canada (Speck, 1945, pp. 76–78). It was performed semiannually at the Bear Sacrifice Ceremony (Midwinter) and at the Green Corn Feast, usually on the last night, in honor of the Nighthawk, whom the Delaware call Pi·ckwolane'o, or Pick^w, which is how the Algonquians hear the booming sound, thinking that the bird breaks wind in flight. The sound is connected with the myth of thunder (Speck, 1946, p. 256). This interpretation takes on significance in relation to the bird-anus motif of the Southern Cult. The organization of the dance resembles the Cayuga variant of Iroquois Eagle Dance: Two to four dancers, rattles in right hand, fans of individually suspended feathers in left, water drum and cow-horn rattle, and the same crouching posture with jumps. A round red spot is painted on each cheek. Speakers appealed for long life and social welfare and made presents to the dancers. The speaker interrupted the dance by striking on the floor. Speck comments that the Delaware account lacks the curing function of the Iroquois medicine society which he studied among the neighboring Cayuga of the same reserve. Sweeping the Big House or ceremonial chamber with an eagle wing ties in with Iroquois council fire symbolism, the great white wing which brushed aside evil from the mat of the law (Speck, 1931, pp. 23–24, 101–103). In Oklahoma, the Delaware Peyote Cult equates a mound of earth with the eagle's body, plants 12 sticks, 6 on a side, and burns them, the stubs being reminiscent of the tail feathers (Speck, 1931, p. 62; Petrullo, 1934, pp. 152, 162–164, 169). Peyotism has gained but a one-time adherent among the Iroquois. The significant fact is that the Delaware revered the eagle and held the Nighthawk to symbolize the antagonism between peace and aerial and terrestrial warfare (Speck, 1946, p. 256).

By contrast the marginal Naskapi, Algonquian hunters of Labrador, have no such legends or ritual connected with serpents or tortoises, or any of the birds associated with Eagle Dance complex—raven, eagle, or hawk (Speck, 1935, p. 80).

The Delaware and Iroquois had already exchanged stone-headed peace pipe with wing attached to a cane shaft by the second decade of the eighteenth century (Hanna, 1911, vol. 1, pp. 101–102), which the Delaware had accepted to show to other tribes as evidence of their subjection to the League. In showing the relic to the Governor and

Council in Philadelphia on June 14, 1715, they opened "the Calumet with great ceremony of their rattles and songs," passed the pipe to all dignitaries present beginning with the English moiety, and then put it up with the same ceremony. The point is that the Delaware had come east from Ohio country where they maintained continual contact with the Shawnee, Miami, and other mobile central Algonquians, gradually drifting west themselves ahead of the frontier. They had ample opportunity to learn the Miami version of Calumet Dance and Eagle Dance too, if that were distinct. The French and Indian War scrambled the Indian population of western Pennsylvania so that in 1767 Zeisberger could report the presence at his mission town of Goschgoschink, a Munsee town where the Geneseo Seneca had re-settled refugee Indians, of such diverse ethnic entities as Cherokee, Fox, Mahican, Shawnee, Missisauga, Nanticoke, Chippewa—mostly Algonquians of one kind or another—and even a "baptized Jew from New England" (Deardorff, 1946, pp. 6–7). This one refugee town provided a setting for the transmission of Eagle Dance from Fox, Chippewa, or Cherokee to the Munsee and Seneca who were settled in adjacent towns up the river.

One division of the Shawnee who formerly lived in the Ohio Valley and now live in Oklahoma formerly had an Eagle Dance, which is quantitatively much like the Seneca form, but lacks several significant traits, and possesses still others such as Eagle suits which may have reached Oklahoma from the Rio Grande Pueblos. The following analysis is based on original materials collected for me in the field by Dr. Erminie W. Voegelin of Indiana University from a much longer checklist of over 50 traits which I submitted to her in 1936–37. The material is here published with grateful acknowledgment.

The one division held the Eagle Dance separately. It is addressed to Eagle who gave the rite to the Shawnee. Roc carried off a man in a hollow log, and the man beat the bird on the head to get home and institute the dance. Three kinds of eagles are distinguished and associated with directions. A preliminary feasting of birds resembles the Seneca method of luring down birds. Shawnee take the third bird, the bundle is there open, and it is later hung on a pole or tree limb. There was no society of those who had been cured of Eagle sickness, or epilepsy, which is caused by wearing untreated feathers or being bitten by bird lice. No ceremonial friendships arose through the rite. The bundle contained 12 feather coats for the dancers, which recall costumes still used in the Pueblo area, besides tobacco, 4 tail feathers, a raven wing—the doctor's emblem as in the South-east—a drum hide and stick, and 1 gourd rattle. There were 12 songs, 12 dancers, and women might watch. Dancers crouched and cried like eagles and picked up objects in their mouths like Onondaga dancers, but the dance more nearly resembled Catlin's Choctaw Eagle Dance than the Iroquois variant, since the Shawnee dancers rest squatting. (The Iroquois dancers perch on chairs, although I never inquired what they perched on, if anything, before chairs came to them.) Raven is messenger, bundle chief, and priest, and conducts the ceremony; there is no whooper, but the 12 dancers cry like eagles; and the conductor appoints 4 singers, and the dancers. The tobacco offering is not burned, and pipe passing is absent, and no honored old men present fans and rattles to the dancers. There is no striking post and beater, and recitation of war records belongs to another dance, and no fans are waved in the dance or laid down with special song. Four is the sacred number, circuits are counterclockwise, meetings are held toward spring, and the rite lacks sex and color symbolisms of the Calumet Dance of the Hako type.

In the list of 25 peculiar features of Iroquois Eagle Dance but 5 outright negatives occur in the Shawnee data—absence of pole and beater, friendship, feather fans, and a song for laying them down. No head is passed. Tobacco is not burned but offered dry, and the dancers cry; there is no whooper. Yet Shawnee Eagle Dance is sufficiently differentiated from Iroquois to have a special quality of its own. (Voegelin and Fenton, in press.)

At the close of such a study one is tempted to speculate on a possible remote connection through a putative ancient Eagle Dance which would tie together the full-suited wheeling Eagle Dance of the Pueblos and the Eagle Dance of the northeastern Indians, which are quite different. The history of the Iroquois Eagle Dance which I have traced with available evidence to the Hako type of Calumet Dance gives a picture of cultural stability over several centuries. The Hako complex was approaching a climax form when discovered by the French in the seventeenth century. Such a vigorous ceremonial institution must have had roots of its own leading into prehistoric times. I think that these roots lead logically to the archeological literature on the Southern Death or Buzzard Cult, so named by the archeologists who view culture history from the remote past forward, but which I think can be reclothed with ethnological reality when time is reversed. Is the complex which underlies Hako what is known archeologically as the Buzzard Cult? (Martin, Quimby, and Collier, 1947, pp. 361–366.)

First of all, the two complexes occur in the same general area, although the Death Cult is more common east of the Mississippi River than west, but Spiro Mound is in the heart of the Caddo country, and some of the tribes with whom the Calumet Dance is associated were living farther east at the dawn of history. The Death Cult is supposed to have flourished about 1600 (Ford and Willey, 1941, p. 358) and to have lasted until after 1700, which clearly overlaps the known period of Hako. Whether or not the two complexes are related, they share a number of traits in common, which I shall now regard from the viewpoint of history and ethnology.

The Hako was held to honor eagles and other birds—duck, hawk, owl, pileated woodpecker, and some lesser birds—who were cosmic symbols and could be appealed to for controlling weather, alleviating sickness, creating friendships, and making peace. Peace and war were but two facets of male aggression in Indian society and so the ritual of one merges into the other; so do the symbolisms. Among the eight motifs analyzed and discussed by Waring and Holder (1945, p. 3), I wish to comment on the Sun Circles, the Bi-lobed Arrow, the Forked Eye, the Open Eye, and the Barred Oval. The circular pallettes of stone remind me of catlinite disks which were brought by Indians from the Upper Lakes to Onondaga in the mid-eighteenth century; restoring the sight of the sun to the bereaved relatives of the dead chief constitutes the burden of the eighth message in the Requickening Address of the Iroquois Condolence Council, a ceremony very much concerned with death; and Pawnee mythology ascribes the Hako to the sun. The sun cult was widespread and occurs in many contexts, as is well known. Could the Bilobed Arrow, thought to symbolize an Eagle-being, stand for the calumet? Weeping and wailing on greeting strangers crops up from the Caddo area, among Central Algonquians, and among the Iroquois it is ritualized in the reception ceremony at The Woods' Edge in Condolence Council. Either the Forked Eye or the Open Eye may represent weeping or clearsightedness which goes with clearmindedness when the ceremony has done its job. The bereaved whose minds were downcast are now requickened. The Barred Oval or Anus Motif, which usually occurs in art forms beneath the tail of the woodpecker, may relate to the widespread Algonquian folk belief that the Nighthawk and Thunderbird break wind in flight. Speck has called our attention to this motif in papers already cited and in conversation.

Some of the decorations on the feathered stems of the Hako, notably the heads of mallard ducks, bring certain archeological specimens to mind. Linton first called my attention to bird-effigy pipes from Ohio-Mississippi drainage, and in particular one pipe from the Hopewell Group is carved to represent the intertwined necks of ducks (Shetrone, 1930, p. 159).

Besides the abstract motifs, the prehistoric ceremonial complex yields full-scale delineations of Eagle and Pileated Woodpecker, whom Omaha mythology made messenger of Sun and leader of the forest birds, as duck was leader on water, owl at night, and Eagle dominated the sky birds. Anthropomorphic eagles, moreover, may represent either eagles appearing to men in dreams or men mimicking eagles in ritual. One who has seen the Eagle Dance in the Pueblos is struck by the near resemblance of some of the Spiro illustrations (Waring and Holder, 1945, p. 20, fig. 5, *b*). The masked dancing Eagle Warrior with head trophy and baton, which again is the Bilobed Arrow (possibly a calumet symbol) (ibid., fig. 5, *a*; Ford and Willey, 1941, p. 358), more nearly resembles the Striking Dance which is the third part of the Calumet Dance. The concept of the head connects with the war complex and is replaced by the rattle in the peace ceremony. Without stretching these parallels beyond the limits of the data, I believe the preoccupation with feathers, bird claws, and the above symbols puts the Calumet Dance in the direct line of descent from the ceremonial complex in the southeastern United States which is known as the Southern, Death, or Buzzard Cult. While not accounting by any means for all the riches which the archeologists have placed systematically at the disposal of the ethnologist, I have hinted at some other institutions known to ethnology such as the Iroquois Condolence Council, the Tutelo Adoption Rite, and the widespread Feast of the Dead which may on similar examination reveal other connections between ethnology and archeology in the eastern United States. In risking criticism for trying to establish these connections I wish to acknowledge the stimulus of one archeologist who provided the lead (Krieger, 1945, pp. 495–496). I trust that this monograph may contribute something to the solution of a fascinating problem.

CONCLUSIONS

The present study of the Iroquois Eagle Dance, an offshoot of the Calumet Dance, warrants some conclusions, a few of which are positive and several of which must remain tentative; and the study raises still other problems which may warrant new research.

First, some general considerations call for comment before drawing conclusions. I believe that the research has justified the viewpoint maintained throughout this study that culture is significant behavior, existing on several levels of abstraction. These levels range from patterns of individual participation in local society, to patterns of local society as affected by the participation of individuals, now dead, who have contributed consciously to innovations and unconsciously to drift, to patterns of tribal society which several related communities share in common, making due allowances for diversity arising from separation in time and space, and finally to culture complexes of wide areal distribution which rephrase and reorder the same culture traits in accordance with those local and tribal patterns which are the guides to what is significant in local experience. Secondly, every individual in final analysis has a culture of his own which the ethnologist can observe and study through the participation of that individual in local society, his interaction with other personalities, and his life history, which is confined to the narrow limits of a single generation to which the ethnologist most frequently belongs. From such observations of participation the ethnologist constructs local patterns of culture which he then proceeds to check with informants for general significance. Discrepancies between native theory and practice arise in this area of inquiry.

The structure of society and of ceremonies is built of such patterns. But a completely functional study of the interaction of the patterns of a culture at a given point of time, while transcending individual participation, does not explain culture as such or the survival of the Iroquois Eagle Dance. The answer to such truly cultural problems lies in history.

History has its levels too. Individuals are the carriers of culture and the makers of history, but an individual's culture is a matter of biographical selection, it is a product of his unique history in local society, and he in turn may alter slightly the course of local history. By observing closely how individuals manifest the local culture, how various types of personality find expression in that culture, and how the culture grants premiums to certain culturally sanctioned personality types, we gain some idea of how the learning process proceeds and how change and stability operate. At various times persons entrusted with preserving ritual have effected changes in its form or content which have enabled the ceremony to survive as an institution in the modern world. Handsome Lake is the most conspicuous example among the Seneca, but we have noted other slight changes by modern innovators. Pattern imposes limits and tolerances for individual behavior, however, and the range of expectable and permissive behavior has been developing during the long history of the local group and the tribe. Save for the slow process of drift, pattern makes for stability. It enables a ceremony like Eagle Dance to go on despite minor innovations and substitutions within its framework. Ceremonies, moreover, are group phenomena, and the individual enjoys participating in them. He enjoys performing the same ceremony again and again, and if he is an Indian he delights in the rhythmic repetition within the ritual, a phenomenon which Goldenweiser called involution, and which contributes to compounding the same pattern by a process of projection into larger wholes without losing the original design. Persons living in such cultures develop a tremendous capacity for boredom, an ability to take the long view, to enjoy the long cycle of songs with very slight alteration in the stanzas or the melody. The individual Indian cherishes the variant of his home locality and he accommodates to other variants only to the extent that they are related or can be related to his own. So what the individual says and does is deeply rooted in his people's past.

The second level of history lies in the past which in ethnological studies is reached through the intensive study of the present. The archeologists have called this method the direct historic approach, and it has the virtue of proceeding from the known to the unknown in a scientific manner, but I have termed my own version of this method "upstreaming" because it travels against the current of time. I believe that its use here is justified, and that the present study would not have yielded significant results had I followed history chronologically. Upstreaming is the method of ethnohistory.

History has a third level, a spatial or distributional aspect, the study of which may be pursued directly with documentary evidence when such is available. Ethnologists have frequently assumed that history was not forthcoming on the American Indian and have consequently made a virtue of indirect methods. Wherever the historical literature and archival materials can be found and combined with an abundant ethnological record the methods of direct history should be followed and balanced with the indirect methods of inferring history from comparative reconstructions. A people are always affected by the history of surrounding peoples, and cultural phenomena like the Eagle Dance seldom occur in geographical isolation, since from time to time innovations reach the second society through exchange of persons in wars, in peace embassies, and marriage. Warriors, ambassadors, husbands and wives, and the wandering male introduce new customs, new ceremonies, new songs, new dances, a new kind of rattle or drum, new techniques—which are usually adopted and rephrased to fit local patterns of culture. This theory, in my estimation, fits the cultural history of the Eagle Dance and its relation to the Calumet Dance.

The following positive conclusions emerge from the study.

(1) The meetings of the Seneca Eagle Dance Society, which I have attended and observed repeatedly at Coldspring, are unique performances depending upon who is invited and how the guests react to each other.

(2) The speeches at Eagle Dance meetings reflect segments of biography which are channeled through an old pattern that comes down from the custom of boasting on war records, and the present speeches function to cheer sick persons, to drain off aggression in a sanctioned manner, and to promote local group ésprit.

(3) Observations and inquiries made in other Iroqouis communities confirm the preceeding conclusions and give breadth and depth to the study.

(4) The Seneca Eagle Dance has its own paraphernalia and a unique

ritual pattern, and its own set of songs which appear to have been borrowed by the other Longhouse Iroquois. Tonawanda is most like Onondaga and Six Nations. Kurath reaches similar conclusions from music and the dance.

(5) The unique local pattern of Eagle Dance meetings fits into a standard ritual pattern for Iroquois medicine societies, which governs all of Iroquois ceremonialism.

(6) The thorough study of a ritual complex requires probing all the roots leading to the past: folklore, personal experiences, dreams which are so important to Iroquois, the examination of museum collections of material culture, the analysis of ritual organization and a study of its precedents in the history of the society, and an analysis of the patterns of sequence which control the program. The study of a major activity in culture touches almost every aspect of that culture.

(7) Traditional history pointed leads which were followed and confirmed with documents. The traditional history of the Iroquois-Cherokee peace has a basis in fact. But documentary history uncovers other paths which tradition has forgotten and these lead to the times and places of contact and sometimes verify the actual transfer of cultural complexes from tribe to tribe. The trail of the Iroquois Eagle Dance, which leads traditionally to the Cherokee, leads historically up the Lakes to the Far Indians of Green Bay, down the Ohio to the Miami and Illinois who had the Calumet Dance. Miami, Illinois, Fox, Chippewa, Ottawa, Shawnee, Cherokee, and Catawba all made direct contact with the Iroquois. The Iroquois, who lacked the Calumet Dance in 1680, received one after another of these tribes at Onondaga, and by the middle of the eighteenth century they had been honored by Calumet ceremony enough times to have acquired it themselves.

(8) Direct history of itself is not enough, for the ethnologist must make certain in diffusional studies through an analysis and comparison of two sets of cultural phenomena that the two are comparable and are generically related. Kurath's and my own independent studies of the history and ethnology of the Calumet Dance reach the common conclusion that historically the Iroquois Eagle Dance is derived from a variant of the Calumet Dance. Musically it seems closest to Fox, ethnologically it has much in common with Cherokee and Shawnee, but all of these modern forms appear to stem from the Miami and Illinois forms which in turn are derived from an ancient Caddoan prototype, of which the Pawnee Hako is the climax form.

(9) Seneca, Cherokee, Fox, and Sioux are the differentiated twentieth-century survivals; Shawnee, Iowa, Omaha, Pawnee, and Osage lasted late into the nineteenth century; Natchez and Miami are eighteenth-century forms, for which time we have Cherokee and Catawba

records; Illinois-Miami-Potawatomi-Iowa are the seventeenth-century links through Pawnee to Caddo; and beyond that point archeology takes over with a putative Buzzard or Southern Cult, which I should like to rename the Eagle Cult, a pan-Indian phenomenon which has the weeping eye, the buzzard, eagle, woodpecker, sun, and other symbolisms of the Calumet complex.

(10) The Roc myth and the practice of eagle trapping have even broader distributions, the former reaching far into the Northwest, the latter into the Southwest, and both cover the riverine distribution of Calumet Dance, and if the myth and the hunting of eagles do not tie directly to the ceremony under investigation in all cases they at least reflect the broad preoccupation of American Indians with the eagle as a symbol of war and peace.

Finally, in all the strife and warfare that characterized aboriginal America, it is important to underscore the Indian's identification of peace with birds and related life forces in nature. Although Indian society was rent with feuds and factions it also had developed some focal factors like the Calumet Dance which stabilized affairs by providing a means for draining off aggression generated internally and stopping intertribal wars. The kinship principle became the basis for creating ceremonial friendships within the tribe, between members of different clans, between moieties, and dual divisions of confederacies, and we find that wherever such mechanisms developed nonaggression followed. People did not fight the communities with whom they played ball or with whom they had made a pact of friendship through the Calumet Dance. Indian society was reaching for a mechanism for extending the peace, and the Europeans avidly seized on it. Such political experiments in simpler societies merit further study.

BIBLIOGRAPHY

BARBEAU, C. M.
  1915. Huron and Wyandot mythology. Canada Dept. Mines, Geol. Surv., Mem. 80. Ottawa.
BARTRAM, JOHN.
  1895. Observations on the inhabitants, soil, rivers, productions, animals . . . in . . . Travels from Pensilvania (sic) to Onondaga, etc. (London, 1751.) Reprinted at Geneva, N. Y.
BEAGLEHOLE, ERNEST.
  1936. Hopi hunting and hunting ritual. Yale Univ. Publ. Anthrop., No. 4.
BEAUCHAMP, WILLIAM M.
  1895 a. Onondaga notes. Journ. Amer. Folklore, vol. 8, pp. 209–216.
  1895 b. Mohawk notes. Journ. Amer. Folklore, vol. 8, pp. 217–221.
  1901. The Good Hunter and the Iroquois medicines. Journ. Amer. Folklore, vol. 14, pp. 153–159.
  1905. A history of the New York Iroquois. New York State Mus. Bull. 78. Albany.
  1907. Civil, religious and mourning councils, and Ceremonies of Adoption of the New York Indians. New York State Mus. Bull. 113. Albany.

1916. Moravian journals relating to central New York, 1745–66.   Onondaga Hist. Assoc., Syracuse.

1922. Iroquois folklore.   Onondaga Hist. Assoc., Syracuse.

1925. The life of Conrad Weiser.   Onondaga Hist. Assoc., Syracuse.

BECKWITH, MARTHA WARREN.

1930. Mythology of the Oglala Dakota.   Journ. Amer. Folklore, vol. 43, No. 170, pp. 339–442.

1931. Folklore in America, its scope and method.   Publ. Folklore Found., No. 11.   Vassar College, Poughkeepsie, N. Y.

BENT, ARTHUR CLEVELAND.

1937. Life histories of North American birds of prey: Order Falconiformes (pt.1).   U. S. Nat. Mus. Bull. 167.

BLAIR, EMMA H.

1911–12. Indian tribes of the Upper Mississippi Valley and Great Lakes. 2 vols.   Cleveland.

BOAS, FRANZ.

1916. Tsimshian mythology.   31st Ann. Rep. Bur. Amer. Ethnol., 1909–10, pp. 29–1037.

1918. Kutenai tales.   Bur. Amer. Ethnol. Bull. 59.

1920. The methods of ethnology.   Amer. Anthrop., n. s., vol. 22, No. 4, pp. 311–321.

BOURNE, E. G., Editor.

1904. Narratives of the career of Hernando de Soto.   2 vols.   New York.

BOWERS, ALFRED W.

1950. Mandan social and ceremonial organization.   Chicago.

BRUYAS, JAMES.

1862. Radical words of the Mohawk language, with their derivatives. Shea's Libr. Amer. Linguistics, X.   New York.

1863. Radical words of the Mohawk language, with their derivatives.   Regents of State of New York, 16th Ann. Rep., App. E.   Albany.

BURTON, M. AGNES, Editor.

1912. Journal of Pontiac's Conspiracy, 1763.   Michigan Soc. Colonial Wars. Detroit.

CANFIELD, WILLIAM W.

1902. The legends of the Iroquois.   New York.

CASWELL, HARRIET S.

1892. Our life among the Iroquois Indians.   Boston and Chicago.

CATLIN, GEORGE.

1844. Fourteen Ioway Indians.   London.

1913. North American Indians.   Philadelphia.

CHAMPLAIN, SAMUEL DE.

1922–36. The works of Samuel de Champlain.   H. P. Biggar, editor.   Champlain Soc., Toronto.

CHARLEVOIX, P. F. X. DE.

1866–72. History and general description of New France.   J. G. Shea, editor. New York.   (Reprinted 1909.)

1923. Journal of a voyage to North America.   L. P. Kellogg, editor.   2 vols. (1st ed., London, 1761).   Chicago.

COLDEN, CADWALLADER.

1727. The history of the Five Indian Nations depending on the Province of New York.   New York.   (Reprinted with an Introduction and notes by John Gilmary Shea, New York, 1866.)

1902. The history of the Five Indian Nations.   2 vols.   New York.

1937. History of the Five Indian Nations, *Continuation*, 1707–1720. *In* The Letters and Papers of Cadwallader Colden, vol. 9, New York Hist. Soc. Coll. for year 1935, pp. 359–434.

CONVERSE, HARRIET MAXWELL, and PARKER, ARTHUR C.
1908. Myths and legends of the New York State Iroquois. New York State Mus. Bull. 125. Albany.

CUOQ, J. A.
1882. Lexique de la langue Iroquoise. Montreal. (Reissued 1883.)

CURTIN, JEREMIAH, and HEWITT, J. N. B.
1918. Seneca fiction, legends, and myths. J. N. B. Hewitt, editor. 32d Ann. Rep. Bur. Amer. Ethnol., 1910–1911, pp. 37–813.

CURTIS, EDWARD S.
1907–30. The American Indian. Cambridge, Mass.

DARLINGTON, WILLIAM M.
1893. Christopher Gist's Journals with historical, geographical and ethnological notes and biographies of his contemporaries. Pittsburgh.

DEARDORFF, MERLE H.
1946. Zeisberger's Allegheny River Indian towns: 1767–1770. Pennsylvania Archaeol., vol. 16, No. 1, pp. 2–19. Harrisburg.
1951. The religion of Handsome Lake: Its origin and development. *In* Symposium on local diversity in Iroquois culture. Bur. Amer. Ethnol. Bull. 149, pp. 77–107.

DENIG, EDWIN THOMPSON.
1930. Indian tribes of the Upper Missouri. J. N. B. Hewitt, editor. 46th Ann. Rep. Bur. Amer. Ethnol., 1928–1929, pp. 375–628.

DIXON, ROLAND B.
1928. The building of cultures. New York.

DORSEY, GEORGE A.
1906. The Pawnee: Mythology (p. 1). Carnegie Inst. Washington.

DORSEY, JAMES OWEN.
1884. Omaha sociology. 3d Ann. Rep. Bur. Ethnol., 1881–1882, pp. 205–370.
1894. A study of Siouan cults. 11th Ann. Rep. Bur. Ethnol., 1889–1890, pp. 351–544.
1897. Siouan sociology. 15th Ann. Rep. Bur. Ethnol., 1893–1894, pp. 205–244.

FENTON, WILLIAM N.
1936 a. Some social customs of the modern Seneca. Social Welfare Bull., New York State Dept. Social Welfare, vol. 7, Nos. 1–2, pp. 4–7. Albany.
1936 b. An outline of Seneca ceremonies at Coldspring Longhouse. Yale Univ. Publ. Anthrop., vol. 9. New Haven.
1937. The Seneca Society of Faces. Scientific Monthly, vol. 44, pp. 215–238.
1940. Problems arising from the historic northeastern position of the Iro-. quois. *In* Essays in historical anthropology of North America, published in honor of John R. Swanton. Smithsonian Misc. Coll., vol. 100, pp. 159–251.
1941 a. Tonawanda Longhouse ceremonies: Ninety years after Lewis Henry Morgan. Bur. Amer. Ethnol. Bull. 128, Anthrop. Pap., No. 15, pp. 139–165.
1941 b. Masked medicine societies of the Iroquois. Smithsonian Ann. Rep. for 1940, pp. 397–430.

1942. Songs from the Iroquois Longhouse: Program notes for an album of American Indian music from the eastern woodlands. Smithsonian Inst. Publ. 3691.

[Record album: same title] Folk music of the United States, 6. [5 records.] The Library of Congress.

1944. Simeon Gibson: Iroquois informant, 1889–1943. Amer. Anthrop., vol. 46, pp. 231–234.

1946. Twi'yendagon' (Wood-eater) takes the heavenly path. Amer. Indian, vol. 3, No. 3, pp. 11–15.

1947. Seneca songs from Coldspring Longhouse [with comment on the music by Martha Champion Huot]. The Library of Congress, Music Division-Recording Laboratory, Folk Music of the United States, Album 17, pp. 1–16. [5 records.]

1948. The present status of anthropology in northeastern North America: a review article. Amer. Anthrop., vol. 50, pp. 494–515.

1949. Collecting materials for a political history of the Six Nations. Proc. Amer. Philos. Soc., vol. 93, pp. 233–238.

1950. The roll call of the Iroquois chiefs: A study of a mnemonic cane from the Six Nations Reserve. Smithsonian Misc. Coll., vol. 111, No. 15.

1951 a. Symposium on local diversity in Iroquois culture. Bur. Amer. Ethnol. Bull. 149. W. N. Fenton, editor.

1951 b. Iroquois studies at the mid-century. Proc. Amer. Philos. Soc., vol. 95, No. 3, pp. 296–310.

FEWKES, JESSE WALTER.
1900. Property-right in Eagles among the Hopi. Amer. Anthrop., vol. 2, pp. 690–707.

FISHER, MARGARET W.
1946. The mythology of the northern and northeastern Algonkians in reference to Algonkian mythology as a whole. *In* Man in northeastern North America. Frederick Johnson, editor. Pap. Robert S. Peabody Found. for Archaeol., vol. 3, pp. 226–262. Andover, Mass.

FLANNERY, REGINA.
1939. An analysis of coastal Algonquian culture. Catholic Univ. Amer. Anthrop. ser., No. 7.

FLETCHER, ALICE C.
1904. The Hako: A Pawnee ceremony. 22d Ann. Rep. Bur. Amer. Ethnol., 1900–1901, pt. 2, pp. 5–368.

FLETCHER, ALICE C., and LA FLESCHE, FRANCIS.
1911. The Omaha Tribe. 27th Ann. Rep. Bur. Amer. Ethnol., 1905–1906, pp. 17–654.

FORD, J. A., and WILLEY, G. R.
1941. An interpretation of the prehistory of the eastern United States. Amer. Anthrop., vol. 43, pp. 325–363.

FRIEDERICI, GEORG.
1906. Scalpieren und Ähnliche Kriegesgebrauche in Amerika. Braunschweig.

GILBERT, WM. H., JR.
1943. The Eastern Cherokees. Bur. Amer. Ethnol. Bull. 133, Anthrop. Pap., No. 23, pp. 169–413.

GILCHRIST, DONALD B.
1936. Manuscript journals and record of Indian letters by Lewis H. Morgan in the Rush Rhees Library. A descriptive table of contents. Rochester.

214

GOLDENWEISER, ALEXANDER A.
    1933. History, psychology, and culture. New York.
    1936. Loose ends of theory on the individual, pattern, and involution in
        primitive society. *In* Essays in Anthropology, presented to A. L.
        Kroeber, pp. 99–104. Berkeley, Calif.
    1937. Anthropology. New York.
HALLOWELL, A. I.
    1946. Some psychological characteristics of the northeastern Indians. *In*
        Man in northeastern North America. Frederick Johnson, editor.
        Pap. Robert S. Peabody Found. for Archaeol., vol. 3, pp. 195–225.
        Andover, Mass.
    1951. Frank Gouldsmith Speck, 1881–1950. Amer. Anthrop., vol. 53, pp.
        67–87.
HANNA, CHARLES A.
    1911. The Wilderness Trail. 2 vols. New York and London.
HARRIS, GEORGE H.
    1903. The life of Horatio Jones. Buffalo Hist. Soc. Publ., vol. 6, pp.
        383–514.
HECKEWELDER, JOHN.
    1881. History, manners, and customs of the Indian nations. Mem. Hist.
        Soc. Pennsylvania, vol. 12. Philadelphia.
HENNEPIN, LOUIS.
    1880. A description of Louisiana. J. G. Shea, editor and translator. New
        York. (1st ed., Paris, 1683.)
    1903. A new discovery of a vast country in America. R. G. Thwaites,
        editor. Chicago.
HEWITT, J. N. B.
    1903. Iroquoian cosmology. First Part. 21st Ann. Rep. Bur. Amer.
        Ethnol., 1899–1900, pp. 127–339.
    1912. Calumet. *Article in* Handbook of American Indians north of Mexico,
        vol. 1, pp. 191–195. F. W. Hodge, editor.
    1928. Iroquoian cosmology. Second Part. 43d Ann. Rep. Bur. Amer.
        Ethnol., 1925–1926, pp. 449–819.
HOCART, A. M.
    1935 a. Blood-brotherhood. Man, vol. 35, No. 127, pp. 113–115. London.
    1935 b. Covenants. Man, vol. 35, No. 164, pp. 149–151.
HODGE, FREDERICK WEBB (editor).
    1912. Handbook of American Indians North of Mexico. Rev. 2 pts. Bur.
        Amer. Ethnol. Bull. 30. (First printing, pt. 1, 1907; pt. 2, 1910.)
HUBBARD, JOHN N.
    1893. Sketches of border adventures in the life and times of Major Moses
        Van Campen. John S. Minard, editor. New York. (First ed.,
        Bath, N. Y., 1832.)
HUNT, GEORGE T.
    1940. The wars of the Iroquois: a study of intertribal trade relations.
        Madison.
JACKSON, HALLIDAY.
    1830. Civilization of the Indian natives. Philadelphia and New York.
JACOBS, WILBUR R.
    1950. Diplomacy and Indian gifts: Anglo-French rivalry along the Ohio
        and Northwest frontiers, 1748–1763. Stanford, Calif.

JESUIT RELATIONS.
> *See* Thwaites, 1896–1901.

JOHNSON PAPERS.
> 1921–1939. The papers of Sir William Johnson, vols. 1–9. Univ. State of New York. Albany.

JONES, WILLIAM.
> 1939. Ethnography of the Fox Indians. Bur. Amer Ethnol. Bull. 125. Margaret Welpley Fisher, editor.

JUNG, C. G.
> 1923. Psychological types. New York.

KINIETZ, W. VERNON.
> 1938. Meeārmeear traditions, by C. C. Trowbridge. (Edited by Kinietz.) Occas. Contr. Mus. Anthrop., Univ. Michigan, No. 7. Ann Arbor.
> 1940. The Indians of the western Great Lakes, 1650–1760. Occas. Contr. Mus. Anthrop., Univ. Michigan, No. 10. Ann Arbor.
> 1947. Chippewa village. Cranbrook Inst. Sci. Bull. No. 25.

KRIEGER, ALEX D.
> 1945. An inquiry into supposed Mexican influence on a prehistoric cult in the Southern United States. Amer. Anthrop., vol. 47, pp. 483–515.

KROEBER, A. L.
> 1904. The Arapaho. Anthrop. Pap. Amer. Mus. Nat. Hist., vol. 18, pt. 2.
> 1907. Gros Ventre myths and tales. Amer. Mus. Nat. Hist. Anthrop. Pap., vol. 1, pp. 55–139.
> 1908. Ethnology of the Gros Ventre. Amer. Mus. Nat. Hist. Anthrop. Pap., vol. 1, pp. 141–282.
> 1917. The superorganic. Amer. Anthrop., n. s., vol. 19, pp. 163–213. Reprinted by the Sociological Press, 1927, 37 pp.

LAFITAU, J. F.
> 1724. Moeurs des sauvages amériquains, comparées aux moeurs des premiers temps. 2 vols. Paris.

LA FLESCHE, FRANCIS.
> 1921. The Osage tribe: Rite of the chiefs; sayings of the ancient men. 36th Ann. Rep. Bur. Amer. Ethnol., 1914–1915, pp. 37–597.
> 1925. The Osage tribe: The rite of the vigil. 39th Ann. Rep. Bur. Amer. Ethnol., 1917–1918, pp. 31–630.
> 1939. War ceremony and Peace ceremony of the Osage Indians. Bur. Amer. Ethnol. Bull. 101, pp. 201–273.

LAHONTAN, A. L. DE D.
> 1735. New voyages to North America. London.

LE PAGE DU PRATZ, ANTOINE S.
> 1758. Histoire de la Louisiane. Paris. English trans., London, 1763, 1774.

LE SUEUR, Jacques Eustache.
> 1906. History of the Calumet . . . dance. R. G. Thwaites, editor. Wisconsin Hist. Coll., vol. 17, pp. 191–200.

LINTON, RALPH.
> 1936. The study of man. New York.
> 1947. The cultural background of personality. London.

LONG, STEPHEN H.
> 1823. Expedition from Pittsburgh to the Rocky Mountains. 2 vols. Philadelphia.

LOSKIEL, GEORGE H.
> 1794. History of the Mission of the United Brethren among the Indians in North America. La Trobe, editor. London.

216

Lowie, R. H.

1909. The Assiniboine. Anthrop. Pap. Amer. Mus. Nat. Hist., vol. 4, pt. 1.

1910. Notes concerning new collections. (Edited by Lowie.) Anthrop. Pap. Amer. Mus. Nat. Hist., vol. 4, No. 2, pp. 271–329.

1913. Societies of the Crow, Hidatsa and Mandan Indians. Anthrop. Pap. Amer. Mus. Nat. Hist., vol. 11, pt. 3.

1915. Ceremonialism in North America. Article in Anthropology in North America, pp. 229–258. New York.

1916. Individual differences and primitive culture. Article in Wilhelm Schmidt Festschrift, pp. 495–500. Wien.

1918. Myths and traditions of the Crow Indians. Anthrop. Pap. Amer. Mus. Nat. Hist., vol. 25, pt. 1.

1919. The Assiniboine. Anthrop. Pap. Amer. Mus. Nat. Hist., vol. 4, pp. 1–270.

1920. Primitive society. New York.

1922. The religion of the Crow Indian. Anthrop. Pap. Amer. Mus. Nat. Hist., vol. 25, pt. 2, pp. 309–444.

1925. Primitive religion. London.

1929. Culture and ethnology. New York.

Mandelbaum, David G.

1936. Friendship in North America. Man, vol. 36, No. 272, pp. 205–206. London.

1940. The Plains Cree. Anthrop. Pap. Amer. Mus. Nat. Hist., vol. 37,. pt 2, pp. 163–316.

Mandelbaum, David G., Editor.

1949. Selected writings of Edward Sapir . . . Berkeley.

Margry, Pierre.

1875–86. Découvertes et établissements des Français dans l'ouest et dans le sud de l'Amerique Septentionale (1614–1754). 6 vols. Paris.

Martin, Paul S., Quimby, George I., and Collier, Donald.

1947. Indians before Columbus. Chicago.

Mason, O. T.

1910. Travel. Article in Handbook of American Indians North of Mexico. Bur. Amer. Ethnol. Bull. 30, pt. 2, p. 802.

McGuire, J. D.

1899. Pipes and smoking customs of the American aborigines, based on material in the U. S. National Museum. Ann. Rep. U. S. Nat. Mus., 1897, pp. 351–645.

1910. Trails and trade routes. Article in Handbook of American Indians north of Mexico. Bur. Amer. Ethnol. Bull. 30, vol. 2, pp. 799–801.

McIlwain, Charles Howard., Editor.

1915. An abridgement of the Indian affairs . . . in the Colony of New York, . . . 1678 to . . . 1751 by Peter Wraxall. Harvard Hist. Stud., vol. 21.

Megapolensis, J.

1792. A short account of the Maquaas Indians, in New-Netherland, . . . written in the year 1644. E. Hazard, editor. Hist. Coll., vol. 1, pp. 517–526. Philadelphia.

Michelson, Truman.

1925. The mythical origin of the White Buffalo Dance of the Fox Indians. 40th Ann. Rep. Bur. Amer. Ethnol., 1918–1919, pp. 23–289.

1927. Contributions to Fox ethnology: Notes on the ceremonial runners of the Fox Indians. Bur. Amer. Ethnol. Bull. 85.

1928. Notes on the Buffalo-head Dance of the Thunder gens of the Fox Indians. Bur. Amer. Ethnol. Bull. 87.

1929. Observations on the Thunder Dance of the Bear gens of the Fox Indians. Bur. Amer. Ethnol. Bull. 89.

1930. Note on Fox gens festivals. Proc. 23d Internat. Congr. Americanists, 1928, pp. 545–546. New York.

1932. Notes on the Fox Wâpanōwiweni. Bur. Amer. Ethnol. Bull. 105.

1937. Friendship in North America. Man, vol. 37, No. 111. London.

N. d. Eagle Gens, Red Stone Pipe. Bur. Amer. Ethnol. Mss. Nos. 1850, 2576.

MILLING, J. C.

1940. Red Carolinians. Univ. North Carolina Press, Chapel Hill.

MILLS, ROBERT.

1826. Statistics of South Carolina: including a view of its natural, civil, and military history, general and particular. Charleston.

MOONEY, JAMES.

1898. Calendar history of the Kiowa Indians. 17th Ann. Rep. Bur. Amer. Ethnol., 1895–1896, pt. 1, pp. 129–445.

1900. Myths of the Cherokee. 19th Ann. Rep. Bur. Amer. Ethnol., 1897–1898, pt. 1, pp. 3–548.

MORGAN, LEWIS H.

1877. Ancient society. New York.

1901. League of the Ho-de-no-sau-nee, or Iroquois. 2 vols. Herbert M. Lloyd, editor. New York. (1st ed., Rochester 1851.)

See also Gilchrist, 1936.

MURDOCK, GEORGE PETER.

1932. The science of culture. Amer. Anthrop., n. s., vol. 34, pp. 200–215.

1949. Social structure. New York.

MURIE, JAMES R.

1914. Pawnee Indian societies. Anthrop. Pap. Amer. Mus. Nat. Hist., vol. 11, pp. 543–644.

MURIE, JAMES, and WISSLER, CLARK.

N. d. Ceremonies of the Pawnee. (In Bur. Amer. Ethnol. Archives, Ms. No. 2520.)

MYER, WILLIAM E.

1928. Indian trails of the Southeast. 42d Ann. Rep. Bur. Amer. Ethnol., 1924–1925, pp. 727–857.

O'CALLAGHAN, E. B., Editor.

1849–51. Documentary history of the State of New York. 4 vols. Albany.

1853–57. Documents relative to the Colonial history of the State of New York. 15 vols. Albany.

PARKER, ARTHUR C.

1910. Iroquois uses of maize and other food plants. New York State Mus. Bull. No. 144. Albany.

1913 a. The code of Handsome Lake, the Seneca Prophet. New York State Mus. Bull. No. 163. Albany.

1913 b. Secret medicine societies of the Seneca, 1909. New York State Mus. Bull. No. 163, pp. 113–130. Albany.

1916. The constitution of the Five Nations. New York State Mus. Bull. No. 184. Albany.

1919. The life of General Ely S. Parker. Buffalo Hist. Soc. Publ., vol. 23.

1922. The archeological history of New York. New York State Mus. Bull. Nos. 235–238. Albany.

1923. Seneca myths and folk tales. Buffalo Hist. Soc. Publ., vol. 27.

N. d. Seneca field notes from Newtown, Cattaraugus Reservation. (MS. 1905.)

PARKMAN, FRANCIS.
1851. History of the conspiracy of Pontiac. Boston.
1897. A half century of conflict. Boston.

PARSONS, ELSIE CLEWS.
1939. Pueblo Indian Religion. 2 vols. Chicago.

PEARSON, T. GILBERT, Editor.
1936. Birds of America. 2 vols. New York.

PETRULLO, VINCENZO.
1934. The diabolic root: A study of Peyotism.... among the Delawares. Philadelphia.

PHILLIPS, PHILIP.
1940. Middle American influences on the archaeology of the southeastern United States. In The Maya and Their Neighbors, pp. 349–367. New York.

PILLING, JAMES CONSTANTINE.
1888. Bibliography of the Iroquoian languages. Bur. Amer. Ethnol. Bull. 6.

POST, CHARLES FREDERICK.
1904. Two journals of western tours. Article in Early Western Travels, 1748–1846, vol. 1, pp. 185–291. R. G. Thwaites, editor. Cleveland.

POTHERIE, BACQUEVILLE DE LA.
1753. Histoire de l'amerique Septentrionale. 4 vols. Paris.

PROVINCIAL COUNCIL OF PENNSYLVANIA.
1852. Minutes of the Provincial Council of Pennsylvania, vol. 2. Philadelphia.

RADIN, PAUL.
1915. Literary aspects of North American mythology. Nat. Mus. Canada, Bull. No. 16, Anthrop. Ser. No. 6. Ottawa.
1920. The autobiography of a Winnebago Indian. Univ. California Publ. Amer. Arch. and Ethnol., vol. 16. Berkeley.
1923. The Winnebago tribe. 37th Ann. Rep. Bur. Amer. Ethnol., 1915–1916, pp. 33–560.
1926. Crashing Thunder: the autobiography of an American Indian. New York and London.
1927. Primitive man as philosopher. New York and London.
1933. The method and theory of ethnology. New York.

RADIN, PAUL, and REAGAN, A. B.
1928. Ojibwa myths and tales. Journ. Amer. Folklore, vol. 41, No. 159, pp. 61–146.

RAINEY, FROELICH G.
1936. A compilation of historical data contributing to the ethnology of Connecticut and southern New England. Bull. Arch. Soc. Connecticut, vol. 3, pp. 1–90. New Haven.

RAMSEY, J. G. M.
1860. The annals of Tennessee. Philadelphia.

RITZENTHALER, ROBERT E.
1950. The Oneida Indians of Wisconsin. Bull. Publ. Mus. City of Milwaukee, vol. 19, No. 1, pp. 1–52.

ROBERTS, HELEN M.
1936. Musical areas in aboriginal North America. Yale Univ. Publ. Anthrop., No. 12. New Haven.

ROBINSON, D.
1904. A history of the Dakota or Sioux Indians. South Dakota Hist. Coll., vol. 2, pp. 1–523. Aberdeen.

SAPIR, EDWARD.
1916. Time perspective in aboriginal American culture. Canada Geol. Surv., Anthrop. Ser., vol. 13, Mem. No. 90.
1917. Do we need a "Superorganic"? Amer. Anthrop., vol. 19, pp. 441–447.
1925. Culture, genuine and spurious. Amer. Journ. Sociol., vol. 29, pp. 401–430.
1928. The unconscious patterning of behavior in society. *Article in* The Unconscious: a symposium, pp. 114–142. S. Dummer, editor. New York.

SCHOOLCRAFT, HENRY R.
1847. Notes on the Iroquois. Albany.

SEAVER, JAMES EVERETT.
1932. A narrative of the life of Mary Jemison. Amer. Scenic and Hist. Preservation Soc. New York.

SENECA OF COLDSPRING LONGHOUSE, THE.
1950. Another Eagle Dance for Gahéhdagowa. (Introduction by W. N. Fenton.) Primitive Man, vol. 22, Nos. 3–4, pp. 60–64. Washington. (Dated 1949.)

SHETRONE, HENRY CLYDE.
1930. The mound-builders. New York.

SKINNER, ALANSON.
1910. Cherokee collection. *In* Lowie, Notes concerning new collections. Anthrop. Pap. Amer. Mus. Nat. Hist., vol. 4, pt. 2, pp. 284–289.
1913. Social life and ceremonial bundles of the Menomini Indians. Anthrop. Pap. Amer. Mus. Nat. Hist., vol. 13, pt. 1, pp. 1–165.
1914. Political organization, cults and ceremonies of the Plains-Cree. Anthrop Pap. Amer. Mus. Nat. Hist., vol. 11, pt. 6, pp. 513–542.
1915 a. Societies of the Iowa, Kansa, and Ponca Indians. Anthrop. Pap. Amer. Mus. Nat. Hist., vol. 11, pt. 9, pp. 679–801. (Kansa organizations, pp. 741–775; Ponca societies and dances, pp. 777–801.)
1915 b. Associations and ceremonies of the Menomini Indians. Anthrop. Pap. Amer. Mus. Nat. Hist., vol. 13, pt. 2, pp. 167–215.
1921. Material culture of the Menomini. Mus. Amer. Indian, Heye Found., Indian Notes and Monogr., n. s., No. 20. New York.
1926. Ethnology of the Ioway Indians. Bull. Publ. Mus. City of Milwaukee, vol. 5, No. 4.

SMITH, ERMINNIE A.
1883. Myths of the Iroquois. 2d Ann. Rep. Bur. Ethnol., 1880–1881, pp. 47–116.

SPECK, FRANK G.
1909. Ethnology of the Yuchi Indians. Univ. Pennsylvania Mus. Anthrop. Publ., vol. 1, No. 1, pp. 1–154.
1911. Ceremonial songs of the Creek and Yuchi Indians. Univ. Pennsylvania Mus. Anthrop. Publ., vol. 1, No. 2, pp. 159–245.
1930. Decorative art and basketry of the Cherokee. Bull. Publ. Mus. City of Milwaukee, vol. 2, pp. 53–86.
1931. A study of the Delaware Indian Big House ceremony. Publ. Pennsylvania Hist. Comm., vol. 2. Harrisburg.

1935. Naskapi. Univ. Oklahoma Press. Norman, Okla.

1939. Catawba religious beliefs, mortuary customs, and dances. Primitive Man, vol. 12, No. 2, pp. 21–57. Washington.

1945. The celestial bear comes down to earth: The bear sacrifice ceremony of the Munsee-Mahican in Canada as related by Nekatchit. Reading Publ. Mus. and Art Gall., Sci. Publ. No. 7. Reading, Pa.

1946. Bird nomenclature and song interpretation of the Canadian Delaware: An essay in ethno-ornithology. Journ. Washington Acad. Sci., vol. 36, No. 8, pp. 249–258.

1949. Midwinter Rites of the Cayuga Long House. [In collaboration with Alexander General.] Philadelphia.

1950. How the Dew Eagle Society of the Allegany Seneca cured Gahéhdagowa. Primitive Man, vol. 22, Nos. 3–4, pp. 39–59. Washington. (Dated 1949.)

N. d. MS. Cayuga field notes. (Written in 1933.)

SPECK, F., and BROOM, L.

1951. Cherokee dance and drama. Berkeley and Los Angeles.

SPECK, F., and SCHAEFFER, C. E.

1942. Catawba kinship and social organization with a resumé of Tutelo kinship terms. Amer. Anthrop., vol. 44, No. 4, pp. 555–575.

SPIER, LESLIE.

1928. Havasupai ethnography. Amer. Mus. Nat. Hist., Anthrop. Pap., vol. 29, pt. 3.

1930. Klamath ethnography. Univ. California Publ. Amer. Arch. and Ethnol., vol. 30.

1933. Yuman tribes of the Gila River. Chicago.

1935. The Prophet Dance of the Northwest and its derivatives: The source of the Ghost Dance. Gen. Ser. in Anthrop. No. 1.

STONE, WILLIAM L.

1838. Life of Joseph Brant—Thayendanegea. 2 vols. New York.

1841. The life and times of Red Jacket. New York and London. (2d ed. 1866).

STRONG, WILLIAM DUNCAN.

1935. An introduction to Nebraska archeology. Smithsonian Misc. Coll., vol. 93, No. 10.

SWANTON, JOHN R.

1911. Indian tribes of the lower Mississippi Valley and adjacent coast of the Gulf of Mexico. Bur. Amer. Ethnol. Bull. 43.

1918. An early account of the Choctaw Indians. Mem. Amer. Anthrop. Assoc., vol. 5, No. 2, pp. 53–72.

1928 a. Aboriginal culture of the Southeast. 42d Ann. Rep. Bur. Amer. Ethnol., 1924–1925, pp. 673–726.

1928 b. Social organization and social usages of the Indians of the Creek Confederacy. 42d Ann. Rep. Bur. Amer. Ethnol., 1924–1925, pp. 23–472.

1928 c. Religious beliefs and medical practices of the Creek Indians. 42d Ann. Rep. Bur. Amer. Ethnol., 1924–1925, pp. 473–672.

1928 d. Social and religious beliefs and usages of the Chickasaw Indians. 44th Ann. Rep. Bur. Amer. Ethnol., 1926–1927, pp. 169–273.

1929. Myths and tales of the southeastern Indians. Bur. Amer. Ethnol. Bull. 88.

1931. Source material for the social and ceremonial life of the Choctaw Indians. Bur. Amer. Ethnol. Bull. 103.

1942. Source material on the history and ethnology of the Caddo Indians. Bur. Amer. Ethnol. Bull. 132.

1946. The Indians of the southeastern United States.   Bur. Amer. Ethnol. Bull. 137.

THOMPSON, STITH.
1929. Tales of the North American Indians.   Cambridge, Mass.

THWAITES, REUBEN GOLD, EDITOR.
1896–1901. The Jesuit Relations and allied documents, . . . 1610–1791. 73 vols.   Cleveland.
1904–1907. Early Western Travels, 1748–1846.   32 vols.   Cleveland.
        See also Hennepin, Louis, 1903; Le Seur, J. E., 1906; Post, Frederick, 1904; Weiser, Conrad, 1904.

TIMBERLAKE, H.
1765. Memoirs of Lieut. Henry Timberlake.   London.

VOEGELIN, E. A., and FENTON, W. N.
[1953?] The Shawnee Eagle Dance.   Unpublished Ms.   Scheduled for publication *in* Anthropological Quarterly [formerly Primitive Man].

VOLWILER, ALBERT T.
1926. George Croghan and the westward movement, 1741–1782.   2 vols. Cleveland.

WALKER, J. R.
1917. The Sun Dance and other ceremonies of the Oglala Division of the Teton Dakota.   Amer. Mus. Nat. Hist., Anthrop. Pap., vol. 16, pp. 51–221.

WALLACE, A. F. C.
1952. The modal personality structure of the Tuscarora Indians, as revealed by the Rorschach test.   Bur. Amer. Ethnol. Bull. 150.

WALLACE, PAUL A. W.
1945. Conrad Weiser (1696–1760): friend of Colonist and Mohawk.   Philadelphia.

WARING, A. J., JR., and HOLDER, PRESTON.
1945. A prehistoric ceremonial complex in the Southeastern United States. Amer. Anthrop., vol. 47, pp. 1–34.

WAUGH, F. W.
1916. Iroquois foods and food preparation.   Canada Geol. Surv., Anthrop. Ser., vol. 12, Mem. No. 86.   Ottawa.
N. d. Iroquois field notes, 1912–1916.   Canada Geol. Surv., Anthrop. Div.

WEDEL, WALDO RUDOLPH.
1936. An introduction to Pawnee archeology.   Bur. Amer. Ethnol. Bull. 112.

WEISER, CONRAD.
1904. Journal of a tour to the Ohio, 1748.   *Article in* Early Western Travels, 1748–1846, vol. 2, pp. 21–46.   R. G. Thwaites, editor.

WESLAGER, C. A.
1944. The Delaware Indians as women.   Journ. Washington Acad. Sci., vol. 34, No. 12, pp. 381–388.

WILLIAMS, RODGER.
1827. A key into the languages of America.   Coll. Rhode Island Hist. Soc., vol. 1.   Providence.   (1st ed., London, 1643.)

WILLIAMS, S. C.
1928. Early travels in the Tennessee Country, 1540–1800.   The Watauga Press., Johnson City, Tenn.

WILSON, GILBERT LIVINGSTONE.
1928. Hidatsa eagle trapping.   Anthrop. Pap., Amer. Mus. Nat. Hist., vol. 30, pt. 4, pp. 97–245.   New York.

WISSLER, CLARK.

1912. Ceremonial bundles of the Blackfoot Indians. Anthrop. Pap. Amer. Mus. Nat. Hist., vol. 7, pt. 2. pp. 69–289. New York.

1915. Material culture of the North American Indians. *Article in* Anthropology in North America, pp. 76–134. New York.

WITTHOFT, JOHN.

1946 a. Some Eastern Cherokee bird stories. Journ. Washington Acad. Sci., vol. 36, No. 6, pp. 177–180.

1946 b. Birdlore of the Eastern Cherokee. Journ. Washington Acad. Sci. vol. 36, No. 11, pp. 372–384.

1949. Stone pipes of the historic Cherokee. Southern Indian Studies, vol. 1, No. 2, pp. 43–62. Chapel Hill, N. C.

WRAXALL, PETER.

See McIlwain, 1915.

ZEISBERGER, DAVID.

1910. David Zeisberger's history of the Northern American Indians. Albert Butler Hulbert and William Nathaniel Schwarze, editors. Ohio Archaeol. and Hist. Soc. Quart., vol. 19, pp. 1–189.

1912. Diary of David Zeisberger's Journey to the Ohio . . . from Sept. 20th to Nov. 16th, 1767. Moravian Records, vol. 2, Ohio Archaeol and Hist. Soc. Quart., vol. 21, pp. 8–32.

PLATE 2

The household of Resting-sky.

Back row: Resting-sky and Voice-above. *Center:* It-dips-water; and (*front*) her grandson.

PLATE 3

Sherman Redeye, Snipe Clan, Coldspring Seneca informant.

PLATE 4

Clara Redeye, Voice-above, Hawk Clan, interpreter, at Coldspring.

PLATE 5

It-dips-water, Hawk Clan matron, wife of Resting-sky, Coldspring Seneca.

PLATE 6

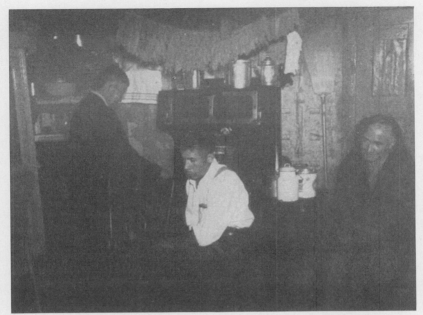

1.

2.

Eagle Dance in 1942 for Big-canoe and He-carries-an-ax.
1, Wood-eater puts tobacco in the fire. *2*, On the last song the dancers lay down the feather fans.

PLATE 7

1.

2.

Eagle Dance in 1942.

1, The second round of speeches for Dew Eagle. *2*, The dancers crouch and sway with the songs.

PLATE 8

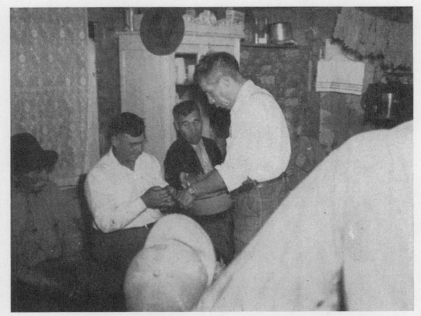

1.

2.

Eagle Dance in 1942.

1, Passing the pig head and crying like crows. *2*, Members carry home pails of corn soup.

PLATE 9

Wood-eater, Bear Clan, Seneca ritualist at Coldspring.

PLATE 10

Corn-husker, Hawk Clan, Seneca of Coldspring, and his two pet hawks.

PLATE 11

Twenty-canoes, Bear Clan, and Stick-lodged-in-a-crotch, Deer Clan, guardians of Handsome Lake's message, as delegates from Coldspring to Tonawanda Longhouse.

PLATE 12

Snorer, Hawk Clan, Seneca of Coldspring.

PLATE 13

Hemlocks-lying-down, Turtle Clan, conductor and singer of Seneca ceremonies at Coldspring.

PLATE 14

Earth-hiller, matron of the Wolf Clan, Coldspring.

PLATE 15

Helper, Sachem chief of the Bear Clan, Tonawanda Seneca.

PLATE 16

1.

2.

*1, He-strikes-the-rushes, Snipe Clan, Seneca ritualist, with gourd rattle of the Medicine Company, in the costume of the Federal Period.
2, Chief Joseph Logan, Onondaga; and Simeon Gibson, Six Nations Reserve, Canada.*

PLATE 17

Djidǫ́gwas, a Seneca of the Wolf Clan, at Coldspring.

PLATE 18

Yankee Spring, a Seneca of the Beaver Clan, at Tonawanda.

PLATE 19

Sarah Snow, Seneca of the Bear Clan, Coldspring's clairvoyant and herbalist.

PLATE 20

1.

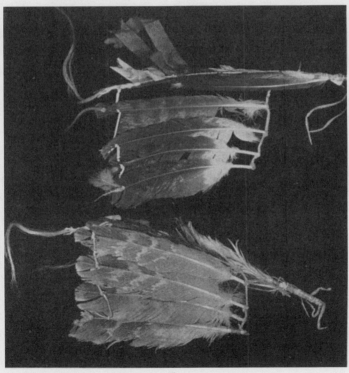

2.

Eagle Society Bundles.
1, Fans and gourd rattles from the bundle of Hemlocks-lying-down. *2,* An old set of fans **in**
New York State Museum.

PLATE 21

Striped emblem pole of Eagle Society, displayed for a meeting of the Society.
(Courtesy New York State Museum.)

PLATE 22

Five-feathered fans from Cattaraugus Seneca.
(Milwaukee Public Museum photograph.)

PLATE 23

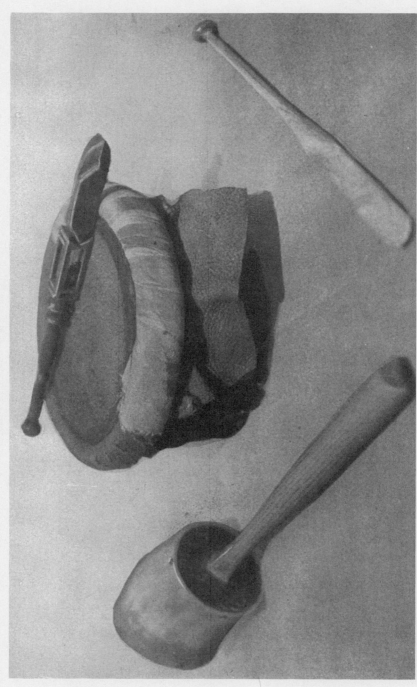

Water drum and horn rattle, by Clarence White of Coldspring, laid out for Eagle Dance singers.

PLATE 24

Horn rattles: *Left*, two by Hemlocks-lying-down; *right*, by Corn-husker.

PLATE 25

Corn-husker's wife leaches white corn for soup.

PLATE 26

Hulled white corn after three washings.

PLATE 27

The Seneca Eagle Dance.

(Oil painting by Ernest Smith, Seneca artist of Tonawanda.)

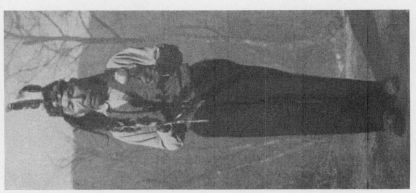

PLATE 28

Cherokee Eagle Dance movements by Will West Long: Approach, holding the fan, and crouch.

An Analysis of The Iroquois Eagle Dance and Songs

By GERTRUDE PROKOSCH KURATH

CONTENTS

FIGURES

ACKNOWLEDGMENTS

The field trips, the choreographic and musicological research preliminary to this study, as well as the work on the manuscript have been facilitated by manifold cooperation. To John Witthoft I owe suggestions for first contacts at Six Nations Reserve in 1948 and at Qualla Cherokee Reservation in 1949. The success of the repeated trips to Six Nations Reserve is due to the cordiality of Deskaheh (Alexander General), Esther Jamieson, Sadie Jamieson, and other Iroquois friends; also to the hospitality of the Rev. and Mrs. John Pryse, of Ohsweken, Ontario. To Dr. William N. Fenton I am indebted for the friendly welcome among the Seneca of Coldspring Longhouse and at Tonawanda Reservation and for counsel and assistance in all aspects of the work.

For the consummation of the research during the year of 1949 I am indebted to the Wenner-Gren Foundation for Anthropological Research for their grant-in-aid.

I wish to express my indebtedness also to Dr. Curt Sachs for invaluable musicological advice; to Dr. Leslie A. White for reading of the manuscript and constructive comments; to Dr. James Griffin for archeological information; to Dr. John O. Brew for permission to reproduce Omaha wawaⁿ songs published by the Peabody Museum; to Dr. George Herzog for permission to reproduce his transcription of San Ildefonso Eagle Dance songs, and for authorizing the duplication of Tonawanda Eagle Dance and Fox Calumet Dance recordings, now in the Archives of Folk and Primitive Music of Indiana University; to Martha Champion Randle for permission to use these records and for texts from her field notes on the Fox; to John W. Gillespie for copies of Cherokee Eagle Dance recordings; and to Carrie Logan Hill, of Six Nations Onondaga Longhouse, and Geneva Jones, of Coldspring Seneca Longhouse, for special information on the ceremony.

GERTRUDE P. KURATH.

Ann Arbor, Michigan.

228

AN ANALYSIS OF THE IROQUOIS EAGLE DANCE AND SONGS

By Gertrude Prokosch Kurath

COMPARATIVE CHOREOGRAHPY

THE QUEST

Fifteen years after William Fenton and Frank Speck, a new guest trudged through the snow to an Iroquois Longhouse. The Sour Springs Cayuga were celebrating their Midwinter medicine rite renewals, and had permitted my participation. On this day—Monday, February 14, 1948—the Eagle Dance was performed as 14 in a series of 20 events. Sober-faced Chief Deskaheh and cheery Willie John accompanied four youths in the same songs and evolutions here reproduced.

This was the beginning of growing friendships and repeated visits, though it was not my first acquaintance with an Iroquois. In July 1946 I had met Chauncey Johnny John, not in his native haunts, but at the University of Michigan Summer Institute of Linguistics. As "professor" for Dr. Carl Voegelin's students, he basked in the scholarly environment. On several free evenings he changed to his artistic role and his ceremonial costume and, in our living room, showed samples of Eagle, War, and other dances and of the songs he had sung into "Bill Fenton's machine." [1]

Several years passed before Dr. Fenton, the ethnologist who believed that the dances and songs required special dedication, found a dancer-musician who was determined to explore these expressions of Indian culture. In 1948, at Allegany Reservation, it was possible for Dr. Fenton and me to collaborate. During the late summer—the Green Corn season—the Seneca had no occasion to enact the Eagle Dance as a ritual. But one memorable evening, September 4, in a one-room cabin, three generations of the Johnny John family demonstrated various rituals, including Eagle Dance, while the fourth generation joined the second Kurath generation in the perusal of comic books.

Eagle Dance remained elusive. At Sour Springs Midwinter of 1949 it was replaced by Striking-the-Stick. But on Monday evening, August 21, 1950, a private ritual took place in the home of Joseph Logan, the kindly and energetic chief of Onondaga Longhouse at Six Nations Reserve. An invitation was extended as a gesture of cordiality.

---

[1] See Fenton, 1942, p. 5, and 1948, p. 3, for an account of Chauncey Johnny John and of the recording.

THE RITUALS AT SIX NATIONS RESERVE

In 1948 and 1950, as in 1933, the same traditional formula governed the procedure and stylized the mimetic imitation of flight. Song and dance, inextricably interwoven, usually alternated with the ritual action. They synchronized only in the tobacco invocation and the final dance song of offering.

ONONDAGA PRIVATE RITUAL

After dark, several Onondaga families and a few friends from other longhouses assembled in the main room of Joseph Logan's home. The male actors chose their places on chairs against the wall. Women, children, and White guests lounged on the beds and chairs of the adjoining bedroom. The following persons were present (fig. 4):

Performers:
1. Joseph Logan, Sr., Deer Clan, *priest.*
2. Bill Johnson (Onondaga), *gift custodian.*
3. Fred Green, Deer Clan, *patient.*
4. Robert Logan, Wolf Clan, age 11, *first dancer.*
5. Marvin Skye, Deer Clan age 8, *second dancer.*
6. Leroy Smoke, Turtle Clan, age 15, *third dancer.*
7. Howard Skye, Wolf Clan (C.), grandfather of Marvin..
8. Alex Nanticoke (Chief of Lower Cayuga Longhouse).
9. Joseph Logan, Jr., Deer Clan,[2] father of Robert, *conductor.*
10. Peter Buck, Deer Clan, *first singer,* with drum.
11. Roy Fish, Turtle Clan, *second singer,* with rattle.
12. A visitor from Tonawanda Reservation.
13. Jake Skye, Deer Clan,[2] father of Marvin.

Spectators:
14. Gertrude Kurath.
15. Edward Kurath, asleep on floor.
16. Joseph Raben.
17 and 18. Women and children, some of them asleep.

The coherence of this ceremony was heightened by the participation of three generations from two families, the Logans and the Skyes. The Logan family dominated the ritual in three significant roles of intercession with the supernatural, intermediary between communicants, and personification of the Eagle spirit. No one appeared in costume. Fred Green had not provided the usual feathered wands. But his mother had cooked a chicken which was placed on a platter and set on the floor in front of the singers. She had also prepared a corn soup for the final communal feast. The omission of mimetic and symbolic paraphernalia did not impair the friendly solemnity of the occasion or its rhythmic continuity.

---

[2] According to Carrie Logan Hill, in both the Logan and Skye families father and son belong to Deer clans from different tribes. They would not belong to the same clan, because of the matrilineal system of descent.

CEREMONIAL OUTLINE

Ritual Action	Music	Dance	Performers
I. Introduction:			
1. Thanksgiving			Priest.
2. Tobacco offering at stove	Chant 1, no instrument		Priest.
II. Body:			
1. Distribution:			
Drum and rattle to singers			Conductor.
	Chant 1, tremolo:		
	A		First singer.
	A B		Both singers.
Wands and rattles to dancers			Conductor.
	Chant 2, tremolo		Singers.
Strike cane, speech			Priest.
2. Impersonation of Eagle:	Eagle cry, shiver rattles	On perch	Dancers, antiphonally.
	Song 3:		
	A, tremolo	Quiver, seated	First singer, dancers.
	A, tremolo	Quiver, lunge	Both singers, dancers.
	B, beat	Hop to singers	Both singers, dancers.
	A, tremolo	Quiver, lunge	Both singers, dancers.
	B, beat	Hop to perch	Both singers, dancers.
Strike cane, speech			Gift custodian.
Chicken placed before singers			Conductor.
	Songs 4–15, same pattern as 3		Singers, dancers.
		In lunge, nibble chicken	Dancers.[3]
After each song, strike cane, speech; gift of biscuits or coins			Society members.
Cane passed around by			Conductor.

[3] Usually Robert sank his teeth into the tender meat. But once Marvin was the successful competitor. On return to his perch, he shouted gleefully, "I got there first!"

CEREMONIAL OUTLINE—continued

Ritual Action	Music	Dance	Performers
II. Body—Continued			
3. Offering:			
	Song 16_____	(See pp. 247–248)_	Singers and dancers.
Lay down wands or rattles	-------------------	-------------------	Dancers.
Collect paraphernalia	-------------------	-------------------	Conductor.
III. Conclusion:			
1. Concluding prayer	-------------------	-------------------	Priest.
2. Distribution of chicken to singers and dancers	-------------------	-------------------	Conductor.
3. Feast of corn soup, served counter-clockwise	-------------------	-------------------	Conductor to all present.

PUBLIC RITUAL AT CAYUGA SOUR SPRINGS LONGHOUSE

Whereas the private ceremony included the entire procedure, the communal observance coincided with only the Body, Part II, of the outline above. The two singers were seated on a bench in the center of the southwestern or men's wall; the four dancers faced them on a bench on the northeastern or women's wall. After the introductory chant, Bill Johnson handed each of them a feathered wand and rattle. The grouping was typical (fig. 5):

1 to 4. *Dancers.*
5. Deskaheh (Alexander General), Turtle moiety, *first singer.*
6. Willie John, Wolf moiety, *second singer.*
7. Bill Johnson, Wolf moiety, *faithkeeper* (Cayuga).
8. Men of Turtle moiety.
9. Women of Turtle moiety.
10. Women of Wolf moiety.
11. Men of Wolf moiety.[4]

Interlonghouse comparisons.—The Cayuga share customs both with the Onondaga and Seneca; hence the grouping of dancers with the former and the moiety association with the latter. My notes give no information on the names of the four Sour Spring youths, but the singers and spectators conformed to a moiety arrangement. The

[4] See Speck, 1950, p. 23, for moiety and sex arrangement.

absence of a fourth dancer and of wands were incidental omissions at the Onondaga ritual. As a rule they should be included, as at Sour Springs. These wands are all handed to the Six Nations dancers after the first chant. The Cayuga use only one chant and the Onondaga follow the second one with a speech. This differs from the Seneca custom of dividing the distribution into two actions, after two songs, by moiety (p. 16). Here again Tonawanda, with the two chants, differs from Allegany with three (figs. 9 and 31; pp. 238, 290). At Six Nations the dancers utter the antiphonal Eagle cry; at Logan's, first Robert, then the other two boys in response. This eliminates the Seneca office of whooper.

The speeches at Six Nations follow the type described by Fenton and fulfill the Iroquois fondness for ritualized jokes and clowning. However, Seneca speakers interrupt the song, whereas the Onondaga and sometimes the Cayuga await the end of the song; Seneca pass the cane in rotation, whereas the Onondaga and Cayuga follow no fixed order. Twentieth century ideas may vary the code of jests: at Logan's the visitor from Tonawanda told how he had heard about the ceremony over the radio and had hurried there. This absurdity was applauded.

THE DANCE: THREE TRIBAL VARIANTS

GROUND PLAN

Seneca—fig. 3.—As the Seneca dancers, be there two or four, are paired by moiety, they always face their partner during the lunge, approach, and retreat, without reference to the singers.

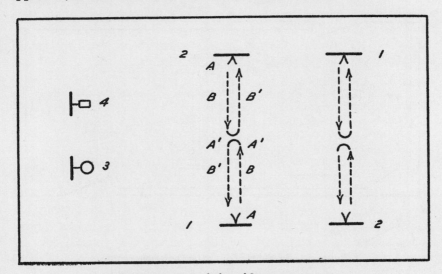

FIGURE 3.—Ground plan of Seneca ceremony.

Six Nations—figs. 4 and 5.—As the square is strung out into a straight line, the four (or three) boys move parallel, always facing the singers and the chicken.

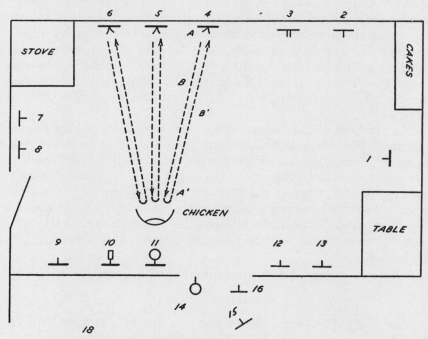

FIGURE 4.—Ground plan of Onondaga private ritual.

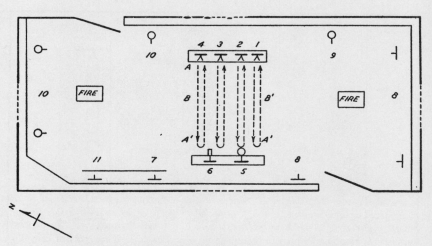

FIGURE 5.—Ground plan of Cayuga Longhouse ritual.

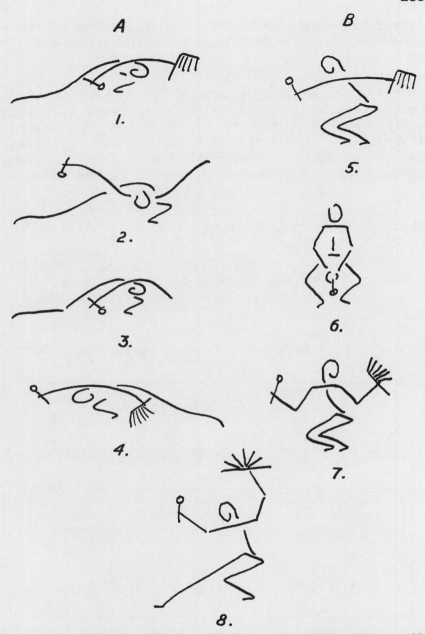

FIGURE 6.—Postures of dancers. *1*, Seneca dancer in lunging position, arms out to side. *2*, Robert Logan, Onondaga, in lunge, arms out in back. *3*, Marvin Skye, Onondaga, in lunge, arms forward. *4*, Cayuga dancer in lunge, right arm forward. *5*, Seneca dancer in hop. *6*, Hopping position in Onondaga private ritual. *7*, Knee twist of Onondaga-Cayuga. *8*, Cherokee eagle dancer. Note various types of wands. For photographs see Seneca, this volume, plate 20; Fenton, 1942, pl. 8; Onondaga-Cayuga, Speck, 1949, plate X, B; Cherokee, Gilbert, 1943, plate 15, 2.

Thus the focus is affected by the type of ground plan. This is absolute, unchanging, for the tribe, no matter who the dancers.

However, the ever-recurrent movement pattern depends not only on longhouse custom, but also on the strength, expertness, and mimetic ability of the individual performers. The step may appear superficially the same, but actually it is never repeated twice with mechanical accuracy. Thus, the choreographies must be considered as paradigms. In figures 7 and 8 the first dance songs of the Seneca and

FIGURE 7.—Seneca choreography to first dance song, S. 4.

FIGURE 8.—Onondaga choreography to first dance song, Oa. 3, 4,

Onondaga cycles are coordinated with the dance script which relates each hop to the corresponding musical beat.[5] The graphic portrayal is supplemented by conventional verbal description.

[5] For dance script and key, see Kurath, 1950, p. 121, and 1951, figs. 22–24.

In addition to this typical choreography, the final dances show definite longhouse variations which call for special outlines.

Seneca: Song 4 (first dance song) (fig. **7**).

A		Seated on perch, quiver wand and rattles.
A		Descend into lunge, right leg extended, facing partner (fig. 6, *1*).
B	Measure 1[6] Count (beat) 1	Starting in oblique position right face, deep crouching hop ahead (i. e., obliquely left). Leave ground on offbeat, land on accent.
	Count 2	Facing forward, hop ahead with half turn left (fig. 6, *5*).
	Measure 2	Two more hops, face left, then forward.
	Measures 3–4	Four more hops, face right, forward, left, forward.
	Measure 5 Counts 1–3	Three heel-beats in place, facing about toward left.
A		Deep lunge, facing partner, quiver.
B	Measures 1–5	Repeat B, in reverse direction, crossing room.

Onondaga: Songs 3 and 4 (first dance songs) (fig. **8**).

A		Same as Seneca.
A		Same as Seneca, in variant postures (fig. 6, *2, 3*).
B	Measure 1 Count 1	Same as Seneca.
	Count 2	Continue facing right, smaller hop obliquely left, crouch less deep.
	Measures 2–4	Continue with 6 hops—3 large, 3 small.
	Measures 5–6	Continue with 4 small deep hops.
	Measure 7 Counts 1–3	Three knee twists, right, left, right (fig. 6, *1*).
A		Without facing about, lunge and quiver (nibble chicken, if any).
B	Measures 1–7	Facing right, with reference to singers, hop right toward perch, as in first B.

Cayuga (fig. 8, and Kurath, 1951, fig. 6).

A A		Same as Seneca and Onondaga, except that more commonly extend left leg.
B		Facing obliquely left (or right), hop continually, as Onondaga, but evenly on each count, as Seneca.
A		Same as Onondaga.
B		Same as Onondaga, but hopping in even accents.

---

[6] On the whole, the concept of "measures" does not fit into Iroquois musicology, and here designates the rhythmic divisions for analytic convenience.

Longhouse.—At all times the dancers' rattles conform to the beat of the singers' instruments, which differs in each longhouse. Skilled dancers also observe this drum pattern in their hopping, as shown in the paradigm. In part their hopping pattern is also determined by the tempo, which the Johnny Johns hold slow enough for a comfortable

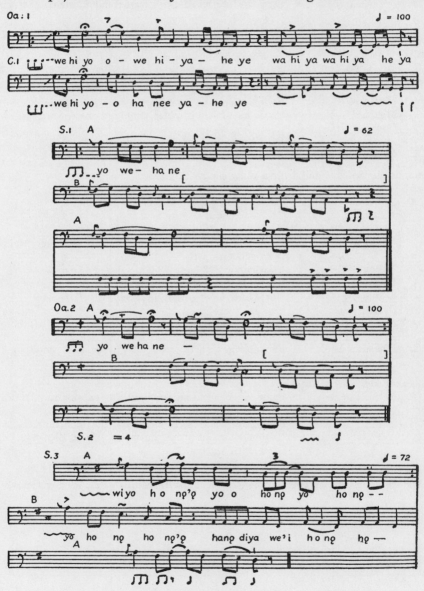

FIGURE 9.—Introductory chants.

hop on each beat, but which Logan snaps up beyond the possibility of a continuous series of rapid deep crouches. Deskaheh's intermediate speed can still be followed by agile dancers in even accents. Less facile performers cannot even execute the alternate hopping pattern of the Onondaga paradigm, but settle for a hop to a measure or an occasional, rather ragged, omission. However, all dancers follow the terminal formula of three sharp beats, variously (Seneca) with stamping or (Onondaga-Cayuga) with knee twists, usually three or, less expertly, two on beats 1 and 3. The manner of advance and return is due to the variations in ground plan, as already stated. But the half turn (or quarter turn) from side to side may as well be an individual idea. Though never observed at Six Nations, it would be possible and even appropriate.

Individual.—Some of the variations of posture have no compulsory foundation in longhouse custom. Either leg can be extended, straight back (fig. 6, *1* and *4*), straight out to the side (fig. 6, *2*), or obliquely with the knee on the ground (fig. 6, *3*). The arms can spread out to

Figure 10.—Dance songs S. 5, Oa. 13, C. 3—comparative.

the side, way back, toward the ground, or with the rattle held forward (fig. 6, *1*, *2*, *3*, *4*, respectively). The fluttering may be confined to the wrists, or involve the shoulders or even the whole torso (Robert Logan).

In the hop, which varies in depth and elasticity, the knees may be held straight forward or somewhat separated (fig. 6, *5* and *6*). At Logan's home the latter angle was caused by the absence of the wand and the consequent grasping and frontal shaking of the rattle with

FIGURE 11.—Dance songs S. 6, Oa. 14—comparative.

FIGURE 12.—S. 7 and S. 14—comparative.

both hands. The arms likewise can fluctuate from an extended to a flexed position (fig. 6, *5* and *7*). These and other apparently insignificant variations actually affect the expressiveness and beauty of the birdlike motions. A droopy eagle is less exhilarating than a sky-dweller with vibrant wings outspread.

FIGURE 13.—Oa. 5, C. 2.—comparative.

FIGURE 14.—C. 4, 6.

242

FIGURE 15.—S. 9, 11 and Oa. 11; S. 10 and Oa. 6, 7—comparative.

FIGURE 16.—S. 12, Oa. 15, C. 7—comparative.

Figure 17.—Oa. 8, 9, 10.

Figure 18.—S. 8, 13, 15, 16.

Figure 19.—S. 17, Oa. 12, C. 5, 8—comparative.

FINAL SONGS

(Fig. 20)

With due allowance for the individual quotient, all of the dances follow the same pattern, but the final deposition of the fans terminates each longhouse ritual in a special way. As in general, the motions resemble those already described, they require no further analysis. They fall into the various outlines here shown. The wand and rattle offerings synchronize with musical phrases labeled on figure 20.[7]

---

[7] Speck describes the position of paraphernalia on the floor (1949 a, pp. 111–112).

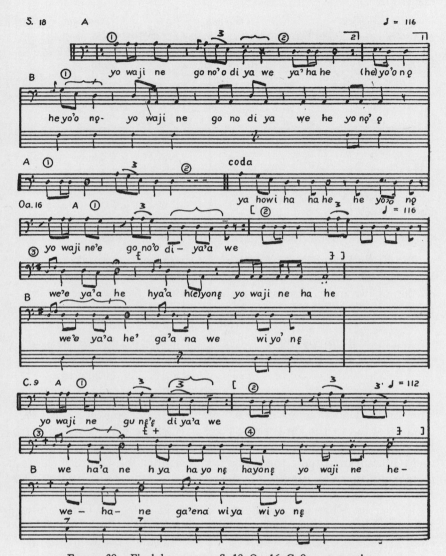

FIGURE 20.—Final dance songs, S. 18, Oa. 16, C. 9—comparative.

Seneca	Onondaga	Cayuga
A A: On perch, lunge	A: (1) On perch	A: (1) On perch.
	(2), (3) Lunge	(2), (3), (4) Lunge.
B: Advance	B: Hop to singers	B: Hop to singers.
A: Lunge face to face	A: (1) Lunge	A: (1) Dancer 1 deposit fan.
	(2) Lunge, quiver	(2) Dancer 2 deposit fan.
	(3) All deposit fans	(3) Dancer 3 deposit fan.
		(4) Dancer 4 deposit fan.
B: Retreat	B: Hop to perch	B: Hop to perch.
A: Lunge		
Coda: Deposit fans		

RELATION TO OTHER IROQUOIS DANCES

The Eagle Dance is atypical both as to ground plan and step, amid a superabundance of shuffling round dances.[8] The approach and recession of two lines constitutes Strike-the-Stick (fig. 29); partner swapping is incorporated in a number of rounds, but these follow a different pattern of musical adjustment and progress with noneagle steps and considerable improvisation. Thus this fine offering to the sky dancer stands alone in Iroquois choreography.

THE SONGS

Iroquois music remains as their superlative cultural expression. The Eagle Dance songs are no exception. Fortunately they have been recorded in the three salient tribal versions which correspond to the dance observations, and consequently they can be studied with greater assurance than the dances, which must be transcribed from memory, from notes made after the ritual, and from descriptions. Dr. Fenton made two sets of Seneca disks: in 1936 at Tonawanda together with Martha Champion Randle; in 1941 at Allegany with Richard Johnny John as chief singer and his grandfather Chauncey Johnny John as assistant and as leader in the last 11 songs from the old man's repertoire.[9] At Six Nations Reserve Dr. Fenton in 1941 recorded Chief Joe Logan's Onondaga cycle as learned from Tom Smoke, Seneca singer of Onondaga Longhouse. In August 1950 Joseph Raben and myself made a tape recording of Deskaheh and Willie John in the Cayuga cycle.

These songs can be translated readily enough into conventional notation because of their remarkably distinct melody, pitch, and beat. However, the process of adaptation must discard the diatonic, harmonic, and metrical concepts of Occidental music. To avoid any

[8] See Kurath, 1951, for description of rounds and cross-overs.
[9] See bibliography of recordings (p. 306).

suggestion of "key" they have been transposed down, variously a third and a fourth, to a uniform level which avoids key signatures. To emphasize the fact that the melodies are not the upper line of a succession of invisible chords, the terminology will bypass terms suggestive of harmony, and will substitute maintone, fifth, five-tone— and numerals—for tonic, dominant, pentatonic—and do, re, mi; tertial for triad, etc. To underscore the flexibility, metric signatures are eliminated and bars are tentative except at definite phrase endings.

The three versions will here be juxtaposed in such a manner as to show analogies and facilitate comparisons. The juxtaposition will carry through the illustrations and analyses. As the Coldspring Seneca version constitutes the starting point of the comparisons, its song order remains intact. The Onondaga and Cayuga versions are presented in rearranged order, so as to place side by side identical or similar songs of the three renderings. As the Tonawanda Seneca version does not feature in the interlonghouse analyses, but forms the basis of the intertribal comparisons, it occupies a separate column in the following tabulation, without connecting leaders.

Here and throughout the paper the following abbreviations represent the four longhouses:

$$S. = \text{Seneca of Coldspring.}$$
$$\text{Ton.} = \text{Seneca of Tonawanda.}$$
$$\text{Oa.} = \text{Onondaga.}$$
$$C. = \text{Cayuga.}$$

The leaders have the following significance:

_____ connects identical songs.
- - - - - - - - - - - - - - - connects related songs.

Coldspring Seneca	Onondaga	Cayuga	Tonawanda Seneca
	1	1	2
1	2		1
3			
4	3, 4		3
	5	2	
5	13	3	
6	14		9
7, 14			
		4	
8	8	6	
9, 11	11		5
10	6		4, 7
12	15	7	
13			
15			
16			8
	9		
	10		6
17	12	5, 8	
18	16	9	10

The interdependent materials and means of manipulation can to an extent be analyzed. The backbone of a song is its tonality, which can be reduced to a scale. This receives plastic form by means of rhythmic units in play against a percussive background. These are welded into patterns of shorter phrases and longer clauses or sections, and finally into an ever-recurrent formula with an ever-variegated melodic contour and individualized coloring.

SCALE SYSTEM

In extracting "weighted scales" each note is checked for its frequency and prominence and then all are lined up in descending order (descending because of the melodic trend) and are labeled from a whole note to a sixteenth in proportion to their significance.

Nucleus.—The predominant note or maintone, here labeled on the level of lower D, as a whole note, may predominate so as to produce a highly focused melody (marked ☺). In all but a few cases it terminates the tune. Sometimes the second or E of the scale ranks next. Sometimes, instead, the third is a runner-up—a neutral third or "blue note," fluctuating between F and F#. Once in a great while the second is the terminal note (Oa. 10), or perhaps the third (S. 7 and 14, Oa. 11). (Initial note ◡, terminal note ◠.)

Secundal and tertial scales (figs. 21 and 22).—Around these nuclei two types of scales take form. Secundal scales, based on the nucleus

FIGURE 21.—Secundal scales.

of a second, include the fourth or fifth as upper tone, next in importance, and an incidental seventh or fifth of the octave below (labeled VII and V). In S. 15 the lower fifth is not incidental, for it ter-

Figure 22.—Tertial scales.

minates part B, phrase (1). This nucleus serves 12 songs from all 3 cycles put together.

Eighteen songs, based on the nucleus of 3 and 1—the third and maintone—constitute what we call the tertial scales. The fifth is sufficiently prominent in all but S. 6, to suggest a "triad" concept, a bugle pattern. This is particularly evident in S. 8 which contains no subsidiary tones. However, in every case the melodic play is tertial, between 3 and 1, or between 5 and 3. This scale type also includes temporary closes of B (1) on a note other than the maintone. These will be listed below.

Though these two scales are constructed on a core of two tones, respectively adjacent and a third apart, yet they are not two- or three-tone scales. Except for S. 8 and C. 6, they all contain four or five tones, namely 5421 plus VII or 5431 plus 6 or VII, with V as duplication of 5. This must be emphasized, for their growth from a central nucleus is reflected in the larger structure and will form the core of that analysis.

Quartal scales (fig. 23).—Thirteen songs require special consideration of their tonal idiosyncrasies. Seven emphasize the interval of a fourth. This is obvious in S. 13 which contains only 541 VII V and thus two inevitable fourths, marked on the weighted scale.

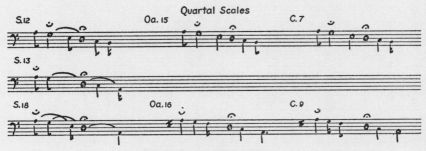

FIGURE 23.—Quartal scales.

T e main theme of S. 12, Oa. 15, C. 7 descends from 4 to 1, with surrounding embroidery of other combinations. These three versions of one song add up to the 5421 of the fundamental scale plus VII and VI. Similarly S. 18 with a 5421 V sequence exploits not only the quartal theme (the first phrase of B), which descends 431, but also in part A the descent of 542 and in B a direct 1 to V. The other two final songs, Oa. 16 and C. 9, explore this interval more timidly in their sequence of 54(3)1 V—a different scale from S. 18. This concept is latent in several other songs with a secundal nucleus, such as S. 10 and 15, Oa. 6, 7, with their frequent progression of a fourth.

Irregular scales (fig. 24).—Two versions of two beginning chants fluctuate in their tonality. Oa. and C. 1 with their introductory play on a third and their secundal coda, interpolate two quartal descents. As in S. 18, this descent is stepwise through an intermediate note. Technically this would be termed a "tetrachord." In the case of Oa. and C.1 an almost diatonic scale results from the combination. S. 1 and its twin Oa. 2 superimpose three stepwise quartal units on a tertial basis, with the intervals of our regular tertial scale.

Two composite songs are in a different tertial scale without a fourth, namely 5321 plus, but in one section they shift their tonal level and introduce quartal descents. S. 3 shifts from a clear-cut tertial section "A" to a cascading "B" in a full scale of 865321 VI, then back again to "A." Oa. 9 terminates both sections in a 65321 scale, but raises phrase (1) of both parts one tone, to a quartal 5421.

All of these scales except one, center around the maintone, and thus may be termed "plagal." Oa. and C. 1 descend to a basic maintone, in an "authentic" scale of modal terminology. As a rule they open

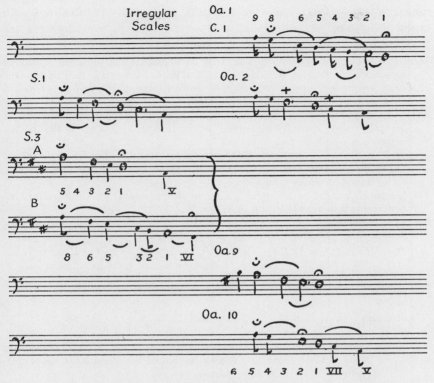

FIGURE 24.—Irregular scales.

on the fifth and end on the maintone. Only four open on the maintone and rise immediately to the fifth—S. 5 and 6, Oa. 13 and 14.
The range below the maintone may be integrated in the melodic
texture or it may form a temporary close, a semicadence in the middle
of part B. The list, already anticipated, is now forthcoming.

SEMICADENCES

On 2 of the scale:	On VII:	On V:
Secundal—	S. 17; Oa. 12; C. 5, 8.	S. 15.
Tertial—Oa. 9.	S. 9, 11,; Oa. 8, 11, 14.	Oa. 16, C. 4, 9.
Quartal—	S. 13.	S. 18.

The more common half-close on VII is of particular interest because
of implications to be expounded in the intertribal discussion.

INTERVALS

The tonal scheme and melodic play of intervals cannot be dissociated, especially in the discussion of quartal scales. They mutually
function as a cause and effect. A survey of the role played by the
various progressions will reiterate the typical nuclear radiation with

direct intervals and the less common stepwise combinations into larger intervals. All of the direct progressions have a moderate compass, and protracted progressions never exceed an octave.

Monotone.—Commonly prolonged in terminal phrases, often pulsated; recurrent in melodic texture in combination with all other intervals, in all positions.

Semitone.—Rare as clear-cut interval, only in S. 12, Oa. 15, C. 7, and in Oa. and C. 1 and C. 4, as transitional ornament.

Three-quarter tone.—Sometimes between adjacent notes and a neutral third or seventh, recognizable by signs of − or +; in reality an interval fluctuating between a semitone and a second.

Second.—In all songs except two with bugle scale, namely, S. 8 and C. 6; in secundal scales as nuclear theme; in Oa. and C. 1 and semicadences on VII as terminal figure, often as transition.

Third.—In all songs; in secundal songs as development; in tertial songs as nucleus; in quartal songs as substratum.

Fourth.—Less common than second and third, but in some form in all but two Seneca, four Onondaga, and two Cayuga songs.

Descends: S. 5, 8, 12, 15, 16, 17;	Oa. 1, 9, 12, 15, 16;	C. 1, 5, 8, 7, 9.
Ascends: S. 6, 9, 15;	Oa. 14;	C. 4.
Rebounds: S. 2, 3, 4, 6, 10, 13, 16;	Oa. 6, 7, 10, 12;	C. 3, 5, 8, 6.
Stepwise: S. 1, 3, 9, 11, 13, 15, 18;	Oa. 1, 2, 6, 7, 13, 14;	C. 1.

Descent in various patterns; ascent usually at phrase beginning; rebound in dive from 1 to V; stepwise in quartal descents (tetrachords), variously as 421 or 431. Commonly hinged on maintone.

Fifth.—Rare as direct interval, especially in Cayuga cycle.

Descends:	Oa. 10.	
Ascends: S. 5;	Oa. 10, 13, 14;	C. 3.
Stepwise: S. 7, 8, 18;	Oa. 1, 6, 8, 12, 15, 16;	C. 1, 6.

Ascent always at phrase beginning; stepwise variously with intervals 521, 541, 531, 5431; always hinged on maintone, except Oa. 10.

Sixth.—Rare as direct interval; never stepwise except in Oa. 6 and 15, S. 12, C. 7. Direct: S. 1; Oa. 2, 6; C. 4, rising, to begin new phrase after a descending melody.

Seventh.—Only once, very protracted, beginning of S. 3 B.

Octave.—Never in one leap; rarely stepwise, such as Oa. 1, C. 1 and 6 falling; S. 10, Oa. 6, 7 rising.

RANGE

The compass of a song naturally lies between the top and bottom note of its scale and is thus evident in the display. Though it contains the intervals, it is not dependent on their size.

Fifth.—S. 5, 7, 17;	Oa. 3, 4, 5, 13;	C. 2.
Sixth.—S. 9, 11, 13, 14;	Oa. 8, 9, 11, 12, 14.	
Seventh.—S. 12;	Oa. 15;	C. 7.
Octave.—S. 1, 2, 4, 6, 8, 10, 15, 18;	Oa. 2, 6, 7, 10, 12, 16;	C. 3, 4, 5, 6, 8, 9.
Ninth.—S. 16;	Oa. 1;	C. 1.
Tenth.—S. 3.		

Songs with a fifth range are mostly tertial, those with a sixth include two secundal scales, those of a seventh are quartal, those with an octave divide evenly, those of a ninth and tenth are irregular. The narrowest range goes hand in hand with repetitious themes. The sixth is commonly caused by a semicadence on VII, with an additional tone in the scale. The seventh is an erratic phenomenon in an odd song. The octave results from a rebounding fourth or from a semicadence on V, without an additional scale tone. Deskaheh's rebounds and semicadences are all of this type and account for the absence of a sixth range and a proportionately large number of octaves. In general, the superabundance of octaves is a conspicuous feature, as is the paucity of larger ranges in all but a few erratic melodies. Some of these observations tie in with the problem of personal qualities.

INSTRUMENTAL PITCH AND TONE

Joseph Logan's opening and closing songs suggest a sense of harmonic instrumental background, for the drum coincides with the maintone, on the G of the same level in recording—D in transcription. Similarly, on the reverse side of the Johnny John recording, their drum is pitched on the minor third, B flat or, in transcription, F. However, on the reverse side of his disk Logan lowers his voice a whole tone; and Richard sings the beginning songs a whole tone lower than Chauncey's continuation. Thus, though the tonic or third furnish a pleasant background to our harmony-accustomed ears, to the Indians the second or fourth are evidently just as satisfactory. In fact it is satisfactory, for the tone of the drum is within the range of the voice and forms an elegant blend. It is not a booming bass drum which brings the blood to a boil and obliterates the melody.

The rattle, while equally unobtrusive, balances the drum with a clear swish in the Seneca and Cayuga recordings. Logan had no assistant. Though its pitch is rather indeterminate, it appears to remain within the vocal range, higher than the drum. Without any effect of chords, the contrasting timbre of the two instruments threads its monotone through the fluctuating melodic texture.

RHYTHMIC FIGURES

PERCUSSION

The drum and rattle also form a basso ostinato of rhythmic pattern matching the structural formula. They always vibrate during the introductory chants, twice as fast in Logan's hands as in Johnny John's. During the dance songs, as we have seen, they alternate tremolo and accelerating duple beat in the alternate A and B sections. But in each cycle they follow a different device, a Seneca play on quarter and eighth notes, an Onondaga stretto of twice-doubled speed, a Cayuga acceleration from alternately accented quarters to eighths. They always conclude with three sharp beats usually coinciding with the last notes, but delayed in C. 2, 5, 8. The Seneca rattle alone does not coincide with the drum, but at times creates its own pattern. All rattles actually sound a faint grace note to each beat, because of the rebound of the "B-B" shot, as written out in S. 5. Both instruments conclude the Seneca cycle with a tapering tremolo, sedate and final.

MELODY

Within their tonal scheme the melodies pulsate in various time divisions, keeping exactly abreast of the percussive background. The smallest time divisions, or rhythmic units, recur within larger combinations or phrases. The most common units, more or less in order of frequency are represented on figure 25. They appear most conspicuously in the following songs:

RHYTHMIC UNITS

(1) S. 2, 9, 13, 16, 18;	Oa. 3, 4, 5, 8, 9, 10, 12;	C. 2, 4, 5, 8.
All conclusions except two.		
(2) S. 5, 6, 9, 10;	Oa. 2, 3, 4, 6, 11, 12, 16.	
(3) S. 1, 3, 4, 9, 10, 13, 17;	Oa. 2, 5, 6, 11, 14, 15, 16;	C. 4, 8, 9.
(4) S. 4, 6, 9, 11;	Oa. 3, 11.	
(5) S. 5, 6, 13, 17;	Oa. 10, 13, 14;	C. 2, 6, 7.
Ends: 7, 14.		
(6) S. 2, 8, 13, 7, 14, 15;	Oa. 1, 10, 16;	C. 1, 5, 8.
Ends: 8.		
(7) S. 3, 6, 9, 13;	Oa. 1, 3, 4, 11, 12;	C. 1, 6.
(8) S. 1, 8, 12, 16, 18;	Oa. 9, 15;	C. 7, 9.
(9) S. 7, 14, 12, 13, 18;	Oa. 15, 16;	C. 1, 7, 9.
(10) S. 2, 3, 4;	Oa. 10.	
(11) S. 10, 18;	Oa. 6, 16;	C. 9.
(12)	Oa. 12;	C. 5, 8, 9.
(13) S. 3;		C. 4, 6.
(14) S. 10, 13;	Oa. 6, 11;	C. 4.

These rhythms are further spiced by vocal attacks and ornaments, grace notes, mordents, and pulsations, particularly in the first chants and in Oa. 9. They are more ornamental and more freely timed not only in these chants but in general in the chantlike parts A with vibrating drum.

The simpler units are more common in conservative songs, with regulated thematic treatment, and the more elaborate and more rapid units characterize rhapsodic songs with free thematic treat-

Rhythmic Units

FIGURE 25.—Rhythmic units.

ment, thus the first chants, and also songs in irregular scales. The former are based on the pulsation, its inversion, prolongation, and delay (units 1–5). The latter are really variants of three-note groupings, even and gracious, or uneven and abrupt (units 9–12). In general, the selection of units seems more closely related to structural than to scale type.

Phrases and clauses.—These units combine by repetition (Oa. 12) or fusion (Oa. 13) into phrases, and two or three of these phrases combine by repetition, development, or contrast, into clauses—the sections A and B. The shortest phrase is S. 18, B, measure 1, of one rhythmic unit of three beats. The longest phrase contains the 15 beats or the entire clause of S. 12. The average phrase contains about 8 beats, as Oa. 14 B. Short and average phrases appear in all kinds of songs, but the longest ones predominate in quartal, irregular, rhapsodic songs, as Oa. 1 and 12.

STRUCTURE

The handling of these units and phrases and their formation into the larger binary frame show consistency and ingenuity, but neither hard-set rules nor improvisation. The greatest expertness is manifest in the development from a central single core, though some interesting contrasts result from the juggling of two themes. In most of the songs, most clearly in those with one theme, the thematic core is identified with the tonal nucleus and dances back and forth on the two central notes of the scale. By this method of analysis, it will as a rule be found in the middle, not at the beginning, and its development can be located before and after the nucleus, as a prelude and coda. Several examples from three scales will be broken up to show their nuclear and concise composition.

Secundal Theme—S. 5, Oa. 13, C. 3 (fig. 8):

Nucleus: Phrase (2), in seconds.
Development: B, phrase (1), in thirds.
A, phrase (1), in fifths.
Coda: Oa. 13, C. 3, phrases (3), monotone after first note; S. 5 no coda, only
terminal three-beat formula.
Labels: S.   Oa. and C.

	A	B	A	B
Consecutive:	a b	c b	a b c	a′ b c
Nuclear:	a″ a	a′ a	a″ a a‴ ′	a′ a a‴ ′
	(1) (2)	(1) (2)	(1) (2) (3)	(1) (2) (3)

Secundal Theme—S. 17, Oa. 12, C. 5 (fig. 19):

Nucleus: A (1).
Development: S. B (2); Oa.-C. A (2).
Coda: S. A (2), B (3) (extension of nucleus).
Secondary Theme: Oa.-C. A (3), B (2).
Prelude: Oa.-C. A (1).

	S.		Oa.-C.	
	A	B	A	B
Consecutive:	a b	c a b	a b c	d c
Nuclear:	a″ a<	a a′ a<	y a′ b	a b
	(1) (2)	(1) (2) (3)	(1) (2) (3)	(1) (2)

Tertial Theme—S. 9, 11, Oa. 11 (fig. 15):

Nucleus: B (1).
Development: S. A (2), B (2);   Oa.-C. A (2), B (2).
Prelude: A (1).

	S.		Oa.	
	A	B	A	B
Consecutive:	a b	b c	a b	b′ c
Nuclear:	y a′>	a a″	y a′	a a″
	(1) (2)	(1) (2)	(1) (2)	(1) (2)

Quartal Theme—S. 18, Oa. 16, C. 9 (fig. 20):

Nucleus: A (1), ii; Oa.-C. also A (2) ii.
Secondary Themes: S. A (1) i and A (2); Oa.-C. A (1) and (2) i, and (4); other
theme Oa.-C. A (3), B.
Development: By thematic alternation, also Oa.-C. A (3).
Coda: Prolongation of theme b at end of all sections.

	S.			
	A	B	A′	coda
Consecutive:	a b a_5<	c a_8<	a_5 b a_5<	c<
Nuclear:	b a′ b_5<	a b_8<	b_5 a′ b_5<	a<
	(1) (2)	(1) (2)	(1) (2)	

	Oa.-C.		
	A	B	
Consecutive:	a b a_5 b	c< a_8<	c<
Nuclear:	b a b_5 a	c< b_8<	c<
	(1) (2)	(3) (4)	

Labels for both the consecutive and nuclear methods:

a, Theme; a', variation; a, nucleus.

a_5 and a_8, Theme transposed down a fifth or an octave.

a< and a>, Prolongation and condensation.

b, Secondary theme.

y, Introduction, in the nature of a call, related to theme.

A (1) i, Section, phrase, subdivision of phrase.

Labels are in themselves irrelevant and are juxtaposed in two ways so as to emphasize the idea of conceiving a composition from the inside outward to the periphery. This is a striking characteristic of most of the Eagle Dance songs, but not of all songs of the Iroquois or other tribes. The first and last songs of the Eagle Dance superimpose consecutive on nuclear structure. That is, in S. 1 and Oa. 2, and in Oa. 16 and C. 9, the main theme is stated in the second phrase, but development and transposition to a lower level follows this statement.

A few comments should point interesting features of the three typical examples:

In those with secundal themes, the theme receives more expansion in part A. In all cases with a "y", this rhapsodic prelude comes at the beginning. S. 5 has no coda.

S. 17 is a different song from Oa.12 and C. 5, but develops from the same nucleus, S. 17 by similar devices as the other secundal songs, except for the position of the nucleus; Oa. 12 and C. 5 by adding a complementary theme to each section.

In the songs with tertial themes, expansion of intervals is similar in A and B, but "y" starts off on the highest note. S. 9, 11 contracts the theme in B (2)—or perhaps conversely the other recurrences can be said to add a rhythmic unit.

Other songs may use these same devices or other means, some of them so subtle as to be subject to several interpretations.

THEMATIC MANIPULATION

The foregoing songs show several devices for developing a theme. These and other devices will be listed with a few examples. They have many other recurrences.

(1) Repetition with slightly varying contour: Oa. 14B.

(2) Expansion of intervals: S. 5, 9, 17; Oa. 10, 13, C. 3.

(3) Dwindling of intervals: S. 5; Oa. 13; C. 3, 6.

(4) Prolongation, usually on monotone: S. 17B; Oa. 5A; C. 4A.

(5) Contraction: S. 9A.

(6) Transposition to lower level: S. 1, 8; Oa. 2; end songs.

(7) Shifting temporal position: S. 7, 14; Oa. 3B, 4B.

(8) Inversion: S. 16 (contour); S. 9; Oa. 11 (rhythm).

(9) Semicadence: see page 253.

STRUCTURAL PATTERNS

The binary formula is only the outer shell. The manipulation of the rhythmic units in various combinations and intervals forms a different mosaic for each song. The patterns can be grouped as follows:

(1) *Parallel Composition.*—In parallel composition the same pattern is repeated in different sections.

> Part A resembles part B:
> S. 2, 4, 5, 6, 8, 9, 17;   Oa. 2, 9, 12, 13;   C. 3, 4, 5, 8.
> Phrase (1) resembles (2) and (3) (if any):
> S. 6B;   Oa. 6A, 8A, 10B, 14B;   C. 2A, 3A, B, 6A.

(2) *Complementary Composition.*—In complementary composition one part mirrors another.

> Contour reversed:
> A and B—S. 10;   Oa. 6, 7, 10;   C. 4.
>   (1), (2)—S. 9, 11B, 10B, 15B, 16B;   Oa. 6B, 11B, 12B, 15B; C.
>   4B, 5, 8B.
> Rhythm reversed:
> S. 4, 9, 11A.

(3) *Asymmetrical Composition.*—Asymmetrical composition has an irregular or rhapsodic pattern.

> One theme:
> S. 7, 14, 9, 11;   Oa. 1, 3, 4, 5, 11;   C. 1.
> Two themes:
> S. 3, 12, 18B;   Oa. 10, 16A;   C. 9.

Some songs belong to two groups, as S. 9 (all three groups) and Oa. 15 (groups 2 and 3). Means of developing asymmetrical compositions are named under Thematic Manipulation. They may appear in any of the song groups. All of the groups include monothematic and bithematic songs. All but 20 have one theme. Those with two or more themes are: S. 3, 10, 12, 13, 18;   Oa. 5, 6, 7, 9, 10, 12, 14, 16;   C. 2, 4, 5, 7, 8, 9. Thus most of the Cayuga songs, but few Seneca songs, have two or more themes.

Tonality also cross-cuts compositional type; but the three scales tend to correspond to the three groupings, namely, secundal scales to parallel, tertial scales to complementary, and quartal and irregular scales to asymmetrical patterns. There are tertial asymmetrical songs (at the same time complementary) and irregular songs (Oa. 9) with parallel form; but on the whole conservative scales and patterns go hand in hand.

CONTOURS

(Figs. 26, 27, 28)

A melodic line, variable and expressive, emerges from the structural process. Its contours, transferred to graph paper, yield geometric patterns. On the graphs a horizontal space represents a sixteenth note and a vertical space a semitone. A notch on the left margin indicates the position of the maintone. The three groups compare samples of parallel structure, asymmetrical designs, and stepwise beginning and

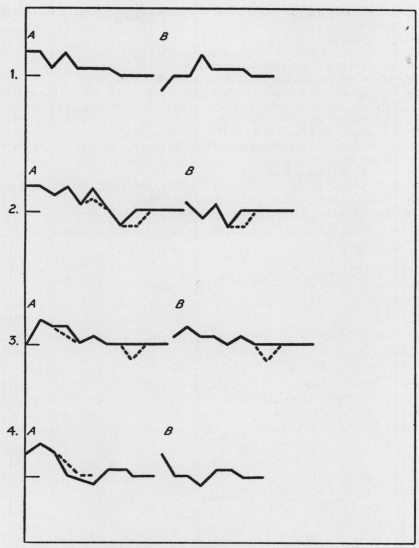

FIGURE 26.—Symmetrical contours, parallel and complementary. 1. Oa. 6, S. 10.
2. Oa. 12, C 5.   3. Oa. 13, S. 5, C 3.   4. Oa. 15, S. 12, C 7.

ending songs. They show a number of structural elements, for
instance:

Parallel endings in the *first group*, with variable developments:
   In fig. 24, *1*, opposite, mirrored beginnings of A and B.
   In *2* and *3* higher level and expansion of opening.
   In *4* parallel pattern of Oa. 15 as a result of added phrase in A, with modified
      mirroring.
   In all, centering on maintone, drawn out in end.

Asymmetrical designs of the *second group*, except for similar endings of A and B in
fig. 27, *7*:
Jagged "hopping" design in *5*.
Complementary pattern in Seneca version of fig. 27, *6*B.
Irregular placement of theme (shown by line) in fig. 27, *7*.
Melodic preponderance above maintone, especially in fig. 27, *7*.
In both groups different song beginnings are evident—opening on the fifth in
1, 2, 4, 6, 7, opening on the maintone in *3* and *5*, with immediate rise to fifth.
Stepwise descents in the *third group*, in contrast with wavering progression of other
two groups.   This betrays the device of transposition.
Steep and bold outlines, ending nonetheless on drawn-out maintone, especially
in figure 28, *11*.
In *9*, octave descent to maintone.
In *8, 10*, and *11*, temporary ending on fifth below, with consequent recapitula-
tion of theme on higher level, notably *8* and *10*.
In *10* and *11* heavy weighting below maintone.

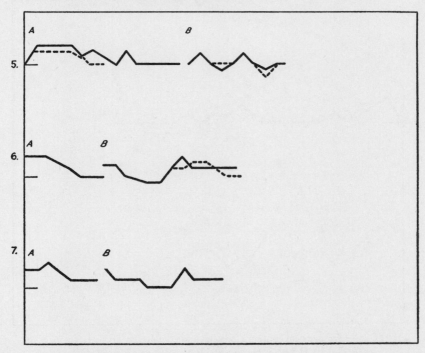

FIGURE 27.—Asymmetrical contours.   5. Oa. 14, S. 6.   6. Oa. 11, S. 9, 11.   7. S. 7, 14.
————————— Onondaga.   ------------ Seneca and Cayuga.   (Onondaga used as norm
because of Seneca and Cayuga similarities.)   Contours represent melodic simplification
for the salient pattern, not detailed graphs by "cents"; for no tonometric apparatus has
been available.   For "cents" see Apel, 1950, p. 126 and pp. 362–3; Thuren, 1923, pp. 17
ff. and pp. 62 ff.

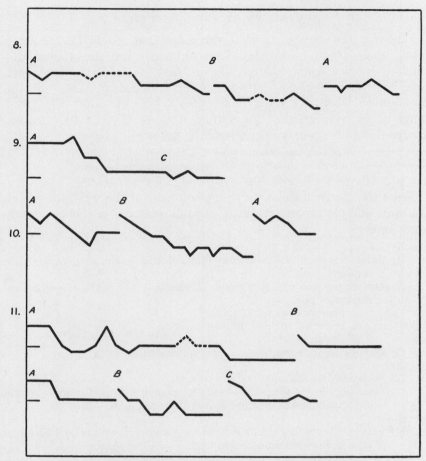

FIGURE 28.—Sequential contours—opening and closing songs.
8. Oa. 2, S. 1.   9. Oa. 1, C. 1 with Coda (C).   10. S. 3.   11. Oa. 16, C. 9; S. 18 with Coda (C).

Scales and rhythmic units.—These cannot be shown on such a simplified graph, except by inference. So we refer to our previous comparisons. In the first group all songs but the last are in secundal scales, the last one (fig. 26, *4*) being quartal. In the second group all examples are in tertial scales. In the third group all examples are in quartal or irregular scales. Similarly, simpler rhythmic units predominate in the first two groups, with triplets in examples 4 and 7. Syncopated and rapid units are confined to the third group.

These observations reinforce our comments on the conformity of conservative or adventurous devices within a song, and also on the contrast between the body of the songs and the chants and conclusion.

Another kind of distinction is also evident, namely, *individual variations* as between versions: lower dips by the Seneca and Cayuga singers, expansion by Logan in figure 26, *4*, by Deskaheh in figure 28, *11*. This subject will form the concluding section of our analysis.

Whoever the singer, in whatever longhouse, Eagle Dance songs retain their peculiar formula. Less obviously but nonetheless distinctly, Johnny John, Shanks, Logan, and Deskaheh imprint each song with their special artistic touch and personality, consistent and pronounced when the versions are placed side by side. The same songs which were graphed for contour outlines (figs. 26–28) also are analysed for idiosyncrasies and bear the following labels:

Variable treatment, by level or rhythm.

A second variable phrase, recurring in other versions.

[   ] An insertion or expansion in one of the versions.

From the study of these varying treatments of the weighted scales, contours and metronome readings, the following distinctive characteristics emerge:

Melody:

(1) Seneca: More focused melodies, range of fifth, lower weighting, gliding contours.

(2) Onondaga: Range of fifth preferred, "hoppy" contours; tendency toward sharpened pitch by:

  a. Sharpened or raised third.

  b. Hastened rise and delayed descents.

  c. Higher weighting.

(3) Cayuga frequent range of an octave, low weighting.

Rhythm:

(1) Seneca: More syncopations and triplets.

(2) Onondaga faster tempo, especially in opening chant. Generally similar melodic units, but different drum patterns in each.

Structure:

(1) Seneca: In opening chants modified ternary form, with recapitulation of part A; in dance songs much juggling with one theme.

(2) Onondaga: In dance songs frequent combination of two themes, tendency toward thematic expansion and embellishment.

(3) Cayuga: In chant free rhythmic play, in dance songs strict adherence to tempo, to symmetrical and parallel forms.

Rendering:

(1) Seneca: Gliding initial attack, free timing, quavering, husky vocal quality, frequent prolongation and anticipation.

(2) Onondaga: Grace note in initial attack, precision, staccato stops and pauses, resonant quality.

(3) Cayuga: Upbeat in initial attack, deliberate, smooth and dignified timing and vocal quality.

Texts:

All: Liquid burden syllables, as "yohawiyonahe," prolonged vowels.

Seneca and Cayuga: Initial attack with soft "(wi)yo" (good?).

Onondaga: Initial attack with more vigorous "goya."

Seneca and Onondaga: In S. 7, 14, 10, Oa. 6, all end songs sibilants. S. 12, Oa. 15, C. 7 different syllables viz;

  S. 12, "honǫdiyo ya'ahe'e."

  Oa. 15, "hanigǫdǫ yohe-i."

  C. 7, "hanigǫdǫ yohawi."

Figures 9 and 28, *8*: Logan fast tempo of melody and drum;[10] Johnny John expansion (exception) and terminal speeding and beat.

Figures 10, 19, and 20, *2, 3*: Johnny John and Deskaheh lower contour line, notably by latter's dips to fifth below. For resultant lower scale weighting, see figure 19, as indicated by greater note values below the main tone of Seneca and Cayuga versions. Shorter Seneca terminal phrase, marked by vertical line.

Figures 16 and 26, *4*: Logan prolonged part A, with balancing dip and surge below and above main tone and parallel endings.

Figures 20 and 28, *11*: Seneca form different, weighted lower. Cayuga extension of part A (exception).

All musical examples show difference in attack on first note, also occasional rhythmic variations as marked.

CHAUNCEY AND RICHARD JOHNNY JOHN

Despite the amazing similarity of the two voices, the different timbre betrays different authorship of the two sides of the recording. Chauncey's voice is huskier and more evanescent in symptom of old age. His greater freedom shows in the two renderings of one song— S. 7 by Richard, S. 14 by Chauncey (figs. 13 and 27), *7*. The melodic differences are subtle, namely, Chauncey's early excursion to a higher note (written as middle B), and more frequent use of short syncopations and triplets. More evident are differences in drumbeat and texts. In the course of the whole record it is curious that Chauncey starts a note higher and slightly speeds up, so as to conclude at about the same tempo as Logan.

TWO SENECA VERSIONS, COLDSPRING AND TONAWANDA

The recording by Robert Shanks of Tonawanda Longhouse became available too late for inclusion in the previous comparative tabulations, but in time for supplementary remarks. The 10 songs are reproduced in juxtaposition with songs from other tribes and will be found in figures 31, 33, 35. Every one resembles a Coldspring relative, except for Ton. 6, which is related to Oa. 10; and Ton. 2, related to Oa. and C. 1.

Ton. 1: like S. 1 with the addition of the rapid ornamental sixteenth notes.
Ton. 2: Similar to Oa. 1 and C. 1, with extended development and greater quartal emphasis: opening phrase descends fourth instead of third; all three recurrences of A descend by fourths, each more rapidly, A' with extension, A'' with condensation. A' and A'' sink to the lower octave (maintone) by play on second and maintone.

---

[10] This may be a longhouse characteristic, for Peter Buck also sang at a good clip.

Ton. 4, 7: Like S. 10 and Oa. 6, 7, especially like the latter, with additional ornamental steplike descent in A, measure 2. Note the rising sequence which, by subsequent descent, creates a bow-shaped contour. S. 10 has no rising sequence in B, S. 6 has sequence of two units, Ton. 4 of three units.

Ton. 5: Like S. 9, except for grace note in A.

Ton. 9: Like S. 6 more than Oa. 14, except triplet in A and semicadence in B. Other songs, though related, show different treatment, thus Ton. 3 and S. 4, Ton. 8 and S. 16, Ton. 6 and Oa. 10. Here Oa. 10 has superimposed two scales by ending A and B on the second; also it has twice attenuated the syncopated unit.

Ton. 10: This final song is most like Oa. 16 in form and treatment of A, but with shortened A and lengthened B, and many melodic variations.

In general, Shanks ornaments and extends even more than Logan, but the fantasy is concentrated in the melody; his rattle usually persists in the same duple beat as Deskaheh's drum. He greatly prefers tertial songs, all but Ton. 4, which tends toward quartal, and the quartal beginning and final songs.

FOUR-WAY RELATIONSHIP

As might be expected, the resemblance between the two Grand River versions is closer than between these and the Seneca songs, and the difference between father and grandson is subtle indeed. Shanks is most individualistic, and stands as middleman between the other repertoires. Deskaheh stands midway in the drum pattern and in structural manipulation, but shares only those Seneca songs which also recur in the Onondaga repertoire. The fundamental conformity can be explained by the avowed Seneca origin by way of Tom Smoke. The divergencies, while associated with the three longhouses, certainly originate in creative personality, in preferences for symmetrical or irregular forms, for vigorous rhythms, embellishments, insertions, or else an even, balanced flow of melody. How these qualities reflect the personality of these Iroquois artists, their mien and gait, stands out as symptom of the Iroquoian freedom within tradition.

MUSICAL RELATIONSHIP WITH OTHER IROQUOIS CYCLES

Is the Eagle Dance isolated musically as well as choreographically? *Scale and Melodic Trend.*—All types of the Eagle Dance scales recur in the great body of songs, though in greatly varying proportions. Rare secundal scales appear in older ceremonial cycles, especially the Medicine Society ritual, also parts of the Drum Dance, and others. Tertial scales occur in these and also in the Feather Dance, Corn Dance, and others. Quartal scales are subordinate in the Bear Dance and predominant in war and modern songs, Striking-a-stick, wasase, modern Women's Dance, and social dances—boldly stated in the last. These last also descend steeply to the maintone, often with a large range to 13 notes, whereas many ceremonial songs hover around the maintone within a fifth to an octave, just like the Eagle Dance. The octave by a dip to the lower fifth is a frequent phenomenon. Semicadence is rare.

Rhythms.—Rhythmic units show a similar distribution. The simpler Eagle Dance units 1 to 5 also predominate in the ceremonial songs, notably those addressed to animals (Bear, Buffalo), and also in the Robin social dance. Syncopations and triplets ornament War Dance types, Fish Dance, and modern compositions. On the other hand, the connection between structure, percussion, and dance pattern is unusual. Cross-over dances similarly alternate beat and tremolo, as Striking-a-stick, or as Fish Dance with a halftime beat instead of a tremolo. But in all dances other than the Eagle Dance the cross-over synchronizes with the chantlike A. In none of them does the percussion beat follow an elaborate pattern such as we have here analyzed.

Structure.—The AABAB form goes hand-in-hand with this percussion oddity and thus with cross-over dances. In the newer ceremonies it appears alongside ternary forms, as in S. 1 and 3; in stomp dances it is commonly replaced by ternary. Both nuclear and consecutive construction recur, the former in the Medicine Dance, the latter in the War Dance, and similar devices juggle the themes, in all kinds of phrases, which are much shorter in Bear than in Women's Shuffle Dance.

Thus musically Eagle Dance fits into the picture, despite individualities of structure and percussion.

THE DANCE AND THE SONGS

Form.—The ceremonial outline and choreographies have already shown the connection between action and song, invocation to chants, and dance progression to rhythmic accompaniment. They have shown the contrasting motion pattern conforming to the song parts which are differentiated by rendering and percussion, though not by melodic character. Legato movement follows legato singing, and hopping follows sharp sound patterns, in every single song. The reciprocal conformity has produced divergent concluding forms: two more sections to complete the Seneca dance and an especially prolonged Cayuga part A to allow for the consecutive deposit of the wands by the four dancers, one on each phrase.

Expression and dynamics.—The contrast of legato and staccato enhances the expressive content of these passages, hovering or hopping. This correlation does not, however, extend to melodic interpretation in movement. The songs may hover in suspense, swoop downward, soar upward, waver up and down, or glide on a level. The dancers pay no attention to these melodic flights. Even the correspondence of the jagged up-and-down jump is very general.

In both dance and song the individual's creative ability contributes to the expressiveness; his personality colors the performance. But in the dance the performer cannot transcend the frame as easily as the singer who is his guide; he cannot interpolate phrases or vary the beat. Within the two contrasting longhouse ground plans, the dancer is more subject to tradition than the singer.

THE WINGED CALUMET

DANCE SURVIVALS

The Iroquois Eagle Dance, a variant of the Calumet ritual, appears doubly significant when we can count on our fingers the tribes that have retained some form of the formerly widely distributed Calumet Dance. Three contemporary types in three key locations have come within my experience, either through observation or through direct description by informants. The three locations are the Midwest, Southeast, and Southwest. The three types are:

The *Calumet Dance* with feathered stem, witnessed among the Fox of Tama, Iowa.

The *Eagle Dance* with feathered stem, described by Cherokee singers of Qualla Reservation, N. C.

The mimetic *Eagle Dance* without wand, witnessed and described in various locations; at home in the Tewa Pueblos, N. Mex.

FOX CALUMET DANCE
(See fig. 33 for music)

The Fox Indians (Meskwaki, Outagami, Rénards) share the Pipe Dance with the Sauk and Winnebago. It is a competition between successive pairs of men or youths who display their best steps of the War Dance type. To a tremolo of the great booming drum, they start with an ambling, clockwise circuit, yelling and vibrating a small tufted rattle in the extended right hand. In the left they hold before them a long-stemmed feathered calumet. They circuit between songs and for their exit. Each song has the same binary form as the Iroquois, a similar alternation of tremolo and beat, and a similar centered tonality. My field notes on several renderings follow.

Two contestants whoop and shake their rattles during an ambling circuit, then place themselves vis-a-vis in the center of the floor.

(1). A. Kneel on one knee, shaking rattle in front.
B. Hop with back pull, turning from side to side.
(2). A. In wide straddle, bend forward and sway with head close to ground.
B. Hopping on left foot, touch right toe, heel, toe, heel. Reverse. (Similar to the jig step.)

(3). A. Forward sway, or change places with partner.
   B. Jump-hop, raising knees alternately.   (Similar to Wasase.)
(4). A. Walk in small clockwise circuit.
   B. War dance step—ball-heel right, raise left knee; reverse, turning from
      side to side.   Pipe held high overhead.

For each combination A and B are repeated.   Each dancer and each song produce a different step, sometimes each half of a song. This variability and the nature of the movements distinguish the Fox Pipe Dance from the Iroquois Eagle Dance, despite the analogy of paraphernalia and of alternate legato and staccato.   Also, the songs receive different rendering in the Midwest, by four or more men seated around a frame-supported drum to one side of the dance ground. The function has lost ritual connotations and has integrated the boast-contest idea into the dance itself.   This is not because of any ritual breakdown among the Fox.   They have retained a good many rites, especially the feasts of gentes.   For instance, the Eagle gens has a ceremony with two calumets but without eagle mime and evidently not connected with the Iroquois type.   (Jones, 1939, pp. 97–98.)

CHEROKEE EAGLE DANCE

The Christianized Eastern Cherokee still attach magic power to the Eagle Dance, in celebration of victory.   Carl Standing Deer and Dave Lawsey of Qualla Reservation were not able to perform it for me, but they described it as a performance by as many as eight men who advance in a line, sway in place, and cross over in two groups They use a deep crouch with one leg extended out in front (fig. 6, 7), thus different from the northern Iroquoian.   According to Fenton (field notes) and Speck (1951, p. 40, pl. 15), each dancer carries a small rattle in the left hand and in the right hand a wand with eagle or hawk feathers attached at right angles, thus also different from the Iroquois.

The Eagle Dance (tsugi'dali) is probably the most important and revered of the Cherokee dances.   The eagles were said to have gathered together and teased each other just as men do now in the Eagle Dance.   The Eagle Dance used to be held in the fall or winter when the eagles were killed but it is now held at any time.   In additon to its celebration of the killing of an eagle, the Eagle Dance has several subordinate elements such as the Scalp Dance which celebrates victory in war, and the Peace Pipe Dance which celebrates the conclusion of peace. The chief function of the Eagle Dance at the present time is the celebration of victory in the Ball game [seven days after the game].   [Gilbert, 1943, p. 263.]

Gilbert includes no dance description; Bernard Mason offers a fanciful version (1944, pp. 175–179).   Thus the only reliable details are recorded by Speck (1951, pp. 39–42).   They are condensed as follows:

An even number of male and female dancers in opposite lines, running east and west, face each other in pairs. . . . Steps range from a dignified walk to the usual shuffling trot, and postures from stooping to crouching with one knee lowered.

First period.—Counterclockwise circling of the fire with stomp step.
Second period.—In early night, concentric circling in opposite directions by male and female groups, with low crouch.
Third period.—Peace Pipe Dance.
    a. Toward morning, two opposing lines of men and women, marking time, then crossing over and returning to place. (cf. Striking-a-stick-Dance). Fan swaying over partner's head.
    b. Lines, separating, in opposite circling, women right, men left. (cf. Pueblo Eagle, Cherokee Quail).
    c. Part (a) back to back.
    d. Same as First period.

Except during the crossover, the wands and rattles were shaken up and down in unison or held above the head. The leading woman used to wear turtle leg rattles, as in the Friendship Dance. In 1929 the women carried empty baskets for feeding the eagle and further placating him.

In an ensuing Victory or Scalp Dance successive soloists led a circling line of men and exhibited mimetic combat steps and boasting enactment of feats (Speck, 1951, p. 64; Fenton, field notes).

Fenton's 1947 field notes, from Will West Long, corroborate Speck's statements in essentials; his quoted song texts resemble those here transcribed in figure 36. All materials add up to fundamental distinctions from the Eagle Dance, not only in ground plans, inclusion of women and stomp step, but even in the type of crouch and the form and handling of the wand.

All three sources add up to inter-Iroquoian formal consanguinity but not identity, and to accentuated contrasts between Southeast and Midwest both choreographically and numerically (Fox two men, Iroquois four, Cherokee eight). On the other hand, the challenge motif, which has been metamorphosed among the Iroquois, unites the Fox Pipe and Cherokee Scalp Dance section.

PUEBLO EAGLE DANCE

The famous Tewa eagle dancers intensify the birdlike illusion of dips and sways and ignore calumet and boast. Two men, symbolizing male and female principals, carry a winglike strip of feathers on their outstretched arms and a half-mask of cap and beak. (See Roediger, 1941, p. 195; Evans, 1931, p. 50.) From the kiva they follow a line of sprinkled corn to the dancing place (Spinden, 1915, p. 111; see also photo).

(1) They circuit the dancing place against the sun to a drum tremolo and almost monotone chant by a chorus of singers in Sioux bonnets.
(2) They step gingerly on half toe, circling in opposite directions or

following one another in a circle, to a syncopated song with even quarter note drumbeats. (3) They sway and twist from side to side, stepping or squatting low to a descending tune with triple drumbeat. (4) They hop from side to side on one foot, toeing with the other, and rotate their wings, to an even beat. (5) They exit as they entered.

This choreographic and musical essence perseveres through local variations, in San Ildefonso (Evans, 1931, pp. 50–60), Tesuque (Buttree-Seton, 1930, pp. 60–63), and even as borrowing in other tribes (ibid., p. 62).

Writers have commonly connected the Pueblo Eagle Dance with the Thunderbird and rain (Evans, 1931, p. 49; Hewett, 1930, p. 128). But Parsons (1939, vol. 1, p. 133) reports it as a communal *curing* ceremony by an Eagle society. "Two doctors dance like eagles and dipping their plumes in ashes, go about the chamber whipping disease away" (Parsons, 1939, vol. 1, p. 539). In San Juan "on the third night of the retreat of the Eagle society, medicine is given to all who come near the altar" (ibid., vol. 2, p. 827). In Tiguan Jemez as an autumn dance it is performed in the open (Parsons, 1925, p. 116). Generally, in Keresan Acoma, Cochiti, and Tewa pueblos, it is performed in the plaza, at Christmas or on King's Day, January 6, along with Buffalo, Deer, Comanche, and Matachina Dances (Parsons, 1939, vol. 1, pp. 494, 533, 542). Never does it include a calumet ceremony, which in fact leads a feeble existence among the Pueblos (Parsons, 1925, p. 122), notwithstanding the San Juan Pipe Dance (Buttree-Seton, 1930, pp. 44–45).

This Pipe Dance is introduced, and the same may be true of the Eagle Dance. It appears along with adopted dances, and has been popularized to performances in a Santa Fe hotel. Parsons (1939, vol. 2, p. 1018) snatches at a possibility of Aztec connections; but she does not follow up in her listing of Pawnee connections (ibid., vol. 2, pp. 1024–25) nor verify her impressions of recent introduction (ibid., vol. 2, p. 1018, ftn.).

THE CALUMET ON THE WATERWAYS TRAIL

These three survivals encompass a large territory, but the calumet ritual spread even further. As the focal object in war, peace negotiations, and barter, it extended its domains from Florida to Canada and to the Rocky Mountains. (See West's list of tribes, 1934, p. 263.) The relatively sedentary Plains Pawnee thought nothing of crossing 600 miles of desert (Tixier, 1844, p. 223). Fr. Hennepin sang Te Deum in the presence of "a great many Iroquese who came from a warlike expedition against Savages of Titonha [Teton]" (Hennepin, 1698, vol. 1, p. 107). The range of Iroquois travel was enormous, but susceptible to exaggeration. (Cf. West, 1934, vol. 1, p. 119; Hodge, 1912; and Fenton, 1940.)

If desert travel held no terrors, the waterways offered a real convenience. Thus Hennepin encountered the calumet in his voyages on the Great Lakes and along the upper Mississippi. The pipe of peace, which he received from the Potawatomi (Hennepin, 1698, vol. 1, p. 124), was a pass and safe conduct even to the Koroa (Hennepin, 1683, pp. 207–209). By the vast tentacles of the great River the calumet connected the Iroquois on the headwaters of the Ohio with the Chitimacha on the Mississippi Delta (Le Page Du Pratz, 1758, vol. 1, p. 108) and the tribes near the remote source of the Missouri; and the dance accompanied the calumet. A few descriptions have accumulated through the miles and the centuries.

BETWEEN THE MISSISSIPPI AND THE GREAT LAKES
(CHIPPEWA, MENOMINEE, WINNEBAGO, ILLINOIS)

The more northerly Iroquois and missionary route was traversed by the Sauk and Fox, as they retreated in 1650 from Saginaw Bay before the Iroquois and in 1733 from Green Bay to the Wapsipinicon River in Iowa, before White encroachment (Kellogg, 1925, pp. 70, 99, 330–333.) As we may expect, their Pipe Dance typifies the area, though modified by time and location.

Fairly recently Miss Densmore witnessed a Chippewa contest dance retained to this day. It is their "good time dance," yet of great antiquity and derived from the manitou.

In this dance a man carried a pipestem and his body was supposed to represent the pipe. The dancer never rose erect, but took a crouching or squatting posture . . . Many contortions of the body were used and the antics of the dancers were considered very amusing. Only *one man* danced at a time. When he had finished dancing, he presented the pipestem to another, who was obliged to accept it and dance; he transferred also the rattle which he carried. . .

A characteristic of the music . . . is that a sharp, short beat of the drum is frequently given, followed by an instant of silence. When this drum beat is heard the dancer pauses in whatever attitude he may chance to be and remains motionless until the drum beat is resumed. [Densmore, 1913, pp. 293–296.]

Three of these songs are reproduced by Miss Densmore. They are in binary form and fairly archaic tertial scales, nonetheless unlike the Iroquois Eagle Dance.

Today "the comedy angle of representing the pipe . . . has given way to plain competition to outdance the others" (Mason, 1944, p. 68).

The Menominee compete in an analagous Tobacco Dance after the Drum Dance or "cawunowin" (Densmore, 1932, pp. 184–187). Two men outdo each other in fantastic acrobatics, shaking their arms like a fish, manipulating a hoop in intricate steps and circlings. A group of men and women dance on the periphery, entirely for amusement, in this "degenerate form of the Calumet."

A century earlier the Winnebago performed a similar dance as a treat to their grandfathers before departing on their fall hunts, as described in General Ellis' Recollections in 1821 (*in* West, 1934).

The whole tribe assembled in front of the house in a large circle, the dancer and the drummer—the master of ceremonies—in the center: first they gave the pipe dance, an amusing affair, a single one dancing at a time, the trick of which seemed to be to keep time with the drum and especially to suspend action instantaneously with the cessation of the instrument—the dancer to remain in the exact attitude in which the cessation of the drum caught him. [West, 1934, vol. 1, p. 249.]

The most eloquent account for this area dates from 1673, by Fr. Jacques Marquette. For the Illinois he gives us not only the dance but song samples as well (Marquette, ed. Beckwith, 1903, pp. 27–29; ed. Thwaites, 1900, vol. 59, pp. 131–137, 311). The calumet was the focal object in peace and honorific celebrations. The stem was—

a stick two feet long, as thick as a common cane, and pierced in the middle; it is ornamented with the head and neck of different birds of beautiful plumage . . . The ceremony commenced with a rhythmic handling by all guests who on their entrance, held the pipe in both hands and danced it in cadence to a song. The ensuing dance consisted of two parts, a variety of gyrations by a special dancer with the "calumet of the sun," to songs by a chorus of men and women; and a mock combat.

Sometimes he presents it to the sun as if he wished to smoke; sometimes he inclines it to the earth; and at other times he spreads its wings as if for it to fly; at other times, he approaches it to the mouth of the spectator, the whole in cadence.

The second [scene] consists in a combat, to the sound of a kind of drum which succeeds the songs, or rather joins them, harmonizing quite well. The dancer beckons to some brave to come and take the arms on the mat, and challenges him to fight to the sound of the drums; the other approaches, takes his bow and arrow, and begins a duel against the dancer who has no defense but the calumet. [Marquette, ed. Beckwith, 1903, pp. 27–29; ed. Thwaites, 1900, vol. 59, pp. 131–137, 311.]

A final part consisted of a speech delivered by the holder of the calumet, relating his battle victories. He received a gift, then presented the calumet to another who handed it to a third, and so on. Finally it was presented to the guest tribe.

The contest element, which has become paramount in the modern versions of this area, forms a secondary section, as among the Cherokee and Iroquois. But eagle mime is absent, except as implied in the spreading of the pipe's wings. We shall never know whether this concept was really absent or merely escaped the good father's attention. At all events, the contribution is of the utmost importance, not only because of its date, but also because of similarities to the Iroquois Eagle Dance in action and music. Of these songs we will say more during a general musical comparison. For the present we continue our westward journey.

In their present Iowa home the Fox Indians adjoin the heart of the calumet cult, though at the time of most intensive diffusion they were located on Green Bay of modern Wisconsin. The material for the pipes came from a very sacred quarry in Minnesota, north of the Falls of St. Anthony (fig. 30); the tobacco originated with the agricultural Pawnee (Wissler, 1912, p. 31; Murie, 1914, p. 641). Among the tribes of the Northern Plains, the calumet served its original function of smoking in almost all ceremonies. The Oglala Sioux shaman divined the outcome of a war party by smoking (Wissler, 1912, p. 59). Special pipe-bearers danced exclusively with their calumets and rattles in the gatherings of the military societies, two bearers in the Oglala tokala, kagi—yoha, sotka, and wic'iska (Wissler, 1912, pp. 31–34); four dancers in the Blackfoot All–Smoking Ceremony, in quadruple presentation to the sun to four songs repeated four times (Wissler, 1913, pp. 445–447). As generally in the Great Plains, women joined male singers who encircled a huge drum.[11]

Despite the importance of these ceremonies, few authors convey any idea of the form. Skinner describes the Plains-Cree observance in a manner reminiscent of the Illinois celebration. In the Sacred Pipestem Dance the bowl was filled and placed beside the stem.

The keeper, standing before the altar, prayed to all directions and then placed the pipe bowl on a pile of offerings of clothes, etc., laid before the altar. He next took up the stem, prayed, and raising the pipe heavenward sang a song in part as follows:—

> Hai ye, ye, ye (four times repeated)
> He, he he he
> Kezikomäskiniyan, etc.

As he sings he turns to all points of the compass holding out the stem. All the others then join in the singing, and the keeper begins to dance, swinging the stem before him over his head and shoulders in a series of graceful arcs. [Skinner, 1914, p. 537.]

The combat idea, here absent, motivated the Assiniboin Pipe Dance of the previous century—an intensification of the Chippewa-Winnebago type. According to George Catlin —

. . . the young men who were to compose the dance had gathered themselves around a small fire . . . One singer commenced beating on a drum or tambourine, accompanied by his voice; then one of the young men seated sprang instantly on his feet and commenced singing in time with the taps of the drum, and leaping about on one foot and another in the most violent manner imaginable . . . brandishing his fists in the faces of each one who was seated, until at length he

---

[11] Other types of Pipe ceremonies: Teton, Densmore, 1918, p. 66; Omaha and Dakota, Lowie, 1915 c, pp. 96–98; Crow, Lowie, 1913 b, p. 150, and 1935, pp. 93, 174, 196, 210; Arikara, Maximilian, 1843 (ed. 1906), p. 407; Blackfoot, Wissler, 1913, pp. 403, 413, 444.

grasped one of them by his hands, and jerked him forcibly upon his feet . . . [This continued] until all were upon their feet; and at last joined in the most frightful gesticulations and yells . . . [Catlin, 1841, pp. 62–63, fig. 32.]

In a very different Mandan ceremony of adoption, the company sing and two special male dancers, "accompanied by the drum and schischihkue'[12] (rattles)" . . . keep time to the music with their pipes (Maximilian, 1843, p. 320).

EAGLE WAND AND CALUMET

Eagle mime and Calumet Dance were combined into elaborate ceremonies among the agricultural tribes around the confluence of the Missouri and Platte Rivers, in the very center of the continent. This prolonged, composite ceremony flowered fully into the hako of the Caddoan Pawnee, fortunately recorded in all its phases by Fletcher, Murie, and Tracy; and into the slightly less elaborate Omaha wa'wa⁷, recorded by Dorsey and Fletcher. Like the much simpler Mandan Pipe Dance, they were adoption ceremonies, but they included a wealth of amazingly combined symbols.

PAWNEE HAKO

The hako, which could take place at any time of year except the winter, was a prayer for offspring, plentiful crops, and long life. Intense reverence was lavished on the ceremonial objects—an ear of corn, a wildcat skin, two squash rattles representing the breast of the mother, above all, two calumet stems: rak'katittu, with brown feathers as the female principle, and raha'takaru with white feathers as the male principle. In addition to the various rites centered on the child, the most important procedures included a smoke invocation in the thirteenth ritual, by the priest or ku'rahus; purificatory sweeping with eagle wings in the eighteenth ritual, by two doctors; an eagle dance of thanks in the nineteenth ritual, by two special dancers; boasting episodes just before and after this dance; and distribution of gifts in this and in the final, twentieth ritual.

The dance of thanks is accompanied by songs which differ from others concerning the pipes and the corn (Fletcher, 1904, pp. 249–253):

When the dance song begins (intoned by the ku'rahus, then the other singers), the two young men rise, each holding in his left hand, high above his head, a feathered stem and in his right a rattle. Both start at the same time and as they leap and dance they wave the feathered stems to simulate the flight of the eagle. The dancer with the brown-eagle feathered stem goes from the north around by the south and pauses when he reaches the place where the dancer

---

[12] This rattle and its name had a wide distribution: Choctaw, chichiquotia (Swanton, 1918, p. 69); Chitimacha chichicois (Swanton, 1911, p. 340); Mandan she-shee-quoi (Catlin, 1841, I: 123), schischique' (Maximilian, 1843, p. 293); Chippewa cicigwan (Densmore, 1910, p. 11); and Naskapi cic'kwun (Speck, 1935, p. 172). It was one of the shamans' tools. Chichigone (Chippewa *shishikwe* "rattlesnake") was a general Algonquian term for *rattle*.

with the white-eagle feathered stem started, while the latter goes outside the path of the former by the south and pauses when he reaches the place at the north where the dancer bearing the brown-eagle feathered stem had stood. There the two dancers stand until the song is finished, when they cross over and take their own proper places. . . Whenever the song is repeated, they rise and dance again in the same manner.

The circle of the white eagle is outside that of the brown eagle, for the white eagle is the male and its place is outside to defend the female . . . the two move in opposite directions so that they may come together; the male and female must conjoin.

There are two dance songs; they both mean the same and there is no order in which they must be sung.

The words mean "Now fly, you eagles, as we give thanks to the Children." [Fletcher, 1904, p. 253.]

(See also Fletcher, 1904, diagram, p. 248, fig. 180; two songs pp. 254 and 255.)

This circular dance and its peculiar melodies did not find an exact equivalent in the same ceremony among adjacent tribes, yet may have served as prototype.

OMAHA WA'WAⁿ

The Omaha Eagle Dance is preceded by a ceremony of the Approach of the Pipes. "In this song the stems are waved to the rhythm of the rattles shaken with an accented beat but no drum is used." (Fletcher and La Flesche, 1911, p. 383.) Eagle Dance also used a duple drumbeat and a whistle from the wingbone of an eagle.

The singers started the music and the two young men, holding the feathered stems high above their heads, with a light, leaping step danced in two straight lines to and from the east, simulating the flight of the eagle. The line taken by the dancers signified that by following the teachings of the ceremony, the straight red line of the pipes, one could go forth and return in peace to his lodge and have no fear. As the young men danced—a dance that was full of wild grace and beauty—it might happen that a man would advance and step before one of the dancers, who at once handed him the pipe. The man recounted his deeds and laid the pipe on the ground. The dance and music ceased, for the act was a challenge. [Fletcher and La Flesche, 1911, p. 399.]

When the pipe was taken up by someone of the party who could match the deed, the pipe was restored and the dance resumed. Then followed gifts of ponies. "When all the ponies had been received the last dance came to an end" (idem).

The Omaha ceremony consisted of the formal presentation of the pipes by a man of one gens to a man of another gens (Fletcher, 1893, p. 35). It focused on a child, called the huⁿga, symbolizing peace. The corn had no place. The eagle was spoken of as Mother (ibid., 1911, p. 379). The two dancers, however, symbolized male and female.

The songs for the dance—Nene bazhan, "shaking the pipes" [13]—were different from those used in other parts of the ceremony. "In these songs there are generally two divisions, an introduction and an accompaniment to the dance movements. As the dancer requires great agility it is of short duration" (Fletcher, 1893, p. 40).

Miss Fletcher's description is confirmed by Dorsey's (1884, pp. 279–281).

Tradition claims the Omaha as comparatively late arrivals in this area, as arrivals from the Great Lakes, as usurpers who displaced the peaceful Arikara and pushed them northward.[14] Peace was cemented between this Caddoan branch and the Siouan Omaha, Iowa, Ponca, and Cheyenne, by means of this ceremony (Fletcher, 1893, p. 74).

IOWA WAIE⁷OWACI

According to George Catlin, the Iowa Calumet or Pipe of Peace Dance was given at the conclusion of peace, in honor of a warrior, or in ceremonial adoption of "brothers" or "sisters." The dancers held the calumet, ornamented with eagle's quills, in the left hand, and a rattle in the other. (Catlin, 1844, pp. 20–21; also Skinner, 1915, p. 709; Miner, 1911, p. xxxiii).

To commence this dance the pipes and rattles are handed to the dancers by the greatest warrior present, who makes his boast as he gives them, and the one on whom the honor is conferred has the right to boast of it all his life . . . the two wand bearers . . . begin a beautiful graceful dance waving the feathered wands through the air before them as they sing about health and prosperity. [Catlin, 1844, pp. 20–21.]

In the Eagle Dance, Hakon-E-Crase, as separately described by Catlin,

each dancer imagines himself a soaring eagle, and as they dance forward from behind the musicians, they take the positions of eagles heading against the wind and looking down, preparing to make the swoop on their prey below them; the wind seems too strong for them, and they fall back, and repeatedly advance forward, imitating the chattering of that bird, with the whistles carried in their hands whilst they sing. [Catlin, 1844, p. 20.]

Again quoting from Catlin:

The drum, with their voices formed the music for this truly picturesque and exciting dance . . . The song is addressed to their favorite bird the war-eagle, and each dancer carries a fan made of the eagle's tail in his left hand, as he dances, and by his attitudes endeavors to imitate the motions of the soaring eagle.

This, being part of the war dance,[15] is a boasting dance; and at the end of the strain in each song some one of the warriors steps forth in an exited speech . . . After this the dance proceeds with increasing spirit. [Catlin, 1852, pp. 17–18.]

---

[13] Compare the Iroquois term gane"odado', "shaking a (calumet) fan."

[14] Lowie reports no comparable ceremony for the Arikara, unless the secularized Hopping Society (kaxkawis) was a vestige (1915a, p. 672).

[15] Called "Eh-ros-ka" by Catlin (1852, p. 19). The Iruska fire handling society?

The chief shaman flourishes a spear during his speech. The ceremony includes the giving of handsome presents.

Early in the twentieth century Skinner (1915, p. 716) reports the Eagle Dance as obsolete but the Calumet Dance still in vogue, but the formal and functional similarity to the hako type suggests that we are here dealing with one ceremony, whose several parts were not recognized by Catlin as connected. The pipe dance, in fact, already suggests bird flight and appears to contrast with the Eagle Dance chiefly by the type of wand and the more realistic mime of the latter.

TETON HUⁿKA

"The Iowa," says Skinner (1915, p. 706), "claim to have originated the ceremony, but it is . . . found in some form among the Omaha, Pawnee, Oto, Kansa, Osage, Plains-Cree," also among the Teton as huⁿka rite (see Densmore, 1918, pp. 68–77; music but no dance allusion). The Kansa mocu watci evidently resembled the Pawnee and Omaha ceremonies (Skinner, 1915, pp. 759–760); and so did the Ponca wawaⁿ watci (ibid., p. 789). All of these tribes considered the wands as male and female except for the Iowa, who considered them both as male. All elements were not equally emphasized, thus the counting coup less among the Pawnee than the Siouan neighbors, but the corn more so.

OSAGE MÉDICINE DU CHARBON

Among the seminomadic Osage the ceremony either escaped recording, or else strongly emphasized belligerence, for the only dance noted even by the observant Victor Tixier is the Médicine du Charbon (Tixier, 1844, pp. 211–215, ill. p. 225). In preparation for war, warriors blackened themselves with charcoal and danced around camp in two opposite groups with "maniacal contortions . . . beating drums or blowing ts-tsêhs (reed flutes); some took up a warlike song which they accompanied by striking their fans on some piece of wood." Among other objects they carried a calumet, a small calabash filled with pebbles, wings of calumet birds (bald eagle) which they used as a fan. In the picture they hop or crouch low. The dance was preceded by a ceremony of striking the post and boasting, and a War Dance by successive soloists, jumping on both feet and enacting battle mime, as in Iroquois wasase (Tixier, 1844, p. 215). It is possible that the Osage devised a different form from that of their archenemies, the Pawnee. Even if this dance does not represent the calumet ceremony, notwithstanding similar paraphernalia and actions, yet it is of interest in showing the merging of the various concepts and the recurrence of the same elements in dances variously for peace and war (Fenton, this vol., pp. 173, 195).

Whereas this last-named dance recalls the Iroquois War Dance type, the other ceremonies of the Central Plains suggests Iroquois Eagle Dance in all essential points—the wand, eagle mime, boast, adoption. Of course, there are differences, especially in the greater length and elaborateness of the Plains ritual (4 days and nights) and calumet.[16] Yet we have noted differences between adjacent tribes and must remember intervening time and space. The Omaha variant would appear more similar to that of the Iroquois, in the pairing of two males, the straight-lined progression, and, as we shall see later, the music. But that does not imply priority for the Omaha. The different sections of the hako type also correspond to the fragments surviving among the Cherokee. Possibly also among other tribes east of the southern Mississippi, along the Tennessee River.

THE SOUTHEAST

In southeastern Illinois the Ohio River forms a fork with the Mississippi, just below the entrance of the Tennessee and Cumberland Rivers, and not far south of the point where the Missouri brings the waters of the Yellowstone, Teton, Platte, Kansas, and Osage Rivers. In the nineteenth century the Shawnee occupied this fork. But they ranged westward to the Pawnee and eastward along the Wabash to Lake Erie, and to the source of the the Ohio River, which they had inhabited next to the Seneca in the late eighteenth century (Fenton, 1940, p. 241). They called the Seneca Elder Brothers, and bestowed other affectionate kinship terms on other tribes which they contacted amicably or belligerently—the Delaware, Cherokee, Wyandot, Sauk and Fox, Ottawa (Voegelin and Kinietz, 1939, p. 9). They had the feathered peace pipe (ibid., pp. 23–24), and they once had an Eagle Dance "where male dancers crouched, hopped, etc."(Voegelin, communication).

In a communication to Fenton, Dr. Erminie Voegelin states that all Θawakila men could dance, but that only 12 middle-aged men executed the Eagle Dance, a different group each year until 1862. They wore feather coats with natural wings attached at the shoulders, but they carried no fans. They moved the wings with their arms, carried eagle claws on their feet, and an eagle bill on their nose. Four singers sang 12 songs, accompanied with a drum and horn rattle, for the 12 dancers. In the morning the dancers came in from the woods and proceeded to an arbor in the western part of the dance ground. Here they hopped around in imitation of eagles (clockwise?). All morning they danced in a squatting position; they hopped around and "hollered like eagles." If someone threw tobacco, they bent over

---

[16] For illustrations of Plains calumets, see: Pawnee (10 splendid feathers), Fletcher, 1904, pls. 84–87; Iowa, West, 1934, vol. 2: pls. 185, 189; Sioux, ibid., pl. 182; Blackfoot, ibid., pl. 182; Assiniboine, Denig, 1930, p. 437, fig. 31, pl. 68 (triple attachments); general, Catlin 1841, vol. 2: p. 98 (8 quills, horsehair). Other types: with eagle effigy, West, 1934, vol. 2: pl. 97; tomahawk pipe, Wisconsin, ibid., pls. 241–245, 256–257.

like birds and picked it up with their bill, preserving a squatting position, upper legs horizontal, weight on toes, arms bent and close to the body. At intervals between dances they would rest squatting down, but would never sit on chairs. Their dances were not surrounded by any of the calumet activities, of pipe smoking, scalp dancing, or whooping, though they might be associated with cure.

In every respect this type resembles the masked eagle mime of the Pueblo Indians, except for multiplied numbers which recall the Choctaw version next on our list.

Happily , the Choctaw Eagle Dance was observed by George Catlin as a celebration after a ball game (lacrosse?), along with other dances held out of doors. His painting shows a crouch similar to that of the Iroquois, but depicts warclubs in the right hand; and the descriptions show other differences, tending toward the scalp dance.

The Eagle Dance, a very pretty scene, which is got up by their young men in honor of that bird, for whom they seem to have a religious regard. This picturesque dance was given by 12 or 16 men whose bodies were chiefly naked and painted white, with white clay, and each holding in his hand the tail of an eagle, while his head was also decorated with the eagle's quill. Spears were stuck in the ground, around which the dance was performed by four men at a time (clockwise), who had simultaneously at the beat of the drum, jumped up from the ground where they had all sat in rows of four, one row immediately behind the other, and ready to take the place of the first four men when they had left the ground fatigued, which they did by hopping or jumping around behind the rest, and taking their seat, ready to come up again in their turn, after each of the other sets had been through the same form.

In this dance, the steps or rather jumps, were different from anything I had witnessed before, as the dancers were squat down, with their bodies almost touching the ground, in a severe and most difficult posture, as will have been seen in the drawing. [Catlin, 1841, vol. 2, p. 144, fig. 227.]

The warclub and circular formation were associated by Catlin with the Pipe of Peace Dance of general distribution, but with a calumet in the left hand instead of an eagle's wing. Farther north this celebrated the closing of hostilities, along with a smoking ceremony (Catlin, 1841, vol. 2, p. 274). We have no way of knowing whether the Choctaw form characterized the Southeast at that time, for dearth of reports. It certainly differs from that of the modern Cherokee, unless we consider it as a blend of the three parts of the Cherokee Victory Dance.

A century before Catlin the Calumet Dance, but not the Eagle Dance, was observed by French travelers all along the lower Mississippi Valley. The Natchez Calumet Dance took the form of a spectacular processional, according to Charlevoix, Le Petit, Le Page Du Pratz, and Dumont (in Swanton, 1911, pp. 134–138). According to Charlevoix, "Treaties of peace and alliances are made with great pomp . . . Commonly the embassy is composed of 30 men and 6 women. Six of the best voices march at the head of this train and sing aloud, the rest follow, and the *chichicoué* serves to regulate the time . . . those who carry the calumet dance as they sing, and turn themselves on every side . . . and make a great many grimaces and contortions . . . then they rub him [the great chief] with their calumet from head to foot." Dumont: "One of them carries in his left hand an earthen pot covered with a dressed deerskin stretched tightly over this pot . . . which serves him as a drum. All answer with cries which they utter in cadence. Some bear *chichicoüas* . . . However, the one who bears the calumet makes it spring about, sometimes low down, sometimes in the air, making a thousand different contortions with his legs and his entire body." There followed a smoking ceremony, a recital of distinguished deeds, and distribution of presents.

The Taensa greeted Pénicaut and Iberville and sang their calumet of peace (Swanton, 1911, p. 268). On approaching a Houma village, Iberville was met by three singers with a calumet of peace, "raised as high as their arms could reach" (ibid., 285). The Koroa gave a calumet to M. de la Salle (ibid., p. 327).

That the Cherokee had the ceremony as early as 1761, we know from Lieutenant Timberlake, who was showered with calumets 3 feet long, ornamented with feathers, deer's hair, and quills (Timberlake, 1765, p. 263). In one dance they "caper, for a minute the music stops, and they relate the manner of taking scalps, then continue the dance" (ibid., p. 92).

All we know of the Catawba ritual is the existence of 5-foot staffs, and the tradition of a dance before 1890, with "feather waving" (Speck, 1939, pp. 55–57). Or is this the Feather Dance, like the great double round of the Creek with feathered sticks (Speck, 1911, pp. 186–189) and of the Iroquois and the eighteenth century Cherokee (Timberlake, 1765, p. 107)?

All we know of an analogous Delaware dance is the Nighthawk Dance of the Six Nations residents, who may have taken it over from the Cayuga or at least have greatly modified it. Nighthawk wings were replaced by feather wands, and turtle rattles by cow-horn rattles. Two to four men hopped in a line as do the Cayuga, as invocation for a healthful season, during the Green Corn festival and the tenth night of the Bear rite (Speck, 1945, p. 76). This is now extinct, as in fact is the Six Nations Delaware ceremonialism, and as, in general, is Southeastern ceremonialism—barring Cherokee vestiges and possible survivals or revivals in Northeastern Oklahoma.

THE THUNDERBIRD

In all of these ceremonies and their remnants the great sky dweller was mimed as he is among the Iroquois, without imitative costume such as we find in the Pueblos. The feathers on a stem, or at times a wing held in the left hand, provide the only palpable illusion of feathered flight, beyond the skilled postures. The Mississippian type also differs from that of the Rio Grande by war associations in contrast to rain, thunder, and cure.

The last-named far-western function prevails among the Iroquois. So does the widespread eagle cult of the Pueblos (Parsons, 1925, p. 68). Comanche (ibid.), Plains (Mooney, 1896, pp. 992–993), and the Southeast.

NORTHWEST COAST

The thunder association, remaining in the Iroquois War Dance, formerly motivated Pawnee ceremonies (Murie, 1914, pp. 559–570), Teton heyoka rituals (Densmore, 1918, pp. 157–170), taken over from the Omaha (Wissler, 1916, p. 866), and the Northwest Coast Thunderbird Dance.

This last phenomenon, which may or may not be connected with the more southerly manifestations, involves realistic costume and enactment to strange archaic songs. In the Klokali dance of the Nitinat tribe, the latter part of July, the performer holds in his extended arms a blanket with eagle feathers suspended along the edge (Densmore, 1943 a, pp. 56–57). In the Bella Coola Midwinter appearance of the Thunderbird, much rumbling, commotion and a beaklike mask intensify the terrifying illusion (McIlwraith, 1948, vol. 2, pp. 146–147). This concept is as old and standardized as any items of this comparatively recent culture.

RECENT ADAPTATIONS FROM PUEBLOS

In addition to these, one might say, "natural" diffusions of the Thunderbird, conscious *adaptations* have carried the Pueblo Eagle Dance type to more easterly tribes. For instance, the young Fox dancers, Charles and Frank Pushetonequa, perform an excellent version which they recomposed from Southwestern prototype, according to their own admission. The Ottawa, Dave Kenoshmeg of Cross Village, Mich., performs a similar dance at the annual August Fair, under the guidance of the local priest, Fr. Bertram. These and possible other borrowings are recent, and independent of the development of the Iroquois Eagle Dance but they show the ease and honesty of such adaptation.

COMANCHE EAGLE DANCE

The modern Comanche version may have a similar recent origin in Oklahoma, despite the legend that has become attached to it. Or it may have been an exchange product with the Pueblos, in the raids that gave rise to the Pueblo Comanche Dance. In the kanani kiyake a single male dancer imitates the eagle (communication Cebyn Dwajty

Maufaunwy). It has also become a show piece, as partly on the Rio Grande, and entirely further East, in contrast with the ceremonialism attached to the Calumet-Eagle dances till they breathed their last.

THE GRASS DANCE

Since the middle of the nineteenth century the Great Plains have developed another, antithetical offshoot of this ceremonial complex; antithetical to the Eagle Dance in the war emphasis, dwindling of eagle references, individualistically-communal and ecstatic though virtuoso execution, as against the set routine of modern eagle dances.

The Teton-Sioux recognize two varieties of Grass Dance, that of the old men, in a clockwise circle, and that of the younger generation without formation (Densmore, 1918, pp. 468–470). In the older version "the men imitate motions of the eagle and graceful birds". According to Lowie (1915 c, pp. 95–96), "only men take part, and they move briskly, sometimes in pairs, sometimes separately, vigorously stamping the ground with their feet, and frequently mimicking martial exploits." The musicians seated in the center around a big drum strike up a tune, later reinforced by the voices of some of the women; and the members of one of the four men's societies arise to perform the vigorous turnings and bendings, described by Mason (1944, pp. 17–40). They give vent to penetrating cries and brandish weapons. Sometimes in the end "the drum continues a moment or two, whereupon one of the men arises and dances around the circle, singing a short phrase, thus "dancing the tail" (Lowie, 1915 c, p. 97). It is an honor to be selected as tail dancer (Densmore, 1918, p. 472).

This Grass Dance or Omaha Dance is so-called because, in the first place, the dancers carry a bunch of grass in their belts as a symbol of scalps (Densmore, 1918, p. 468); and in the second place because it came from the Omaha to the Teton Sioux, by way of the Yankton, about 1860 (Wissler, 1916, p. 866). It spread to all of the Plains tribes, as far as the Shoshone (Lowie, 1915 b, p. 822), and it bounced back to the Omaha and their neighbors, and by way of the Potawatomi reached the Central Algonquians as the Drum or Dream Dance (Wissler, 1916, p. 868, and Barrett, 1911, pp. 251–406). The Central Plains tribes have called it the Chief's Drum Dance (Iowa, Skinner, 1915, pp. 720–724), or the Modern Iruska (Kit'kahaxki Pawnee; Murie, 1914, p. 628). Indeed, Grass Dance combines features of the Calumet Dance and ancient Iruska, with its four pipe-dancers (Pawnee), bird-headed stick (Crow and Cheyenne), and iruska trick of fetching dog meat out of a boiling kettle. After a feast the dog bones are placed on the ground by four successive dancers who count coup on them (Murie, 1914, p. 624; Wissler, 1912, pp. 48–52; Lowie, 1913 b, pp. 200–206; Skinner, 1915, pp. 720–724). There follows much gift-display with boasts, blankets, and horses instead of the coins and crackers of the Iroquois.

The songs, which Murie claims to be of Pawnee origin, disseminated among the Arikara, Crow, and Dakotas, and were lately supplemented by original compositions (Murie, 1914, p. 629). They are attributed to the Omaha by Miss Densmore's Teton informant, also alongside new compositions. These songs, fortunately reproduced by Miss Densmore (1918, Nos. 95–200), are Siouan in character, yet in an interesting way show affinities with hako and Iroquois Eagle Dance songs. This affinity corresponds to the special baroque development of the dance itself, apparently so far progressed from the dignified Eagle Dance. A similar breaking up is manifest in the Iroquois wasase (War Dance), which may be a peripheral form of the Grass Dance, as suggested by its steps and songs.

The Grass Dance and its derivatives proved a significant, non-narcotic emotional outlet in a time of stress, during the large-scale land sessions in 1860–87 (see Billington, 1949, pp. 651 ff.). Its spectacular spread, observed by able scholars and interpreted by Wissler, practically coincides with that of the Calumet Dance (see fig. 30).

THE CATTARAUGUS BIRD DANCE

Our round trip concludes with a historical relic of the Eagle Dance at Cattaraugus Reservation. Among the sources already scoured by Fenton, two pages contribute to our search. About 1890, when Harriet Maxwell Converse observed the "Bird Dance" and the Seneca boy artist, Jesse Cornplanter, sketched the ritual, the four dancers squatted and pecked, faced each other in two pairs, and bore fans much as they do today (Converse, 1908, pp. 71–72). But the song "arranged" by Frank B. Converse, the musician husband of the writer, cannot by any stretch of the imagination be equated with any of the recorded songs. Its sequential outline and tonality and its return to the original level relate it to the first introductory Coldspring chant, but its range of 11 notes and its bold intervals exceed those of surviving melodies. The absence of percussion notation, of texts, and of comments precludes further identification of this tantalizing fragment.

At the turn of the century the Eagle Dance featured as one of the most prominent and admired Iroquois dances, confined, because of its difficulty, to a few virtuoso performers. In this statement Mrs. Converse is backed by Arthur C. Parker, another devotee to Seneca ceremonialism (Parker, 1909, pp. 174–176).

GANEGWA'E AND ITS RELATIVES

DANCE

Of the diverse forms we have passed in review, not one corresponds exactly to the Iroquois Eagle Dance; yet all of them find an echo in one or several of the elements listed by Fenton (p. 179). These elements are here listed and are followed by their distributions among tribes to the West.

ELEMENTS

(1) *Pairs of youths or men . . .*
> Single pair West of Missouri, all types, including modern Fox.
> Male and female symbol, Central Plains and Southwest.
> Doubling on periphery—four Iroquois, Choctaw, Blackfoot.
> Doubling on periphery—eight Cherokee.
> With Seneca moiety opposition; Onondaga, Cayuga, Cherokee linear.
> Successive soloists, older forms East of Mississippi.
> Simultaneous soloists, newer form of Grass Dance type.

(2) " *. . . holding a rattle in the right hand and a feather fan in the left . . .*"
> General distribution except on northern and southern periphery.
> Choctaw and Osage wing in hand, Choctaw warclub in right hand.
> Southwest and Northwest mask and winged arms.

(3) " *. . . crouch swaying and advance . . . retreat hopping . . .*"
> General distribution even in recent nonmimetic forms.
> Advance usually in straight line; circular—Pueblo, Pawnee, Choctaw.

(4) " *. . . a speaker . . . strikes a pole . . . to recite some record of personal achievement . . .*"
> Boasting, a Northern Plains characteristic, enacted everywhere, anciently among Iroquois, in hako area and in Far West; speeches everywhere East of Rockies. General in war dances.

(5) " *. . . he distributes presents . . .*"
> Gifts, formerly pretentious, everywhere except in Southeast and Southwest. Not confined to war-calumet-eagle complex.

(6) " *. . . After the dance, the master of ceremonies passes an animal head.*"
> Terminal feast, formerly dog meat, generally in pipe war, Iruska, and Grass Dance ceremonies of Missouri-Mississippi-Great Lakes.
> Modern Iruska combined with counting coup.
> Dog variously replaced by beef, pig, or chicken.

PATTERNS

Figure 29 shows the distribution of salient ground plans: circular patterns in Southwest and in hako, and in older War Dance forms; straight lines in easterly area, with opposition in the Seneca Eagle Dance and the Striking-a-stick Dance, breaking up in recent War Dance derivatives.

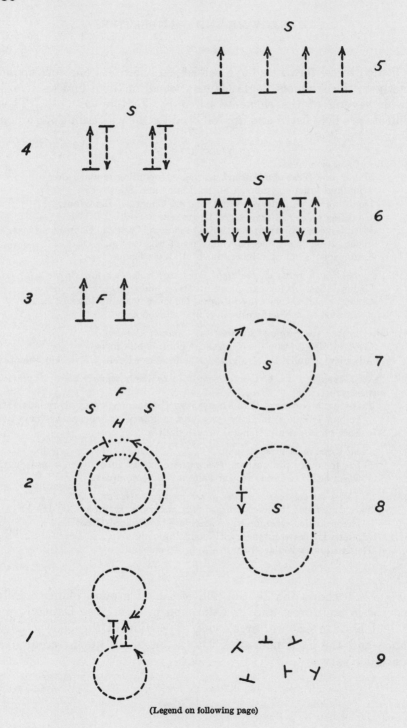

(Legend on following page)

The map (fig. 30) shows concentration and combination of all forms in the "Hako area," among the Central Plains agriculturalists; pairing in this center and in Pueblos, with multiplication on the periphery; prevalence of eagle mime among southerly agriculturalists, Pueblos and hako area, with easterly fanning out; and northerly fanning out of Pipe and Grass Dance, notably among hunting tribes. The pipestone quarry, north of the Pawnee, is in the territory of Dakota Sioux.

MUSIC

Musical comparisons are limited by even more fragmentary material than are dance forms. Whereas no detailed choreographies are available, yet the verbal descriptions and solitary ground plan, scattered through the centuries, provide us with some working basis. But song renditions are completely absent before Alice Fletcher—with one illustrious exception—and are furthermore of doubtful accuracy before the days of the phonograph and of the scientific attitude.

Thus in reading back the music that accompanies Father Marquette's description of the Illinois Calumet Dance, we must remember the missionary opinion of these ceremonies, and furthermore, the courtly Pavanes composed in 1735 by Marquette's compatriot of the next generation, Jean Phillipe Rameau, for his "Indes Galantes." Nonetheless, the "song" makes musical and textual sense if considered as three songs of varying tonality and character, the last one with the largest range. No percussion accompaniment was reproduced.

Edwin Tracy's hako transcriptions and Frances Densmore's Sioux and Chippewa songs inspire confidence. But John C. Fillmore approached the Omaha songs with the conviction that "melody is a product of the natural harmonic sense and that all efforts to reduce primitive music to scales without reference to the natural harmonies implied in them prove futile" (Fletcher, 1893, pp. 61–62). Thus we cannot know what he may have done to the songs besides harmonizing them and we mistrust accuracy while respecting his perception of their sacred nature.

FIGURE 29.—Intertribal dance patterns. S = singer. F = fire. H = hunka. *1*, Pueblo Eagle Dance. *2*, Pawnee Eagle Dance. *3*, Omaha Eagle Dance; Siouan Calumet Dance, Fox Calumet Dance. *4*, Seneca Eagle Dance. *5*, Onondaga Eagle Dance; Cherokee Eagle Dance; Blackfoot Calumet Dance (with 8 men). *6*, Iroquois Striking-a-stick (Shawnee?); Cherokee Eagle Dance. *7*, Choctaw Eagle Dance; Sauk and Fox Victory Dance; Plains Scalp Dance; Older Grass Dance. *8*, Iroquois Feather, Thanksgiving, and *wasase* Round Dances. *9*, Iroquois *wasase* War Dance (usual plan); newer Grass Dance.

In figs. 31–36 the Tonawanda Eagle Dance songs are placed side by side with analogous Calumet and Eagle Dance songs of other tribes. The Tonawanda introductory chants show more striking resemblances with the western songs than do the chants of the other three Iroquois versions; but the actual dance songs are deficient in secundal scales. Hence a few Coldspring and Onondaga excerpts are included in these illustrations. The Central Plains examples show two contrasting tendencies as clearly as the Iroquois songs, namely, rhapsodic and formalized songs.

RHAPSODIC SONGS

The introduction in the Omaha wawa⁷ and the pipe-waving invocation in the Pawnee hako (fig. 32) resemble the Tonawanda introductory tobacco invocation chants and concluding song (fig. 31). So far as one can judge from the transcription, song 3 of the Illinois Calumet ceremony belongs to this same type of free, vertical songs. This type is united by the following characteristics: a full scale, with a quartal skeleton and concluding secundal play; a wide range from 8 to 11 notes; syncopations, triplets, and rapid rhythmic figures interspersed with simpler units; consecutive structure with sequential descent; percussion tremolo, broken at phrase endings and terminating in even beats at the end of the song; a slower tempo than dance songs; steep descent, sometimes stepwise, sometimes direct, centered around the maintone in Tonawanada 1 and wawa⁷ 1, ending on the maintone as the lowest note in the other instances. These traits are not typically Iroquoian but, as we shall see later, they pertain to the Northern Plains.

FORMAL DANCE SONGS

The dance songs of the Pawnee, Omaha, and Fox resemble those of the Iroquois in their level trend, with moderate stepwise descents of 421 or 532; simpler rhythmic units; a similar concluding formula of two short and a long; the recurrence of similar motifs but with a variable formula of repetition (figs. 33 and 34). The drum synchronizes with the voice, with a pause in the middle of the Omaha songs. The Cherokee, Illinois, and Pueblo examples stand between these conservative songs and the rhapsodic type, by their more descending trend, conclusion on the lowest note, and syncopated units. However, tertial scales prevail. In general these add up to a triad scale,

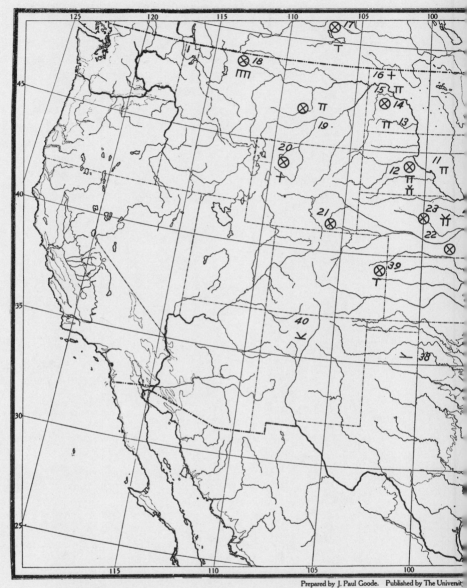

Prepared by J. Paul Goode. Published by The Universit

FIGURE 30

Numbers indicate location of tribes in the middle of the 19th century:

1. Onondaga near Syracuse
2. Coldspring and Cattaraugus Seneca
3. Tonawanda Seneca
4. Iroquois of Six Nations Reserve
5. Seneca and Shawnee joint locations in 18th century
5a. Shawnee
6. Miami—1670-1750

6a. Illinois—1673
7. Meskwaki (Fox)
8. Winnebago
9. Menominee
10. Chippewa
11. Yankton Dakota
12. Teton Dakota
13. Arikara

14. Hidatsa
15. Mandan
16. Assiniboine
17. Cree
18. Blackfoot
19. Crow
20. Shoshone

LEGEND DISTRIBUTION

T *1 PIPE DANCER.*
TT *2 PIPE DANCERS.*
TTT *3 PIPE DANCERS.*
TTTT *4 OR MORE PIPE DANCERS.*
⋋ *1 EAGLE DANCER.*
⋎ *2 EAGLE DANCERS.*
⋇ *4 OR MORE EAGLE DANCERS.*
⑂ *BLENDED EAGLE AND PIPE DANCE.*
+ *CONSECUTIVE CONTEST DANCERS.*
⊗ *GRASS DANCE TYPE.*
○ *FEATHER DANCE TYPE.*
⊕ *COMBINED EAGLE AND SCALP DANCE.*
△ *PIPESTONE QUARRY.*

SCALE

stribution.

21. Cheyenne and Arapaho	28. Osage	35. Taensa
22. Pawnee	29. Cahinnio (Caddo)—1687	35a. Houma
23. Ponca	30. Cherokee	36. Natchez—1758
24. Omaha	31. Catawba	37. Chitimacha—1758
25. Iowa	32. Creek	38. Comanche
26. Oto	33. Choctaw	39. Kiowa
27. Kansa	34. Koroa—1683	40. Rio Grande Pueblos

specifically in the Tonawanda songs in figure 35. Cherokee songs descend in chained thirds of 7531, producing a range of seven notes instead of an octave (fig. 36).[17] None of the songs except the Pawnee are preceded by calls, though some of them start with an introductory phrase like an extended call. Though on the surface all of the cited examples appear different, the South and West are united with the Iroquois by fundamental characteristics. Tribe by tribe, they can be summarized as follows:

Pawnee and Iroquois.—Hako song 1 (fig. 34) has a nucleus of a second, a semicadence on VII, the simpler Iroquoian rhythmic units 1, 5, and 7, parallel structure, an accented duple drum beat, a tempo only slightly slower than that of Tonawanda, and a level melodic contour. Song 2 combines a descending second with an ascending third, in a focused melody. Its essentials resemble the first song, but it has no semicadence, and plays its rhythmic motif (unit 3) in two complementary phrases.

Omaha and Iroquois.—The actual dance of wawa[7] is in two parts, which we term songs 3 and 4. Song 3 precedes a modified quartal nucleus by a tertial phrase and repeats its simple rhythmic units (1, 8, and 14) in parallel structure with a gentle descent to the maintone (fig. 34). Song 4 more closely relates to Pawnee and Iroquois examples by virtue of its secundal nucleus, preceded by a tertial phrase, by a semicadence on VI, simple rhythmic units 3 and 14, and complementary centered structure with a mirrored contour. Both Omaha songs use a drumbeat and tempo characteristic of Iroquois Eagle Dance.

Illinois and Iroquois.—The first and second Illinois Calumet Dance songs notated by Fr. Marquette give no indication of their structure or percussion pattern, but they appear related to Eagle Dance songs by their tertial scales with a terminal play on a second and the effect of a semicadence on VII in Illinois song 2 (fig. 34). Song 1, however, appears quartal with a terminal second, and both have a descending contour. The rhythm has to be inferred. Song 1 seems to fit into a triplet pattern and song 2 into units 1 and 14, but their phrasing is blurred.

---

[17] For discussion of chains of thirds, specifically as applied to Europe, see Sachs, 1943, pp. 385–386 and 388–393.

Tonawanda 1

FIGURE 31.—Tonawanda 1, 2, 10; scales. (See p. 296.)

FIGURE 32.—Song excerpts: Pawnee, Omaha pipe invocation; Pueblo Eagle Dance, Illinois Calumet Dance. Compare Tonawanda songs in figure 31. Also compare Sioux Grass Dance songs in Densmore, 1918, No. 195, and Sioux Sun and Grass Dance in recordings by Willard Rhodes. (See Bibliography.) (Key signature was inadvertently omitted from Pawnee 1. This should be the same as for Omaha 1.) (See p. 296.)

FIGURE 33.—Tonawanda 9, 4; Fox songs 1, 2, 3; scales. (See p. 296.)

FIGURE 34.—Pawnee Hako, Omaha Wawaⁿ, Illinois Calumet Dance songs. Compare Tonawanda Eagle Dance and Fox Calumet Dance in figure 33. Also compare Chippewa Pipe Dance (Densmore, 1913, No. 171) and Menominee Pipe Dance (Densmore, 1932, Nos. 109–112); also Teton Sioux Hunka (Densmore, 1918, Nos. 2 and 3). (See p. 296.)

FIGURE 35.—Tonawanda 3, 5, 6, 8. (See p. 296.)

FIGURE 36.—Cherokee songs 1, 3, 4; scales of tertial Tonawanda and Cherokee songs. (See p. 296.)

Texts to Figures 31–36

Tonawanda Seneca—see Fenton pp. 67–68.

Pawnee Hako
1. Hooo. 'Hare ra . . . (Young children coming).
2. Hooo. Ha! Ira hirura . . . (Behold! Yonder he is coming).
3. Hooo. Rawa sa wari! Iri i hare . . . (Now you eagles fly. You children).

Omaha Wawaⁿ
1. 2. Kawae tha . . . (burden syllables).
3. Kae tha kae tha . . . ho kae thu nae na ha . . .
4. Ho kae tha . . .

Illinois Calumet Dance (probably untranslated meanings).
1. Nina hani . . . (refers to pipe?).
2. Cahoua hanogue atchicha . . . he he.
3. Mintingomi tade pini pinihe atchichale matchi minamba mictande pini pinihe.

Pueblo Eagle Dance
3. Ohaowiya heneya . . .

Fox Calumet Dance (burden syllables and meanings).
1. Yuwe yuwe yuwe . . . aiyaiye *ho tce* (pipe dance syllables)
   aiyai aiyai nik' gan di k ɛn nɛ ma nō mi nɛ wi nɛ ma nō mi nɛ wi *ho tce*
           (All my friends, I am a Menomini) [A full tribal member].
2. kwĭ kwoᵈ tca ha·n wĭ na wĭ w°, nuwiyuwi . . . (Three times).
   Jack Snipe, he can't pull to fly [too full of food, this bird].
   wĭ ha·ni sɛːᵈ tce *ho·ᵈ tci*
   Can't use his wings.
3. aiyai aiyai mɛ nā gwi a·si (Twice)
   aiyai aiyai mɛ nā gwi a·si e *ho tce* aiyai aiyai
           spoiled buffalo meat
Obtained by Martha Champion Huot from Bill Leaf, singer.
Song 1 refers to a young man just returned from first war experience.

Cherokee Eagle Dance (burden syllables).
1. had'ehona . . .
2. ha'yniho' ha'yniho'ge (twice) nu'wiga'nina ya'niho'ge. Repeat.
3. yo'we hoyowe . . .

Literary References to Figures 32 and 34.

Hako—1. Fletcher, 1904, p. 251; transcription by Edwin D. Tracy.
      2. ibid., p. 255.
      3. ibid., p. 254.
Wawan—1. Fletcher, 1893, No. 51, p. 117; transcription by John C. Fillmore.
      2. ibid.
      3. ibid., p. 118.
      4. ibid., pp. 118–119.
Illinois—1, 2, 3. Marquette, Thwaites ed. 1900, v. 51, p. 311.
Pueblo of San Ildefonso—Evans, 1931, p. 53; Transcription by George Herzog.

Melodies are quoted as transcribed, except for occasional transposition to a common level for comparative purposes. All other transcriptions are by G. Kurath.

Fox and Iroquois.—We have previously commented on the affinity between Fox Pipe Dance and Iroquois Eagle Dance songs, particularly in the bipartite structure, with tremolo during A and duple beat during B. This similarity is emphasized by the focused contours with a mild descent within a range of a fifth to an octave, and dwindling intervals toward the end of each section. The three Fox songs show even more conservative tendencies than Tonawanda 9 and 4 (fig. 33), and tie up with hako examples in the secundal scales the effect of a semicadence in song 1, simple rhythmic units, and repetitious forms, consisting in each section of a high statement, the theme, and a monotone coda. The tempo of A is slower than B, which proceeds at the rapid clip of the Onondaga dances.

Cherokee and Iroquois.—The Cherokee examples in figure 36 show more contrasts than likenesses with the Tonawanda songs in figure 35. Besides the difference in scales, noted above, the Cherokee songs introduce syncopation and rapid unit 12, also a curious 7/8 phrasing in song 3. The structure consists of thematic repetition in mildly descending sequence and contour variations, to a low maintone. The drumbeat is erratic and different in each song, progressing from absence to a slow irregular pattern to an even duple beat.

Pueblo and Iroquois.—The Pueblo transcriptions by Dr. George Herzog (1935) show Plains rather than Iroquois tendencies in the sequential descents, syncopations and triplets, and the quartal scale of the first, third, and fourth songs. Song 3, however, uses a tertial scale, level passages, a tempo similar to the Seneca, and a pattern of triple tremolo and accented single beat to the two parts of the melody.

TRENDS OF DEVELOPMENT

A comparison of two sets of songs shows the following schemes, in order of increasing ingenuity: (1) Pawnee 2 and 3 : nucleus with initial call and sally. (2) Omaha 3 : nucleus with initial development and monotone coda. (3) S. 5, Oa. 13 : nucleus with initial development and terminal monotone coda, duplicated in A and B. (4) Ton. 9 and S. 13 : secondary theme; nucleus, variant. Again (1) Omaha 4 : nucleus with initial overlay. (2) Fox 1 : nucleus with initial development and monotone coda. (3) Oa. 12 : development, complement; nucleus, complement. (4) Ton. 4 : development, nucleus, coda; complement, sequential ascent of nucleus, coda (figs. 33 and 34).

In the Fox songs, the two parts A and B form one consecutive whole, whereas the Iroquois A and B contain parallel but varying restatements of two themes.

The Cherokee, Illinois, and Pueblo songs show different tendencies. The Cherokee songs merely tend toward the binary form; the tertial scale consists of chains of thirds adding up to a seventh, in distinction from the octave's dip of the Tonawanda "triad" scale (figs. 35 and 36). Relationship to the hako nucleus is not out of the question, considering the flexibility of Indian intervals; but such stages of growth cannot be demonstrated by intervening tribes. The Pueblo songs do not obviously hark back to Pawnee hako, but, like the Illinois examples, exhibit Plains characteristics (fig. 32).

RELATIONSHIP TO OTHER SONGS OF THESE TRIBES [18]

Placement of these songs in their tribal setting will here be most summary and can be followed up by perusal of the detailed analyses.

Pawnee.—Hako Eagle Dance songs stand alone in the great treasury of Pawnee ritual songs. Hako contains a few equally archaic chants, as the chant to the sun (Fletcher, 1904, p. 135). Most of the songs show greater development, chants to the corn with a tertial trend (ibid., pp. 162–163), in chained thirds at times (ibid., p. 188); with a quartal trend in pipe songs (ibid., pp. 101, 111, 249–251). Miss Densmore stresses the generally greater simplicity of melody and rhythm as compared with Siouan songs, preference for 5-note range, two-thirds proportion of descending intervals (Densmore, 1929, pp. 14–18). In fact, we find a preponderance of the simpler rhythmic units, but also many songs with triplets and syncopation, and descending melodies up to 14-note range. These tendencies are exhibited in the pipe songs. (See also songs in Densmore, 1929, Nos. 19, 20, 22.)

Omaha.—Omaha songs similarly combine two tendencies but with a minority of simpler even units and compact ranges, and a majority of complex rhythms and great drops (Fletcher, 1893, Hethuska songs Nos. 17, 19, 23 with triplets, No. 22 with syncopation and a range of 12 notes). Virtually all of the songs are quartal. Thus the Eagle Dance songs, though less archaic than those of hako, contrast with the general tendency; but the introductory chants emphasize the Siouan qualities. Considering the derivation of wawa[7] from hako, the paucity of precise analogies is surprising. They do exist (Fletcher, 1893, pp. 392 ff.; 1904, pp. 268 ff.), but the Omaha have certainly exercised creative talent.

Great Plains.—These bold qualities burst into full glory in the music of the Teton Sioux, especially in the Grass Dance. Here the downward transposition of longer phrases is carried to an extreme (Densmore, 1918, No. 195–199). No. 195, with its range of 17 notes, transposes the theme and subtheme four times, down two octaves, in strikingly consecutive structure.[19] The characteristics

---

[18] It is too early to generalize on cultural implications of tonality, as so competently presented for Eurasia in Sachs, 1943. "Triads," for instance, appear from the Cherokee to the Eskimo (Thuren, 1923, pp. 86–87).

[19] For typical Plains structure, see Herzog, 1935, p. 409.

have been summarized by Densmore (1918, pp. 42 ff.) and the melodic line of a number of songs has been plotted. Some of these compare with the contours on our figure 28, particularly page 204, Nos. 49 and 56 (Dreams about Animals) and page 245, Nos. 59 and 71 (Treatment of Sick). The songs dealing with the hako-derived hunka form an exception, with their simple "triadic" pattern (Densmore, 1918, Nos. 2 and 3). They do not, however, resemble the Eagle Dance, for they deal with other parts of the ceremony.

Northern tribes.—Similar tendencies are evident in the music of the Mandan and Hidatsa, for whom, however, we find no pipe songs (Densmore, 1923); and in Cheyenne and Arapaho songs, more pronounced in the Cheyenne repertoire (Densmore, 1936, Nos. 23 and 29) than in the Arapaho with their agricultural background (ibid., No. 18). The sequence is also a characteristic of Chippewa and Menominee songs, but with more preference for simpler units, notably in the Chippewa pipe songs which differ from the Menominee Tobacco Dance (Densmore, 1913, Nos. 171–173, and 1932, Nos. 109–112). We have noted a similar melodic line in Chippewa No. 171, "O'gima" and Fox Pipe Dance songs.

Throughout this northern area we find many songs with discrepancy of vocal and instrumental tempo, also frequent iambic drumbeats (long-short), especially in the war songs and Grass Dance.

Fox.—The Sauk and Fox escaped Miss Densmore's attention, but their songs have been recorded by Martha Champion Randle and some of them were notated by ear during my attendance at their festivals. The general similarity to Iroquois music is apparent in the tonality and in the level trend of their ceremonial music and also in the peculiar structure of A A B A B with alternate tremolo and beat corresponding to static and crossing dance patterns, notably in Bean Dance and Bear Dance. The Pipe Dance songs fit into the musical frame as well as do Iroquois Eagle Dance songs.

Cherokee.—Cherokee songs have also to date escaped exhaustive publication, but some samples appear in Kurath, 1951, figures 5 and 7; and recordings by Lucas Moser and John W. Gillespie are on hand. These are predominantly tertial: Corn Dance and Masked Dance descend in chains of thirds, just as Cherokee Eagle Dance; but as a rule the rhythms of both melody and drum are relatively simple and the tonality and line recall songs of the Northern Iroquois. Chains of thirds appear to be a characteristic of the Southeast. They are in evidence in songs of the Creek, such as medicine chants (Speck, 1911, p. 227 ff.) and the Feather Dance (ibid., p. 192), of the Yuchi (Ball Game, ibid., p. 209), and of the Choctaw (Densmore, 1943 b).

Pueblos.—Miss Densmore's collection of music from Santo Domingo

Pueblo shows some use of syncopation and of quartal scales, notably in the Buffalo Dance (1938, No. 59 ff.), but a strong tertial tendency particularly in the Corn Dance, with chained thirds in Nos. 39 and 46. They also show a preference for level or rising contours, but again Buffalo Dance No. 65 and others descend. On the whole, the Eagle Dance is closer to Plains music than to typical Pueblo songs.

SUMMARY

The comparisons indicate two easterly paths of musical diffusion: a horizontal development from Pawnee and Omaha through Fox to Iroquois, and an oblique trend from the Missouri area through the Illinois southeast to the Cherokee, thence in an arc to the Iroquois. Secondly, they show the fusion of introduced songs with the local style, in contrast with the dance patterns which remain esoteric to the Eastern Woodlands. Thirdly, they emphasize the role of the individual artist in adherence, transference, and creative modification: the Cherokee, Will West Long; the Iroquois, Johnny John, Shanks, Logan, Deskaheh, and generations of forgotten singers.

TRANSMISSION AND RECEPTION OF RITUAL CURRENTS

Choreographically and musically the Iroquois Eagle Dance has more in common with the Calumet Dance of the Northern Plains hunters than with the Eagle Dance of the Southern agriculturalists. With the North it shares the rectilinear pattern, the introductory chants, the wand, boast, gifts, and feast; with the South it shares only the birdlike mime. It shows closest relationship with the blended ritual of the agricultural Central Plains tribes. To the Omaha pipe-shaking it conforms in all respects; to the nineteenth ritual of the Pawnee hako in all essentials except for the Pawnee circles and maize-symbolism. The three types are united by a feathered sway and by pairing.

Of these three types the Eagle mime appears as an ancient and possibly extensive substratum. Its origin is lost in prehistory. Parsons' and Fletcher's Mexican hunch remains a theory.[20] A Southeastern ceremonial complex is variously traced by archeologists to Central America (Waring and Holder, 1945; Nuttall, 1932), to indigenous roots (Krieger, 1945). These prehistoric birdmen resemble the

---

[20] For Aztec parallels, see Parsons, 1939, vol. 2, pp. 1019–1025, specifically, reference to Sahagun, 1932, pp. 146–147. Birds were impersonated in the semihelmet mask of the Eagle Knight dancers during the rain ceremony, also by masked dancers during Tentleco, the arrival of the Gods (Sahagun, p. 120). See also Sandi, 1938, pp. 611–612. Magnificent fans of stout wing-feathers of rare birds were carried by chiefs in ceremonial dances, by envoys to neighboring tribes as official badge and exchange-gifts. Feathers of the green quetzal bird were especially prized (Nuttall, 1888, p. 24, pl. 2, figs. 13, a, b).

At the time of the Conquest, as today, the Volador was the most realistic and spectacular bird imitation (see Toor, 1947, pp. 317–323 and pl. 152 ff.). These and the gorgeous Quetzales emphasize sun associations. (See Quetzales in Toor, p. 353, pl. 160.) These dancers carry small rattles but no fans. As witnessed, they appeared different choreographically and musically from the northerly Eagle dance forms.

modern Western vestiges in mask and posture.[21] Direct descent in their own area has been obscured by discontinuance of the eagle masks among the Shawnee and Cherokee (Fenton, field notes).

The second type, the Calumet Dance, already enjoyed a wide favor in the seventeenth century on the advent of the missionaries who helped to spread its acceptance to distant tribes. The pipe as such can be traced to the Hopewellian Period, 500–1000 A. D. (Setzler, 1940, p. 260) and to the pipestone quarry in Siouan territory (see map, fig. 28). For the feathered pipe, facts display not only general diffusion, but three well-defined paths of transmission to the Iroquois, by way of the Central Algonquians, the Ohio Valley via the Shawnee, and through the South via the Cherokee. Among Plains tribes the cult has died out, simultaneously with removal to Oklahoma and with the rise of the Grass Dance. Vestiges survive among Central Algonquians.

The impact of the Calumet on the ancient Eagle Cult may have fashioned the third blended ritual before the era of White encroachment, though Marquette and Allouez and their fellow travelers spoke only of calumet waving and were unaware of any eagle mime they may have witnessed. The new composite of ancient forms appeared as hu^{n}ka among the Teton Sioux in 1801 (Densmore, 1918, p. 69) as a legacy from the Pawnee. Thus the dance was certainly included in the age-old hako by the end of the eighteenth century. This feather-waving ritual survives, modified, in the eastern periphery, among the Iroquois with shrinkage of the wands, doubling of numbers, and melodic elaboration. Futhermore, in the different longhouses the geometry and practices are undergoing continuous development.

In the drama of transmission and reception the circles and squares, the seconds, thirds, and fourths function not as inert mathematical formulae but as symptoms of tribal dance and music culture. Inevitably they have changed and continue to change with the passage of time, with transmission across great areas and through intervening tribes, and with filtration through local and individual personalities.

---

[21] For dancing eagles, on copper plates from Temple Mound C of Etowah, see Willoughby, 1932, fig. 13, p. 32, 14, p. 34. Eagle paraphernalia includes a pair of huge wings, claws, a beak, a fan in the right hand, sometimes a head in the left, on shell gorgets of Eastern Tennessee, sometimes also deer antlers (Willoughby, fig. 26, p. 54 and fig. 29, p. 57). The raised-knee posture could appertain to almost any Indian tribe, but is especially reminiscent of the Pueblos. On a Tennessee shell gorget two eagles engage in combat (ibid. fig. 27. p. 55).

BIBLIOGRAPHY

APEL, WILLI.
1950. Harvard dictionary of music. Cambridge, Mass. (Musical terms.)

BAKER, THEODOR.
1882. Über die Musik der nordamerikanischen Wilden. Leipzig.

BARRETT, S. A.
1911. The dream dance of the Chippewa and Menominee Indians of northern Wisconsin. Bull. Milwaukee Publ. Mus., vol. 1, pp. 251–406.

BARTRAM, WILLIAM.
1791. The travels of William Bartram. Philadelphia.

BILLINGTON, RAY A.
1949. Westward expansion. New York.

BUTTREE-SETON, JULIA M.
1930. The rhythm of the Red Man. New York.

CATLIN, GEORGE.
1841. The North American Indians, 2 vols. London. (1926 ed., Edinburgh.)
1844. Fourteen Ioway Indians. London.
1852. Adventures of the Ojibbeway and Iowa Indians in England. London.

CONVERSE, HARRIET M.
1908. Myths and legends of the New York State Iroquois. Arthur C.
Parker, editor. New York State Mus. Education Dept. Bull. 125,
pp. 1–195. Albany.

DENIG, EDWIN T.
1930. Indian tribes of the Upper Missouri—the Assiniboin. 46th Ann.
Rep. Bur. Amer. Ethnol., 1928–1929, pp. 395–628.

DENSMORE, FRANCES.
1910. Chippewa music. Bur. Amer. Ethnol. Bull. 45.
1913. Chippewa music. II. Bur. Amer. Ethnol. Bull. 53.
1918. Teton Sioux music. Bur. Amer. Ethnol. Bull. 61.
1923. Mandan and Hidatsa music. Bur. Amer. Ethnol. Bull. 80.
1929. Pawnee music. Bur. Amer. Ethnol. Bull. 93.
1932. Menominee music. Bur. Amer. Ethnol. Bull. 102.
1936. Cheyenne and Arapaho music. Southwest Mus. Pap. No. 10. Los
Angeles.
1938. Music of Santo Domingo Pueblo, New Mexico. Southwest Mus.
Pap., No. 12.
1943 a. Music of the Indians of British Columbia. Bur. Amer. Ethnol. Bull.
136, Anthrop. Pap. No. 27.
1943 b. Choctaw music. Bur. Amer. Ethnol. Bull. 136, Anthrop. Pap. No. 28.

DORSEY, J. OWEN.
1884. Omaha sociology. 3d Ann. Rep. Bur. Ethnol. pp. 207–370.

EVANS, BESSIE and MAY G.
1931. American Indian dance steps. New York.

FENTON, WILLIAM N.
1940. Problems arising from the historic northeastern position of the Iroquois.
Smithsonian Misc. Coll., vol. 100, Essays in the Historical Anthropology of North America, pp. 159–251.
1942. Songs from the Iroquois Longhouse: Program notes for an album of
American Indian music of the Eastern Woodlands. Smithsonian
Inst. Publ. No. 3691 (see musical bibliography, Album VI).
1948. Seneca songs from Coldspring Long House: Program notes for Album
XVII, folk music of the United States, the Library of Congress.

FILLMORE, JOHN COMFORT. See FLETCHER, ALICE C., 1893.

FLETCHER, ALICE C.
1893. The study of Omaha Indian music. (Aided by Francis La Flesche, with a report on the structural peculiarities of the music by John Comfort Fillmore.) Archaeol. and Ethnol. Pap. Peabody Mus. Cambridge, Mass., vol. 1, No. 5, pp. 7–152.
1904. The Hako: A Pawnee ceremony. (Assisted by James R. Murie; music transcribed by Edwin S. Tracy.) 22d Ann. Rep. Bur. Amer. Ethnol., pt. 2.
FLETCHER, ALICE C., and LA FLESCHE, FRANCIS.
1911. The Omaha Tribe. 27th Ann. Rep. Bur. Amer. Ethnol.
GILBERT, WILLIAM H.
1943. The Eastern Cherokee. Bur. Amer. Ethnol. Bull. 133, pp. 169–413.
HENNEPIN, LOUIS.
1683. Discovery of the River Mississippi. Ed. 1846, Historical Collections of Louisiana. New York.
1698. A new discovery of a vast country in America. R. G. Thwaites, editor, 1903. Chicago.
HERZOG, GEORGE.
1935. Plains Ghost Dance and Great Basin Music. Amer. Anthrop., vol. 37, No. 3, pp. 403–419.
HEWETT, EDGAR LEE.
1930. Ancient life in the American Southwest. Indianapolis.
HODGE, FREDERICK WEBB, Editor.
1907–1912. Handbook of American Indians north of Mexico. Bur. Amer. Ethnol. Bull. 30.
JONES, WILLIAM.
1939. Ethnography of the Fox Indians. Margaret W. Fisher, editor. Bur. Amer. Ethnol. Bull. 125.
KELLOGG, LOUISE P.
1925. The French regime in Wisconsin and the Northwest. State Hist. Soc. of Wisconsin, Madison.
KRIEGER, ALEXANDER D.
1945. An inquiry into supposed Mexican influence on a prehistoric "cult" in the Southern United States. Amer. Anthrop., vol. 47, No. 4, pp. 483–515.
KURATH, GERTRUDE P.
1950. A new method in dance notation. Amer. Anthrop., vol. 52, No. 1, pp. 120–123.
1951. Local diversity in Iroquois music and dance, pt. 6 of Iroquois Symposium. Bur. Amer. Ethnol. Bull. 149.
LA FLESCHE, FRANCIS. See FLETCHER, ALICE C., and LA FLESCHE, FRANCIS; also FLETCHER, ALICE C., 1893.
LE PAGE DU PRATZ, ANTOINE S.
1758. Histoire du Louisiane. 3 vols. Paris.
LOWIE, ROBERT H.
1913 a. Dance associations of the Eastern Dakota. Anthrop. Pap. Amer. Mus. Nat. Hist., vol. 11, pt. 2.
1913 b. Societies of the Crow, Hidatsa and Mandan Indians. Anthrop. Pap. Amer. Mus. Nat. Hist., vol. 11, pt. 3.
1915 a. Societies of the Arikara Indians. Anthrop. Pap. Amer. Mus. Nat. Hist., vol. 11, pt. 8.
1915 b. Dances and societies of the Plains Shoshone. Anthrop. Pap. Amer. Mus. Nat. Hist., vol. 11, pt. 10.

1915 c. American Indian dances. Amer. Mus. Journ., vol. 15, pp. 95–103.
1916. Societies of the Kiowa. Anthrop. Pap. Amer. Mus. Nat. Hist., vol. 11, pt. 11.
1935. The Crow Indian. New York.

McIlwraith, T. F.
1948. The Bella Coola Indians. 2 vols. Toronto.

Marquette, Jacques.
1673–1682. Voyages and discoveries in the Mississippi Valley. Transl. John G. Shea, ed. H. W. Beckwith, 1903. Coll. Illinois State Hist. Library, Springfield, Ill.

Mason, Bernard.
1944. Dances and stories of the American Indian. New York.

Maximilian, Alexander Phillip, Prince of Wied-Neuwied.
1843. Travels in the interior of North America, R. G. Thwaites, editor, 1906. Cleveland.

Miner, William H.
1911. The Iowa. Cedar Rapids, Iowa.

Mooney, J.
1896. The ghost-dance religion. 14th Ann. Rep. Bur. Ethnol., pt. 2.

Murie, James R.
1914. Pawnee Indian societies. Anthrop. Pap. Amer. Mus. Nat. Hist., vol. 11, pt. 7.
See also Fletcher, Alice C., 1904.

Nuttall, Zelia.
1888. Standard or headdress? Archaeol. and Ethnol. Pap. Peabody Mus., vol. 1, No. 1, pp. 5–52, Pl. III.
1932. Comparison between Etowan, Mexican and Mayan designs. Etowah Pap., pp. 137–144. Phillips Acad., Andover, Mass.

Parker, Arthur C.
1909. Secret medicine societies of the Seneca. Amer. Anthrop., n. s., vol. 11, No. 2, pp. 161–185.

Parsons, Elsie Clews.
1925. The Pueblo of Jemez. New Haven.
1939. Pueblo Indian religion. 2 vols. Chicago.

Roediger, Virginia M.
1941. Ceremonial costumes of the Pueblo Indians. Berkeley and Los Angeles.

Sachs, Curt.
1943. The road to Major. Musical Quart., vol. 29, No. 3, pp. 380–404.

Sahagun, Bernardino de.
1580. A history of ancient Mexico. Fanny R. Bandelier, editor, 1932. Nashville, Tenn.

Sandi, Luis.
1938. The story retold. Theatre Arts Monthly, vol. 22, No. 8, pp. 611 ff.

Setzler, Frank M.
1940. Archeological perspectives in the northern Mississippi Valley. Smithsonian Misc. Coll., vol. 100, pp. 253–290.

Skinner, Alanson.
1914. Political organization, cults, and ceremonies of the Plains-Ojibway and Plains-Cree Indians. Anthrop. Pap. Amer. Mus. Nat. Hist., vol. 11, pt. 6.
1915. Societies of the Iowa, Kansa, and Ponca Indians. Anthrop. Pap. Amer. Mus. Nat. Hist., vol. 11, pt. 9.

SPECK, FRANK G.

1911. Ceremonial songs of the Creek and Yuchi Indians. Anthrop. Pap. Mus. Univ. Pa., pp. 157–245. Philadelphia.

1935. The Naskapi. Norman, Okla.

1939. Catawba religious beliefs. Primitive Man, vol. 12, No. 2. Washington.

1945. The Celestial Bear comes down to earth. The Bear Sacrifice ceremony of the Munsee-Mahican in Canada as related by Nekatcit. Sci. Publ. No. 7, Reading Public Mus. and Art Gallery, Reading, Pa.

1949 a. Midwinter rites of the Cayuga Longhouse. Philadelphia.

1949 b. How the Dew Eagle Society of the Allegany Seneca cured Gahéda-gowa. Primitive Man, vol. 22, No. 3. Washington.

1951. Cherokee dance and drama. Berkeley and Los Angeles.

SPINDEN, HERBERT J.

1915. Indian dances in the Southwest. Amer. Mus. Journ., vol. 15, pp. 103–117.

SWANTON, JOHN R.

1911. Indian tribes of the Lower Mississippi Valley and adjacent coast of the Gulf of Mexico. Bur. Amer. Ethnol. Bull. 43.

1911. Indian tribes of the Lower Mississippi. Bur. Amer. Ethnol. Bull. 43.

1918. An early account of the Choctaw Indians. Mem. Amer. Anthrop. Assoc., vol. 5, No. 2, pp. 21–28.

THUREN, HJALMAR.

1923. On the Eskimo music in Greenland, pp. 1–45; Melodies from East Greenland, pp. 47–112. W. Thalbitzer, editor. Meddelelser om Gronland, Copenhagen.

THWAITES, REUBEN GOLD, Editor.

1896–1901. The Jesuit Relations and allied documents. Travels and explorations of the Jesuit missionaries in New France, 1610–1791. 73 vols. Cleveland.

TIMBERLAKE, HENRY.

1765. Memoirs of Timberlake. London. (Ed. 1927, Johnson City, Tenn.)

TIXIER, VICTOR.

1844. Tixier's travels on the Osage Prairies. Ed. John F. McDermott, transl. Albert J. Salvan. Norman, Okla., 1940.

TOOR, FRANCES.

1947. A treasury of Mexican folkways. New York.

TRACY, EDWIN S. See FLETCHER, ALICE C., 1904.

VOEGELIN, ERMINIE, and KINIETZ, VERNON.

1939. Shawnese traditions. Michigan Univ. Mus. of Archaeol. Occ. Contr. No. 9. Ann Arbor.

WARING, A. J., and HOLDER, PRESTON.

1945. A prehistoric ceremonial complex in the Southeastern United States. Amer. Anthrop., vol. 47, No. 1, pp. 1–34.

WEST, GEORGE A.

1934. Tobacco, pipes and smoking customs of the American Indians. 2 vols. Bull. Publ. Mus. City of Milwaukee, vol. 17.

WILLOUGHBY, CHARLES C.

1932. Notes on the history and symbolism of the Muskhogeans and the people of Etowah. Etowah Pap., Phillips Acad., Andover, Mass., pp. 7–67.

WISSLER, CLARK.
  1912. Societies and ceremonial associations in the Oglala division of the
      Teton-Dakota. Anthrop. Pap. Amer. Mus. Nat. Hist., vol. 11, pt. 1.
  1913. Societies and dances of the Blackfoot Indians. Anthrop. Pap. Amer.
      Mus. Nat. Hist., pt. 4.
  1916. General discussion of shamanistic and dancing societies. Anthrop. Pap.
      Amer. Mus. Nat. Hist., pt. 12.

RECORDINGS

Seneca—Coldspring—Chauncey and Richard Johnny John, 1941. Recorded by
    William N. Fenton, Library of Congress No. 56.—Tonawanda—
    Robert Shanks, 1936. Recorded by Martha Champion Randle and
    William N. Fenton, L C Nos. 9, 10. Archives Indiana Univ.
Onondaga—Six Nations Reserve—Joseph Logan, 1941. Recorded by William N.
    Fenton, L C, Nos. 23 and 24 A. Published in Album VI, Songs
    from the Iroquois Longhouse, Folk Music of the United States,
    1942.
Cayuga—Sour Springs Longhouse, Six Nations Reserve—Alexander General
    (Deskaheh) and Willie John, 1951. Recorded by Gertrude Kurath
    and Joseph Raben. Reel 3, now in National Museum of Canada.
Fox—Tama, Iowa—Bill Leaf, 1933—Recorded by Martha Champion Randle,
    L C, No. 37. Archives Indiana Univ.
Cherokee—Qualla, N. C.—Will West Long, 1946. Recorded by Artus Moser,
    forwarded by John W. Gillespie. Private Collection.
Sioux—Wanblee, S. D.—Recorded by Willard Rhodes. Publ. Ethnic Folkways
    Library, E F 2. Omaha (Grass) Dance—1420 B (transcribed, but not
    reproduced).

INDEX

Aaron, Jerry, informant, 94
Abenaki Indians, 157, 158, 176, 184
Abram, Cornelius, Seneca, 32, 33
Abrams, Chauncey, Seneca, 57
Adoption Rite, 206, 275
Aiaoua, Indian tribe, 192
Akansa Indians, 183, 195
Akŭks, mystic birds, 95
Alabama Indians, 175
Algonquian Indians, 49, 105, 109, 114, 117, 154, 155, 159, 175, 176, 178, 185, 199, 202, 203, 205
    Central, 154, 155, 156, 268, 269, 272, 273, 283, 301
Allegany Indian Reservation, 5, 11, 41, 43, 47, 57, 74, 78, 81, 115, 118, 129, 134, 150, 229, 233, 248
    later celebrations at, 31–37
Allegheny River, N. Y., 5, 42, 46, 50, 75, 99, 116, 144, 153
Allouez, Father, explorer, 170, 182, 187, 300
All-Smoking Ceremony, 274
American Museum of Natural History, 130, 200
American Philosophical Society Library, 3
André, Father Louis, 192
Animal abductors, mythical, 175
Animal's head, served at dances, 76, 106, 119, 144, 174, 191
Anthropomorphic beings, 114
Anus motif, 205
Apples, offered at dance, 35, 36, 37, 61, 137
Approach of the Pipes Ceremony, 276
Arapaho Indians, 175, 188, 189, fig. 30, 299
Archaic residue, 173
Arikara Indians, 179, 188, 189, 191, 192, 277, 284, fig. 30
Armstrong, Jesse, Seneca, 34
    John, Seneca, 17
Arrow, Seneca brave, 29, 42, 51, 101
Arrows, 94
Arrowshafts, 195
Assiniboin Indians, 175, 186, 188, 274, 279, fig. 30
Atkin, Edmond, 168
Awl-breaker, Indian man, 55, 56, 61, 65, 95, 96, 114, 127
Aztecs, 271, 301

Bad Boy and Giant Crow, legend of, 89–90
Banker, Captain Evert, 158
Barred Oval motif, 205
Barrett, S. A., 131, 284
Basketmaker, 43
Basketry, knowledge of, 39

Baskets, 17, 50, 52
    hand, 7
    pack, 7, 137
    splint, 7, 34, 137
    washing, 7, 137
Battle-ax, 183
Beads, 165
Bean Festival, 77, 299
Beans, pole, 7, 137
Bear Dance, 266, 267, 299
Bear rite, 281
Bear Sacrifice Ceremony, 202
Bear Society, 112, 124
    dance, 19, 112, 122, 266, 267
Bear's head, served at dances, 177
Bear's meat, served at feasts, 107, 129. 137
Bearskin, 197
Beauchamp, Rev. William M., 79, 156, 157
Beaver, 156
    Indians, 175
    skins, gifts of, 155, 156, 160, 163, 182
Bella Coola Midwinter festival, 282
Belt, peace, 169
    Road and Peace, 169
    wampum, 102, 123, 134, 156, 157, 159, 164, 165, 166, 167
Berdaches, 183
Berries, wild, 44
Bibliography, 210–222, 301–306
Big Bird Dance, 31, 33
Big Birds, celestial beings, 31, 32, 33, 35
Big-canoe, Seneca man, 34
Big Crow, mythical being, 81, 116
Big-leaf, mother of Hemlocks-lying-down, 49
Big Miami River, 163
Big Porcupine, Seneca Indian name for Speck, 35
Big Raven, dance conductor, 173
Big Sioux River, 189
Big-Women's Dance, 51
Billington, Ray A., 284
Bilobed Arrow motif, 205, 206
Bingham, Robert W., 3
Bird Abductor Legend, 74
Bird Dance, 83, 284
Bird lice, beliefs regarding, 95, 100, 173, 199, 200, 203
Bird Society, 33
Black, Chief Barber, informant, 4
    Chief Edward, informant, 4, 55
Black Coat, Indian chief, 200
Blackfoot Indians, 186, 188, 189, 274, 279, 285
Blacksnake, Seneca leader, 78
Blair, Emma H., 155
Bloodroot, 134

307

318

Meskwaki tribe, Fox Indians, 268, 274, 279, 282, 287
Message sticks, 42
Messenger, Dance official, 14, 23, 55, 57, 58, 60, 62, 116, 134, 135, 136, 139, 179, 182, 190, 194, 196, 204
Method, comparative, 172 ff., 185, 199, 208
   ethnohistory, 2, 208 (upstreaming)
   field work, 10–11, 199
   functional, 2
   historical reconstruction, 172, 178, 188, 204, 208
Mexican bird dances, 300
Miami Indians, 154, 155, 156, 159, 160, 161, 162, 163, 164, 167, 171, 172, 181, 182, 186, 203, 209, 210
Michelson, Truman, 184
Michilimackinac, French settlement, 183, 188
Micmac Indians, 175
Midwest, location of survival of Calumet Dance, 268, 269, 270
Midwinter Festival, 21, 35, 36, 40, 42, 43, 53, 56, 73, 110, 113, 117, 123, 144, 177, 229
Milwaukee Public Museum, 131
Mingo Indians, 160
Miniatures, ceremonial use of, 123, 124, 142
Missionaries, opinions of, 287
   relations with Indians, 40, 41
Missisauga Indians, 203
Mississippi River, 271–272, 274, 279, 282, 285, fig. 30
Mississippi Valley, 165
Missouri River, 279, 285, fig. 30
Moccasins, 148, 161
Modern Iruska Dance, 283
Mohawk Indians, 79, 100, 106, 157, 159, 166, 167, 168, 169, 177
Moieties, 8, 14, 15, 20, 23, 24, 26, 28, 29, 30, 32, 35, 46, 48, 55, 60, 71, 72, 119, 122, 123, 124, 125, 126, 134, 136, 137, 138–144, 150, 174, 179, 181, 191, 232–233, 285
Money, distributed at dance, 35, 61, 62, 72
Montagnais-Naskapi Indians, 175
Mooney, James, 96, 100, 101, 197, 199, 200, 282
Morgan, Lewis H., 3, 76, 77, 78, 102, 104, 105, 142
Morning Star sacrifice, 180
Morris, Thomas, adopted by Indians, 104
Mortar, corn, 7
Moser, Lucas, 299
Mosopelea Indians, 194
Munsee Indians, 202, 203
Munsee-Mahican Indians, 202
Murdock, George Peter, 2, 144
Murie, James, R., 188, 275, 283, 284
Museum of the American Indian, Heye Foundation, 5
Music, see Songs.

Musical instruments, 52, 230–232, 238, 255–256
Musical range, 254–255, 264, 266–267, 284, 288, 297–298
Musical recordings, 227, 248, 255, 286, 291, 299
Musical sequence, 238, 252, 263, 266, 288, 298
Musicians, 186
Muskogeans, 201
Myths, 103, 145–146, 200, 202

Nadoessi (Sioux), 192
Names, patrilineal English, 8
   personal, 8
Nanticoke Indians, 78, 203
Narragansett Indians, 177
Naskapi Indians, 202
Natchez Indians, 175, 194, 195, 198, 201, 209, 280, 281
National Museum of Canada, 3
Ne-ho-sa-den-dat, Squat Dance for Males, 76
Neuse River, 159
New Fire Ceremony, 180
New Religion, 78, 79
Newtown Longhouse, 4, 11, 26, 29, 30, 42, 47, 49, 50, 54, 58, 65, 74, 75, 80, 81, 109, 112, 116, 127, 133, 135, 138, 139, 140, 141, 142, 143, 144, 148, 150
New Year, Seneca, 9
New Year Dance, 21, 29, 37, 48, 52, 69, 83, 125
New Year's Festival, 29, 51
New York State Museum, 4, 116, 131
Niagara gorge, 95
Nicotiana rustica, 34, 132
Nighthawk, celestial being, 202, 205
   Dance, 202, 281
   wings, 281
Nitinat tribe, 282
Northern Plains Indians, 12
North Star Bundle ceremonies, 180
Nuttall, Zelia, 300

Ochre, yellow, used for paint, 134
Ofo, Siouan-speaking tribe, 194
Oglala Indians, 189, 193, 274
Ohio River, 159, 195, 279, 301
Ohsweken, 43
Ojibwa Indians, 108, 170, 174, 175, 186, 187, 188
Okanagan Indians, 175
Oki, familiar spirit, 118
Omaha Dance, 283
Omaha Eagle Dance, 276–277
Omaha Indians, 175, 179, 188, 189, 190, 191, 192, 195, 196, 205, 209, 228, 275, 276–277, 278, 279, 282, 283, 284, 287, 288, 289, 300
   music, 291, 293, 297, 298, 300
Omaha wa'waⁿ, 276
Omens, belief in, 201
Oneida Indians, 104, 106, 127, 133, 159, 166, 167, 168

322

○